IN
THEIR
OWN
WORDS

IN THEIR OWN WORDS

Contemporary American *PLAYWRIGHTS*

DAVID SAVRAN

THEATRE
COMMUNICATIONS
GROUP

In Their Own Words: Contemporary American Playwrights is published by
Theatre Communications Group, Inc., the national organization for the
nonprofit professional theatre, 355 Lexington Ave., New York, NY 10017.

The publications and programs of Theatre Communications Group, the
national organization for the nonprofit professional theatre, are supported by
Actors' Equity Foundation, Alcoa Foundation, Atlantic Richfield Foundation,
AT&T Foundation, Citicorp/Citibank, Columbia Pictures Industries,
Consolidated Edison Company of New York, Eleanor Naylor Dana Charitable
Trust, Dayton Hudson Foundation, Exxon Corporation, The William and Mary
Greve Foundation, Home Box Office, Inc., The Andrew W. Mellon
Foundation, Mobil Foundation, Inc., National Broadcasting Company,
National Endowment for the Arts, New York Life Foundation, New York State
Council on the Arts, The Pew Charitable Trusts, Philip Morris Incorporated,
The Rockefeller Foundation, The Scherman Foundation, Shell Oil Company
Foundation, the Shubert Foundation, Inc., Consulate General of Spain and
The Xerox Foundation.

Condensed versions of interviews with Richard Foreman, David Mamet and
Luis Valdez appeared in *American Theatre* magazine.

Library of Congress Cataloging-in-Publication Data
Savran, David, 1950–
In their own words.

1. Dramatists, American—20th century—Interviews.
2. American drama—20th century—History and criticism.
3. Playwriting. I. Title.
PS352.S28 1988   812'.54'09   88-2118
ISBN 0-930452-69-0
ISBN 0-930452-70-4 (pbk.)

Design by The Sarabande Press

First Edition: April 1988

To Paula

ACKNOWLEDGMENTS

F irst and foremost, I want to thank the playwrights interviewed for their insights, generosity and candor.

My thanks to Martin Bergbusch, Associate Dean of Fine Arts, and my colleagues in the Drama Department at the University of Regina for indulging my frequent absence from campus during the past year. My special appreciation to William Dixon for taking over as Acting Department Head during the summers of 1986 and '87. My thanks to Bonnie Jackson and Jeanette Groenendyk, to the University President's Fund and to my students in Twentieth-Century Drama, winter semester 1987, for their encouragement and support.

I want to express my gratitude to the many people who, in the past year, helped me clarify my ideas, prepare for the interviews and plan the introductions. Special mention must be made of Stacie Chaiken, Joan Duncan, Beth Eisenberg, Wesley Gibson, John Hirsch, David Hult, David Hutchings, James Leverett, Gwen Parker and Laura Ross. Finally, I want to thank the three people who have been most deeply involved in this project: M. Elizabeth Osborn, my wise and compassionate editor at TCG; Paula Vogel, who instigated the project and advised me every step of the way; and Ronn Smith, who provided sharp insights and support when and where they were most urgently needed.

The photographs in this book are reproduced by the kind permission of the following photographers: p. 3, Ilaria Freccia; p. 51, Ricardo Block; p. 84, Robert Mapplethorpe; p. 100, Jeffrey Davenport; p. 117, Ophelia Y.M. Hwang; p. 132, Brigitte Lacombe; p. 145, Dennis Behl; p. 178, Langdon Clay; p. 193, Ed Betts; p. 207, Bobbi Hazeltine; p. 223, Gerry Goodstein; p. 240, Cynthia MacAdams; p. 257, Marek A. Majewski; p. 272, Susan Cook; p. 288, William B. Carter; p. 306, Diane Gorodnitzki. All uncredited photographs courtesy of the individual playwrights.

CONTENTS

CONTENTS

Imagine that you enter a parlor. You come late. When you arrive, others have long preceded you, and they are engaged in a heated discussion, a discussion too heated for them to pause and tell you exactly what it is about. In fact, the discussion had already begun long before any of them got there, so that no one present is qualified to retrace for you all the steps that had gone before. You listen for a while, until you decide that you have caught the tenor of the argument; then you put in your oar. Someone answers; you answer him; another comes to your defense; another aligns himself against you, to either the embarrassment or gratification of your opponent, depending upon the quality of your ally's assistance. However, the discussion is interminable. The hour grows late, you must depart. And you do depart, with the discussion still vigorously in progress.

—Kenneth Burke

PREFACE

On a cold afternoon in February 1986 I sat with my friend Paula Vogel, playwright and teacher, in a Blarney Stone tavern in the heart of the Broadway theatre district. Together we surveyed the American theatre in dismay. Although we'd read and seen some brilliant and powerful new work, we wondered why so many fine plays either remained unperformed or received inadequate productions and failed to find an audience. Why has it been so difficult, we asked, to get challenging new work produced? Why has the American theatre become so tame? Why has it cut itself off from its social context? Why has it so neglected drama that attempts serious historical analysis? Why has money been the only thing at stake in so many productions of new plays?

I recalled when we were in graduate school and we believed — maybe somewhat naively — the theatre to be a vehicle for social change, a locus for political and cultural dialogue. I thought about the following years, after Paula moved to New York to write and I started teaching in Canada, about the thrill of discovering new work at the Public Theater or La Mama, the exhilaration of seeing Stephen Sondheim's *Sweeney Todd* or Caryl Churchill's *Cloud 9* or John Guare's *Gardenia*. Ten years and three beers later, the situation looked completely different.

Trying to account for the crisis in the American theatre from New York's narrow perspective, we noted many causes, including the severe economic constraints that set the priorities of many producers, the myopia of the most powerful critics and the success of a reactionary regime in debasing the level of political dialogue, both on and off the stage. We wondered how the situation differed in other parts of the country. When Paula asked me how the American playwrights we most respected felt about this crisis, I told her I knew only what I could deduce from their plays because there was no book detailing their views. Paula then suggested I edit such a collection, soliciting essays from playwrights about their craft and sense of social responsibility.

I was then too busy revising my Wooster Group book for publication to begin work on another project. During my annual summer sojourn in New York, however, I reconsidered Paula's proposal, recognizing that a book of essays could — and should — provide an effective tool with which to diagnose the theatre's malaise. I approached Theatre Communications Group with the idea and quickly realized that it was impractical to solicit essays from playwrights. We agreed instead on interviews, to be accompanied by short critical introductions. TCG gave me a go-ahead in August and I drew up a list of questions that, I believed, would expose the nature of the crisis in the American theatre and the position of each of the leading writers vis-a-vis this crisis. Together with TCG, I selected the playwrights.

The process of deciding who was to be included was a difficult one, divided as I was by my own strong predilections and my desire to represent the American theatre fairly. I felt it reasonable to restrict the list to those who have written a significant body of work (as opposed to one widely performed play) and remain at the peak of their creative activity. While attempting to develop further criteria, I recognized immediately how subjective they became, that what is a "significant" body of work to me will be inconsequential to others. After much deliberation, I chose playwrights with vital and distinct voices — acknowledging, of course, that there are many others. Together, I believe, they personify the diversity of theatre in America, from regional to Broadway, holding divergent views of dramatic form, style, the creative process and the theatre's political function. All except Sam Shepard graciously agreed to be interviewed.

The goal in each interview was to obtain a clear sense of each playwright's position: in relation to the history of dramatic literature, to the heterogeneity of American theatre and to the prevailing cultural and political order. To that end, I asked all the playwrights first about their early experiences in theatre, their training and influences. I then questioned them about their way of writing, their experiences in production and attitude toward the critics. Finally, I asked them to articulate their view of the American theatre and their plans and goals for the future.

I supplemented the general questions with specific ones about their plays and the broader dramatic and cultural issues raised by their work. Because I believe that dramatic form and style — subtly and powerfully arousing and fulfilling audience expectations — are crucial to understanding a playwright's ideological position, I have attempted either to secure from each his or her sense of the relationship between aesthetic and moral mission, or to give the reader enough information to make the connection. Due to the wide variety of subjects, however, it was impossible to follow up all the provocative or contentious issues that arose.

The interviews ranged between one and four hours but averaged roughly ninety minutes. All were edited and cut, some quite heavily, to eliminate redundancy and confusion and reduce them to manageable length. In all cases I tried to retain a sense of the movement of the conversation and the dynamism of the playwright's speaking voice.

The introduction that precedes the edited transcript of each interview is an attempt to set the scene. It provides basic biographical information, an overview of the development of the playwright's career and an analysis of a dramatic strategy that I believe is a key to understanding the playwright's singularity and the impact of his or her work on an audience. All of the citations in the introductions are drawn from other interviews or published writings. Unless specified otherwise, the dates given for plays are for first productions.

As I was preparing this book, I quickly realized that there are no clear-cut answers to the questions that Paula and I raised, nor are there unimpeachable positions. The voices of the playwrights are diverse and distinct, providing multiple and sometimes conflicting perspectives. Their interplay comprises what Kenneth Burke calls the "drama" of history — understood as the interminable and heated discussion he so elegantly details in the quotation that serves as epigraph to this book. Each voice must be heard as a reply, not just to the questions I've asked but to the activity of predecessors, other theatre professionals, critics, the public and each other. Each describes, justifies and attempts to redress his or her position within a complex institutional and artistic system. In the process, each offers an acute analysis of the causes and sustaining mechanism of the crisis in what is, in fact, a multiplicity of American theatres, each with its own objective and methods. I have — for now — attempted to moderate my own voice, suspending evaluation to allow the playwrights' strategies to come forward. However, if this book is to accomplish its goal, the reader, realizing how much is at stake in this "heated discussion," must judge and evaluate carefully and then join in, recognizing that he or she shares the power to fashion a more vital and responsible theatre.

December, 1987
New York City

IN
THEIR
OWN
WORDS

LEE BREUER

Before discovering the European avant-garde at UCLA, Lee Breuer was headed toward becoming, in his own words, a "fifties version of a yuppie, pledging a fraternity, pre-law, all that shit." Instead he began reading Camus, Beckett and Genet and inaugurated the first of his three phases as a writer by composing a "quasi-existentialist, surrealistic" play. The decade after UCLA he divided between San Francisco and Europe, continuing to write in the European tradition. He embarked on the next phase of his career in January 1968, when he sat down to write what was to become *The B. Beaver Animation*. The next year he cofounded Mabou Mines, the theatre collective for which he has written and directed the series of plays which comprises the minimalist-conceptualist portion of his work. These include *The Red Horse Animation* (1970), *The B. Beaver Animation* (1974), *The Shaggy Dog Animation* (1978), *A Prelude to Death in Venice* (1980) and *Hajj* (1983). In recent years Breuer has begun the third phase of his career, producing work independently of Mabou Mines (in fact, all members of the collective work independently) and developing as a pop-classicist: *Sister Suzie Cinema* (1980), *Red Beads* (1982), *The Gospel at Colonus* (1983) and the as yet unfinished musical epic *The Warrior Ant*.

3

Despite the changes in Breuer's work, it all coalesces under his dictum "that you are never one thing, that you are constantly giving off energy the way an atom would radiate. All of this energy is characters: they come back to find you." Breuer describes his Animations series as a *via negativa*, eliminating the characters which were once, but are no longer, valid self-images. In each he explores a perspective on consciousness and exorcizes a part of himself, using an animal metaphor—"I see myself in everything that walks and talks and crawls on its belly," begins *Red Horse*. Drawing on Kafka's fables and on animated cartoon characters, each piece examines man as a particular social animal. *Red Horse* is about romance, opposing freedom to being taken for a ride, being taken over; *B. Beaver* is about the dam that breaks creative flow and about speaking through a stutter: "b-b-beaver"; *Shaggy Dog* is about the master/slave relationship, running the stories and memories of the filmmaker/dog, Rose, against those of her filmmaker/master, John.

Breuer's Animations are composed of interweaving voices: of individual characters, of narrative and of the writer/performer reflecting on his own activity. *A Prelude to Death in Venice*, a development of Part III of *Shaggy Dog*, is perhaps Breuer's most sophisticated exercise in dramatic counterpoint. The play is essentially a monologue delivered by the puppet John Greed, standing between two pay phones, manipulated by a looming figure, Bill (played by Bill Raymond). Breuer explains that because actor and puppet are "aspects of a single person," the dialogue becomes "a study in manipulation" with "textual reverberations." In effect, the piece performs the schizophrenic composition of a theatre text, the "idea of 'producing' reality," through the string of telephone conversations and the interplay of voices. In this ingenious and wildly comic piece, John's shifty, finagling characters are unmistakably the many personae of a single actor/stand-up comic/shyster—Breuer's image for the writer at work.

The Animations make extensive use of popular culture in both a satirical and a nonparodistic way, attempting both to critique and to capitalize on the emotional force of popular music, comic strips, Hollywood cliches. Beginning in the late 1970s, however, Breuer became increasingly preoccupied with using popular culture in a new way, trying, as he describes it, to combine "pop culture with my growing knowledge and sensitivity to the classics— kinda like putting rock 'n' roll together with Dante." In both his gospel revision of Sophocles, *The Gospel at Colonus*, and his rock 'n' roll epic, *The Warrior Ant*, he attempts the fusion of the popular and the esoteric.

In *The Warrior Ant*, with music by Bob Telson, Breuer combines theatre and concert forms to create "a carnival parade," an "active rather than a meditative experience." The piece's structure is based loosely on *The Aeneid*, with a bit of Dante thrown in ("Midway in its life the Warrior Ant/ Found itself in a dark hole"). Set in a giant ant colony, it uses live actors, Bunraku puppets and African and Caribbean musicians to explore the relationship between the individual and the social unit, asking the question: which is the real organism? Using a variation of the *terza rima*, Breuer classicizes the jive lyricism he has developed over the years, alternating between narrative, invocation and prayer. The epic, a mystical journey, charts the life of an ant from conception to its not-quite enlightenment and death. In the final moments the ant ascends, riding upon the back of the moth on the way to its final rest: "Ant flows into moth, moth into ant, / across the line of void, until each / annihilates the other with annihilating love."

Behind the wealth of performance styles, forms and subjects, through his six-part *Realms* (of which *The Warrior Ant* is Part V), Breuer has attempted to devise a series of comprehensive metaphors both for an inner, spiritual process and for the diversity of human relationships. Each of his pieces is an artist's self-portrait: as horse, beaver, dog, puppet, ant. However, the self-portraits of the seventies and those of the eighties move in opposite directions. The Animations are highly sophisticated, deconstructive of consciousness and of the act of writing, while his later work returns to innocence, attempting to recover an incantational theatre that would break down the distinctions between classic and vernacular, African and European, sacred and profane, performer and spectator. In a strange amalgam of the lyric and the grotesque, *The Warrior Ant* synthesizes rather than analyzes. It is a statement of political unity, an activist "black/white classicism," and at the same time a giddy, glittering apocalypse.

■　■　■

MARCH 12, 1987—KAVANAGH'S RESTAURANT, NEW HAVEN

What led you into theatre?

My ego. I had a big turn in my life at sixteen. I started UCLA, and that same year my father died. I moved out of the house and was pretty much on my own. That was the end of my middle-class life.

You grew up in L.A.?

Yes. What happened was I started leaning toward creativity as a support structure. At that time there really were not too many other options for anybody who didn't want to enter the system. There weren't any politics. There weren't any drugs.

5

When was this?

The fifties, Eisenhower. You chose art or a criminal life or the system. I had one pivotal experience at UCLA. I remember almost nothing about my five years there except that I worked in a parking lot at the Sunset Towers on Sunset Strip and lived in an apartment on the Strip with four other guys. But I had one class given by a guy named Oreste F. Pucciani. The wonderful thing about Pucciani was that he looked like Albert Camus and of course everyone wanted to be *l'étranger*. Among the avant-gardists at UCLA in the fifties, the going number was Existentialism; Oreste seemed to embody the idea of European avant-garde hipness. You must remember that at that time theatre was Miller and Williams, period. In this one course I was introduced to Beckett, Sartre, Camus, Genet, Giraudoux, Artaud and about ten others. I became very interested in Existentialism and wrote a naive, so-called Existential play based on Camus. It took the UCLA theatre arts department by storm. I was instantly famous on campus. They were still doing the play ten years later. I didn't get the same sort of emotional boost until the *Shaggy Dog Animation* in 1979—twenty-two years is a long, long time to keep the faith. Anyway once I was considered the Rimbaud of the theatre department, I got locked in. The image was so enticing, I couldn't kick it. It was like a drug. I went on to win a Samuel French award, won some campus awards, did three plays and was seen as a radical.

From UCLA I went up to San Francisco and became close to McClure, Ginsberg, Ferlinghetti, did Larry's first play *The Animations*, even met Kerouac before he died. I hung out at City Lights a lot and did the Beat trip.

Had you done any work in theatre before UCLA?

No, and I didn't direct until some three or four years later. I was just a playwright then. Ruth Maleczech and I went up to Big Sur and hung out at what later became the Esselin Institute. We were making up cabins and I was washing dishes and tending bar. Henry Miller was there a lot. This was the sixties before the sixties. That's where it all started. This was the same world and life that became clarified around 1964 with the advent of the San Francisco scene. It was very exciting because those people, in that first Evergreen book, kind of formed the Beat Generation.

So many of them have been winding in and out of my life. I hadn't seen Terry Riley, the composer, for twenty years; we bumped into each other in Japan and now we're going to do a piece together. San Francisco between 1960 and 1965 was phenomenally creative. When I got back from Europe in 1970, half of my San Francisco friends were dead. The drug scene was very, very heavy. But it was also an incredibly creative time. You take the Music

Center in 1962, when I was working with Pauline Oliveros, Mort Subotnick, Ann Halperin, Ronnie Davis. Their stuff was still heady ten years later.

I'm fifty now and very luckily situated in that I'm old enough to have been part of the entire American theatrical avant-garde which began in 1959 or 1960 and crystallized around the Living Theatre's *The Brig* [1963]. Though I wasn't part of the Living Theatre's scene on the East Coast, I met all of the people who were part of *The Brig*. I saw the original production with JoAnne Akalaitis. I was pretty much on the scene from its inception and it's been the center of my whole life. Now that it's turning into another scene, the performance scene, you can really see a shape to it.

What theatre were you involved with in the early sixties?

Ruth Maleczech was working at the San Francisco Mime Troupe and the Actor's Workshop and I got real lonely and started hanging out, trying to learn how to direct by working with some of the Mime Troupers. Eventually I found I had a great flair for directing. But at that time I was just playing around. I just didn't want to stay home and write while she was rehearsing.

And then you went to Europe?

In '65, and stayed there till '70.

You worked with the Berliner Ensemble?

Not so much worked as studied with them for a month. Helene Weigel was very kind to us. We were permitted to attend a number of rehearsals. We met everybody. We walked across Checkpoint Charlie every day. At the same time Ruth and JoAnne studied with Grotowski and later, with David Warrilow, I went to visit Grotowski in Poland. Those are the two major formative experiences in Europe, the Berliner Ensemble and the Polish Laboratory Theatre. Back in the States, one of the things that affected me most deeply was seeing Giorgio Strehler's Piccolo Teatro when it came to San Francisco.

What specifically excited you about the Berliner Ensemble?

I was introduced to Brecht by Ronnie Davis, in the Troupe. And I suddenly felt a tremendous identification and a deep understanding of his ideas about a narrative theatre, as opposed to a dramatic theatre. That narrative theatre has been the basis of all my work. But I think I've developed it in a variety of ways that Brecht didn't, for different reasons and different purposes.

Later I realized where Brecht got all his stuff. Now Brecht for me is 90 percent the Peking Opera. I didn't realize that then. My interest in the great Asian theatres—the Bunraku, the Kabuki, the Peking Opera, Kathakali—is just the next step after Brecht. Why study Brecht when you can study the

Peking Opera? But I was deeply affected by his literary formalism and the Meyerholdian acting style. When I first became interested in acting, the tradition in America was the Method and I studied it—I have a deep respect for Stanislavski. But here was a wonderful alternative. And little by little I began to understand that this was the storytelling style as opposed to the motivational style. I am now involved in writing mock epics, like *The Warrior Ant*. I became more and more fascinated by the question, how does a great epic poem turn into theatre? It turns into a narrative style of theatre. Brecht was the hook.

What about Brecht's politics?

I certainly feel that my sympathies are, in a strange way, with the left. But I have a kind of cynical objectivity about politics in general. I don't feel that politics is the deepest metaphor for my perception of living. And I feel that Brecht himself was deeply confused and that what he stood for was deeply confused. I will give you one example. When we went to the Berliner Ensemble, it was filled with upper-middle-class West Berliners. Joking around with the Ensemble, I asked, "Where are the workers?" They were at the girlie shows around the corner. I think Brecht was on one level naive, much more so than Mao, about how to reach the so-called proletariat. I think he was naive about science too; the more I learn about science, the stupider Brecht's so-called scientific perceptions become. The philosophical and metaphysical basis for Brecht's so-called scientific theatre was deterministic, Newtonian, classical. That all ended with Einstein. By the time Brecht was writing, people were into quantum theory. Science was a crap shoot and Brecht was still thinking there were laws about behavior. But Brecht wasn't naive about art.

I'm terribly interested in the great art of storytelling. And yes, the politics, sure, on the level of day-to-day behavior. I certainly feel that there's much more of me that's lower class than upper class. I grew up in a liberal atmosphere. Once I left home, I struck more toward a radical idea. But I was really leaning toward the influx of spiritual energy coming into the United States by way of Japan, the first tidbits of Buddhism and the first spiritual longings of the sixties. I was in Europe when the heavy political activism of the late sixties was developing. I was more interested in the psychedelic love-ins of the early sixties and so I never got involved in marching around and raising cain about Vietnam. My statement about Vietnam was to do *Mother Courage*. That doesn't say anything. Everybody's full of a tremendous number of illusions and I tried to cop a Brechtian activism and found out that I was being rather elitist and foolish.

I have a deep mistrust of the right and the far right, but not of a spiritual fundamentalism that is often to the right. I've hung out a lot now with members of the black Baptist church and the Church of God and Christ who are basically fundamentalist, but they're not the kind of highly energetic wealthy right that I have no communication with at all. The United States now is thoroughly disgusting politically and a total bore and I can't wait for somebody to get it over with, just clean the fuckin' shit out. What's happening now on Wall Street is mentally and spiritually primitive, greedy animals and greedy children. It's not even worth thinking about.

Did the work with Grotowski feed more into the spiritual side?

Grotowski was not yet on his spiritual search. His trip now bores me. I was tremendously interested in his elucidation, in fascinating ways that I still use, of the last motivational ideas of Stanislavski. But that was a revelation I received second-hand. Ruth Maleczech and JoAnne Akalaitis went to study with Grotowski at his Avignon workshop. We had great respect for his work, particularly with his original company, and we felt that he had extraordinary insights into the idea of how to motivate abstractions. You see the trick with Stanislavski is that basically it is so Freudian, tied to the psychology of Realism. Grotowski led us toward the possibility of working internally for abstract form. How do you motivate style? That was a question that Ronnie Davis and I debated all the way back in 1960 and that he never really solved. It was always, you motivate with realistic psychology and then you impose style.

Through Grotowski, we hit on a way of motivating style by going deeper than Realism into the internal process. When you see a bag lady—we saw a lot of them in the sixties in New York—spinning in the middle of the street with three garbage bags on her head, or doing a dance up and down a curb, that's totally real, but it's not Realism. We felt that there was an emotional truth to every formal idea—Surrealism, Expressionism, Primitivism—and that somehow each of these forms comes from a deeper level of the subconscious than the form of Realism. In other words, there wasn't Realism plus form. Realism *was* a form just like Surrealism, inching toward the idea of a formal view of the universe. But the Grotowski who came over here and started hanging out in trees and rhapsodizing...I don't need that.

When did you found Mabou Mines?

Mabou Mines was founded by five of us, as a collaborative: Philip Glass, David Warrilow, JoAnne Akalaitis, Ruth Maleczech and myself. January 1, 1970.

What impact has that had on your development as a writer?

It was an incredible privilege to have a company of great performers working on my stuff. It was a very important phase for me as a writer. Also very, very difficult. The great formal innovations in theatre have come usually when a writer found himself with a company at his disposal. Shakespeare and Molière are two prime examples. The great thrill was to write for specific people. The *Red Horse Animation* was written for JoAnne, David and Ruth. The *B. Beaver Animation* added Bill Raymond and Fred Neumann.

The company hung in with me long enough so that I could write and direct at the same time. In other words, I usually began to direct before I had written the script. I had an initial idea and preliminary material to improvise with. That's why the *Shaggy Dog Animation* took four years. When I started out, I had just barely written the prologue. We rehearsed and performed it as a work-in-progress at Paula Cooper's. Then, while JoAnne did a play, I went back and wrote for nine months to a year until I had Part I and some of Part II. We did that as a work-in-progress. Then Mabou Mines did another play and I went back and finished it. That's why the *Red Horse Animation* took nine months even though it's a rather short piece. The *B. Beaver* already existed as a short story but it was totally revised over a period of a year and a half.

It's an incredible learning process and this is the great advantage, most clearly demonstrated by *A Prelude to Death in Venice*: when I was working with Bill, for a period of about eight weeks, I would change lines every night. Because Bill was situated between the two telephone booths, he could paste up dialogue and I could add whole new pages that he would put right into performance. I could test out the audience response, what lines worked, what gags worked. It was a living laboratory. And little by little we hulled it down so that it all worked. This is classically what the out-of-town tryout period did for a Broadway play. The writer, the composer and the director had these sessions until 6 A.M. after every preview and the changes would go in the next day. That's exactly what I was doing with Bill. That is an unbeatable process. And you need a company that will bear with you.

The negative aspect is that because we're conceptually so collaborative, everybody's ideas got into the act, not only in the directing but in the writing. When we finished the *B. Beaver Animation*, I thought there were serious errors in the continuity. Choices were made that muddied the script. I really preferred, for narrative clarity, the single-actor version on tape with Fred Neumann. I had much more control over that than over the multichoral version that was so incredibly complex. Because we worked it over so much, and had so many high-powered, complicated actors who had so much wonderful stuff, ultimately the narration was overpowered. I got tired of hearing reviews of how great the performing was but that the script was a series of non sequiturs and fake Beckett. It deserved better than that. It's one of the clearest things I've ever written. It was made incomprehensible because the emphasis was on the comedy and the performing style. The script was, in a way, trashed.

So I have found that I've gotten much more out of my scripts when I work less collaboratively. But I never can top the tremendous dedication of a group of people who've worked years on my work and have allowed me to develop and change. The situation was far more positive than negative. I learned that I wanted to control the script, to make it more of a literary event, with more concentration on the story and the language, only because it had veered too far in the other direction.

How do you think of your writing now?

It took me a long time to figure out what I was doing. I think now that I'm writing epic poems that I have found an intricate way to dramatize. Therefore, I am an epic-theatre person the same way Brecht is an epic-theatre person. I didn't know for a long time whether I was writing poetry or prose. I believe I'm writing a very loose, free form of poetry. It's tighter with *The Warrior Ant* because I'm writing in tercets with a certain metrical scheme. But the earlier pieces are all dangerously close to so-called prose-poems. I think they're prose-poems because the formal rules are related more to poetry than to plays. This is why I feel that it's correct to call them performance poems. They're not plays, except perhaps *Prelude to Death in Venice*.

Realms, a six-part work, of which the Animations are just the first three parts, is the big work of my life. I began it in 1968-69 with the first draft of *B. Beaver*. And I'm now at part five with *The Warrior Ant*, but it's an enormous part. The whole series is concerned with the six realms of spiritual existence in the Buddhist wheel of life. You have your choice. If you want to understand what living is all about, you can divide it in the Freudian sense and write about id, ego and superego. Or you can divide it in the Christian sense and write about Heaven, Hell, Earth and Purgatory. Or you can divide it in the Buddhist sense and write about six realms. Man is supposed to exist at different times in each of these realms. There's the animal realm; the human realm; two heavens, the one of the passionate or angry gods and the one of the peaceful gods; and then below earth is not only hell, but the realm of the hungry ghosts, a kind of purgatory.

I've worked on *Realms* for so long a time that I'm able to wait, before I continue, until I sense that my life is settling into a different realm. For example, *The Warrior Ant* is the realm of warriors, that of the angry gods or heroes. The motivation came when my work started to get on a roll and I started to fight for a certain kind of position, kicked off by producing *Gospel at Colonus* and deciding not to work for anybody anymore. I confronted the whole issue of who owns what and who gets paid what, deciding what sort of position I want in theatre and trying to hold on to it. I hope ultimately I will find a way to write about peace, for part six.

In your work, where do characters come from?

For a long time I thought that developing a character was like peeling off an onion skin, a part of yourself you want to get rid of. Now I think you can't peel it off. You peel off a layer but it still stays with you. I write parables about so-called animal characters or characters inspired by Kafka's parables, which is the key to the whole structure—stories like "The Burro" and "Jackals and Arabs." The great animal parables of Kafka inspired me to try all these little animal stories, the Animations.

I'm always looking for a metaphor for a certain sense of myself. It can be of either sex or human or animal or insect or anything. But it's quite literal. I write about an ant because I feel antlike, in a very complex way. *The Warrior Ant* is about culture. I'm interested in sociobiology and the question: What is the real animal, society or the individual? In other words, how controlled are you? How much free will do you have? In particular, how much free will do you have as an artist? An ant's a classic example. An ant can't live more than a few minutes separated from the society, the culture, the hill. The irony is that I'm sure—or fantasize—that individual ants feel they're individuals. But they're so totally a part of the social animal that one can perceive the anthill as the real animal and the ants as no more individual than the cells in the human body. Does each cell in your body feel it's an individual? Each cell is programmed to go and fight disease and die. Like each ant is pro-grammed to die if the hill is invaded by termites. But is not each human being programmed to die if the country's invaded? So the idea here is to find a metaphor for my deep intimation of lack of freedom.

My only writing teacher, ever, at San Francisco State, was named Herb Willner and the only thing I remember him telling me is, "write into the metaphor." I really believe that. I don't think I've ever followed any other advice about writing. The key is the moment I can formulate the metaphor, when it reverberates. A dog. A dog as the precise metaphor for the male-female sociopolitical entity in terms of feminism today. A dog and a master. A leash. A chain. That kind of a thing. I really feel I'm writing a parable.

So the specific characters are determined by what is needed to tell the parable.

The characters *are* the parable. They're like a position paper, an embodiment of a philosophical stance, of a certain idea about consciousness. They represent the first nuance of objectivity. I might feel and feel and feel and then suddenly I'll have a view of what I feel. I'll say, "Oh, I've been feeling like a rat." Boom! Write a story about a rat. It's that click that says, "You can finally take all these feelings and embody them in a metaphor." Once you have the metaphor, you're able to objectify. It's therapeutic. It's a release. It's like passing the buck into literature, into art.

How do you see the relationship between your work as writer and as director?

For a long time, I couldn't put that together. Then, just about the time I started Mabou Mines, I realized they were the same thing. That was a revelation. I doubled my options. Instead of being locked into a position where I can only fix, adjust and formulate directorially, I now have the option to change it on the writing end. If I can't solve a writing problem, I can change it directorially. It's like dual pipes on a car. You have two ways out from the motor. At one time I tried to formulate a kind of dialectic which I still use a little bit. Once the script was out there, I approached it as if it had been written by an asshole and only I, with my great directorial skill, could save it. But that is a paranoid way of dealing with yourself and I decided that maybe I should adjust to the fact that I think I've got a pretty good script. When I was working the other way, I was allowing a lot of persiflage and obfuscation in the script and a lot of games and tricks. Many people felt that I did myself a tremendous disservice. *Gospel* was a big transition, as is *The Warrior Ant*. I'm just letting it talk and stay clean. I'm casting better and directing less. Ultimately, I feel I'm a writer who directs, not a director who writes.

Can you say more about the impact of Asian theatre?

When I was a kid, sixteen or seventeen, I was introduced to my twin pillars, Beckett and Genet. I've always had a secret contact with Genet that was much more important than anything I felt about Beckett. I didn't do Genet because he was so expensive and Beckett was very cheap—a couple of characters and a stalk of celery. For Genet you had to have an extravagant production. What moved me very deeply was Genet's deep confrontation of illusion itself. I thought Genet was at the vanishing point of theatre. He symbolized theatre to me. In other words, if you believe that there's a void and that there's *maya* or illusion, theatre students would have to study *maya* because the more you know about illusion, the more you know what is not real. With Genet I started out at that point, trying to understand reality as play.

The great Asian theatres, particularly Bunraku—a Buddhist theatre— proceed from the same point. What I find most fascinating and brilliant, and a great spiritual statement about theatre, is that the Bunraku is a conscious manifestation of illusion, holding up before your eyes something obviously and presently dead, a piece of wood. Out of this piece of wood an entire world that appears to be real is constructed, by means of the semiotics of theatrical

13

convention, all the signs and gestures of life and psychology. But the fact that you are being presented with a dead thing, a piece of wood being manipulated by three puppeteers, is constantly enforced. It's the perfect symbolism of the theatrical convention, the manifestation of the illusion of reality or a world of *maya*, ultimate illusion out of something absolutely and visibly lacking spiritual and biological existence. It's a perfect dialectic: all life proceeding out of all death.

Also, since I've been working with Bob Telson and have become involved with African musical and narrative forms, I've become fascinated by what I sense now as the transition from narrative to theatre. The key in African music is the idea of call and response—response the beginning of choral narration, and the lead singer the equivalent of the actor.

The two facets of all Asian or Third World theatre are the metaphysical or spiritual aspect and the hook back twenty-five hundred years to when theatre was in the transitional state from narrative to dramatic, about 500 B.C. in Greece. In the great Asian theatres, the most elaborate and magnificent means of telling a story have been devised. But still, instead of motivating the character, they motivate the oratory. It's still basically a singing tradition.

How do you see the Bunraku puppet and operator? So many Westerners look at the relationship metaphysically, like that between God and his creation.

You can see it a lot of different ways. You can see it deterministically, these black, hooded figures manipulating human beings. Or you can also see the id manipulating the personality, or the unconscious manipulating the social mass. But what I'm most fascinated by is the idea that puppetry, costuming, makeup and characterization all come from the same source. When the storyteller began to characterize, change his voice to say certain lines, dance with certain gestures for the mimesis of characterization, the idea was to represent and bring to bear out of the self another self, another entity. In candomblé and voodoo, the idea of characterization is literally being entered by a god. This was prevalent in Greek theatre too, but in candomblé and in voodoo, you call the god in and change character. Your voice changes, you speak another language, you dance a different way.

The formal ideas and additions are, of course, mask, characterization, make-up, costume—but all these are various stages in a single process. When the entity finally leaves the body, it becomes a talisman, or the costume that extends the height of an African dancer, or the puppet that sits on a shoulder. It's the incredible excitement of another entity emerging from the human being and finally popping loose, but still manipulating us psychically. The excitement is in giving birth to a god. It might be better to say, giving birth to the archetype. It's not so much the god as the archetypal sense of self, or of the social unconscious, giving birth to a higher manifestation of the living force than can be embodied in an individual actor. A god is maybe a cheap way of putting it, it's more a social archetype.

With the idea that man has created God in the image of his archetypes.
Right.

Can you explain the evolution of your writing?
I had a hot period as a kid that hooked me in, and then a long period of nothing. I tried to write a book. I threw that away. I tried to write another one that was much better, much more metaphorical, kind of Kafka-inspired again, but I never finished it. And all during this time I was in a lot of conflict because I found that I had a flair for directing. It was easy for me and I had a lot of success. While it was hard for me to write and I had absolutely no success. I was a professional director when I was twenty-one years old. I always told myself, "You'll talk people into doing your plays." But it never worked out. I always got talked into doing their plays. I left the States in '65, hoping that in Europe I would figure out if I was a writer. That took three or four years.

In '68, after a real crisis, when my self-esteem had fallen to zero, I wrote the first draft of the *B. Beaver Animation* and I knew I had written something on a new level. From then on, I had confidence and I knew it was just a matter of getting it together to start a theatre. I knew I had enough to say to ask people to do my work. Then I could bring all of my directorial, organizational and producing skills into it because I knew that I had something to organize, produce and direct. I really didn't want to run a theatre that did other people's work.

I'm a real late bloomer as a writer. I feel that I'm just coming into my own. I didn't get a fully confident writer's stance until *Shaggy Dog* won a best American play Obie in '79. Then I thought, "Okay, here's an award that Beckett and Shepard won and I'm in stride here." I finally had a book out and national recognition as a writer.

The phase that began in '68 with the *B. Beaver Animation* carried through the *Red Horse Animation* in '72. Then in '75 my whole writing style changed and, for the first time, it wasn't derivative. I completely cut off literary influences and with *Sister Suzie Cinema* in '75, I was finally on my own. With *Sister Suzie Cinema*, the *Shaggy Dog* and *Prelude to Death in Venice*, I was almost totally influenced by music, pop lyrics, antiliterary and anti-intellectual sources, Mohammed Ali's poetry, comic books, things like that. It was a pop-culture take on writing without literary pretensions. That lasted until '81-'82 and then I made another turn with pieces like *Hajj* and *Warrior Ant*, which are an attempt to write bona fide poetry. *The Warrior Ant* is patterned on the *Aeneid*. It's mock-epic, tongue-in-cheek classical literature.

Is there a favorite among your pieces?

The Warrior Ant's my favorite. Theatrically, it's the most complete, finished work I've ever done. The most ambitious was the *Shaggy Dog* but I'm in the process of revising it now and there's going to be much more music in it. The most exciting try, where I attempted to reach for everything, was *Hajj*. That was an attempt at a live-video mix on the level that I had done live-audio mix before. It was an attempt to establish a dramatic work in the realm of poetry and to keep it there. I think it was the most successful, fully abstract thing that I've tried. When it's done, *The Warrior Ant* will certainly be the longest, and I hope the best.

When will it be finished?

It's a twelve-part work, a trilogy performed over three nights. Parts I and XII are done. Part IV is virtually done. The first night, Parts I through IV, will hopefully be ready to go into rehearsal next fall because Part II is quite short and I have a draft of it. And I just got an idea what Part III's all about. So we're looking at two to three more years.

How do you see the American theatre today?

I really have isolated myself from the theatre. I don't think I've attended a performance in two years. I'm totally unqualified to comment on the state of the American theatre. I know the work of my friends from the old time. Richard Foreman's work I respect a great deal, the Wooster Group I respect a great deal. I don't really know of a great theatrical statement at the moment. I do know that the so-called avant-garde theatre has become the world of performance. I believe that the clear, precise examination of the difference between performance and acting is very important if the performing arts are to continue to have an impact.

How do you see your own work?

I'm interested in projecting a theatrical metaphor that is radically different from the rest of the American theatre. It will reach its most developed stage in Part I of *The Warrior Ant*. It hearkens back to African tradition, unifying audience and stage. In African theatrical, dance or musical works the performance has so much impetus that the audience takes part responding or singing alone. *Gospel* achieves this. People are flabbergasted at the audience response and involvement, at the fact that the tradition is not post-Cartesian. You don't just sit there and analyze, you take part. *The Warrior Ant*'s going to go a step further. We did it in concert at S.O.B.'s with people dancing to the music. I would love to do *The Warrior Ant* at some place like the Palladium, or at a theatre where the apron could be a dance floor, so that the audience can get up and dance during the songs and then sit back down so the puppet show and the story can continue.

Telson and I are always looking for a form where we aren't limited by the tradition of short songs. The excitement of music is hitting a groove for fifteen or twenty minutes. That's why *The Warrior Ant* stretched into three nights instead of one. Half concert, half party, half play. In other words, Bob and I want to break down the rules of American theatre and to reinvent a social, storytelling, formal style.

When I go out, I go to hear Arabic or Caribbean music, or to see African dancers. When we were in Trinidad, we hung out with a steel band. This is theatre to me. One of the greatest theatrical experiences I've ever had was Carnival in Trinidad. Because I like narration, I like films; in a way, I think I've always done live films. I'm interested in the fact that theatre's getting more involved technically, that sound systems are getting better.

So your work now is grounded almost exclusively in participatory, non-European forms?

In Caribbean music and theatrical traditions, the Carnival mask. Great fifteen-foot costumes, incredible tableaus and displays, floats, bands. Theatre's a parade. Part I of *The Warrior Ant* is a parade.

What are your goals for the future?

I want to finish *Realms*. That's the most important thing. I want to finish *The Warrior Ant* and the six pieces tucked into it, the story of a redwood tree. For ants, trees are gods, so the redwood tree is the greatest god. I'm interested in working in video, I'm making a videotape of *Prelude to Death in Venice*. And I'm interested in music and I like writing song lyrics and working with musicians. Telson and I have a number of projects planned. One is a work based on Kafka's *Letters to Milena*. Another is a version of *Red Beads*, my little fairy tale, for which Telson would compose classical music. My project with Terry Riley is to work on the Irish epic, *The Tain*. With Mabou Mines, I'm planning to do a woman's *Lear*, starring Ruth Maleczech. Most of all, I want to write a book and I have a really good idea for one. It'll be a short novel—an answer, somehow, to Camus' *The Stranger*.

CHRISTOPHER
DURANG

The American theatre's most savage farceur, Christopher Durang, has described his daily routine during his three-year "sophomore slump" at Harvard as skipping classes, sleeping all day, cleaning bathrooms and going to movies. In his senior year, 1971, he broke out of his depression by writing a venomous comedy, *The Nature and Purpose of the Universe*, and a musical burlesque of the Gospels. During the next three years at Yale Drama School he wrote among other works a short one-act, *The Marriage of Bette and Boo* (1974), and *The Idiots Karamazov* (1975), a satire of Russian drama and fiction in collaboration with Albert Innaurato. These were followed by indictments of the movies (*A History of the American Film*, 1976), Roman Catholic education (*Sister Mary Ignatius Explains It All for You*, 1979), psychotherapy and urban romance (*Beyond Therapy*, 1981), hereditary lunacy (*Baby with the Bathwater*, 1983) and homegrown and nurtured neurosis (full-length version of *The Marriage of Bette and Boo*, 1985).

If Durang is best known for his assault on the ironclad morality of the Catholicism on which he was raised, it is because of *Sister Mary Ignatius*, his most successful and notorious play. However, this interrogation of Catholicism should be seen as part of his more general questioning of authoritarian personalities, social structures and belief systems, ranging from psychoanalysis to the well-made play. Durang's favored dramatic method is the satirical sketch, which develops a single grotesque idea in unexpected ways to an unexpected end. In most of his work the model for the sketch is clearly perceptible: either an immediately familiar situation or a well-known dramatic device. Each of his plays is a more or less tightly coordinated series of sketches whose impact finally is the result more of accumulation than linear development.

The Nature and Purpose of the Universe is a brutally comic attack both on the rationalization of suffering by those who believe it will be rewarded and on the dramatic forms, from soap opera to *Death of a Salesman*, that exploit and furtively glorify female anguish. In a succession of very short scenes the play dramatizes the abuse of its eternally patient and submissive heroine by her vicious husband and sons. Eleanor's passion play begins at breakfast, while she scrambles eggs and cries softly into her dish towel. Her son Donald, a dope pusher and pimp, hurls her to the floor and starts kicking her: "Did you throw my hypodermic out? Did you, you slut? Slattern! Trollop! Tramp!" By presenting an impossible succession of ills, *Nature and Purpose* finally transcends satire. It appropriates dramatic models and allusions ("Attention must be paid, my ass!") to create a surrealistic counter-mythology that pays a demonic tribute to the modern world's boundless potential for cruelty.

As in Durang's other plays, the comedy arises in large part from the use that characters make of various deceptive or obscure orthodoxies to rationalize their brutality. *Sister Mary Ignatius* is the apotheosis of this strategy, its title character a woman who uses the catechism of the Church to justify her vicious view of human relations. Through Sister Mary, Durang criticizes less the Roman Catholic church per se than the violent imposition on others of some Catholics' disturbed view of the world, the insane assurance that allows this woman to shoot dead a former student who, although gay, had just been to confession, and then exult, "I've sent him to heaven!"

The autobiographical *Marriage of Bette and Boo* relies much more heavily on empathy than Durang's early plays and takes a more compassionate view of human foibles. Despite its sometimes ferocious satire, its characters have emotional depth and seem misled rather than malignant. It is the first of Durang's plays which eschews self-contained scenes for a larger and more traditional structure in which characters evolve and change. The satirical indictment of various repressive institutions falls into the background. Instead, the emotional focus is on the destructive relationship between Bette and Boo and what can be salvaged from it by Matt, their son and the play's narrator.

The play ends with no grand moment of illumination, but—and this is a significant change for Durang—with a sense of the possibility for growth.

Throughout his career, Durang has used comedy to provide distance, to encompass personal pain and the horrors of modern civilization. He explains that when he started to compose *Nature and Purpose*, "suddenly the extremity of suffering made me giddy, and I found the energy and distance to *relish* the awfulness of it all." In their most fully realized and astute moments, teetering between anguish and glee, Durang's plays subvert both the conventions of realist drama and the strictures of the middle-class culture that savors it. In so doing, they speak directly to the fragmentation of self in modern society, to the relentlessness with which the world estranges the individual from his own pain and to the institutions that attempt to naturalize that estrangement.

■ ■ ■

DECEMBER 1, 1986—CHRISTOPHER DURANG'S APARTMENT, NEW YORK CITY

What led you to become a playwright?

I started writing when I was really young and I don't know why. In the second grade I wrote a two-page play, and I continued to write plays through grammar school and high school. In eighth grade the seniors did a play of mine. It gave me my first taste of the fun of audience response. I wrote another play that they did my sophomore year.

Where was this?

Dell Barton School in Morristown, New Jersey, run by Benedictine priests. It was a boys' school but we were able to borrow girls for the plays from neighboring Catholic girls' schools.

What kind of plays did you write then?

Versions of Broadway musical comedies. With my parents I occasionally went to Broadway musicals, and to the Paper Mill Playhouse in Millburn, New Jersey. My eighth-grade play was called *Banned in Boston*. I had forgotten it but was amused later when *Sister Mary Ignatius* had censorship problems in Boston, among other places. *Banned in Boston* was extremely innocent. It ended with four marriages—very Shakespearean. It was about a sweet girl living with her two maiden aunts. The aunts connected up with the Protestant minister to close down a local show that they thought was offensive. There were songs in it for which I wrote lyrics.

And then you went to Harvard.

And at Harvard I had expected to keep writing but I went into my sophomore slump early and it lasted until the beginning of my senior year. It was a rather serious depression. I wasn't certain that I was going to continue writing. I did put on two things at Harvard. My freshman year a play called *Diversions* was done in the Loeb Experimental Theatre, and then *The Greatest Musical Ever Sung* in Dunster House my senior year. Putting that on was a shot in the arm for me. In the summers back in New Jersey I had been in a couple of musicals including *Annie Get Your Gun,* in which all the songs are very good. I really thought I had Irving Berlin coming out of my ears and got to joking with a friend about making a musical out of the story of Christ and the Gospels. Through sophomore and junior years I wrote songs for this mythical musical I had no intention of ever putting on. I would sometimes sing them to people over dinner and senior year the Drama Society helped me put it on. I got a big kick out of the audience response.

That year William Alfred was offering a playwriting course, but I didn't have any plays to submit. However, in December I started writing *The Nature and Purpose of the Universe.* After all the strikes and uproar at Harvard, they put out a brochure called "The Nature and Purpose of the University." When it was put under my door I looked at it and thought it said "The Nature and Purpose of the Universe." I wrote that play in a great rush of energy, in two days or something. It really burst through the suppression of the previous two years. I submitted that for Alfred's class, even though he had signed a letter to the *Crimson* against *The Greatest Musical Ever Sung.* At Harvard, which is quite open to different points of view, I did not expect protests. But the Catholic chaplain was offended by it. I don't know whether he saw it or just read the favorable review in the *Crimson.* In any case he got various people to write letters saying that the musical was offensive.

The Nature and Purpose of the Universe wasn't totally about Catholicism but it did have this crackpot, radical nun, someone who had taken the Second Vatican Council very seriously. She smoked cigarettes and decided that the present Pope wasn't the right Pope so she kidnapped him and ended up killing him. I thought "God, Professor Alfred is going to think I'm a psychotic anti-Catholic" and then it turned out that he liked the play. So I did get into that class, and then went through a period of several years of being prolific. I applied to Yale Drama School with *Nature and Purpose.*

And what was your experience there?

Very good. The timing was just right for me. I didn't have a lot of confidence and I found Yale a good workshop. I didn't find the classwork all that inspired but I had become doubtful at Harvard about what you could learn in a class. I also found that I just wasn't very scholarly. So one of the nice things about Yale was that there was a lot of practical experience available. If you went around getting your plays on in the Yale Cabaret, that delighted the playwriting department, particularly Howard Stein, the head, and also Robert Brustein, the head of the school.

Also, because of some combination of shyness and looking exceedingly young, I rarely got cast at Harvard. So I presumed that I would not do any acting at Yale when there were people there preparing to do it professionally. But I ended up doing a lot of acting, initially because the Cabaret, which had a different show every week, had great need of actors. Because the actors' programs were extremely time-consuming, nonacting majors sometimes got a lot of work in the Cabaret. I found being in plays instructive. I was usually more interested in what the actors and directors had to say about my plays than what the other writers said. Some writers can be good teachers because they have a nurturing quality. But I find in writing classes that often another writer will explain how he or she would write the play. That's simply not very useful. Also, I had a good time at Yale because, as various articles have said ad nauseam by now, my fellow students were an exciting batch and a number went on to become quite famous.

During that period, what writers were you particularly influenced by?

Joe Orton. I get restless at a Feydeau farce. They're fun but I always find that they're almost two acts too long. There isn't any strong comment about life going on. There's something more acrid and biting about Orton. Although one doesn't see it in my writing, I was also influenced by Fellini movies, particularly the ones before and including *8 1/2*. The way he would bring in Catholicism was of interest to me because, in Broadway musicals and television, people tended to be very nondenominational. Everybody was like the *Donna Reed Show* and that was supposed to make whatever it was more universal. Between Orton and Fellini, I got the idea that Catholicism could be interesting to a general audience rather than something to hide.

You came to New York after Yale?

I stayed one extra year in New Haven because I got my Actors' Equity card through Brustein, who hired me to play Alyosha in *The Idiots Karamazov*. So for six months I was working as an actor at Yale Rep and for the other six months had three part-time jobs. One was working with a doctor at the medical school indexing a book on schizophrenia. One was teaching acting twice a week at Southern Connecticut College, which was intimidating because I didn't feel qualified. The third was sending out form letters to people who had donated their bodies to science, saying that the medical school had a surplus of bodies and they had better make alternate plans. That was an odd period. I was frightened of New York.

At the end of that year, Brustein gave me a CBS playwriting fellowship. I had to write a play that Yale Rep got first dibs on doing and I taught a class in playwriting. Getting that money was the impetus to move to New York. I got involved almost immediately in a production at the Direct Theatre, which no longer exists. They had an 11:00 P.M. show and did *The Nature and Purpose of the Universe* and later *Titanic*. By that time I was ensconced in New York.

And then you wrote History of the American Film?

History of the American Film was the first thing that people tended to hear about. I started it at Yale and submitted it to the O'Neill National Playwrights Conference in Connecticut. I had been turned down there three or four times—I often use this to tell playwrights to keep trying. I got in with *American Film* right after *Titanic* moved to Off-Broadway, where it got horrific reviews, for me in particular. But *History of the American Film* was quite a success at the O'Neill.

In 1977 I worked on three regional productions of the play. They were staggered so that I got to work, somewhat confusingly, with three different composers on the songs. I had two Broadway offers, one from a good mainstream producer who wanted me to bring in Marvin Hamlisch and lots of stars, and one from two beginning producers who had seen it at Arena Stage and wanted to keep a lot of what they saw there. I opted for the latter. About that time, I started getting put in those articles about up-and-coming writers. I also started to get movie offers. They all tended to be parody-related because that's what *History of the American Film* was. I didn't take any of the offers, deciding that I wanted to work on the show coming in to Broadway and thinking that if it was a success, it would be more advantageous for my career.

The Broadway production wasn't a success and when it closed, it felt a little bit like a stillbirth. It was my first experience of these periods of going hot and cold in terms of how you're perceived. When one is hot, one is asked for things that are really inappropriate. There had been a show called *Beatlemania*. Elvis Presley had just died, and this producer called me up and said he wanted me to write *Elvismania*. I said I thought the idea was pretty crummy. I didn't even like Elvis Presley. As soon as *History of the American Film* closed, all that interest stopped.

At the same time my mother, who'd been having bouts with cancer for several years, went into the final year of her life. That year was an extremely difficult one. I felt discouraged about writing, not sure of where to go next. I was feeling depressed about how the play was received, also about how hard it is to control things. I did see that we made errors in the production of the play and yet I knew that all those errors came out of good will and good thoughts.

In the midst of that year, I began *Sister Mary Ignatius*. I hadn't gone to church since the end of my freshman year. Late in high school I became a "radical" Catholic. I was a pacifist, I was against the war in Vietnam, I wasn't hanging around the Cardinal O'Connor Catholics. I was hanging around the Daniel Berrigan Catholics. When I went to Harvard I presumed I'd find a lot of Catholics like that. But the Catholic Student Center was very clubby. Eventually I heard there was a Jesuit house up by the Harvard Divinity School where every Sunday they had a more experimental mass, and were politically concerned. I went to this mass most of the second half of freshman year. There were only about twenty people and instead of the priest giving the sermon, everybody shared their thoughts Quaker-style. Anyway, this particular Sunday—my depression had come upon me during this period—there was a nun, who wasn't wearing a habit, who said that even though there were more civilians dying every day in Vietnam and even though we kept trying and trying and didn't seem to effect any change in the government, nonetheless she still had hope. And just quietly to myself, I thought, "I don't." So I never went back [laughs]. Then I went into a two-year depression. I stopped believing in the God of both the conservative and the liberal Church—this God who, though mysterious, has some sort of plan and is watching over us. I just didn't see the point anymore.

I hadn't thought about religion since then. But religion is one of the few things that one can offer someone who's dying. My mother was averagely religious, she hadn't stopped going to church. The rest of her family was more religious than she was. I watched them all try to make sense out of it, try to use religion to comfort. And I got to thinking again that when you accept Catholicism, there really is an answer for absolutely everything. Watching my mother's death, I felt that I didn't have an answer for anything. That was the initial thought for the play.

I started with the image of a sole religious figure who teaches children simply coming out and explaining it all. But it had been such a long time since I had thought about the rules. Because you're taught them when you're six or seven, you take it as fact rather than interpretation. You learn that if you put your hand on the stove you burn it, and that if you masturbate your soul turns black and you go to Hell unless you go to Confession. There were so many rules that I became somewhat incredulous. I wasn't actually angry writing the play. The play comes off as angry, I see, but I was incredulous and amused. I just found all that so strange. My mother was ill and I wasn't feeling good about theatre. I began it and didn't know if I thought it was good so I put it in a drawer and didn't write any more of it.

Then my mother died in March of '79. *History of the American Film* had opened in March 1978. My mother, who started with breast cancer which then progressed to bone cancer, became less and less able to walk. She managed to get well enough to come to the opening on Broadway. And the next week she really couldn't walk again. Strange what will can do. When she died I was actually greatly relieved. I was sorry but she was in so much endless pain and discomfort that it was better, if she couldn't get better...it really was time to let go.

Then two things happened. Somewhere in the interim I had applied for a Guggenheim fellowship and I got it a week after my mother died, which was fortuitous because I had very little money. And then I needed to take time off to rest and "heal." So I went to stay with a friend in Washington, D.C. and I started writing again. I wrote the first expansion of *Bette and Boo*, a one-act I wrote at Yale. And then sometime after that, I went back to *Sister Mary* and I put a little boy in it but I didn't know how else to make it a play. Then I came up with the idea of her ex-students showing up. I didn't feel that it could become full-length—I almost didn't finish it because I was aware that it's hard to make any money from a one-act. I didn't even know if I would get it done. It ended up being my most financially successful play. It's funny, both *History of the American Film* and *Beyond Therapy* are easier for audiences to take. There's something friendly or lighthearted about them. I always expected those two to be the hits.

How do you write?

I've always written in spurts, when I felt like it, which has usually made writing enjoyable. I don't mind going back to rewrite as long as it's for a production or if I have a specific idea, or if I hear an actor reading aloud. *History of the American Film* was hard because it was such a sprawling structure and I had so many options for rewriting that I got somewhat lost in it. After *Sister Mary* I put myself on a schedule, Monday through Friday, writing every afternoon for at least two hours. And I went through a period of exercising. I jogged in Central Park and forced myself to write.

When I wasn't feeling inspired, when I'd get stuck on a line or decide what I was working on wasn't very good, I often found, when looking at it the next day, that it wasn't nearly as bad as I thought. Sometimes it would be good. And other times, some section would be good. (I've been thinking I better put myself back on that schedule because I haven't been doing much work lately.) *Beyond Therapy* was done in that period, on a schedule. It was hard for me to end it and I think maybe that was because I was forcing myself to. I like the ending as it's written for Broadway but Off Broadway there were two extra scenes: one got cut in previews and one when we moved to Broadway. I didn't have a sense of where the play peaked until we went into production.

I take it that when you start a play, it comes to you more as an idea than a fully developed plot.

Yes, and this has been giving me problems working in Hollywood, where they want you to pitch an idea with a conclusion before you start work. I usually start with an idea and discover where it's heading as I go along. It does make for some awkwardness in structure sometimes. In *Sister Mary Ignatius*, until I came to the page on which one student pulls a gun on Sister and Sister pulls a gun back on her, I had no idea anyone had guns. It came as much of a surprise to me as it does, hopefully, to the audience. My mind doesn't work in outline form very well.

When you get into rehearsal, do you do a lot of rewriting?

It depends on the play. I'm not someone who does incredible rewrites in rehearsal. Some writers go in with one play and come out with a totally different one. I don't like working that way either as an actor or a writer. Usually before production I have a reading with actors well cast—they have to be right for the parts to tell what's right for the play. And I do rewrites based on the reading.

The Marriage of Bette and Boo was written over such a long period of time and rewritten so many times. I had a reading at the Public Theater about a year before the production and remembered that a couple of things didn't work. So I did my best to address them shortly before we went into rehearsal. After that, we had very few rewrites.

You mention in the script that the production at the Public was a particularly happy experience. Can you say more about that?

In terms of collaborating with people in the theatre, it was an exceptionally positive and smooth experience. In *Sister Mary Ignatius* and *Baby with the Bathwater*, I think both the director, Jerry Zaks, and I made casting errors. Very close to opening we replaced an actor for the betterment of the show. That's always a traumatic thing for everybody involved. But with *Bette and Boo* we were exceptionally happy with the cast.

I first wrote the play as an exercise. So much of it was so close to my parents' life that I thought, "I can't have this done." But I did show it to my playwriting teacher, Howard Stein, who then, unbeknownst to me, showed it to one of the directing students. Suddenly I was being offered a student production, which at Yale was a big deal because the students got assigned to it as part of their work. I decided it was too good an opportunity to pass up so I didn't tell my mother about it. My parents were separated and my father didn't follow my doings that closely anyhow.

Up until that time, my plays seemed to alienate at least some segment of the audience. *Bette and Boo* seemed to have "real feelings" in the midst of the dark comedy. I was aware that the audience response was very strong because of that. Also, it had ten characters, which is a lot for a one-act. I thought I could probably expand it to a full-length. So when I got offers to have it done in New York I turned them down. When I did expand it, shortly after my mother's death, I had a reading at the Actor's Studio and again the response was very strong, although the play didn't quite seem finished. I brought it to Joseph Papp and he decided to do it, but I didn't want it done while my father was still alive. I got very self-conscious about how he would feel. Then my father, who's in his early seventies, had a series of strokes which made him more or less senile so I realized that he wouldn't know about the play. At that point I decided it would be all right to have it done. There was a real sense of specialness among us. It was interesting to act in it and I thought the cast accepted me pretty fast.

Do you read the critics?

Yes, I have read the critics. But with *Bette and Boo* I read them less. In fact, initially I wasn't going to read any of them. But I heard such bad things about Frank Rich's review in the *Times* that after a couple of weeks, it started to prey on my mind. I started to fantasize that it was worse than it might have been. So I had to go read it. Reviews are a problem I haven't solved yet. There are many actors—Elizabeth Franz, who played Sister Mary, for example—who don't read them and just do their work. I think that's healthy, if you can get to it.

I used to think that since I didn't have to get up there the next night and perform, I should be able to read reviews and digest them. What's written does have an awful lot to do with whether you're going to run or not. The critics can make a show a hot ticket or important to see. I think that initial aura lasts for about four months. If audiences genuinely like your show and if the producer has enough money to hang in there for four or five months, you can run regardless of the critics. I feel that two of my plays, *Beyond Therapy* and *The Marriage of Bette and Boo*, could have run longer. *Beyond Therapy* was on Broadway in the late spring and it was very expensive. But my perception was that audiences loved it. I feel the same way about *Bette and Boo*. We almost continued running. We sold just fine, but the Newman

Theater is Papp's main theatre and he had other things scheduled. You couldn't have moved our set and the direction was very much geared to it. So that was frustrating. I think if we'd had a flexible set, he probably would have moved us to another space. He also said that had Rich's review been good he would have moved it, and that had it been earlier in the year he might have moved it anyway.

So you don't see anything positive coming from the critics?

No, I really don't. The only thing is that when you get a good review, it's good publicity. For the last four months I've not read the theatre sections because they irritate me too much. But I must say, as a corollary, that I don't know what's playing. With movies it's a different situation. No one film critic has as much power as Frank Rich does in theatre. There can be a consensus among critics that carries more weight.

The *Times* writing style is pontifical—in their news articles, too. In theatre reviews, opinion is presented as fact. There's actually a house style. You never get the sense that the critic is a person with his own prejudices. It's odd, on the one hand *The Marriage of Bette and Boo* really was a success for me. It won all these Obies. I won an award from the Dramatists Guild which, interestingly enough, the *New York Times* wouldn't publicize. And yet I also ran into people who go to the theatre a lot and had not seen it. I thought, "I bet they read the *New York Times* and believed it." I would have preferred that people miss *Baby with the Bathwater*, which Rich liked.

You've mentioned that you believe some of your plays are more disturbing than others and I must say I've always responded to the darker ones. I'm fascinated by the horror of Nature and Purpose of the Universe. *As you said in your note in the script, it's difficult to get the balance of cruelty and comedy right.*

The first time I saw a production of the play was about the same time I got into Yale. I had submitted it to a Smith College playwriting contest and won. So I got on the bus to Northampton to see the production. College students were doing the first scene in their rehearsal clothes very nonrealistically. There wasn't any stove but the woman had a big, heavy frying pan and a fork and was pretending she was doing eggs. And when the sons and the father would call her slut and trollop and throw her to the floor and the big pan would bang around, I found it hilarious. I was beside myself laughing [laughs]. It was almost embarrassing. When I later saw a production in New York, some nights the actress would hit it just right and it would be both funny and touching. Other times you'd see too much pain.

Of all the playwrights in this book I feel you're the closest to being a satirist. Your criticism comes less from a generalized skepticism than a deep-seated moral sense. I find that interesting in relation to the attempts to ban your work. The morality in Sister Mary Ignatius *is, I think, clear-cut. It just doesn't happen to coincide with the official morality of the Roman Catholic church.*

Sister Mary, I think, came out of being really honest—there can be a brutality to honesty. I was naive enough to think that most people would agree with me. When I left the Church, a strong element of liberalization was going on, which I hoped would hold its own. I thought that more liberal Catholics would say, "That's how the Church was back then and we're lucky that it isn't that way now." And presumably, the people who still were that way would not come to see it or maybe not even hear of it.

People who were upset with *Sister Mary* often said that all Catholics aren't like that. Well I know all Catholics aren't like that but I'm not writing a documentary. Mother Teresa doesn't belong in this play. Although I'm not even that crazy about Mother Teresa. I'd like her better if she were in favor of family planning [laughs]. Instead she's just going to let the world populate all over the place and deal with the poor starving masses, which is nice of her, but...[laughs].

It's rare that anyone deals with a belief system. Sister really goes through the beliefs, not just the behavior. Walter Kerr, who is not a fan of my work, nor I of his, kind of liked *Sister Mary*. One of the things he said, as a dyed-in-the-wool Catholic, is that it was interesting how little of the dogma I had changed. So the fact that people laugh at the dogma must be infuriating to people who believe it.

The controversy is a sign that it's working. The most acrimonious was in St. Louis, wasn't it?

Yes. Now it seems there are going to be problems anywhere it's done, particularly if public funding is involved. The country has become so conservative—maybe the Iran story will stop people deifying Reagan. What I do find serious and startling is the entry of religion into politics the last few years. A lot of my civic teaching came from nuns who told us that the Communists were terrible because they didn't let people practice their own religion or criticize the government. I can understand people hating my play and saying it's garbage and shouldn't be seen, but the notion of actually using the law to silence it strikes me as shocking.

It goes back to one of the things that *Sister Mary* is about. When Sister

Mary kills the gay guy she genuinely believes she's sending him to heaven. She realizes that his free will isn't going to get him there and so she takes it upon herself. I feel the people who protest the play, saying that it's genuinely evil, that it harms people and might harm their children, are doing the same thing. They don't have any interest in understanding the dangers of limiting speech. I thought my play would become dated, because of the Vatican Council, but with this Pope and Cardinal O'Connor it isn't.

I'm reminded of your evocation of Chekhov in Beyond Therapy: *"It's all how you look at it. If you take psychological suffering in the right frame of mind, you can find humor in it." The darkest plays—*Nature and Purpose, Sister Mary—*have apocalyptic endings. In* Beyond Therapy *there's an accommodation made. The characters don't really change but they do adjust to the situation.*

It's funny you're saying that because I really did love Chekhov's plays when I was in college. I think I related to the sense of despair, of loss.

But they also can be extremely funny.

You are probably right about *Sister Mary*'s strong sense of morality. Diane's speech about her mother dying of cancer, about why she's angry at Sister Mary, was probably the first time I ever wrote what I thought to be the truth dead on, as opposed to something fiddled up with dark comedy. It's hard to act that speech, to keep it from sounding like a speech. For someone who isn't threatened by what's said about the dogmatism of religion, it's clear that the author feels that suffering from cancer is not a good thing. People sometimes thought of my early plays that I must be this absolute moral idiot, as well as a moral monster. Those people who can't laugh at *Nature and Purpose* think that I'm just laughing at suffering. They don't see I'm laughing at how awful it is. In *Sister Mary* you do get a sense of how to relate to it. There is suddenly a realization, "We've been laughing at these rules but they're actually harmful." The fact that you think something's harmful gives you a moral base.

I liked the word you used, accommodation. In *Beyond Therapy* the accomodation is realizing that people are lonely and that sometimes half a loaf is better than none. It's a cliche, and it's nowhere to be found in *Nature and Purpose of the Universe* [laughs]. One of the things that interests me about *Bette and Boo* is that there's an awful lot of anger about how these people treat each other. They are vicious yet there is something about the end of the play...you can't quite get over the fact that there are connections that happen in families that have something to do with love even if you have to reject a great deal. You don't get that from *Nature and Purpose*. *Nature and Purpose* was written out of a real lack of belief that people change. It's not that I think now that people change easily, but I do believe that people can change somewhat. I'm not as bottom-line hopeless as I was in college. Actually [laughs], my getting through college was one of the reasons why I became more hopeful.

There are three very serious ways to admit that life is just going to be hell. The first one is suicide—very confrontational [laughs]. The second is to go to a mental institution. And the third is to live at home, with your parents. A great many of my aunts and uncles lived with their parents. There was always pressure on me, after my mother got divorced, to come home and live with her because she was "alone." I viewed this as a living death. There was just something very wrong about these families who were living together. Because I didn't do any of those three things, I feel that I succeeded somewhat in changing the route that was mapped out for me.

Feelings of hopelessness keep you from attempting to change a situation. A director I worked with early on was very tempestuous and it made me very unhappy. The directors I've worked with recently, Jerry Zaks and John Madden, happen to be extremely kind and logical people. That was a change and a reason for my mostly positive thoughts about collaboration. I have a problem with the critics because I can't change the critics. I can choose not to read them but I cannot take away their power.

Your plays concentrate on societal attitudes, with the implication, I believe, that in order to change the position of the individual, one must change society. It was interesting to read in your note to Bette *and* Boo *your dislike of a production that turned the play into Matt's private psychodrama.*

Having played Matt, I can say he really is like a Brechtian narrator in Act I. He just comes in and introduces the scene, has a couple of wry things to say and that's it. Then in Act II, he has some actual scenes with other characters. However, in the last segment of the play, starting with the divorce, suddenly the play does focus on what happens to him. I remember Joe Papp gave me a comment that made me do a small but interesting rewrite. All along Matt is trying to analyze upsetting things and to use his college work with Thomas Hardy to make sense out of them. And part of the humor in the speech is that he's doing so badly at it. Papp said that he wished there were some neat way to finish with Hardy. And I came up with the speech where Matt suddenly says, "I can't make sense out of these things anymore." It's an accommodation. He's given up trying to change them.

There was something I really liked about what Jerry Zaks did to the last scene. When we were rehearsing the hospital scene where Bette is dying, he said we shouldn't play sadness, we shouldn't play illness. This is a visit and actually as visits go, it's not so bad. Bette and Boo seem to have a lot of ease talking to one another, in some ways, that they never had before. Zaks, as an audience member, said he found himself wishing that they'd found it earlier. What was interesting is that I didn't write it saying, "Now they're at ease." My parents had some visits like that in the hospital. Again, it's an interesting accommodation—Bette has stopped trying to change Boo and so her stakes are lower, which allows her just to let him be.

I've recently befriended some people who are positive thinkers—telling the universe what you want, that kind of thing. It does surprise me that things can be changed sometimes, if you just tell someone what you want and what you're disagreeing with. I came from a family where either people didn't tell anybody anything or, in the case of the alcoholism, tried to change something that couldn't be changed.

How do you see the American theatre today?

I'm presently depressed about theatre in New York. The quality isn't good. I wrote off Broadway quite a while ago. I have my sights more on Off Broadway. But something odd is happening. I seem to be wanting to blame it mostly on the *New York Times* although I don't know if that's accurate. Maybe it's even more serious than that.

It's awkward for a playwright to speak against other works but I will in this instance. It's so expensive to go to the theatre and the audience is dwindling. That awful thing still happens with the snob hits, usually imported from Britain. That's fine if there were room for other plays, but there isn't. I think a snob hit like *Equus* is fine because the audience enjoys it, whatever limits its philosophy might have. But last year the two snob hits that Frank Rich tried to get people to go to were *A Lie of the Mind* and *The Iceman Cometh*. I have rarely spent eight more boring hours in the theatre than at those two plays. The Shepard play did have a couple of good scenes with Ann Wedgeworth, but they're similar to scenes in a couple of his other plays. *Iceman* may be a great play, but something was very wrong with it in that production. It was hell to sit through. I feel that audiences that chose those two plays because of the critics aren't going to come back to the theatre.

I feel that Frank Rich and the audience have gotten very separate from one another. Rich has very little response to emotion. When Walter Kerr was in his heyday, with *My Fair Lady* and all, he was very much in sync with the audience. I think Rich isn't and has become less so. I also think that there's a critical burnout—it may have happened to him. A big part of me doesn't feel like getting back on the horse, going up in front of the critics again. I think I'm perceived as a successful playwright so if I'm feeling this way, I think it's a serious sign.

Bette and Boo and *Sister Mary* are the two plays that I've gotten really strong letters on. I didn't get as much hate mail with *Sister Mary* as you might think. They just tried to close it down. I remember the first Saturday matinee of *Bette and Boo*, before we were reviewed. We had been getting good audience response and we reminded ourselves, "This is a matinee and the audience will be older and we don't know if they'll like it, so gear yourselves." It went very, very well. When we left for a dinner break, there were four of what I would call theatre ladies, with gray hair, in their fifties or sixties. They were waiting to say hi to all of the actors. They particularly wanted to tell me, "We really think you've done it this time. We thank you and we just loved it." I said, "I'm so glad you liked it." And they said, "We didn't like it, we *loved* it." What I got from that was the sense that the emotional quality in *Bette and Boo* reached most of the audience, including that group that used to go to the theatre. So I'm frustrated that they didn't get more of a chance to see it in a longer run.

Did you like Aunt Dan and Lemon?

Yes. Wally Shawn is one playwright whose work I like. *Aunt Dan and Lemon* was challenging for audiences. The fact that he doesn't put the rebuttal in is dangerous and caused him a lot of trouble. It's a difficult play, not easily entertaining. I found some of it quite funny, when Aunt Dan would go on about Henry Kissinger. I realize that Wally and I have certain things in common. I sometimes have the ability to tell the same joke over and over which drives some people crazy. But it's kind of like Gracie Allen, who always did the same thing and always made me laugh. That was true of *Marie and Bruce* too, another play I liked. That also connects to the psychological stuff I'm talking about, growing up with people doing the same thing over and over again. I relate to that unrelenting quality as being true to life. Rich's review of *Aunt Dan and Lemon* is one of the very few that I would be in alignment with. But the play is very intellectual.

Do you think the situation is better in the regional theatres?

I hope it is.

Do you get a lot of productions in the regionals?

I do. *Beyond Therapy* has been done a great deal. *The Marriage of Bette and Boo* is starting to be done. *Baby with the Bathwater* not too much but occasionally. It's been done abroad quite a bit. But I don't know where theatre is. The Broadway musical has become like Las Vegas. I don't look forward to going to theatre very much.

What are your plans for the future?

I almost feel like I don't have any. I wrote a one-act play about a year ago called *Laughing Wild* that I had a reading of with Katherine Kerr, who was so good in *Cloud 9*. I was excited by how that went. I want to write a companion piece but I keep not doing it. I don't have any other ideas for a full-length play at present. I would like to get involved in low-budget filmmaking where one theoretically has control over the output. They keep almost making a movie version of *Sister Mary*. Sigourney Weaver and I worked together on a screenplay we haven't finished, kind of like *My Dinner with Andre*.

There are two things I like about film. One is trying to reach a larger audience and the other is the permanence of it. When I see my plays done in ways that I don't like, I wish that I had my hand in getting a film version. There is a film of *Beyond Therapy* that Robert Altman has just made but the tone couldn't be worse. The rough cut that I saw was a desecration of the play. The actors are all good, they could be good in the parts, but Altman rewrote the script a great deal and so the tone is totally out the window. It's really bizarre.

Is there a favorite among your plays?

I think *Sister Mary* and *The Marriage of Bette and Boo* are my two favorites. Also I am occasionally extremely amused by *Titanic* because it's so crazy. It's not as angry as *The Nature and Purpose of the Universe* but it comes from the same pathological place [laughs]. Reading this play, you think this person needs therapy desperately, he really needs help [laughs].

RICHARD FOREMAN

T he nine-year-old Richard Foreman became hooked on the theatre when he was introduced to Gilbert and Sullivan during a visit of the D'Oyly Carte company to New York. Four years later he became convinced that Tennessee Williams' *Camino Real* was "the greatest thing in the world." His enthusiasm led him to work actively in school and community theatres in Scarsdale and to become president of his high school drama club. After training at Brown and Yale universities, he moved to New York in 1962 to pursue a career as a playwright. For several years Foreman wrote absurdist boulevard comedies and tried to break into the commercial theatre. Then he suddenly began to compose a kind of play radically different from anything that Broadway offered. In 1968 he founded the Ontological-Hysteric Theatre and, in a tiny space on Wooster Street, produced the first of his groundbreaking pieces, *Angelface*. That same summer he began the other half of his double career, collaborating with the composer Stanley Silverman on *Elephant Steps*, the first of a series of musical plays that would follow over the next twelve years. In 1972 he started working with his long-term partner Kate Manheim, whose powerful and mysterious presence has dominated almost all of his pieces since then.

35

In comparison with those on which he was raised, Foreman's plays are marked by what appears to be an almost total absence of character development or plot. Composed in a language richly allusive and yet utterly concrete, they abound in absurdities and discontinuities. His style, deeply resonant and sometimes very difficult for an audience, results not from a nihilistic rejection of narrative or the tenets of literary theatre, but from a desire to explore, through performance, the workings of consciousness itself. Foreman's plays are about neither the intricacies of an objectively real world nor the psychological peculiarities of character; they are about perception, feeling, understanding, expression. They *perform* consciousness—understood as being itself a performance, a play of intuition and expression, external stimuli and endless reflection. For Foreman, consciousness is a labyrinth of mirrors in which images magically change shape as they are reflected across the silvered walls.

Consider the opening of *Angelface*:

Max: The door opens. I don't even turn my head.
Walter: Does it turn?
Max: What?
Walter: Heads turn.
Max: Heads turn. My head is a head. Therefore: my head turns. Open the door a second time.

In this scene Max is seated in the center of a room. A door opens revealing Walter standing there. Max speaks. Watching, we expect something to happen. But instead Walter questions Max. Max doesn't understand. He questions Walter. Walter tries another maneuver, he makes a statement, he makes sense. Then, composing an absurd syllogism, Max turns it into non-sense. Here are (the fragment seems to be saying) the workings of consciousness: statement, reflection, non sequitur. Then it all begins again, "Open the door a second time."

Foreman's plays from the late sixties and early seventies explore consciousness by deconstructing the dramatic situations that dominate boulevard comedy: rivalries and erotic triangles. In the next phase of his writing, beginning with *Vertical Mobility* (1973) and *Rhoda in Potatoland* (1974), Foreman's focus shifts to a deconstruction of the act of writing itself—the act of bringing material to consciousness and putting it down on the page. These pieces dramatize that inner dialogue, the characters taking up the different, shifting voices within consciousness, manifestations of the various selves vying for control of the pen. They tease, question, change the level of discourse and call attention to the status of the written text, only to be constantly interrupted by false starts and stops, seemingly random intrusions and black-outs. These scripts, hostages not to real but to written time, document Foreman's attempts "to notate at every moment, with great exactness, what was going on as the writing was written." They read not like imitations of a real world but "like notations of my own process of imagining a theatre piece."

In the early 1980s, with *Penguin Touquet* (1981) and *Egyptology* (1983), Foreman's work shifted again. His most recent pieces are both more exuberant and less explicitly reflexive than his earlier ones, making greater use of anecdote, alliteration, rhyme and music. They still explore consciousness and the act of writing, but focus as intently now on an external object: political process in *Miss Universal Happiness* (1985), forms of media and control in *Film Is Evil, Radio Is Good* (1987). The fatalistic undercurrent in many of his earlier pieces, derived from the paralyzing force of incessant reflexivity, has given way to a sense of the sheer delight of using language, song, characters and stage space, to a celebration of the free play of the mind and of the world.

Watching Foreman's theatre in cluttered lofts or nonproscenium theatres, stage lights shining in their eyes, spectators will feel disoriented. Observing the fantastically detailed scenic environment, filled with strange cultural artifacts, they may recall the complexity of the mind itself. Studying Foreman's celebrated use of strings to demarcate space, they may be reminded how vision processes experience and places grids over reality. Seeing the familiar made strange and the unexpected become the inevitable, they will struggle to make logical connections. Deprived of the opportunity of responding to character empathically, they will work actively to understand, to interpret the action. As they do, they will discover that their own perceptual process repeats Foreman's process of creating the work. They will become participants not in an insular aesthetic event but in "the work of art as a *contest* between object (or process) and viewer." They will find themselves as enveloped in their own reflections as in the piece itself, their consciousness split, like the theatre itself, between watching and doing.

■　　■　　■

SEPTEMBER 28, 1986—RICHARD FOREMAN'S LOFT, WOOSTER STREET,
NEW YORK CITY

What were your early experiences in theatre that led you to write your own material?

I was interested in the theatre long before I became a playwright. When I was a kid my grandmother took me to see a musical revue, *Call Me Mister*, with music by Harold Rome. I came back to the fourth grade and staged my own version of it, using the records and lip-synching it with the other kids. I directed it, made the scenery and did everything else. When I was in junior high and high school I designed scenery for community theatres around Westchester and acted in high school plays. Then I went to Brown University and did a lot of acting. I remember one day when my friends who were taking playwriting courses showed me their plays to see what I thought of them. I remember reading all the plays and saying, "This is ridiculous. I can do better than this." [Laughs] So I started writing plays. Even at that age, I pretentiously had ideas about the theatre that I thought were in advance of what I was being asked to do at Brown. I thought, "If I write the plays, I can really control things."

This was in the early sixties?

Earlier than that. I graduated from Brown in '59. My last year at Brown, they refused to allow me to do a Brecht play. The Dean said that he was a Commie author. So I started my own group and wrote my first play for it. It was a kind of Yeatsian lyric drama. Then I went to Yale as a playwright and wrote my imitation Arthur Miller, my imitation Murray Schisgal (believe it or not), my imitation Brecht, my imitation Sartre.

I came to New York, still trying to write Broadway-style, sort of absurdist comedies. I actually had one play optioned for London that Alec Guinness seriously considered doing. Then I remember one day coming back to my house and saying, "This is ridiculous. I've got to find my own voice. If I walked into a theatre, what would I really like to see going on in front of me on the stage?" I remember specifically asking myself that question and specifically, at that moment, seeing the image of a kind of tension between two performers which, in one way or another, relates to everything I've been doing ever since. So I began writing my kind of plays as the result of a specific decision out of a specific frustration, deciding to do what I really wanted to do and not caring if everybody thought I was a fool. Nobody could make heads or tails out of what I was trying to do. So I decided I had to direct for myself.

That was my introduction to the theatre. I should add that I started making theatre because I was a shy kid and it was the only way that I could live out a fantasy life of being more comfortable with people. Not that I was a recluse. I always found ways to be a leader. I belonged to many clubs. Believe it or not, I was voted most likely to succeed in my high school class. [Laughs] But I was always uncomfortable, inside, in my relationship with other people. I still am.

You've mentioned several influences—Brecht, Sartre, Yeats. What impact did they have on your early work?

None except Brecht was an influence for a long period of time. Back in about '53, when I was in high school, I happened upon Mordecai Gorelik's book, *New Theatres for Old*, in which he had a chapter about Brecht. I don't think many people in America had heard of Brecht in 1953, much less a fifteen-year-old kid. But I was immediately and totally seduced by Gorelik's discussion of the alienation effect and Brecht's desire for a kind of emotional coldness. For the next twenty years Brecht was, I suppose, my god. I tried to find out everything I could about him. His rather flatfooted, aggressive literary style influenced the way I wanted to write. I thought that his was obviously the way to work in the theatre. He was absolutely my greatest influence. But not anymore. I stopped liking Brecht that much when I turned thirty or so.

What was the effect of your studies at Yale?

I studied under John Gassner, whom I found to be an extremely rigorous teacher. I liked him very much, although even at that point my aesthetic was different from his. He thought I had talent, which was gratifying. He said that my one problem was that I tended to go for a big dramatic effect and would then repeat it and repeat it and repeat it. For a long time I tried to correct that until I realized, "How silly. If that's what I want, I should turn it into an asset, or at least try to."

What about the other, nontheatrical influences?

When I came to New York, I met the underground cinema people. They were interested in contemporary American literature, which up until then I had denigrated completely. I thought of myself as a rigorous, vicious European intellectual and had contempt for what I thought was the more primitive, naive American approach. But through these people I was introduced to Charles Olson, Robert Duncan, that whole school of poetry, and to Gertrude Stein, who became the second big influence in my life. It was really the combination of Stein and Brecht, I suppose, that produced the first thrust of my work—with one other bizarre contribution.

Because of the interest of some of these filmmakers in various esoteric matters, I got interested in alchemy. I began thinking of the attempt to write a play as the attempt to work and rework the same material again and again, much as the alchemists would keep working on their combined metals to transform them into gold. I really thought of writing a play as taking certain basic physical givens of the situation in the play and repeating them with slight variations again and again and again.

Formally each of your works proceeds not through a linear, causal development but through a series of variations.

Yes, that's the way I think. Of course, the earlier plays—from about 1968 until about 1975—were a bit different from what I'm doing these days. Now the writing tends to break down into aphoristic fragments of, I think, a kind of elegant language, even though there's no narrative progression. When I began, the characters spoke a flatfooted notation of the physical sensations in their bodies: "Oh, my hand is now heavy. It's still heavy. Why is it heavy? Why does it feel like it's growing?" Discussions like that would go on and on and on. It was almost as if I wanted to start from scratch. I wanted to start from the ground of matter before I dared to use a more aphoristic style, a more comic style, which spoke more openly about all of my real metaphysical concerns.

Were you interested in using Brecht to provide that concrete, material base?

I wasn't thinking of that aspect of Brecht, I was thinking of him totally in terms of the alienation effect, the desire for a nonempathic theatre. The language, meanwhile, was derived from Stein and from this alchemical approach to manipulations. Stein also, in trying to write in a continual present. The move into a more aphoristic style was a move away from that continual present into recycling all the inherited garbage and treasures of Western culture, which I think has been the emphasis of my work in the last ten years or so.

How do you start working on a piece?

That has changed radically over the years. First of all I must explain that I work as a poet works. I think that's the cause of one of the problems I've had with the critics. I don't think that people who go to the theatre spend much time pondering contemporary poetry. If they think of another literary art form, they think of novels. They do not think about the implications of language and what can be done with it. And that, rather than narrative, has always been my concern, as well as the psychological implications of what the words do to the person who is speaking them, the way that they hit associations and strike off other trains of thought.

John Gassner taught me that plays aren't written but rewritten. You would write your first draft, read it to the class and then go back and rewrite. And actually, it used to be a lot of fun. I would fix and fix and fix and fix. At a certain point I noticed that in rewriting I was trying, among other things, to eliminate the tone of my mother's voice from my texts. When I read the plays to myself all I could hear was my mother, who used to read me bedtime stories, speaking all the lines of dialogue. I didn't like that, so I tried to get Arthur Miller's tone in there, or Brecht's.

When I began writing the style of plays that I write now—that happened in '68—I still believed that a play had to be written from an outline and then rewritten. So I began with an outline delineating normal boulevard theatre: triangular domestic situations that I would then try to de-write. Scene 1: Ben and Rhoda in the living room are arguing about whether or not Max should be allowed to come to dinner because Ben is jealous. Knowing that that was the driving emotional force, I would then in writing the scene try in every way possible to deny it. That was my psychological intent. For the first four years, I worked that way. Then I came increasingly under the influence of a lot of theoretical work by artists about how twentieth-century art should be produced. And I decided that it was perhaps interfering with other sources of creativity to work from the constriction of an outline. And also, philosophically, I was not convinced that one should manipulate an audience to that extent, knowing at the beginning where you want to get at the end.

So I began writing without an outline. However, what happened was that I would get an idea for a play and start to write it out in scene form and after two pages, ten pages, sometimes twenty pages, it would dry up. And I'd say, "That play's not going anywhere. I've got to start again." I worked that way for a period of about five years. About once a year—after sitting down every day to write—suddenly a play wouldn't stop and I'd go through to the end. That left me with notebooks and notebooks full of plays that never went anywhere. I remember, after about five or six years, saying, "Why can't I use all these false starts and actually stage them?" I believe the first play that was made up of false starts was *Hotel China*. But I made myself one rule. I said, "These false starts are indications of where Richard really was *at* when he was trying to write these plays. So I've got to be honest. I'm going to stage all of my false starts as they were written, in sequence, not changing anything, to give the audience evidence of what was going on in me trying to make a play." So for the next six years or so, anything that ended up in my notebooks would be staged exactly as it appeared there.

The next logical step: One day I said to myself, "This is ridiculous. Why make these rules for yourself?" I began to feel free to take pages from last year's work, shuffle them around, do anything that I wanted to do, treating them as raw material to manipulate. And that, essentially, is the way I work now. For many years I was shy about admitting how loose my compositional methods were getting. I began to feel guilty, thinking of all those parental figures out in the world who would say, "You're not sitting down and working like a good solid honest workman, the way Ibsen did." So I didn't come right out and admit my increasing belief that the most interesting writing would simply come to you at odd moments. You had to pick it up on the fly, as it were, and then organize that random material, much as you would select and organize the random material of life in order to write an Ibsenite play.

Now, this is not at all different from the way that most twentieth-century poets work. The reason I work this way is simply that I have different metaphysical interests, different therapeutic interests in making art, than Herman Wouk might, if he's writing a novel that he hopes is going to sell a lot of copies and be bought as a movie.

In the last year and a half, I have tried more and more to integrate into plays song forms that I've been writing to specific tape loops. I write under the influence of that looped music very repetitively, and try to let come whatever comes through the motor input of those musical rhythms. I also started feeling freer about taking my amassed collection of five hundred pages and putting them out on the floor to see how I could combine them in a collage. I was interested in various strategies that would allow different material through. At one point, for example, as I was writing from left to right, I tried to imagine that there was something else that I couldn't read being written by an invisible hand going from right to left on the same line. And somehow I thought that imagined collision, or superimposition, produced a different kind of material.

Now, through all of this, I believe that a thematic center emerged for each play and that the texts have the same kind of coherence as the words of someone in psychoanalysis, free-associating on the couch month after month. The director Richard Foreman is finding in these texts the same kind of coherence that a psychoanalyst finds in the material his patient is producing when he thinks, "I'm just saying whatever comes into my head." But of course necessity is always at work. And it's my job as a director to find the necessity at work in the text that I am trying not to control as I produce it. Because what is reflected in my text is, I hope and think, all the forces that are operative in the world at this moment, seen from the particular perspective of Richard Foreman. I think the task of the twentieth-century artist is to tell his fellow human beings, "This is what it's like to experience the universe from this position. Is that relevant? Is it of interest to you? Does it relate to the way that you experience the universe?"

When you're writing a play, how do you conceive characters?

You have to understand that I don't write a play anymore. I put things down in notebooks. When it comes time to produce a play, I look through the notebooks to find interesting language, interesting sections. I haven't written characters except perhaps during the first years I was writing. For the first eight years or so, even when I wrote in the notebooks, I would write down who was speaking. These days, when I give a text to the actors there's no indication of who is speaking. It looks like a poem on the page. I feel casual about it because I have always believed along with Max Jacob, the French poet who's one of my favorites, that character is an error, that our characters are determined by the accidents of our birth and our social circumstances. If you go a step further, you can say that they're the accidents of our genes. I have always been interested in trying to write from and evoke that level of the self that underlies character, that level of consciousness that we all share, upon which is superimposed the accident of character.

When I assign the lines I think of the collision between the particular character of my performer and what I consider to be the more universal thrust of my language. I will ask myself, for example, how a universal statement about fear collides with the particular characteristics of Kate Manheim, or of Ron Vawter, who has other characteristics. Let's say that Kate and Ron were in a play together. I could totally reassign the lines, I could restage the play and I profoundly believe that it would be just as true. For the last ten years, the scenario is evolved in rehearsal. Not the language, that stays pretty much the same.

I noticed that in Miss Universal Happiness *you used the members of the Wooster Group in their more or less traditional roles, the ones they've developed over the past few years.*

Yes, and that's what interested me. I must admit I'm not interested in helping an actor discover how to play a type totally different from himself. If actors are interested in that, they may be frustrated working with me. If I give them something to do and they try it twice but don't do it well, I'll say, "No, instead of that, do a tap dance." They might say, "Oh Richard, let me work on it. In a week or two I'll get what you want." But that's not what I'm interested in. I'm trying to make ever more vivid and present what they are and allow that to inhabit the particular environment of my text.

I have also written eight or ten musical comedies with Stanley Silverman, the composer. When I'm writing them, I try to work in a somewhat more conventional mode with more conventional aims. A lot of people deny that, people who don't particularly like my musicals. But there, I think, I'm writing characters in a more classical sense. I imagine the characters and try to write lines and songs appropriate to them. So, just as I stage conventional, classical plays, I think of myself as having a double career as a writer: the totally explorative writer who's trying to get himself in as much trouble as possible writing poetic texts, and the more audience-oriented writer doing musical comedies with Stanley.

When you work with Stanley, does the text come before the music?

Yes, always. Basically by Stanley's choice. I would be willing to work the other way around.

As a director you try to bring out a certain level of coherence in the text you have assembled?

That's right. I'm trying to find it for myself. Before I go into rehearsal, I don't study the text much. I think the truth of the text should be discovered on its feet, in the theatre, with the actors. I don't make lots of notes, I go in kind of naked with the language. If a character says "Oh, my foot is heavy. Yes, but will this handkerchief help?" I have to decide: Do I want to use a real handkerchief? Is the foot really heavy? Or when he's talking about his foot, is he holding his head? Is his foot symbolic of his sexual organs?

As director you make those specific choices.

Right.

Where does designing the set come into the process?

That comes first. When I have the fifty-odd pages I'm going to use, the next thing I do is start to make a set. That's a long, laborious process. I generally go through ten, fifteen little models, each of which seems wonderful to me until I look at it three days later and think it's boring. I cannot really explain how it evolves. The first thing I do is make a model of the room I'm going to work in and try to make it resonate somehow. When I decided to do *Miss Universal Happiness* with the Wooster Group, I thought it probably took place in some of kind of revolutionary, Latin American setting. So I started imagining different kinds of rooms. At first I imagined a sort of hovel the peasants lived in with a big horse painted on the wall. Then I thought of a back room with lots of shelves, like in a general store in South America. The set went through all kinds of metamorphoses. I generally find that a set finally works for me when I arrive at the point where I have erased or made a counterstatement to the original, easily imagined visual thrust of the play. In *Miss Universal Happiness* we ended up with a set that, before I decorated it a lot, was almost a Diaghilev kind of colorful series of children's building blocks. I have to live through, I have get out of my system the obvious, more realistic response to what the text is suggesting and take what seems to be coming in from left field. I think that response is to something deeper, to another level of the text.

So is the designer more the analyst than the poet?

The analyst, if one remembers that there are many different schools of psychoanalysis. I would be prone to agree with those, including the Lacanian, which say that the analyst's task is not to come with great cerebral artillery to what his patient is saying, but to float in an unfocused way and to let arise in him whatever arises from what the patient is saying. But it's still the artist—and I think a good analyst is an artist, open to finding out what his own unconscious is telling him about what the patient's unconscious is saying.

So a piece is always staged for a particular situation.

Yes. However, I'm always typing up new pages, recollating old pages, thinking, "Oh my God, now I'm set for the next year and a half. But what am I going to do after that?" [Laughs] That's mostly a neurotic response, because when I'm planning that far in advance, I know perfectly well what happens is going to be very different from what I've planned. Unfortunately, since we all live in a world of grants and applications, we're often forced into deciding too far ahead of time what we're going to do. This sometimes causes difficulties for the real creative process, which I think is a much more improvised activity.

What impact does your work as a director have on your scripts?

I imagine that every artist dreams of creating in the most organic way possible. I don't know if that means that ideally I would like to write the play in rehearsal. But I do know that I specifically leave out many narrative keys in my writing because I feel that they can be more suggestively, imaginatively fulfilled in the staging. I know that I'm staging the play and that this is part of the same process. Whereas when I pick up Ibsen or a contemporary author, I often think, "It's all here in the text. Why bother doing it?" I think that's one of the reasons why a lot of directors come up with things like doing *Hamlet* underwater. How boring to do a play unless you can do it differently!

There are a lot of people who have said, "I like his directing—well I don't *like* his directing, but his directing's okay—but his texts, well, not much to his texts." I have confidence, though, that in time people will be able to relate to my texts and see that they have the same coherence and density as a lot of twentieth-century poetry. I'm not saying I'm as good as Ezra Pound. I am saying that my texts operate in the same way and are not incoherent and meaningless. The fact that I generate them differently from the way people usually generate texts for the theatre is, I think, irrelevant.

I became a director only because no one else would direct my texts. That's lucky in a way, because I think that whatever small contribution I have made has had something to do with my confidence that, however far out I went with my texts, I could solve the problem as a director. Indeed, for many years I would say to myself, "Okay, Richard, take these pages, combine them to make a text that will make you think, 'My God, nobody could possibly direct that.' And then see if you can do it." I have often said that I'm a more conventional director than I am a writer. I think I tend to domesticate texts that are wilder than my staging.

It seems to me that as a director, your work attempts to move beyond simply illustrating a text, whether your own or somebody else's.

More than I like though, I do fall into the trap of illustrating the text. I have to remind myself that, when I read my texts, what delights me is that at every moment I see several different things at once. Sometimes I forget that when I'm staging them and I overemphasize one line. I made a specific effort in staging *The Cure* to avoid a lot of the gestures that I had fallen back on in my recent plays. I was trying to keep *The Cure* cooler, more minimal, but also more suggestive. One reason I could do this was that I wasn't trying to control twelve people at once on the stage. I felt more relaxed, having to worry about only three.

I saw The Cure *at both the beginning and the end of the run, after two cast members had been replaced, and I didn't notice any major changes.*

There were none. We replaced one male character with a female one and ideally, we should have reassigned the lines and done a whole new production. But I get bored easily. Staging something again, such as I'm doing now with *Africanis Instructus*, is one of the tortures of my life. I always like to move on to something new.

Do you read the critics?

Yes. But I've always wished that I didn't. I hope that maybe this year I won't. I'll tell you this, I used to read each review twenty times over [laughs]. Now I read them only once and throw them out. So I'm making some progress. I get very upset, as I think most people in the theatre do, when they are negative, even though I may think the critic's a fool and what he's saying is clearly foolish. I agree with Gertrude Stein that artists don't need criticism, only encouragement. All you can do as an artist is try to radicalize your impulses and strip away everything that isn't you and make whatever *is* you that much stronger. Critics who write for the newspapers are interested in talking about how well the audience has been manipulated, not about how rigorously a specific vision has been presented on stage. So it's frustrating, but that's life.

As the years go by, I must admit that I find the critics sillier and sillier. Now that we're moving into a more conservative political era, there has been a lot of criticism not only of me, but of the kind of directors and writers I represent, saying that we're self-indulgent. I'm accused again and again of solipsistic vision. I find that absurd. It simply means that the people reviewing me don't recognize my cultural references. For instance, *Africanis Instructus* is about the discovery of Africa and about how the modern world destroys all the exoticism of foreign cultures, about how the energy goes out in this collision between societies. There's one scene in which a black man from Africa brings in a red telephone on a platter. A critic in the *Village Voice* said, "He just picks out of his unconscious these meaningless images and they're singing about a red telephone. What does that have to do with Africa?" As if a red telephone doesn't have to do with all the hang-ups of the West and the hot line to Moscow and our emergency-oriented life. All of the symbols have reference to culturally inherited preoccupations. Maybe the critics just aren't as well read or as well informed as they should be.

I also think it's because they're not used to dealing with such loaded images outside of a narrative framework.

Yes, I suppose that's true. But good Lord, if you've had any exposure to the other contemporary arts, you know that that is the way material is organized these days by artists.

How aware are you of the social implications of your work?

Immediately—after the fact. Maybe there are some artists who proceed purely by calculation. I don't. I talk about my work afterwards—or I have in the past quite a bit—and I can analyze intellectually as well as anyone else and see what is operating in my work. But I think an artist sort of blanks out and does it and then sees what he has. And he either throws it out or goes on. Of course as a director there are certain things that I'll notice, highlight and develop. All the calculation and the organization that Ibsen or Arthur Miller do is in writing and rewriting. I do that as a director because I feel a need for that collision of raw, more unconscious material with the conscious control of the director.

How do you see the American theatre these days?

I don't go to the theatre. I don't find theatre interesting. Occasionally when I have a friend in something I think, "I have to go or he'll be mad at me." I suspect many people in the theatre are in that position. As one gets older and gets involved in the world of one's own work, one is just irritated that other people aren't doing what you want done in the theatre. However, I do pay attention to many other arts and I continue to be stimulated by painting and poetry especially. Also, occasionally, by film and music, though less so now, perhaps because I'm making so much of my own music that I almost consider myself a composer. I read continually, obsessively, especially in the areas of philosophy and psychoanalysis, and a lot of—how shall I put it?— therapeutic, religious, mystical writings. That's what I do mostly: read. I read five, ten books a week.

You've mentioned the more conservative political climate. Do you think it's had an impact on your own work?

I think it is impossible that it has not. I would like to think that it hasn't and that I'm holding out for something other and different. But I believe that you are a product of your time and you're going to reflect that. For instance my last play, *The Cure*, got much quieter and, for many people, more accessible than some of the more hysterical, frantic things I've done in the last few years. I'd like to think that was a choice that had nothing to do with trying to be in tune with the eighties. But we are beings who respond to the contingencies of the circumstance and we cannot predict, we cannot really analyze what is making us do what we do. I certainly don't approve of the climate of the eighties. I'm horrified to see reports and articles in the press now saying that the sixties was the worst period America ever went through. I think the sixties was the one decent, healthy period in American life. My task is to try to resist everything spiritually deadening about the eighties and to keep something else alive.

This is why I did the play with the Wooster Group two years ago. I had been doing my plays at the Public Theater for Joe Papp. And I love Joe, he's been very good to me and I love everybody over there. But there's no question but that slowly I was getting pulled into an orientation a bit less combative, a bit less confrontational. When I'm working at the Public Theater, dealing with my friends there, I know they don't really share my aesthetic. Therefore, I wanted to come back to SoHo. And the one group that I respect in New York, that I think is as interested in getting into trouble as I am, is the Wooster Group. I wanted to immerse myself in an environment where I didn't have to worry about stepping on anybody's toes. I don't like to offend people. I'm a friendly guy. I didn't want to feel even an unconscious inhibition about getting myself in trouble. And that, indeed, is what happened [laughs], which is fine.

I'm going to do another play with them next year. I think that's a healthy thing for me to do because I had started to become part of the establishment avant-garde, the token avant-garde. I'll certainly never be as acceptable as some of my co-token avant-gardists because I still manage to do things that a lot of people have difficulty with. But it's a problem: to resist the horrible corruption of the theatre which is, finally, to want to be loved. You've got a whole group of people out there and you sense whether they love you or they don't. It's hard for a human being to say, "I don't care if you don't love me."

What are your goals for the future?

I have absolutely no goals anymore, except maybe to get out of the theatre. I'm not alone in having said for quite a while, "I hope I'm not doing the same thing ten years from now." But increasingly I'm not sure that I ever will get out of the theatre, though I suspect that getting out would be a healthy thing for me. I think that one should change and I think the remaining opportunities for change in the theatre are not great. Anything I dreamed of doing in the theatre, I've done. I'm not the most successful person in the world but I've worked a lot in Paris, which was a dream of mine. I've done something at the Paris Opera. I've worked on Broadway. I've worked at Lincoln Center. I've done huge productions. I've done my own rigorous work in all the places I've wanted to do it. And since, in my own work, it's like I'm up to Chapter 27 of the same novel, I have no more dreams.

Except, of course, I've always thought that my work (and most interesting twentieth-century art) is therapy on some level. None of us lives anywhere near the potential that is built into us. We're all asleep, me included. If you're a good artist, your art tends to be better, more rigorous, more alert than you are when you're alone in your apartment eating dinner. If I have any goal, it would be to make some of the rigor of my art pertain more in the other hours of my waking life. I'm very aware of the fact that when I make a work of art, I'm making a place where I would like to be. I wish the world had the same rigor. And I don't think that's particularly healthy. I realize increasingly that to hope that a work of art is going to solve your life's problems, or any life problems, is not very sensible.

Up until about six years ago, I approached every production saying unconsciously, "This one is going to do it. It's got to be perfect. Because if it is, it's going to change everything." I now deeply, fully understand that no matter how good it gets, it's not going to change anything. And that realization, sinking into me slowly, has had a profound effect on the way I think of the future. I no longer think of it as doing bigger and better theatrical production. If I have a dream, it is to transcend that final trap of art when you're making the most honest art that you can, thinking that *that* is something tremendous. I don't think it is.

Looking back at your work, do you have a favorite piece?

I like *The Cure* very much and a lot of people seemed to like it. I told the cast about four weeks into rehearsal that I was willing to be judged on *The Cure*. But there were two other pieces that I think were equally good, neither of which were that well liked. One was in New York many years ago, called *Vertical Mobility*. And one was in Paris a couple of years ago, called *La Robe de Chambre de Georges Bataille*. Both of those pieces I thought were very deep, very mature.

Do you hold out any hope for the theatre?

I wish more people who are concerned deeply with language would work in the theatre. In America now there's a group of young poets who are great artists, part of this so-called language movement in poetry.

I don't think we need any more plays. There's so much material to do but one never gets a chance. I think the greatest American writer this week [laughs] is probably an eighty-year-old lady in Florida by the name of Laura Riding. Someday I'd like to do some of her work but I can't while she's alive because she's very difficult.

I think I will always be interested basically in writing. Last year I said to myself, "How boring to be a director. This year you do your version of *Hamlet*. Next year you do your version of something else and compare it with Strehler's version." That doesn't interest me in the slightest. I'm interested in generating language and then some gesture, music, staging. Or the balance can change. But to me, it's all the writing of a text, whether or not the staging is a part of that text. So even as a director, as a person who makes his scenery, makes his music, I think of myself as a writer making texts.

MARIA IRENE
FORNES

Born in Havana, Maria Irene Fornes came to New York with her mother
in 1945, when she was fifteen years old. She studied painting in night
school and with Hans Hoffman in Provincetown before going to Paris to paint
for three years, returning to New York in 1957 as a textile designer. Three
years later, having read only one play—*Hedda Gabler*—she suddenly got the
idea for *Tango Palace*. "I stayed home for nineteen days and only left the
house to go buy something to eat," she recalls. "I slept with the typewriter
next to me." In the 1960s she was active in the Off-Off Broadway movement
and wrote a series of dazzling, inventive fantasies, including *The Successful
Life of 3* (1965), an almost comic-strip version of an erotic triangle; *Promenade*
(1965, revised and expanded 1969), a vaudevillian celebration of unexpected
juxtapositions, with music by Al Carmines; and *Molly's Dream* (1968), about
a waitress's wistful fantasies.

In the early seventies she went through a fallow period, which came to
an abrupt end in 1977 with the first production of *Fefu and Her Friends*, a
play much more somber and emotionally violent than her early works. It was

51

followed by a series of passionate and political works, including *Evelyn Brown* (1980), based on the diary of a servant in turn-of-the-century New Hampshire; *The Danube* (1982), about nuclear war; *Mud* (1983), an examination of a lethal erotic triangle; and *The Conduct of Life* (1985), about women held in thrall to a petty Latin American tyrant, torturer and rapist.

Despite the sharp differences between her early and her later plays, all of Fornes's work can be seen as a relentless search for a new theatrical language to explore what theatre has always been about: the difference between text and subtext, between the mask and the naked face beneath it, between the quotidian and the secret, between love and the fear and violence always threatening its fragile dominion. Fornes's early plays are filled with a slightly melancholic cheer, the result of an interplay between a sequence of fantastic and whimsical interactions and the underlying knowledge of unrequited desire and unfulfilled hopes—or in the words of her Dr. Kheal, "Contradictions compressed so that you don't know where one stops and the other begins." *Promenade*, for example, is peopled by a variety of symbiotic pairs, escaped convicts and a jailer, rich socialites and servants, ladies and gentlemen, a mother and her children. It is a comedy about the failure to make connections, searching for its plot in the same way that the jailer searches for his prisoners or the mother for her lost children. Throughout the play the pairs keep missing each other and although they delight in the unexpected turns, there is an intimation of a darker reality always held at bay. At the end the mother asks the two convicts, "Did you find evil?" And when they tell her "No," she assures them, "Good night, then. Sleep well. You'll find it some other time."

Even in these early works Fornes's revolutionary use of language is evident. From the first, she has honed speech to a simple, concrete and supple essence, whether in dialogue or as here, in the song of the convicts from *Promenade*:

> When I was born I opened my eyes,
> And when I looked around I closed them;
> And when I saw how people get kicked in the head,
> And kicked in the belly, and kicked in the groin,
> I closed them.
> My eyes are closed but I'm carefree.
> Ho ho ho, ho ho ho, I'm carefree.

This is language surprisingly capable of expressing complex shades of emotion and mobilizing a rich and understated irony.

One way of approaching Fornes's recent work is to see a reversal in the relative tonalities of surface and depth, the action now much more ominous, the characters no longer the "cardboard dolls" of *Promenade* but beings who breathe and sweat. The change is heralded in the first scene of *Fefu* when the title character, discussing her husband's belief that women are "loathesome," compares her fascination with it to turning over a stone in damp soil. The exposed part "is smooth and dry and clean." But that underneath "is slimy and filled with fungus and crawling with worms. It is another life that is parallel to the one we manifest." Fefu warns, "If you don't recognize it...(*Whispering.*) it eats you." All of Fornes's later plays are explorations of the dark underneath. In *Fefu* Fornes unearths the workings of a furtive misogyny and its destructive power. The seven women who join Fefu at her country house are all, to some degree, victims of the men, with their "natural strength," hovering just offstage. "Women have to find their strength," Fefu explains, "and when they do find it, it comes forth with bitterness and it's erratic." Those among them unable to recognize their internalization of masculine attitudes are destroyed.

The plays since *Fefu*, written in a great diversity of styles, explore the workings of violence—psychological, political and sexual—and the self-destruction toward which it leads, with the aim of teaching, of asking the spectator to understand and to make another choice. *The Danube* was conceived when, by chance, Fornes came across a Hungarian-English language record. "There was such tenderness in those little scenes," she recalls. When asked to write an antinuclear play, Fornes thought of the sadness she felt for "the bygone era of that record, and how sorrowful it would be to lose the simple pleasures of our own." Set on the eve of World War II, the play charts the gradual decay of a civilization along with the emotional and physical destruction of its well-meaning protagonists. It ends with a "brilliant white flash of light," and then, darkness.

Fornes's plays differ from those of most of her contemporaries in that almost all are set either in a preindustrial society or on the far edge of middle-class culture. They are filled with a deep compassion for the disenfranchised, for whom survival—rather than the typically bourgeois obsession with individual happiness and freedom—is the bottom line. They do not delight, even covertly, in suffering but take a stand unequivocally against dehumanization and violence in its myriad forms. Perhaps it is in this context that her revolutionary use of language is best understood, its simplicity and beauty signaling, in the midst of violence and decay, a verbal utopia in which things are called by their proper names and brutality is so embarrassingly evident that it can no longer hold sway.

■　　■　　■

IN THEIR OWN WORDS

OCTOBER 29, 1986—RIVIERA CAFE, SHERIDAN SQUARE, NEW YORK CITY

What got you interested in theatre?

A play that I wanted to write got me interested in theatre. I was not a playwright. I was not in theatre because at that time theatre was not a very interesting art.

When was that?

1959, '60. At that time the most advanced writers in the American theatre were Tennessee Williams and Arthur Miller. That *was* the American theatre. Important theatre took place on Broadway. The beginning of the avant-garde theatre came from Europe: Samuel Beckett, Eugene Ionesco and Jean Genet. It was as if those European writers were inviting us. But even when these writers became known here, it took a few years before we actually started doing their work.

For years most of my friends were in the arts. They were writers—novelists, poets—or painters. I didn't know anybody in theatre. So I was never at a rehearsal of a play. I never knew an actor who would talk about rehearsals or auditions or anything like that. Very few people I knew went to the theatre. I do remember going to see *A Streetcar Named Desire* because word filtered down that it was interesting. But when I started to write a play, although it did have something to do with some theatre I had seen, it had nothing to do with a general affection for or interest in the theatre.

So you were more attracted to European theatre?

In '55, I think it was, or '54, I saw the original production of *Waiting for Godot* in Paris, directed by Roger Blin. I'd just arrived in Paris and I didn't know a word of French. But I was so profoundly upset by that play—and by upset I mean turned upside down—that I didn't even question the fact that I had not understood a word. I felt that my life had been turned around. I left the theatre and felt that I saw everything so clearly. Maybe it was just a clear night, but it was such a physical experience. I felt that I saw clarity. Maybe that night something in me understood that I was to dedicate my life to the theatre. My feeling was that I understood something about life. If you'd asked me then what it was I'd understood, I couldn't have told you. If I had understood the text it still wouldn't have been clear. Of course, I knew the play had something to do with slavery and freedom.

I was a painter and lived in Paris for several years. I was not interested in writing. I came back to New York in '57 and the next year, I think it was, I saw a production of *Ulysses in Nighttown*, with Zero Mostel, directed by

Burgess Meredith. It was performed in a place—on West Houston Street, I think—that was not ordinarily used as a theatre. And that too had a profound effect on me. But still I didn't think I wanted to write a play. I just thought, "How wonderful, what an incredible thing."

Then in 1960, or maybe it was 1959, I had an idea for a play. I was obsessed with it. And I started writing it. Most of the people I knew, especially writers, said, "Theatre's a very difficult medium. You have to learn how to write a play, otherwise it won't be put on." I thought that was very funny because I never thought that I would write a play to put it on. I had to write this play because I had to write this play. It was as personal as that. I never thought of a career or a profession. So I wrote it. And writing it was the most incredible experience. A door was opened which was a door to paradise.

Which play was that?

That was *Tango Palace*. I imagine there are few writers who have such a sharp beginning. Usually a person's interest in theatre or literature starts early. Then one day you decide that you'd like to do something. It's very gradual. For me, it was like when you miss a step and fall into a precipice. I didn't even decide that I was going to step into it. And there I was, flying up!

What about other influences? Arthur Miller, Tennessee Williams?

I don't like Arthur Miller at all. I don't like Tennessee Williams' plays very much either, because it seems to me that he celebrates a kind of feminine neurosis, that he sings praise to it. I don't like that. But I don't dislike him the way that I dislike Arthur Miller. I feel love for Tennessee Williams, like someone I knew. In his writing you see the spirit of somebody with delicate feelings who was beat up as a child and lives in a world of pain and tears with a kind of complacency. Maybe complacency is not the right word. Maybe it's masochistic—the feeling that you cannot escape it. So you have a longing for beauty and for romance, you dream that Prince Charming's going to take you away from it all. I don't see the point of that at all. I feel we're fortunate that no matter how terrible things are, we live in a society where we have the freedom to take action, even if some people make this difficult for you, or if you're disabled from your upbringing. I understand how one can be mangled psychologically, but still your effort should be to find your vitality and move on.

I don't romanticize pain. In my work people are always trying to find a way out, rather than feeling a romantic attachment to their prison. Some people complain that my work doesn't offer the solution. But the reason for that is that I feel that the characters don't have to get out, it's *you* who has to get out. Characters are not real people. If characters were real people, I would have opened the door for them at the top of it—there would be no play. The play is there as a lesson, because I feel that art ultimately is a teacher. You go to a museum to look at a painting and that painting teaches you something. You may not look at a Cezanne and say, "I know now what I have to do." But it gives you something, a charge of some understanding, some knowledge that you have in your heart. And if art doesn't do that, I am not interested in it.

I don't know what my work inspires, because I'm never the spectator. But I'm horrified to think that my work in any way would suggest there is no way out. I've been told by some women, for instance, that by killing Mae in *Mud*, I have robbed them of the possibility of thinking there's a way out. "If she cannot escape," they said, "how can we?" I feel terrible that I have made them lose hope. The work that has most inspired me to action or to freedom is not work that's saying, "Look, I'm going to show you how you too can do it."

Kafka's *The Trial*, like *Waiting for Godot*, gave me the experience of a remarkable energy inside me. Pozzo beats on Lucky and at the end Lucky doesn't get free, but it doesn't matter because I do! I've never been anybody's slave but when I see that I understand something. Josef K. may get guillotined or go to the electric chair but, rather than saying "I'm doomed," I learn from his behavior. I know what my intention is, but I don't know if, after seeing *Mud*, it would be difficult to feel, "I'm getting out." I know that most people don't feel depressed by it.

So many of your plays have apocalyptic endings, where an amazing thing happens, like the burst of light at the end of **The Danube**. *It's as though you're not so much ending a situation as producing a shock wave directed at the spectators, which makes them deal with what they've seen.*

Maybe I have to be a little more careful with that. As I'm writing the play, I suffer with the characters and I share their joys—or else I can't write. I am dealing with them for a long time and then analyzing, breaking the play down, trying to see if it works. I become a technician and start moving things around. It could be that the shock is more violent to the audience than it is to me, because often that violent moment has to do with the violence of ending the work. That's a violence to an author.

Often, when you've become very involved in the life of a character, when you're riveted, and the play ends, you have a feeling of rupture. This world has died. But maybe that feeling of rupture is deeper in me...after all, audiences are involved in it for an hour and a half or two hours. But I've been involved for one to three years. I don't know how to end a play unless...who's going to kill whom? It could be that it's so violent for me that I transfer it to the stage. But to a member of the audience who doesn't have the same sense of loss when it's over, it's a shock, right? You say it is startling. I experience Mae's death, for instance, as a natural thing. I don't see how they could possibly let her go.

In retrospect it becomes an inevitability. The ending makes me go back to discover why.

I think usually the people who have expressed to me their dismay at Mae's being killed are feminist women who are having a hard time in their life. They hang onto feminism because they feel oppressed and believe it will save them. They see me as a feminist and when they see Mae die, they feel betrayed. I say "they," as if it were a multitude of people. A couple of people have said, "How could you do this to me?"

They expect positive role models. This also comes up in regard to black theatre. Some people are disturbed to see, for example, a black man who is as oppressive as the white man he's fighting against.

I don't believe in role models because I don't believe in that expression. I've never played a role in my life, and role playing to me is the beginning of death. You have to be yourself and you have to find wisdom and enlightenment within yourself. The moment you're playing a role, you're faking it, pretending you're this or that. I know that's not what they mean but the choice of the word is unfortunate.

We have the potential to learn by example or by demonstration. If you're trying to teach people to be careful when they cross the street and not just trust the light, and you show them a film where someone doesn't look and a drunk driver comes by and kills him, you're not saying, "You're going to get killed." You're saying, "Look what happened to this person. You look and don't get killed." That is a classic way of teaching. But maybe that's old-fashioned and I am an old-fashioned person.

How do you begin a play? Plot, characters, a situation?

Usually characters, but not characters that I choose or people I meet and about whom I say, "I'm going to write a play about them." They're characters that come to the page. I was so inspired when I wrote *Tango Palace*. I didn't ask for it, it just came into my mind and possessed me. Considering that it was my first play, it was easy to write. And it received a production at the San Francisco Actor's Workshop, very well directed by Herbert Blau and very well acted by Robert Benson and Dan Sullivan. Then it was published shortly afterwards in a college book of literature, among writers like Aristotle and Shakespeare and you can imagine....When you have a first experience like this, you're always looking to repeat it.

I tried to find ways to be possessed again. I devised writing games—I put descriptions of characters on a number of cards and places on other cards, and shuffled them. I wrote *Promenade* like that. I took one card and it said The Aristocrats and I took another card and it said The Cell. All the locations followed the cards I was getting. And I found that it was possible to be caught up again in a kind of writing where the characters take over and they do what they do and you have nothing to do with it. All you do is write down what's happening. If I don't write that way, the dialogue is very flat and tedious. I have to force the writing out. When the characters take over, it's fluid and fast and interesting. And you are as surprised as when you see something in the theatre and don't know what's going to happen next.

For six years now, I've been teaching playwriting at INTAR. I have an ideal situation there. This year we are meeting every morning at 9:30 for thirteen weeks, which is very intensive. Usually we meet three times a week for six months. First thing, we do half an hour of yoga. Then I give them a writing exercise. I have invented exercises that are very effective and very profound. They take you to the place where creativity is, where personal experience and personal knowledge are used. But it's not *about* your personal experience. Personal experience feeds into that creative place. It's wonderful to see that people can learn how to write.

My writing has been coming from the lab for the last five years. It has changed my style of writing. *Tango Palace* was very passionate. I realized after I wrote it that I didn't know yet how to write painful things without going through agony myself. So I started to write things that were lighter because I just didn't want to suffer. I'm not going to jump into fire so that I can be inscribed in the roster of great writers. But now, through my exercises, I know how to do it. My students know how to do it.

Right now we're in the second week of work. Today we were doing an exercise and one of the writers started sobbing. He was in the lab last year so he knows how to go into that and come out. It's not unusual for me to look over and see someone filled with tears. And you say, "Oh wow, I wish I were there because that must be something good." But he was sobbing and he stopped writing. So I went over behind him and said, "Are you okay?" He said yes. And I said, "Do you need anything?" because I thought maybe he needed comforting. He was okay; he was going through pain, but so what? After a while he went and blew his nose. He looked in the mirror and said he didn't look as pretty when he cried as Natalie Wood so he better stop [laughs]. Pain can be channeled—it's like what actors do. Actors go into the most agonizing thing and they're shaking and you think, "My God, how can they do this every night?" You want to say, "My poor darling. Let me hold you for a while to comfort you." And you go back to the dressing room, and they look like they've just been swimming in the Caribbean. They look radiant, and you're a wreck. So that's how I write [laughs].

It's wonderful to have that every day, with a group of people. We do our yoga quietly. I give them an exercise. We hardly ever talk. We write all morning. The last half-hour, they read. At first, I have a lot to say but I don't criticize the writing. I see if they are trying to write according to some other person's rules. You can tell from the dialogue—if it doesn't have any real life, you know they're following some idea of how people write.

Writing every day is wonderful. You may feel, "I'm not inspired," but maybe after half an hour you begin to be able to write. At home I would say, "Okay, I'll do something and then I'll write." And then I don't write that day. I don't write the next day. After a month of not writing, I don't know how to write. I forget. If you write every day, it's like another kind of existence. There's something in you that changes. You're in a different state.

How long have you been directing your own scripts?

Since 1968 with *Molly's Dream*. That summer there was a workshop for playwrights at Tanglewood in connection with Boston University. They had a company of fine actors. The plays were done in elaborately directed readings, with a lot of people memorizing as much as they could. Robert Lewis was the director of the program, but he wasn't directing any of the plays. I told him I wanted to direct and he said, "No. The directors will direct." I said, "But this is a playwrights' project and, as a playwright, I need to direct this play." He said no. I was annoyed, but I asked Ed Setrakian because I knew him as an actor and liked him and thought, "Why not?"

Then Ed started doing things that I didn't think were right. The play was very simple and he was making it too abstract. So I went to Bobby Lewis and said, "This is not right. He's asking people to do this bizarre behavior. The play's a kind of movie fantasy where people behave normally." So Bobby Lewis said, "You have to ask Ed to do it the way you want. And if you have any problems, I'll talk to him." So Ed did what I asked and then he said to me, "I haven't been able to sleep because of what you're doing to me." And I looked at him and said, "Ed, I'd rather you don't sleep than I don't sleep."

I'd always been so timid. When a director would say "Boo," I would acquiesce. But that situation taught me never again to give in. I didn't want to make Ed not sleep. I wanted to do it myself. If then it doesn't come out right, I did it wrong and nobody else has to suffer. I promised myself that I wasn't going to let anyone else direct my work. And I didn't care if it never got done again.

So I went to New Dramatists—I was a member there—to do *Molly's Dream* again. I wanted to do it with Julie Bovasso. They said, "All right, but we have to get you a director." I said, "No, I want to direct it." They said, "There's a rule here that playwrights are not to direct." And I started screaming, "I'm directing or I'm quitting. If this is a playwrights' organization, you have to do what is good for the playwrights. What are you going to lose?" So they made an exception for me. I directed Julie Bovasso and it was a bumpy ride. I didn't know her history of quitting and throwing chairs at directors. It worked because I didn't have a director's ego. I just wanted her to do my play. And she was wonderful.

I direct the first production of my plays and often the second. *Sarita's* going to be done a second time in San Francisco. They wanted me to direct it but I can't. It's too exhausting and I have too much writing to do. I wish I were directing it because I usually make changes in the second production. With the first production, sometimes I haven't finished the play.

So you're active as a writer while you're directing the first production.

Often I'm writing the play. Since *Aurora*, the play after *Molly's Dream*, I have never had a finished play before I started rehearsal. Usually I have a first draft of most of the play. It still needs a lot of rewriting but at least the scenes are there. *Aurora* and *Fefu and Her Friends* were not finished until three days before opening. For *Eyes on the Harem* I had something like three little pages written when we started rehearsal.

During the summer when I work at Padua Hills Playwrights' Workshop in California, we're supposed to write a play for a particular place, a particular grove. For me that's a first draft, or not even a first draft, because usually they want only forty minutes. Then I write more and it becomes a longer play. *The Danube* and *Mud* came from California. *The Mothers* I did last summer at Padua. It may be called something else when it's a big play.

The printed version of *The Conduct of Life* is different from the performance you saw. Orlando's speeches about his sadism were written after the play was first produced.

When I saw the play I really disliked the character, he's such a horrible man. But from reading it, I understood him much better.

The difference is partly in the writing, and partly in the fact that the actor was a young man without much experience. When you work Off-Off

Broadway—which means there's no money—there are a number of excellent actresses available. It's much harder to get men. Men don't work for nothing. There are more parts for them, more jobs. If they don't start making money from acting after, say, a couple of years of acting classes and one or two more of auditioning, they quit. Women don't because either they have a husband to support them or they are dedicated to the theatre. They will spend their whole life working a job and acting wherever they can.

Do you read the critics?

I never read a review until people tell me whether it's good or bad. It makes me too nervous. So if people say, "It's excellent," or "It's so-so," or "It's terrible," then I can read it. But I usually read it quickly. Maybe a year or two later, I pick up a review and say, "Oh, I thought this was worse, actually it does say things that are good, that are interesting."

I'm sure critics hate to have a playwright think this, but I find there's very little I learn about my work from reading the reviews. A lot of the critics—not from the *New York Times*, but the *Voice*—are talking to the playwrights, as if we're having a conversation and they're saying, "Look, Irene, it's time you did this." But I don't find that they are usually insightful enough. Maybe I'm being unfair, since I find when I read a review a few months later, it reads differently from the way it first did. Maybe I never find it insightful because I'm so guarded. But I think I'm right to be guarded because there's a difference between having a private conversation and a public one. A negative review is read by everybody. And not only that, but the people who read a negative review—"It was terribly slow"—won't go to see the play. You lose your audience because the critic wanted to have a conversation with you. When you have the power of the media and you tell everybody I'm stupid, that's not a conversation.

But the Village Voice *has been very supportive of your work.*

I owe my life in the theatre to the *Village Voice*. If the *Village Voice* did not exist, I don't know if I would be writing now. Richard Eder was positive about my work when he was with the *Times*. Since he left, about nine years ago, the *Times* never comes and when they do come, it's just hell. Marilyn Stasio has been supportive but she doesn't get much of a chance at the *Post*. They print Clive Barnes and they print reviews that she writes when they feel like it. I complain about the *Voice* because to me they are the only paper. I don't complain about the *Times* critics because to me they don't exist. They don't say anything.

They fulfill a function in the marketplace. Frank Rich doesn't have anything to offer people working in the theatre.

It's just for businessmen. They say to this guy: yes, no or so-so. They should just print that in the newspaper: SO-SO, in large type. I think a journalist, a critic of value, is someone who can teach, who can persuade people to stretch themselves a little bit. I don't mean doing the playwrights a favor or art a favor, I mean helping the audience understand something. Critics are not doing that.

Aunt Dan and Lemon *was one of the very few recent plays for which, I think, Rich did fulfill that role.*

I didn't like the play because I feel it is promoting fascism.

I didn't read the play as promoting fascism but forcing the spectator to confront his own fascist sympathies.

But you know who Wally Shawn is. You know he's not a fascist. How do ordinary people know who he is? It's not that he has to say straight out, "I'm showing you how stupid people are. Listen to how stupid this girl is who's saying it's decent and normal to be fascist." But there is something about where the heart of the author is. When your heart is dubious and perhaps you take a little too much pleasure in sadistic things, it may be confusing.

I don't know anything about Wally Shawn's politics. I know of his father and I saw him in *My Dinner with Andre*, where he was playing a poor writer. Well, he's not poor so I thought, he's playing a part. I don't know whether he's a fascist or so intellectual, so sophisticated, like Andre with his thing about burying himself to experience death. You don't know how far these people can go with, "Let's experience it." Maybe he thinks it's a good idea to go around and kill people. I don't know! I bet you that most people left the theatre saying, "I think Reagan is right. We have to eliminate all the people in Honduras and Nicaragua that are standing in our way."

I saw it as being about Reagan too, but about the incredibly seductive power of his fascism.

But how do you know that Wally Shawn is not pro-Reagan? That girl was a little too convincing for me. When she said, "We're not really compassionate, we are, maybe, a little embarrassed"— something like that—there was something so intelligent about that line. This is too dangerous. If he means to say, "Watch out, look how quickly you can turn," he shouldn't do it so convincingly. Don't hypnotize me into believing that it's right because then, what are you doing? You are creating murderers, the same way they do when they brain-wash men who join the marines.

In the theatre I wanted to shout, "No!" I felt outraged. Then I looked around and I became more interested in watching the audience. I don't think people were thinking, "How wrong this girl is." I thought they were thinking, "Is it true, what I'm being told?" You know how many people in that audience actually don't have compassion, but only a little disgust? And you know how many are liberal, just because they think it's right? I felt him convince half that audience. I thought, "The reviewers didn't think that because either they know Wally and they know he has a tender heart or because they think, 'Wally Shawn couldn't be writing this fascistic thing.' " And they all saw it as you feel it was intended. Let's hope most people read the reviews.

When I wrote Orlando's speeches in *Conduct of Life*, I worked very hard to try to imagine the experience of a sadist. I went through hell. It was so difficult. It was so ugly. I have written violent things and they all come out of me...easy, natural. I have a monster in me. I have many monsters in me. But that particular one, Orlando, is not in me, I don't understand it. It was a nightmare for me to write those speeches. But I hope that I didn't write them too convincingly. If I did, I would eliminate them from the play. And I feel that Orlando is less dangerous because not many people, especially people who go to the theatre, are going to abuse little girls.

What Wally Shawn is proposing, that they support Reagan, is not as drastic as that. You just go into the voting booth and think, "I want to keep my comfortable life, so I won't tell anybody." That's easy.

In The Danube *you use some Hungarian, in the sections of translation. That makes me think of your own position. How is it for you writing in a second language?*

I came here when I was fifteen and that is precisely the time you begin to become your own person, when you are no longer a child. You begin to go outside your family or school and venture on your own, you start thinking thoughts that you can't share with your family. So when I started thinking independently—or rather, when my thinking connected to society rather than home—it all happened in English. If I want to talk about simple things, I can do it equally well in Spanish or English. When I start talking about thoughts, if I speak Spanish, I have to translate all the time.

For many years I've admired your use of a language that's simple and straight-forward, and very poetic.

My vocabulary in English is very limited. When I read a newspaper or mag-azine article I'm constantly finding words that I don't know. I don't mean

63

technical words. But words I don't use. So I look them up and then I forget what they mean. And it may be that because my knowledge of the language is limited, I always have to be sure of what I'm saying because I have nothing else. I can't say, "I'll put a fancy phrase in here and cover up," because I don't know how to write a fancy phrase. So I have to think, "What does the character want to say? What is the reality of what's happened? What is the need? What is it inside him that can be said to depict him?" I think more of painting, of a character painting a picture, getting a picture clear.

At the same time, it seems your plays are about the impossibility of language to comprehend experience, about the difference between text and subtext. Doctor Kheal says that you can't talk about beauty.

It's become fashionable to say that about language and I'll tell you why I object. Evidently the directors of some productions of *The Danube* believe that I use the language tape to show how we're prisoners of language and how we repeat, as if there were a recording going and we were puppets. Unfortunately, there's also the image of puppets in the play which confirms this for them. Can you imagine? Language is the greatest gift that we have. We've been sitting here talking for two hours. And to think that I would say, "We are imprisoned by language"?! But they have people act like puppets. Don't they understand that this play is about life and the destruction of life? You can't blame language if you don't know how to use language, if you stop thinking. It's like a computer, you just press a key and you get a whole sentence. That's how so many people use language. It's gotten to the point if you don't use set paragraphs, people don't understand what you're saying.

People often speak about my work as being singular. What's singular is that each person's speech is full of little pieces, how they really think, one word at a time. People are very simple. But they are specific about each little detail. Even if it's just, "Oh, good morning, how are you? How's your daughter?" Maybe I leave out one word that, when I talk, I don't. Words that are useless, like "actually." I take those little words out.

But you were asking me about *Doctor Kheal*. Of course, language is language and life is life. There's no question about it. The number of things you can experience and don't know how to express are infinite. And it is true that sometimes we think we're experiencing only those things we know how to talk about. But that doesn't mean that language is shit. Language is a miraculous thing, probably the greatest gift we have. But it doesn't substitute for life. People who try to use it that way are in trouble. They have to know what experience is. But also they have to try using this incredible tool to clarify what they are experiencing. Because I'm a writer, I know how much work that is. Doctor Kheal has a hard time explaining beauty. So? He explains everything else. It's just that for a moment he would rather experience it. He's saying, "How could one ever come near it? I bow my head in front of it." A way of expressing your awe is to say, "Words fail me." That's language.

How does the American theatre look from your perspective?

You could say that the regional theatre, the Broadway theatre and the Off-Off Broadway theatre are schools of theatre. The theatres are training writers they've never seen, young artists who see whose plays get done all the time and whose plays don't get done at all.

You can go to the school without walls, which is Off-Off Broadway. There's more freedom there. There's more variety. But there, nobody's paid, so you can't demand too much.

I feel that the regional theatres have betrayed the playwrights. Their training has turned too many into documentary writers. Some people are doing actual documentaries, like Emily Mann and Adrian Hall. But that's just journalistic, those pieces are not going to last. That's not theatre literature. It may be serious and subtle work but it's not a play. Plays are written with a bit of that mentality, too. Even if the story is not about a current situation, there's a correlation with something happening right now, like corruption in City Hall.

The regional theatre depends too heavily on subsidies. It's inevitable. I'm not saying that they should do something different. There are less brains on Broadway but more energy. It's a business. I think that the regional theatre is more frightened than the Broadway theatre.

Do you think that's true of the Off-Broadway companies here? Manhattan Theatre Club, Playwrights Horizons, Second Stage?

Those are part of the regional-theatre aesthetic. But I don't go to the theatre enough to be able to say that with great conviction. The timidity comes from being afraid of losing your subscribers. If you lose your subscribers or your single-ticket buyers, you lose part of your funding. Because the more money you make at the box office, the more money you're given. It makes a certain business sense but it has nothing to do with art. And they're afraid, especially when they get into bigger expenses. Part of this has to do with the Equity scales. They have every reason in the world to be afraid. I think that they would put on *anything* that they could get an audience for.

Just recently, I've seen some of the regional theatres opening up to my work. I know my work has changed. It's more accessible, more emotional. There's more of a plot. Maybe they're not changing and I'm changing. I don't know. Maybe they're looking for something and writers who are less conventional will have an opportunity to be done on this large a scale. But it's not all good news because if the audience doesn't like it. . . . Of course any art always depends on sales. Theatre has become an unnatural thing, unlike television or film. So it has to be subsidized.

When I wrote my first play, I was writing because I wanted to write. And I still feel that a little bit. I do it for my own evolution. That doesn't mean I don't want theatres to put on my work, that I don't want audiences to flock to the theatre, that I don't want critics to write fantastic things, that I don't want to get every award there is. If it happens, it's part of my evolution.

Was there a time when you felt you weren't making progress?

After *Promenade* was done at the Promenade Theatre. Actually, I think it had started a little before. Up through *Tango Palace, Successful Life of 3, Dr. Kheal* . . . some of those were humorous but there was more there too. And then I started to repeat. I think in *Aurora* I tried to repeat *Promenade*. It wasn't conscious. And *Molly's Dream*, too, in a way. Those plays were more charming than substantial. They had less muscle. That's why I find my exercises in writing are so important. I think the worst thing for a writer is to write in only one way. It's not from being lazy or clever, you just get into a rut. You don't know you're in a rut. You say, "That's how I write." But if you do those exercises, you write from so many different places and your writing seems so peculiar. Afterwards, you look at it and say, "No, it's not peculiar. It was just peculiar for me. I'd never written from that place before."

Also, the Off-Off Broadway writers started to feel indifference from the people who had been our producers. They started getting excited by directors.

You're talking mid-seventies.

Even earlier, late sixties. The period when the writers were the main energy source in the Off-Off Broadway theatre was only two or three years. I think that '65 was really the beginning of the flowering. I don't know if Sam Shepard, Lanford Wilson, Rosalyn Drexler or Rochelle Owens was writing before that. I started in '65. The first thing that I heard about was Rosalyn Drexler's *Home Movies*. That may have been '64. By '69 already the directors had taken over—Tom O'Horgan, Open Theatre.

Richard Schechner founded the Performance Group in '67.

It's so important to have interest from outside, to have a theatre that wants your work, actors who ask, "Can I be in your play?" And we had Michael Smith in the *Voice*. He was our critic in our paper. You need that. A group of people coming with excitement to the theatre, that's all I need. But I do need that. I cannot write in isolation.

Are there any favorites among your plays?

There are favorites but usually it's the one that I'm working on, the one that I don't really understand yet. Like when you're in love, it means you don't really understand the person. When you understand the person, it's *a* love, rather than *in* love. I think *Fefu* is a very beautiful play. I did it in Minneapolis in May and working with it again, I find it's a very moving play without being sentimental. Men who are more feminine in their nature, more artistic, feel it as deeply as women. There are some men who don't know what's happening. They say, "What? Is there a play there? Is there anybody on the stage?" *Mud* I think is a little jewel.

I'm worried about *The Conduct of Life* because I only did it once. When I do a play once I feel that I don't yet understand it fully. And I worry whether it would work as well if I didn't direct it. I know *Mud* would work. I saw one production of it which wasn't good and yet it worked. But *Conduct of Life* may have a strange soul to it.

How so?

I don't know how it reads. Recently there was a reading of it at Los Angeles Theatre Center. I got a call from the director. He wanted to talk about casting, so I said, "Please, above all, Orlando should look like a very ordinary person, a nice guy. You meet him and he's like someone who works in an office and has a nice job." And he said, "Fine." For Letitia he said he had a very strong woman. Then he asked, "How old is Olimpia?" I said, "Olimpia's a middle-aged woman." He had cast a young girl. I said, "She's a housekeeper, a woman who cleans. She's short and heavy." An attractive girl would throw the balance of the play. I don't even know if the play would work.

He was thinking, too, of women being oppressed. All those women are strong. Nena is a strong woman, a strong child. It's not just women being oppressed. When you have a nut, a crazy person like that, everybody's oppressed. It's the oppression of a sadist. It has nothing to do with women. So a playwright has to be careful. I thought it was so obvious that Olimpia is an illiterate housekeeper that I didn't specify that she's middle-aged, overweight and unattractive. How can you say Olimpia's being oppressed? She runs the house! A servant is a job like any other. You work. When you go to work in an office, are you oppressed? You think that everybody should be a boss?

People like to draw a clear line between victim and victimizer. It's frightening for people to recognize their role in the maintenance of this system.

I don't think Olimpia, Nena and Letitia are maintaining the situation. I remember shortly after the Castro takeover there was a group of Cuban exile artists. They wanted me to go to meetings, to have readings, and they said, "It's not political." So I went. They had readings of poetry and discussions of painting and stuff like that. Then one day they passed an anti-Castro manifesto around that we were supposed to sign. It talked about the Red monster and the language was extreme. I said, "No, I don't want to sign." They were indignant and asked, "Are you in favor of Castro?" I said, "Not really. I'm not in favor of Castro but I'm not against him either. I don't know enough." And they said, "If you're not against him, you're for him." I'm not for him and don't tell me what I am because I know what I am. It's like saying if people don't fight the system, then they are for the system. That's not so. People have to survive. If you don't go out and get a gun and shoot the general, it doesn't mean you're supporting the system.

Letitia is in love with Orlando, but I don't think she's a masochist. She discovers horrible things, that he's in love with a child. She discovers what he is and she shoots him, because she cannot live around him. Before that she has enough information to realize what he is, but she cannot face it. But that doesn't mean that she's supporting the system. There is an oppressor in that play, but it's not Orlando, who is just a peon in the political system. It's the generals.

I don't think everybody there is supporting the system. What are they going to do? Olimpia has a job. She has to survive. You think she's going to say, "You son of a bitch. I'm not going to work in this house anymore. I'm going to go out and starve." We can do that in this country. Here, if Olimpia leaves a job, she's employed the next day somewhere else, because she's a good housekeeper and knows how to cook. But not in other places. So you cannot say, if you don't fight it, you're with it.

It may not be true in Latin America, where survival is the bottom line. But in this country so many people are passively complicit with an oppressive regime. That's a very serious problem.

Are you supporting Reagan because you don't go out and shoot him?

No.

Do you know how many people in other countries think that you are? Because you are going around with your little tape recorder and doing your little interviews instead of fighting.

There are ways of being politically active besides picking up a gun.

Letitia is just an ordinary woman who doesn't know anything. She's just in love with this guy. She's not political. She's not even intelligent. And Olimpia is an imbecile! Do you expect her to be political? And Nena? You expect her to be political? I expect you to be political. I expect me to be. We're supposed to be. It's been going on how many years now?

Six.

It's getting worse and worse. There isn't even a strong opposition as there was in the sixties. I would say that we are parties to this, but not them. We have the knowledge, the intelligence, the perspective. We know what's right and what's wrong.

What does this mean then in terms of bringing about social change, for people who don't have the perspective we have?

They cannot bring about social change. They don't know what's possible.

What can they do?

The only thing they can do is act emotionally. Letitia acts emotionally. She kills Orlando. Not because he has betrayed her, but because he attacks her physically. When he does, she shoots him.

CHARLES FULLER

Born and raised in Philadelphia, Charles Fuller considered becoming a musician when he was growing up, but his passion for literature eventually brought him into the theatre. He majored in English at Villanova and then served in the army from 1959 to 1962, stationed in Japan and South Korea. Several years later he cofounded the Afro-American Arts Theatre in Philadelphia and in 1968 wrote his first play, *The Perfect Party*, a drama about intermarriage and racial intolerance. This was followed by a series of plays including *In My Many Names and Days* (1972), a fifty-year family history; *Candidate* (1974), about a black mayor running for office; and *In the Deepest Part of Sleep* (1974), which began his long association with the Negro Ensemble Company. His first major success was *The Brownsville Raid* (1976), an exploration of the dynamics of racism and fear set in 1906 Texas in which a group of black soldiers wrongly accused of murder are dishonorably discharged on President Roosevelt's orders. Fuller explained that he was not interested in writing a two-dimensional melodrama, "the usual black-and-white confrontation piece," but in putting "blacks and whites on stage as people."

All of Fuller's plays deal with complex situations that do not admit easy resolution. They study the circulation of violence within a society, concentrating both on the development of motives and on the impact of violence on the community. *Zooman and the Sign* (1980) documents the breakdown of the social fabric and the triumph of fear following the accidental murder of a young girl, Jinny Tate, on the front steps of her house by Zooman, a vicious teenager wielding a ten-inch switchblade. The play charts her family's turn from grief to anger and their decision to place a sign on their lawn: "The killers of our daughter Jinny are free on the streets because our neighbors will not identify them." Although beginning with a random act of violence and ending with a premeditated one, the shooting of Zooman by Jinny's uncle, *Zooman* does not provide a tidy denouement. Instead, it leads the spectator to ask a series of questions: Why does violence flourish in the black community? How can the health of the community be restored? Can revenge do anything other than extend the chain of violence?

In the Pulitzer Prize-winning *A Soldier's Play* (1981) Fuller poses an even more complex series of questions. In structure, the play is a mystery, told in scenes of interrogation and flashback. Set in 1944, it begins with the shooting of Sergeant Waters and ends with the apprehension of the murderer. Fuller's treatment of the formula, however, is anything but traditional. As Captain Davenport, the black investigator, begins to put the pieces of evidence together, the situation at Fort Neal is revealed to be corrupted by racism on so many levels that the identity of the murderer becomes increasingly unimportant. Waters himself is portrayed as an extremely ambiguous figure. On the one hand, he is deeply aware of the difficulties facing black people in America. "We got to challenge this man in his arena—use his weapons," he admonishes one of his men. "We need lawyers, doctors—Generals—Senators! Stop thinkin' like a Niggah!" Yet he is hated for his cruelty and the indirect murder of one of the men. He has become as oppressive as the white officers who tyrannize him. Peterson (who, it turns out, is his killer) describes his type, "White man gives them a little-ass job as a servant—close to the big house, and when the 'boss' ain't lookin' old copy-cat niggahs act like they the new owner!"

When Peterson's guilt is discovered, one is left wondering if justice has been served. Had Davenport not pursued the investigation so assiduously, the white command would have accepted "the unofficial consensus" that the local Ku Klux Klan was responsible and let the matter drop. Instead, another black man becomes a victim and the white colonel can write Washington dismissing the events as "the usual, common violence any Commander faces in Negro Military Units." By the end Davenport's role is as problematic as Waters'. Davenport, too, is a victim of racism, disdained by his white boss, Captain Taylor: "Being in charge just doesn't look right on Negroes." Again one is left

71

asking questions: Why did Davenport pursue the investigation to its bitter end? His desire to prove Captain Taylor wrong? His hunger for justice? But whose justice?

Zooman and *Soldier's Play* thoroughly explore the workings of racism and demonstrate how deeply corrupted all parties become. In both there is no moral high ground, no vantage point within the action from which a character may survey brutality, dehumanization and murder in an objective way and offer simple corrective measures. In both all participants are implicated. Fuller's plays testify to the problems confronting American culture in transforming its racist heritage. They call into question the efficacy of the criminal code in putting an end to the cycle of murder and revenge. They point up both the futility of violence and the desperation that is so often its cause. "I feel outrage all the time at the violence around us," Fuller has said. "It's growing in epidemic proportions. Random violence especially. It seems to be the only demonstration of self left to so many people."

■ ■ ■

NOVEMBER 28, 1986—CHARLES FULLER'S APARTMENT, NEW YORK CITY

What drew you to playwriting?

I had been working in Ludlow, a Philadelphia community, as a housing inspector, and was writing short stories and poetry. A group of us got together and decided to start a theatre—this was in the sixties. We needed a place out of which to operate, to be a part of rebuilding the community. There was a lot of that going on in the sixties. At that time I wasn't really writing plays, but skits connected to community issues. I was interested in how you save your community—blacks and Puerto Ricans were living side by side and going to war every day. We did the skits in a church and I then began to write little playlets. People came down from Princeton, from the McCarter Theatre, and saw them. They told me that for the first time they were going to open their season with a new play, from a new playwright, and did I have anything to submit? I recall telling them yes, although I didn't have a thing. But I wrote a play, *The Perfect Party*, and they did it.

When was that?

October 1968. John Lithgow's father, Arthur Lithgow, was then the director of the McCarter Theatre. When I was there I got to meet the Negro Ensemble Company. They were doing *Song of the Lusitanian Bogey*. Meeting them and working in the theatre was something, after opening night, that I wouldn't ever give up. I was hooked. From that time to this, I've worked in the theatre.

Have you ever directed?

No, nor acted. My major interest is writing. I've never had any interest in directing. There aren't enough good plays.

When you started, were there many influences on your writing?

I don't think there are many writers in the United States who have not been influenced by Joyce, Stendhal, Hermann Hesse. I read everything I could get my hands on. I wanted to duplicate something like Franz Kafka's *Metamorphosis*. I was so fascinated with what the man was able to do, I wanted to come up with things that described my world in the same manner. [Laughs] I'd imitate *Ulysses*, writing stream-of-conscious thought. And the more you read, the more you understand that you must do something different, something as exciting as the things that you're enjoying so much. After college I went into the service and kept reading. By the time I got out of the army, in 1962, I was pretty certain that writing was what I would do.

So it was the theatre in Philadelphia that solidified your plans?

Yes, quite by accident. At the time we began, I had no intention of expanding what we were doing to include full-length pieces. That only happened as a consequence of taking a chance. And at Princeton Arthur was generous enough to give us all apprentice training. He took our lighting people, our actors. We went there not just to do a play but to learn theatre.

The influences you've mentioned are mainly European writers. What about American playwrights?

I made it a point to try and read everything. So plays were part of that process. After a while, it wasn't any individual's influence, it began to be the influence of literature in the world, and wanting to be a part of this great body of work that survived everything. I read to learn about history, about what people were doing.

When did you come to New York?

1969. Surprisingly enough, I've always worked here. Since I arrived I've never opened a play outside of New York City. And I don't ever intend to. I started working with the Negro Ensemble Company in 1974. I had worked down at Henry Street. I had done some plays in Harlem. But the Company is really a place for playwrights. They make sure the playwrights get what they want.

When you sit down to write a play, how do you start? Characters? Plot?

I can tell you what I'm doing at the moment. I'm starting a play and at the moment what's of most concern to me is telling an enormous story, an incredible story. I'm not so sure how it fits in terms of my decisions about characters. I need to tell a remarkable story and to do it in whatever way I can. The heart of it is to tell a story that no one else has ever told. And since I'm not sure that human beings have changed very much through the centuries, I mean to do it differently, to put the things we are accustomed to in the theatre—relationships between human beings—in a different light.

For me the opening moments of a play are most important, in terms of form. I might begin a play a hundred times until I get it absolutely right. Because if I don't get you in those first few minutes, I've lost you. I want to get you caught up as fast as possible. You hear something, you see something, there's enough to drag your butt into that play. And that might take me months, before any story comes out, before anything else happens. Once I'm dead certain of the opening moments, the rest is a lot simpler.

A Soldier's Play *begins as a mystery that you want to see solved.*

You have to keep watching. I'm never sure that people are going to follow you if you're just walking along. I'd rather rush them, push them, without giving them an opportunity to back away from it.

How do you proceed once you've written the opening?

I don't know what's going to happen beforehand. The story has to be created as I'm doing it. The process is one of discovery from beginning to end. Even when I do history. Events take place but they do not in any way describe the people involved in them. John Wilkes Booth shot Abraham Lincoln in April 1865 but no one knows what the guy in the first row of Ford's Theatre was thinking when he heard the shot. You can chronicle historical events but the reporting of the event in no way describes the human emotion going on around it. You can describe the facts or the context in such a way that you discover new things about them.

Do you do a lot of reworking before you get into rehearsal?

No. Working at the NEC has, in many ways, helped a lot of us because you don't have the money to fiddle around with a play. I sit here at my desk rather than in the theatre and do it. I don't know which is better. I've never had the opportunity to test a play over a period of weeks, to workshop it.

So you don't do much rewriting in rehearsal?

No, very little. There's not enough money to be able to do it. In a very real way, it has changed the way I see a play. When I first began to write plays, I was *in* the play. But knowing that you don't have a lot of time to play around with it makes you start thinking about sitting in the seats. So you start seeing the piece as you write it, which is very different from being inside the piece and writing your way out of it. You're really concerned with how it's going to look. I think that takes a lot more time in terms of structuring the piece.

Do you work closely with Douglas Turner Ward?

Once it's done Douglas and I sit around and talk for days, weeks, decide some things, argue some things. By the time we get in the theatre we're fairly well agreed on how the piece is going to look. Again, the question of finance is involved. Our work saves a great deal of time for the actors.

Do you do much rewriting after a first production?

No. When it goes up, it's finished. I'm not going to touch it again, I don't care what it looks like. There must be a time in a writer's life when he lets go. Since life is not perfect, it's reasonable to assume that no work you do is ever going to be perfect. For me writing is an extended process, a kind of evolutionary process. I compare the things I wrote ten years ago against the things I'm writing now and they really are different. It's a learning process. If I made mistakes, I hope I'll change them in the next one.

Can you explain the changes you've seen in your writing?

It's more mature, thank God. The things I'm trying to do on stage are different. At one point I was trying to learn how to handle large numbers of people, how to move them around the stage successfully, how to keep all this life going on at the same time. Then at one time I was concerned with how to handle small numbers. I did a play once with only four people.

As time passes, I find myself concerned with continuous action. Blackouts and crazy things like that unnerve your audience. I'd like to eliminate them entirely so that you never lose touch with what's going on. Your eyes don't have a chance to slow down, to stop, to relax. Very much like music.

For as long as I can remember, I've wanted to describe black people in a new way, to destroy all the stereotypical ideas about black people. The idea that anybody, anywhere, can always be described in the same terms is irrational and insulting. It's very important for me as a black writer to change how Western civilization—which includes black people—perceives black people. That's at the heart of what I do. So you might say the work hasn't changed but that I've developed new ways to approach old problems. Racism, for example, doesn't disappear, but one's approach to racism changes. How to fight it changes.

How do you think it should be fought now?

If attitudes change then fewer people are involved in racism. I don't believe that writers can change the world by themselves. But we can change the climate. You must get people to the point where certain ideas can be perceived. For example, in 1977 they introduced the personal computer. That allowed people to perceive new things, or old things in new ways.

One thing that interests me in your writing is your use of temporal ambiguity. At the end of A Soldier's Play, *it's made clear that what you're writing about happened in the past and that, implicitly, times have changed. But at the same time I'm struck by how much times* haven't *changed. I think that ambiguity ties in with the way you use stage space, keeping it flexible and dynamic, being able to move in and out of different locales, as well as different times.*

Flexible time is part of the whole structural nature of a play. I don't believe in "Scene 1: August 1, 1931, 8 A.M. Scene 2: Two weeks later. Scene 3: The next day. On the porch." For me life is ebb and flow. Images can merge. Time should merge. A character in a play should be able to walk through time, to go from one year on one side of the stage to another on the other side. If you begin these things properly, the audience will connect to that without difficulty. For me the idea of real time has totally disappeared as a tool for writing a play of any kind.

I've always wanted actors to put more into character than into messing around with a lot of props. I'm trying to reduce the amount of junk on the stage—set, props, all those things that get in the way of creating magic. The more you give actors to do, the better they get, when they don't have to turn upstage and pick up a picture and look at it and turn back and sit down. It's not that that's not part and parcel of very good plays. But I want the play to become a creation of the actors, with the playwright furnishing the imaginative backdrop for everything. If the play says you're in the year 2021, that's where you are. I work with some of the finest actors in the world and I like to give them more and more to do. If you tell your audience you're in a modern apartment, they will believe it. What reason do they have to doubt you?

Also, I want my plays performed. The black community doesn't have a lot of money to spend on sets. It's ludicrous to be writing plays with black characters that call for elaborate sets. I want people to say, "Let's do it on a blank stage because that's what the author wants us to do. All we have to do is pay actors." There's no need to limit the opportunities for a play by its setting. How crazy can you get?

A formal limitation also limits the potential of the material itself.

You have to understand you're limited to begin with. The stage is only so big. You don't have the world of the motion-picture screen to play with. You know that 99 percent of the time your play will be performed in a proscenium theatre. Every piece of wood you put on that stage limits you further. I try, as much as possible, to put the whole world up there. I'm attempting to get plays out of the constriction that they seem to be in and have been in for centuries. The influence of film on theatre I think will be felt more and more.

Did that feeling come out of writing the screenplay for A Soldier's Story?

To a certain extent. I want to do something on the stage that transcends time and space, which is what movies do very effectively. You can't cut on stage but something of that rhythm, which is so much a part of how people see, should be transferred onto the stage. *Soldier's Play* was an attempt to link past and present, to go back and forth rapidly. The more we are caught up in television and movies, the more you'll see the form of a play change. Performance pieces, too, approach theatre in a different way. I'm not a performance writer but I think that movement is important.

Good storytelling is essential. In a good story, you accept the terms in which the story is told. Theatre audiences are good at that, suspending their belief for two hours. My aim is to give them more, in a sense, by giving them less. Furniture and doors have an enormous influence on how you see characters. I'd like you to see them in a different way.

Without doors.

Not even suggestions. If they're not needed, why use them? One day I may go back to them. But now I'd like to continue reducing, creating purer characters who come at you just by virtue of what they're saying. That's what the Elizabethan theatre was, the Greek theatre. I'm not doing anything new. A religious ritual has the same potential. A minimal number of things are used—a knife, a bowl—but each has such enormous value that the people using them don't even have to wear costumes. I think that character can have the same power. There's a problem when realism is so much a part of what you're doing that the details overwhelm the story. Everyone has details of their own, in their own homes. Why should they need someone else's details in a play?

Is there any production that you look back on particularly fondly?

Soldier's Play. It was a joyful experience for all of us—although I'd like it to be out of my life. A *Soldier's Play* stayed with me a longer time because of the movie. Normally I would have gone on to something else much, much faster. You can get stale, playing the same music over and over.

I come out of the bebop school of writing where you always try to top yourself, like the musicians I grew up with—Miles Davis, Charlie Parker. If you listen to their music over an extended period of time you realize that they're changing with the music and they're always playing different things. It's important always to keep trying to play the music in a different way. I write with music, it's always there, it's always a part of my life. I don't find it unusual to describe a play as I would describe playing by Thelonius Monk or Miles Davis. They're my models much more than writers. Davis has been an inspiration to me for years and years, as long as I can remember. If I could only write like they play.

Do you read the critics?

There's a service that gets us all the reviews at once. I read them. Anyone who takes the time to write about something I've written is of interest to me. I write for people and there's no reason to believe that critics aren't people. I want people to see what I do. Once you risk putting something in the public domain you ought to risk hearing what people say about it. If you don't like it, then you shouldn't be out there. If someone doesn't like my play, that's all right with me. You don't have to like it. There's no way to predict human behavior. I try not to do it with my characters because I know you can't do it with people in the world. Critics are entitled to their feelings. Some I enjoy more than others. I don't have any animosity toward them. They can say what they want. It's not going to stop me from writing.

What are you working on now?

I'm writing a five-play history that begins around the Emancipation of 1863 and will end, hopefully, around 1900. The facts are easy enough to cull. There are millions of books on the Civil War and Reconstruction but I've never heard of a description of those events from the point of view of black people.

There are some things you always know about people no matter when you look at them. Shelter and clothing are a need of people in the temperate zone, throughout all times. If you understand something about the nature of those items and how they're used, then you can also understand something about how people moved. For example, if you're a slave and the bottom of your shoes is wooden and the tops are leather, you make a lot of noise when you walk. Somebody had to not like the clacking sound of wooden shoes on the stone roads of the South during the time of slavery. It had to have gotten on somebody's nerves. Many things can cluster around something as tiny as wooden shoes.

One assumes that people in a state of slavery will be bent over and as timid as they can be. But it's totally unreasonable to believe that when they turn the corner and go into their own houses, they will still be bent over. From the time they turn the corner life is lived out in a reasonable way. The men stand up and talk to their women. There's no reason to believe that families did not operate as families. There are lots of things you can cull from the circumstances of the times. What would you do if you never saw money, because nobody ever paid you anything? Those kinds of things we must deal with when we start playing with history. We must not assume that the events, as described, also describe the people caught up in them. Since human nature is always the same, you can tell remarkable things about something that you never dreamed you could know.

History has become for me a way of reexamining black people in the long journey of the United States. Events have always been described from another point of view, simply because we couldn't write. Now we can reexamine these events, to define ourselves rather than to be defined. Everything that was written about those recently freed slaves should be examined in light of the opinions that white people had of black people. The social sciences at the time, describing the truth of the Negro, have to be understood in terms of who was telling it, the advantage to him or her in the telling.

It's enjoyable to go back over those events and reexamine and redescribe in terms of what I know about human nature. You can't argue with the events. But you understand something about the nature of human beings. All the stereotypical things white people used to believe about black people just can't be true in the light of reason. If you lead people to rethink the past, that may change how they perceive black people in the future.

In examining the world, you find that stereotypes of white people don't exist either. You have to understand that even in the worst of circumstances, even in a lynch mob, everybody's human. Maybe that kind of madness is part of the human condition. You understand people in terms of their idiosyncrasies, that very often determine their destinies. Even the worst man has something in him that is admired and loved by somebody else. If you understand that, you can't in a play describe characters as, for example, the racist police commissioner or the black-power black. I've stopped using character descriptions at the beginnings of plays. Read the damn play. If you've got to know beforehand, forget it. The story, the acting out tells you. When you try to overturn stereotypes, it's easy to be foolish enough to believe the same things about white people that white people have for so long believed about blacks. The work has to become more complex. We ought to understand that our differences are describable and that they all speak to our being far more human than we might think.

Both Zooman and the Sign *and* Soldier's Play *are about revenge and yet the situation is not resolved at the end of either play.*

Nothing is ever really resolved. Do you really resolve a murder by sending somebody to jail, or killing him in the electric chair? Television resolves the most extraordinary problems in two hours. Movies do it. I just don't believe in that. I think stories have gray endings. We don't simply close the door and step into a new life. A lot of things have prepared you to open the door in the first place. Plays often come to pat endings. I think you can tell audiences only, "This part of it's over." We all go on and look back with regret or joy or whatever. I think that revenge is a formidable and a fundamental quality of human beings. As is violence.

Your plays observe the complexity of the social network that produces violence. Is there a way out?

I'm not sure that there needs to be. It seems to me that the evolution of the human animal is toward greater complexity. The most extraordinary thing we do is learn. The more you give people to learn, the better off they are. Sometimes providing them with a more complex image allows them to grow. The more information you have to use, the better you are at moving through the world.

In other words, by becoming aware of how this works, one is no longer simply trapped?

Even if you don't use the information, it is better to have it. You might be able to give it to someone else. The idea of television, that you can reduce human emotions to a half-hour, that you can tell any story in two hours, is a financial necessity. The people in charge don't deal with complex things because they don't think the audience is capable of handling them. That seems to me insulting. I deal with as complex a situation as I can find and hope that the people in the seats can understand it.

Even if the characters on stage can't.

Yes. Why should the people in the play understand everything? I certainly don't understand everything. The play is, after all, my voice, and there's no reason to tell you a lie. I have faith in folks. I really believe in the audience.

But just because you picture a situation in which people do rather badly doesn't mean that you intend to dash the spectator's sense of hope.

Finally, it's about putting what you believe to be the truth on stage, however wild and fantastic it is. People are benefited by the truth, no matter how ugly it is. Anything that we are misled by or misinformed about or afraid to confront limits us. My best friend once told me: "The job of a writer is to see to it that everybody in this world remains free." The more information you give people, the more likely it is that they will not allow themselves to be enslaved. If you aren't doing this job, you're wasting a lot of time. I'm certainly not writing for the money.

How do you view the American theatre today?

I've been seeing a lot lately. I don't believe that the arts are ever in trouble. Societies go through periods of time when not a whole lot is produced. I don't think that's a catastrophe, that's just in the nature of things. It's unreasonable to believe that every year all these great plays will be done. Life in America is, for the most part, mediocre. There's no reason to believe that theatre's going to be any better. I don't find the state of theatre terrible. I think it's going to get better, because it always does. It's in need of money, a good product, more playwrights, more directors, more theatres. It hasn't really changed, at least not in the twenty years that I've been associated with it. You can only write more, work harder to raise money, all those things.

Never get the idea that a national policy for theatre is somehow going to solve problems that theatre has never been able to solve on its own. I've sat through so many meetings about setting a national agenda for theatre. I just don't think it's possible. People can dedicate themselves to certain things. My goal is to change how you see black people. Someone else's may be to get more people into the theatre. All of that taken together works to make theatre what it is. It's unreasonable to believe that it's going to change overnight into a financially viable institution. We forget that the players who used to travel through the old West were lucky to get $3.50 for a night's performance. They had to drum up business even then. Why think that theatre is suddenly going to become the major cultural institution in this country? It never was, it never will be. Movies, technological things, excite people.

What work have you seen the past few years that you particularly admire?

I saw some stuff that the South Africans did at Lincoln Center—incredible! Motion connected to language, the music of that was marvelous. There's nothing in our history that can imitate it. Perhaps work songs, but America doesn't have a culture where dance is part and parcel of how people live their lives. The whole South African experience is dance, music and rhythm. Prior to that, some productions I saw last year at a theatre festival in Lithuania were really exciting—people on stilts, light, motion coming across the stage. Both things were exciting because of what could be done in the staging, not just the language.

I've always been like a delighted kid at the circus. What the circus can do with three rings is remarkable—the excitement, the magic. I've always wanted to make things happen that fill you with awe. You're learning something, the story is going on, you're feeling the emotion, and there's magic! You come away feeling, "Wow!" You won't hold on to the experience if it only comes out of sadness, if you remember only how it made you cry.

In a lot of American work I've seen lately I find the same old political arguments, coming out of a time when people were helpless, or believed they were helpless, and had to do something to alleviate their helplessness. The way to do that was to reexamine yourself, to find your own inner spirit and to fly up out of that condition. Well, the truth is that most people never stop examining themselves. Hell, let's get on with it. The world is still in front of us. We have to combat the selfishness that results from all that mirror-looking. This recognition is coming from outside the literary community, from those who said, "Let's raise money, let's sing our way to feeding a couple million people in Africa." Let's stop feeling sorry for ourselves for being so confused. Too many writers are just rehashing things.

Which is one reason why you're going back to history.

The United States is really a creation of the post-Civil War period. For me, *our* birth is the Emancipation. Our relationship to this nation is fundamentally a post-1863 phenomenon—as is our beginnings as people, actively operating on government. Prior to that, we have only slave stories. After that, we have a free human being operating in a society that is beginning to accept his or her freedom. There was enormous interest in "the Negro" at the time of the Civil War. What was going to happen now that he was free? By about 1890 everybody was saying let us forget the infernal Negro, and America turned to Imperialism, another form of subjugation. So we were the object of a lot of attention, theories, attitudes that persist today. Part of dispelling that is to go back to where it started and dispel it forever from that place and time. Given the nature of the history and the facts, there's no denying it: these were real people. You have to start thinking differently about them, and about yourself in relationship to them. You begin to change at the root.

So by doing that you are, in effect, providing the way out for the characters in Zooman *and* Soldier's Play.

When you provide a new launching pad for those people, they leap forward into history along a different path. And everyone associated with them has to see themselves in a more practical and rational way. We are all better off for that, if for no other reason than that we can be more comfortable with each other.

JOHN GUARE

T he story that Ronnie tells in the second act of *The House of Blue Leaves* really happened to John Guare. His producer uncle, Billy Grady, was searching for "the Ideal American Boy" to play Huckleberry Finn in a movie. When he arrived at the Guare home, the twelve-year-old, without warning, auditioned for him, dancing and singing, standing on his head, laughing, crying, and finally taking a deep bow "like the Dying Swan" on Ed Sullivan. Uncle Billy turned to Guare's parents and said, "You never told me you had a mentally retarded child."

Guare didn't get the part and became a playwright instead. During the sixties he wrote a series of one-acts for Off-Off Broadway and in 1970 had *Blue Leaves*, his first full-length play, produced, as well as a musical adaptation of *The Two Gentlemen of Verona*. These were followed by *Rich and Famous* (1976), *Marco Polo Sings a Solo* and *Landscape of the Body* (both 1977), *Bosoms and Neglect* (1979), and a cycle of four plays set between the Civil War and the end of the nineteenth century about the intertwined lives of four characters: *Women and Water* (1985), *Gardenia* (1982), *Bulfinch's Mythology* (not yet finished) and *Lydie Breeze* (1982).

Guare's early plays—through *Marco Polo*—are whimsical comedies with a dark undercurrent, peopled by unpredictable eccentrics, alternately foolish and violent, for whom everything goes wrong. In *Blue Leaves*, written under the aegis of Strindberg and Feydeau, the director friend of Artie Shaughnessy, the protagonist, flies in to New York from Hollywood to mourn his incinerated girlfriend and ends up leaving with Artie's, who's very much alive. *Rich and Famous* takes place on the disastrous opening night of the first produced play (but the eight hundred and forty-third written) by Bing Ringling, the world's oldest living promising young playwright, whose parents end up deserting him for his archrival, the boy next door. *Marco Polo*, set on an island off the coast of Norway in the year 1999, ends just after Tom, whose legs have been eaten by piranhas below the ice floe, makes a remarkable observation: "I've been reading Chekhov. *Three Sisters*. Those poor girls, all the time trying to get to Moscow. The town they lived in was only forty-eight miles from Moscow. In 1999 that town is probably part of Greater Downtown Moscow. They were in Moscow all the time."

The evocation of Chekhov is more than coincidental. Guare stands out among his contemporaries for his intricately plot-driven playwriting, filled with both the major reversals and the little ironic surprises—so common in Chekhov—that force characters incessantly to reevaluate their situations. Events never turn out as planned, his characters never get what they want and yet, almost inevitably, they turn their losses into unexpected gain. In a theatre dominated by dramas of disillusionment and perdition, Guare has almost single-handedly renovated the classic ironic formula, writing dramas in which recognition issues out of suffering, understanding out of dismay.

The first of Guare's plays to realize fully and powerfully this ironic pattern is *Landscape of the Body*, written in two days and optioned forty minutes after it was finished. On the Nantucket ferry Betty, recently fled from New York's Greenwich Village, recalls how many of her friends, employers and family, including her own son, have died in violent and mysterious ways. Out of this horrific yet comic series of disasters, Betty reaches a new level of understanding and forges a bond with her former persecutor, the police captain she meets on the ferry. She never learns who murdered her son, she learns rather not to expect answers. "My life is a triumph of all the things I don't know," she says. "I read Agatha Christies and throw them away when the detective says 'And the murderer is....' The mystery's always greater than the solution."

In the "Lydie Breeze" tetralogy Guare writes the history of a generation, the men and women who came of age during the Civil War. In chronicling the relationship between Lydie Breeze and three men—Amos Mason, Dan Grady (whom she loved) and Joshua Hickman (whom she married)—and their attempt to establish a socialist utopia on Nantucket, the playwright depicts their hopes and dreams, and the failure of their plans to build a better world. The cycle explores the interrelationship between the personal and the political as well as a series of changes—from innocence to insight, idealism to corruption, civil war to imperialist venture. *Gardenia* shows how materialism destroys the community: the desire not simply for money and commodities, but for people, the will of both Dan and Joshua to possess Lydie. Only in his prison cell, after killing Dan, does Joshua find the freedom he had never known on the wide Nantucket beach. "We mistook the size of the ocean, the size of the sky for the size of our souls," he tells Lydie. "It's taken this prison to show me our true horizons. I want to look our petty furies in the face and name them and lose them."

Joshua's desire is fulfilled in *Lydie Breeze,* Guare's most retrospective play, set eleven years later. Finally understanding the web of desires and careless betrayals that led to murder, despite (or perhaps, because of) his disillusionment, Joshua is able to help Lydie, his young daughter, exorcise the spirit of her dead mother. "You make yourself smart. And you dream," he tells her. "You don't let it destroy you. You...don't listen to me!" And he teaches her to read, repeating the lines from the Walt Whitman poem with which the cycle began: "On the beach at night alone....A vast similitude interlocks all."

In chronicling late nineteenth-century America, composing a vast network of characters, events and images that recur and evolve, Guare is renovating poetic drama. Simultaneously, he is writing a covert history of American drama itself: both *Gardenia* and *Lydie Breeze* are filled with subtle echoes of and references to O'Neill. "Your own past is valuable," Joshua is advised, in phrases that Guare hearkened to long ago: "Damn it, man, you're an American. Illuminate our future."

■　■　■

SEPTEMBER 30, 1986—OFFICES OF THE VIVIAN BEAUMONT THEATER,
NEW YORK CITY

What first got you interested in the theatre?

My parents were crazy about the theatre. And I had two great-uncles who toured from 1880 till 1917 with their own stock company. My father worked on Wall Street, despised it, said, "Whatever you do, never get a job." I was lucky to have a family who thought my going into the theatre was a really pleasing choice. Their support was terrific. When I was eleven I saw in *Life* magazine, during a summer vacation, that two boys had filmed *Tom Sawyer*. The boy across the street at the beach and I said, "We want our picture in

Life magazine." So I wrote three plays— we didn't have a camera. *Life* wasn't interested, but *Newsday* Long Island did a story on me—it reported that we were going to give all the money to the orphans of Long Beach. Seeing the story, in 1949—that was it. For my twelfth birthday my parents gave me a typewriter that I still use. It's as simple as that.

You were involved in the Off-Off Broadway movement in the sixties.

You couldn't *not* be. I came out of the Air Force Reserves, came back to New York, and a play that I wrote was done at the Barr-Albee-Wilder workshop, a profoundly important place for a number of people. Then in 1965 the O'Neill Playwrights Conference started. They called around to various theatres to say, "Name three writers of promise," and picked the twenty names that appeared the most times. I was one of those people. I went up to the O'Neill and they asked us what we wanted. I was assigned a date and trusted to have something to produce on that day and I did, the first act of *House of Blue Leaves*.

Off-Off Broadway was a psychic reality which meant: *anybody can have a play done.* I once wrote a play on Thursday and gave it to a friend. She said, "Come down to Theatre Genesis. They're doing new plays on Monday." My play was done that very Monday. There was a real energy in the air. Writing a play was a thing of great pleasure and fun—more like singing. The theatre was not Broadway, not so serious. The plays were not reviewed. That, in retrospect, gave one a great deal of confidence.

But it was the O'Neill that provided the real confidence and focus for me. I had a play read there in '65 and I wrote a play there in '66, '67 and '68. Then they made an enormous change. Instead of picking the playwright, they picked the play. That was a psychic sea-change, because the strength of the O'Neill had been recognizing writers of merit. They trusted that you would come up with something. Then—and they had to do it to keep people moving through—it got to be, "You're only as good as your play." Your play became a property. Luckily, by this point I was able to move on.

Were you ever tempted by directing?

Never. I like having someone else to talk to. I don't have the ability or patience to recognize the way that actors have to build a performance. Directors like Jerry Zaks or Mel Shapiro or Gregory Mosher will say, "The actor needs more time." I'm a good audience. I love to be around rehearsals. But I don't like to be the link between my material and the actors. I think that a playwright should always have an objective view, should be someone to do battle with. Someone should force you to say, "This is what I really mean." When you're doing your work you know what your play means in a kind of shorthand way so you don't have to make the extra step of translating it. And sometimes you make the wrong cuts. You have the play so fully in your head that you could cut anything and it's still there for you. A director can say, "We really need this beat. This is a hinge to get from here to there."

I do like being involved with the design. I think that everything should go through the director, but I don't want to hand my play over to a director and say, "Do what you want, this is a libretto for your intentions." I work with the director and the lighting designer, the set designer, the costume designer, to focus in so that everybody's telling the same story. That to me is what the theatrical experience is—the audience watching a group of people all trying to produce the same effect. It's truly democratic.

What other playwrights have had an impact on your work?

There's a story that Milos Forman tells about the two ladies who used to run the Cinémathèque in Paris. They said to him once, "We have decided that we have seen every movie ever made, and you know what? There's never been a bad movie." I'm a junkie. I love to see plays. There are a lot of plays I really hate but I don't think there are any I haven't learned from. If you hate something, you have an obligation to ask, "Why do I hate it? What does that represent to me?" With every play you see you ask, "How does that relate to my own work?" From a very early age I felt that whatever play I was reading—whether it was Chekhov or a musical comedy—was telling me something about my own work. Every play, in a sense, is a play with problems. How do you solve those problems? I always love to tell the story of what I've seen back to myself. If you like something, you incorporate that into your work.

What about specific writers?

Feydeau, Strindberg. Reading *Crimes and Crimes* was an extraordinary event. There was a play, when I was a kid, called *The Wisteria Trees*. Joshua Logan had done *The Cherry Orchard* but set it down South. So I took *Three Sisters* and I typed it out and for Moscow I put New Orleans, thinking of Kim Stanley, people you saw on *Playhouse 90*, because plays were done on television. The softest part of Chekhov is always the honey that attracts us. It takes us a long time to understand the rigor of Chekhov. It takes us a long time to understand the juice of Ibsen. And it takes a long time to get the construction of Chekhov. One perceives it as molasses at first, it seems so easy.

Strangely, for learning about the structure of plays, I read the record jackets of show albums. I recognized that the first or second number will always be a "want" song. "All I want is a room somewhere." "We've got to have, we plot to have, because it's so dreary not to have, that certain thing called the boy friend." "Something's Coming." It was such a revelation, in the record store, reading those notes. You really can tell how the story is told through the songs. "Guys and Dolls" contains the three themes of that show. Recognizing that was a revelation. Therefore, beginning a play, what is my "want"? I came to Stanislavski through record jackets, at age twelve, thirteen, fourteen. So I always approach plays in a practical way.

When I was at Georgetown, Washington was a strong tryout town. I went to plays all the time. Then I went to Yale Drama School. New Haven was also a tryout town. We spent all our time arguing because every play that came in was a play in trouble. You never saw a finished play. Or you'd sneak into a play, you'd miss the first act. So you'd try to figure out how the play began.

Who did you study with at Yale? John Gassner?

Yes, but the key thing was studying with people like Donald Oenslager, learning set design. I was a terrible set designer. But I learned about the light in which a play should take place, learned what a set had to be. That was tremendously valuable. The setting for the play: not just the set, but the life in the different styles, the fact that everything that appears on the stage comes from the writing—that was a revelation to me.

How important, then, was Yale for you?

Not at all. I always think of it as putting life on hold. The draft kept me at Yale. When I got out, I was so proud, smug, with my MFA from Yale, and I got drafted. It was remarkable to go into the Air Force because I was twenty-five and everybody else in my group was in their teens, and I was almost the only one to have graduated from high school. Very quickly everything that one part of me valued was rendered completely valueless.

If you're going to be in the theatre, you either have to be some kind of primitive, some kind of naif, or you have to know as much as you can. I loved school for leaving you alone. It was a place where you could sit and read and let your instincts lead you. School seemed to be a delayed adolescence. College was a repeat of high school. I liked being at Georgetown because I wrote a play every year. I was editor of the literary magazine. I sold orange juice and checked coats at the National. I loved that. I loved being at Yale just to work on shows. Writing is my way of working in the theatre.

When you write, what elements come first to you?

Each play is different. I write and write and write and write. I find it very comforting just to write in a notebook. Many years ago—this was a revelation for me—I had to write a play for the O'Neill and I didn't know how to begin it. I had no idea. So I went through notebooks, which I'd never done before, and found a speech that I'd written three years before in Rome. It was a speech about how, if I could have been born anybody I chose, I would have been born an Etruscan. I'd written that speech when I went into an Etruscan museum to get out of a terrible downpour. It was just waiting for the rest of the play. I learned from that that our inner life is so rich. I realized that I'm always working on a play and my obligation is just to keep going back and finding it, recognizing the thread. That speech I'd forgotten was the beginning of *Muzeeka*.

There are many different ways in which a story will reveal itself. You may work and work and work on a play and then another comes in the middle. You always have a play that comes as a gift, that's just waiting there and pops right up. You always have to be working on something because you have to trust your unconscious life, to be ready to deal with a play when it says, "Here I am."

What about with the Lydie Breeze tetralogy? Did you have it all plotted out in advance?

No, not at all.

Was Lydie Breeze *written before* Gardenia?

Yes.

And that's the last in the series.

In order of writing, it's four, two, one, three.

When does Bulfinch's Mythology *take place?*

A year after *Gardenia*.

But in starting with Lydie Breeze, *you ended up mapping out the basic action.*

Yes, the action is there. One thing, though: Moncur, the boy who holds the key to it, dies in *Women and Water*. And after I lost him, I realized that he must be alive. It was a mistake. He is a key for *Bulfinch's Mythology*. I couldn't carry the plot without him. So I had to go back and unravel that. But generally the characters were all very clear in my head. Their pasts were very clear.

You compared Women and Water *to the other plays in the cycle by explaining that, while the other plays are retrospective,* Women and Water *picks them up in the present, so to speak.*

It's when we first meet them. Each play is, in a sense, in a different style. That was one of my tasks. Much of the action in *Gardenia* and *Lydie Breeze* concerns people dealing with the consequences of the past. So my obligation was to show them before they had a past. That's the rule—we had to see them in action.

But what surprised me was that in showing them in action, you showed them dealing with the past. So much of the play is devoted to discovery.

But at least they deal with the past in first-person terms, in current terms. The key image in each play is a journal. The cycle is all about books, about the printed word. The final action of *Lydie Breeze* is Joshua taking out the mother's journal and giving it to his daughter. The key image in *Women and Water* is the father's journal, and the lies told in that, and then Lydie writing a journal. *Gardenia* is about the destruction of two manuscripts. In *Lydie Breeze* nobody's writing anything down or keeping a record. There is no narrative. It's all dispersed. But at the end, they return to the book.

Seeing Women and Water, *I felt a great deal of anxiety for the characters, knowing what's going to happen to them.*

Writing it has always been a matter of deciding what they know and what they don't know. I'm having one more go-around with *Women and Water*, making a cut. Then when I have *Bulfinch's* done, I'll figure out what the next step is.

I find your plays closer to the well-made play model than those of many of your contemporaries, because of the importance of revelations about the past. And they're very carefully plotted.

That's a new perception. Before they were perceived as not being plotted. It's funny.

I always imagine you sitting down to write with the plot carefully laid out.

No, because if you know what the plot is, there's no fun in writing it. You write to surprise yourself. You've got all this material and in putting it together, you recognize that the consequences can be completely different from what you had planned. You have to be prepared for that. You have to have the freedom to follow the consequences of the work rather than bending it into a preordained scenario.

Letting the plot make itself as you go along.

Yes, and finding justifications and support for where the story is taking you. If the story's taking you so far away you end up in the Boxer Rebellion, you say, "Wait a minute. I have to go back and control this." But generally, it's about realizing what a person wants, realizing that this is the consequence of that action. And then recognizing the cut-off point. The arc of the play is always the hardest thing to recognize.

At what point does that usually become clear?

It can make itself evident very quickly or take years. I stumbled on the arc of *Gardenia* when I realized that the action of Act I was that of a man having a manuscript and destroying it. Then I said, "What a good idea. I must repeat that action but have the action produce a completely different response." It's a mirror image.

It's also a before and after, with the murder of Dan Grady in between. It's a very strong dramatic structure.

You have to approach your work in a double way. You have to write it on an unconscious level—just let it come out. Then you have to get a distance from it, and come back to it almost as a collaborator. The hardest thing to do is to listen to your work, putting your ear against it and answering the questions, "What is this material trying to turn into? What is the underlying rhythm in this?" It's always a question of the balance between intuition and conscious choice. It is the obligation of the playwright to account for every choice, so the director or an actor can ask you, "What is the meaning of this?" I don't think you can say, "It doesn't mean anything. I just write. I'm just a vessel through which it passes."

Do you feel this obligation even when your point is to leave the audience wrestling with a problem, as in Bosoms and Neglect? *A central issue is resolved at the end of the play, but at the same time the human situation is pointedly not resolved.*

It's resolved in a very conventional way and then quickly unraveled.

So there's a big difference between spelling things out for the director and actors and spelling them out for the audience.

The minute that you resolve something, you open up a whole new question. When you've got a great curtain, you must always ask yourself, "What would happen if something broke and the play had to go on?" I took a summer school class in college in which we had to write the fourth act for a play, we had to continue it. I remember writing the fourth act to a Sean O'Casey play. That was a great revelation. You have a snazzy ending, but what are the consequences of that snazzy ending? In murder mysteries, which I love, I always wonder what happens to people's lives *after* they've figured out who did it. Every solution intimates the start of something new.

That's the status of each of the plays in the tetralogy.

That's been the problem with the plays. How do you make the plays act independently without the ending of the cycle?

Have you always had a hand in choosing directors and actors for your work?

I always have. I've always tried to work with the most interesting people.

And you always attend closely to the rehearsal process.

One has so few productions. What's a rehearsal period? Four weeks. Ten plays is forty weeks—not even a year. In a lifetime, you're lucky to have ten plays done. So it's all precious time.

Do you rewrite a lot during rehearsals?

I was once given a shirt that said "Captain Rewrite." I love to rewrite because I keep finding out new things. I want to underline things, find the right rhythms. I'm always trying to hear the music. Sometimes you learn that the problems you're trying to solve can't be solved in that play. So that's what the next play will be.

And you rewrite after productions, as with **Women and Water.**

It's not finished yet. It's been done in L.A. in one version and at the Arena in another version. It's not the kind of play that you can solve just in reading. I need to see its effect. It presents new problems that I have to develop a new vocabulary to deal with. I went into each production with specific tasks.

Are you working on **Bulfinch's Mythology** *now?*

I like to carry it around with me. I like to think about it. I have to see what adjustments to make in all four plays. Last May when we were here at the Beaumont, with the success of *Blue Leaves* and the Tony nomination, I said, "This is the time to back away, to vanish and write a new play." I started with seven pages. I wanted something brand-new to happen.

What productions do you look back on as particularly successful?

The original production of *Blue Leaves* was as wonderful an experience as the Lincoln Center revival. Our *Two Gentlemen of Verona*, which was built in rehearsal, was a great thrill. We had a theatre in Nantucket where we did the first version of *Marco Polo* and it was one of the most hilarious times I've ever had. *Landscape of the Body* in Chicago, when we first did it with Shirley

Knight and Murray Abraham. Most of the time productions are a great pleasure.

I'm struck by the fact that recognition of your work is coming rather late, with this production of Blue Leaves. *Some of your more recent plays have not fared too well with the press. How do you feel about this belated acclaim?*

It's great. It's unreal. You know, you can't learn anything from reviews. They're just telling you what the quality of your life is going to be in the next year. Success is immensely more pleasurable than failure. I mean failure in the sense of being perceived as having failed to connect. That's terrible. The best thing about *Blue Leaves* here at the Beaumont is that it's not just a commercial production. The energies are going into rebuilding a theatre and making other work possible. I feel very much at home here, as I did early on at the O'Neill. Originally Gregory was going to do *Gardenia* here because he had done a wonderful production of it in Chicago. But those actors were not available.

What you want from a play is for the energy to go on to the next one. There are people who write an immense success and then they can't write again. And there are those who've had plays fail and the failure was so brutal that they can't risk it again. But this experience has been wonderful. It validates the past and creates some life in the future.

How do you see the American theatre today?

Strangely, I think it's very healthy. I say this as we're about to move to Broadway. If we had started *Blue Leaves* on Broadway, it would have been deadly. We're moving to Broadway only because we have to get out of here. The new season's beginning at the Beaumont. That's a wonderful way to come to Broadway.

The expense of a production, the real estate-ness of it, is ludicrous. When I was a kid I dreamed of having a play on Broadway. But that dream has been progressively defused. Now I think, "Hey, I'm having my play *done*." That's the important part. Broadway is just a tourist marketplace. My play is there by virtue of a crapshoot, rather than a decision to present it at the "shrine of excellence." It's all real estate and marketing and I'm glad the production will be going there with our people in it. We haven't had to make adjustments or compromises. Nobody's said, "What do you mean having a Broadway show with John Mahoney and Swoosie Kurtz. Let's get a star." It's a very fortunate situation.

That old-time dream that when you *get* there, it has to be on Broadway, has been abandoned. You now say, "I'm really excited about going to L.A. to work on my play." I think that people have much more sense of the development of a play. They understand that a play is more a part of your life than it is a piece of real estate. When you open in New York it takes a long time to realize that a play should not have to bear so many dreams...that are not part of the play. The decentralizing of the theatre is the most important thing that's happening today. That's getting us back to something that existed twenty-five years ago. The best of the Off-Off Broadway movement was the fun of getting plays on, being involved in a body of work, not just one play.

So you see the current situation as healthy.

I think that the lines have never been so clearly drawn between commerce and the fact of being a playwright. They were blurry there for a while.

It seems that there's not much life left on Broadway for more serious theatre, compared with the situation fifteen years ago. **Big River** *is not a terribly substantial play, but it's a critical success.*

But that's a musical. And what's interesting is the channels that it came through—American Repertory Theatre and La Jolla. I'm not defending Broadway, but it's the place we've seen Glen*garry* and—albeit with an all-star cast—*Hurlyburly.* I think the more important fact is the vanishing of Off Broadway, because of economics. It's interesting that a comedy like *The Foreigner* formerly would have been seen on Broadway. Now it's Off Broadway. And *Glengarry*, with its bite, in the old days would have been somewhere Off Broadway. I find that, in a way, very healthy and remarkable.

I have a friend who had a play done Off Broadway that cost something like $300,000—one set, five characters. This to me is more alarming than spending millions of dollars for a Broadway play. That it costs so much to put on a play in a 200-seat theatre is really scary. Broadway is a marketplace but Off Broadway has traditionally been daring. It's not there waiting for you, it's an adventure even to get to. Your theatregoing experience begins the minute you see the poster and look at the address to see where you have to go. Maybe it's in an unfamiliar part of town. You behave and dress differently from the way you do for a Broadway show. But the Off-Broadway producer now cannot afford something daring or experimental. The sensibility is that of Broadway.

The traditional Off Broadway has turned into the Public Theater doing Wally Shawn's *Aunt Dan and Lemon* or *Marie and Bruce.* And the not-for-profit theatre can produce Wally Shawn only because of the income from *Chorus Line.* You need an *Edwin Drood* to support the new drama. When we did *Two Gentlemen* I was most struck by the fact that Joe Papp wanted it to be a success so the money could go into *Sticks and Bones.* Manhattan

Theatre Club needed an *Ain't Misbehavin'* to give them the rest of their season.

The established Off-Broadway theatres in New York have become so cautious, for the most part, that it seems more the responsibility of the regional theatres to develop new talent.

The problem with the regional theatres is their relationship to subscribers. When I first went to Washington, you would go to the Arena to see a Brecht or an *Epitaph for George Dillon*. And then you'd go to the National and see some star vehicle. But last year when I went down the Arena was doing an elaborate production of *The Philadelphia Story* and the National was doing a stripped-down version of *Long Day's Journey into Night*. What is the regional theatre's debt to the people who are supporting it? What is the role of the audience to the theatre?

Do you anticipate your entire tetralogy being performed in New York?

We'll just read it together. Gregory did *Gardenia* on a bare stage and I've seen *Lydie Breeze* done on a bare stage. We'll find a bare stage somewhere and do it. If you have illusions that that evening will be repeated five hundred times, to universal love and admiration, you're crazy. But I know that I will see it somehow. One has to become one's own producer, in a way. The rules are clear. The responsibility is yours—which is why you have to know the actors you need to do your work. Productions come about in all manner of ways. Look what's come from David Mamet and Gregory Mosher in a room in Chicago doing plays.

Are there any favorites among your plays?

No. I understand the reason for them all, I understand how they interconnect.

Like many other playwrights, you focus on the effects of the past on the present. Unlike you, many playwrights show how the present simply repeats the past. To quote O'Neill, the past is the present.

No it's not. The past was then and the present's now.

Your plays are about transformation and people taking control of their own lives and making their own futures.

Everybody's trying to find a way out. Everybody is under the delusion that there is a way out and everybody is using what slender tools they have to invent their way of thinking they've escaped.

I think your understanding of the future as transformation is quite different from that of many other playwrights—Miller, for instance. Willy Loman is dreaming, like Hickey in The Iceman Cometh, *not envisioning a real future. Compare that with a play like* Night of the Iguana *where characters make their own lives. This is why I see a connection between you and Williams. Your material is about characters confronting the past and moving on. The tetralogy is, in part, about inheritance. But at the end it's clear that young Lydie is not a reincarnation of her mother.*

I remember being shocked seeing *Sweet Bird of Youth*, at the fact that at the end the movie—all that Princess was fleeing—is a success. When she finally has the courage to call up and find out how it went, she learns it was a triumph and she goes back to it, leaving everybody behind. That's one of my favorite reversals. In a sense you've forgotten about the movie, you just assume it's a disaster. I can still remember the astonishment I felt. The boldness of that!

Like Gussie going off at the end of Lydie Breeze.

Out of the geometry of our lives she has picked up something. It's like what I said about listening to the material and saying, "Oh, here's a new consequence I never would have expected." It's taking what's at hand, saying, "Wait a minute. Lucian is right here. I could go away with him."

So you had not planned that ending?

No, it was a great surprise. But that had happened in my family, that event, to a great-aunt.

I've read that the cycle is based on your family history.

It's a way of using things overheard. It's a way of using things that one could never put together, that no one ever questioned, facts that just were there. There were no books destroyed. But there are certain events that are as happened and others that are inventions.

Seeing Gardenia, *I thought that in writing about the 1860s you were, in part, writing about the 1960s—the characters coming out of a national disaster with so much hope. I couldn't help but relate it to my own experience of the sixties.*

You felt that you made a difference. If *you* burned your draft card, or burned the flag, or traveled to Washington and marched, there would be a difference. The only time I've ever seen people dance in the street is the day LBJ said, "I'm not going to run again." People danced on 57th Street. We said, "We did that!" That was a magical feeling. But it's a feeling found in—if you read *Sentimental Education*—the 1840s. It was part of the 1940s, the thirties—*Waiting for Lefty*.

It's an attitude toward history.

You feel paralyzed by history or by the present, or else you believe that the future is waiting for you to come into it: *we need you to be there.* You will make a difference, believing that instead of saying, "Oh, screw it. What difference does it make?" When you say that, they've won. That's what's happening right now—the sense of powerlessness, the feeling that they'll do whatever they want to. But that will change. You do not know how, but you know that this generation of yuppies will pass. We needed a new class of philistines, so that there will be a future avant-garde. Ten years from now the next generation will look at their parents and say, "You don't understand what *we're* trying to do."

Your plays keep the Utopian impulse alive. There's so much trashing of the sixties right now.

That feeling of revolution is still the most dangerous of all. The credit card has done so much to destroy it—when you've got your card, you can buy anything! How quickly people are co-opted into the system. What better way to manipulate the youth of today than to have their education cost so much that they've got to spend a good part of their lives paying off the investment.

My plays are not nostalgic for the sixties. They celebrate the feeling that comes along every thirty or forty years, that belief that "I can make a difference." I think of the poignance of our attitude toward South Africa. We're not aware of the reality of South Africa. We feel we can force our government to impose sanctions against the country but we don't know how to make them deal with the homeless or with drugs here. Still, South Africa is a start. What's important is to honor that revolutionary spirit: "I can change. I will make a difference." And it's important to look back and consider people who were trapped in their past.

Your work focuses on the danger and exhilaration of that revolutionary moment. This is, of course, connected to the idea of producing the future. A revolution entails not getting rid of the past but dealing with it in a different way.

The reins are handed over to you. That is ultimately what David and Goliath is about, and Jack and the Beanstalk—who is it that said there are only two plots, Cinderella and Jack and the Beanstalk? It's the message of Christ, in the best sense. You, the little man, now have value. The Christian ideal is,

"You have value and can topple the empire." Now in this country we have a smug empire that one hopes gets toppled.

I feel privileged to be involved in an arena where you are not dreaming about things but dealing with problems and people on a day-to-day basis. I feel privileged to be dealing with them, instead of saying, "Oh God, if only I could be a playwright." I *am* a playwright, and that's a great thing to be able to say.

JOAN HOLDEN

J oan Holden is unique among the playwrights in this volume because all of her plays have been written for a theatre collective, the San Francisco Mime Troupe, with which she has been associated for twenty years. Not only does she enjoy extensive feedback from actors and directors on her scripts, she writes most with one or more collaborators. Nonetheless, she remains the primary literary focus of a company which, in her own words, "has never moved to abolish the writer, director, or the designer, but only to allow more people to play those roles."

The San Francisco Mime Troupe was founded in 1959 by Ronnie Davis, dedicated to effecting political change. Under Davis's lead, the company developed a performance style modeled closely on the conventions of *commedia dell'arte*, vaudeville and carnival sideshows, presenting pieces ranging from pure *commedia* to a celebrated blackface *Minstrel Show* (1965). Davis continued to lead the Mime Troupe until 1970, when he resigned and it reorganized as a collective, refusing the domination of a single creative imagination and dedicated to the refutation of the bourgeois notion that art is "above" history and politics. Joan Holden, who had written her first script for the Troupe in 1967, took over as principal writer. Since 1970 she has directed the composition of a body of work that has explicitly addressed political issues. Pieces include *The Independent Female* (1970), a feminist parody of melodrama; *The Dragon Lady's Revenge* (1971), about CIA drug smuggling in Southeast Asia; *Frozen Wages* (1972), an indictment of Nixon's economic policies; *False Promises* (1976), about the birth of American imperialism; *Hotel Universe* (1977), a protest against real estate speculation; the Factperson/Factwino trilogy (1980-82), a tale of comic-book style superheroes; *Steeltown* (1984), about plant closures; *Spain/36* (1986), an examination of internecine strife during the Spanish Civil War; and *The Mozamgola Caper* (1986) about CIA-backed counterrevolutionaries in Africa.

For twenty-five years the Mime Troupe has been a populist theatre, performing every summer in San Francisco's parks and immediately responsive to the political and theatrical needs of its audience. To maximize its accessibility, all of Holden's work is written in comedic style, drawing freely upon many different popular entertainments—circus, puppet shows, parody, comic strips, melodrama. Holden has used these forms to expound what she calls the "basic theme" of all the Mime Troupe's plays: "There is a class system in this country that is not run in your interest. It is run in the interest of rich people and they fool you about your interest." She writes to provide the working class with an understanding of how it is blinded and suppressed, and to instill in people the belief that they can change the system.

In her years with the Troupe, Holden has written both historical and contemporary plays. The former are designed to provide an awareness of how a particular oppressive structure arose; the second, of how to deal with it. *False Promises* is a history play that dramatizes the destructive consequences of the working class's failure to recognize where its interests lie. Like most of Holden's plays, it contains several lines of action which finally converge, contrasting the economic imperialism of J.P. Morgan and President McKinley with the effect of their most successful venture, the Spanish-American War, on Colorado copper miners. The play demonstrates how disaster befalls the ethnic and ideological opponents within the union when they fail to band together. Only as the army arrives to occupy the town do the people begin to understand how they have been used and betrayed. At the end a black soldier comes forward and pronounces what is a crucial point for Holden: "When the time comes, you don't get to pick who's on your side—history decides that for you. You just got to understand history."

One of the Mime Troupe's most successful plays, *Factwino Meets the Moral Majority,* has a contemporary setting and focuses on the problem of education. This second part of the Factperson/Factwino trilogy introduces a superhero of clarification who with his magic "zap" is able to transform myopic reactionaries into clearsighted progressives. A succession of scenes loosely tied together, related more by the opposition between falsehood and clarity than the presence of Factwino, the play climaxes in a confrontation between the superhero and Jerry Falwell. "Zapped" by Factwino, Falwell reconsiders the truth of the Bible: "How come it contradicts itself three times inside the first two chapters?" He reasons that "If there are errors, there are not absolutes! No absolutes, no morality!"—and promptly takes a hit of bourbon.

Like all of Holden's plays, *Factwino* is unabashed agitprop, designed to raise political consciousness and produce change. As such, it assumes that the correct and the incorrect can be separated, that progressive social champions can be divided from repressive villains. Like many of her other scripts, it makes use of magical conversions to change enemies into allies—knowing, certainly, that conversion in the real world is much more problematic. At the end of the trilogy, it is clear that Factwino's victory over Armageddonman is only provisional, more setback than outright defeat for the beast with two heads—Business and War. The hero's last line to the audience is a recognition of the political difficulties which only begin when the play ends: "We all going up against Armageddonman. And *everybody* got to find their power." With its immediately recognizable point of view, such work is, as Holden recognizes, effective political action for its outdoor audience, largely the already converted. That its power to persuade its indoor audience is uncertain poses a difficult question that the Mime Troupe is not alone in wrestling with: can political theatre, addressed to the American middle class, actually change people's beliefs?

■   ■   ■

MAY 6, 1987—SAN FRANCISCO MIME TROUPE OFFICES

What got you interested in theatre?

I've always been interested in theatre, always gone to plays. I remember my first play: being six years old in Mary Janes and taken to see *The Mikado* at the Curran in San Francisco. I remember the all-yellow set. I remember the buzz of the full house. I always wanted to be in school plays, but the thing I was most interested in was the lights. Then in the fifties the big theatre experience for me was the Actor's Workshop. I remember seeing *The Crucible*, I guess in the mid-fifties. It was such a catharsis. The audience was full of McCarthy victims. I remember my mother sobbing beside me. Then I realized something could happen in the theatre besides lights and beautiful music and costumes.

I never dreamed that I would be a playwright. But my husband at the time, Arthur Holden, started acting—it was the fifties, we got married in

102

college. When we moved down here to go to graduate school, he joined the Mime Troupe. I took a great course from a professor at U.C. Berkeley in comedy. He started with Cornford's *The Origin of Attic Comedy* and Bentley on the psychology of farce. This was a new dimension that reaffirmed my feeling that there was something ritual going on in theatre. But I was planning to be an English professor. I had gone to Reed College, where if you were a good student, you were going to be a professor, and if you were mediocre, you'd go into government service. I was a good student and totally miserable in graduate school. The only thing I liked was reading all the plays. I had a few brilliant courses that taught me to write essays, but mostly I hated it. In 1964, after I'd passed my M.A. orals, I was going to take a year off and go to Europe. Driving east to catch the Yugoslav freighter, round about Reno I realized, "I don't ever have to go back there." So I decided to be a writer. But I still never thought of playwriting.

I saw the Mime Troupe for the first time at the Encore Theatre—they did a midnight show of *Dowry*, a commedia play. They were still attached to the Actor's Workshop, which by this time was getting very high-toned and ready to fly off to Lincoln Center and self-destruct. I had heard of *commedia dell'arte* but I had no idea what it looked like. The life of this performance made it my number three fantastic experience in theatre. Ruth Maleczech was in it, and Bill Raymond was the Pantalone. Ronnie Davis was the Brighella. Joe Bellan, who's the dean of comic actors around here, was the Dottore. *Dowry* was the funniest, most energetic, most alive thing I'd ever seen on stage.

We went to France in 1964 and lived in Paris for two years. I saw Ruth Maleczech again in *Dutchman*—I think Lee Breuer directed it in English. That was hot. I went to plays all the time. I was going to be a fiction writer, but I never finished a piece of fiction, never had any adventures worth writing about, so I came home, intending to be a public servant—a high school teacher or public health administrator or social worker. Arthur went back into the Mime Troupe and Ronnie mentioned one day that he was looking for someone to adapt a script and Arthur said, "My wife can write." That's how I became a playwright. I adapted a Goldoni script, *L'Amant Militaire*. Number four primal experience in the theatre was going to the first reading. I had very good actors—I didn't know how good. Sandra Archer, who was the great leading lady of the Mime Troupe, and Peter Coyote read a scene. It was hilarious. There they were, acting words I wrote, and people were laughing.

What playwrights influenced you during that period?

I think Molière's the master. The *lazzo* or comic bit or comic conflict in a scene just seemed to come naturally to me, but it probably came from reading so much Molière. I think you are born either comic or tragic. When I was little, the pictures I drew weren't pretty but they were always funny. I've always been a cartoonist.

What about Brecht?

Everybody asks me about Brecht. You're a political playwright, aren't you influenced by Brecht? Brecht is fantastic, but hard to imitate because he's a poet. You can't imitate Brecht any more than you can imitate Shakespeare. But you can make epic scenes which teach a lesson, which are over when the point is made. From Brecht I have pillaged many ideas. But he pillaged them from Shakespeare. In 1969 the Mime Troupe did *Congress of the White-washers*, a deservedly seldom-produced Brecht play, based on the opera *Turandot*. There are forty scenes with epic characters—crowd scenes, market scenes. Ever since then, I've written many of my plays in this epic style of comedy—a scene can happen anywhere and anything can happen.

Adapting the Goldoni play, I got an important idea from Ronnie Davis. The play was about the Spanish army occupying Italy, a natural for a satire on the Vietnam War. Ronnie said, "What are you saying here? What is this about?" And I said, "It's about the war." "What about the war?" "It's bad." "Big deal, big news, why is it bad? What should we do about it? You can't just talk about something, you have to have something to say." That was a big lesson, that an idea is precise. I've been teaching graduate playwriting for years and the idea that you must have something to say is completely foreign to a great number of beginning playwrights [laughs].

What modern playwrights influenced your writing?

Dario Fo. He has this surreal imagination you can't imitate. He does what I do, only much better. He's the comic master of our time. To find such a great artist doing this is an inspiration. Political theatre, after all, is pretty much out of fashion. Almost nobody does political comedy.

What about Arthur Miller?

The public seriousness of his great plays is something I admire—not his style.

From whom else have you learned?

I never took a course in playwriting. When I had to teach the first time, I didn't know what to call anything. In desperation I took *The Poetics* down from the shelf—it blew my mind. When I read it after seven or eight years of writing, it explained all my failures and all my successes. I think you're born either a classicist or an avant-gardist. I'm a classicist. So Aristotle con-

firmed everything that I was hazily thinking. Whenever I have to fix something, I think: Does it have a beginning, middle and end? Is something
unnecessary? Is everything that's necessary there?

Gilbert and Sullivan are another important influence. They dare to be
silly. We did a lot of Gilbert and Sullivan in college.

How did working with the members of the Mime Troupe influence your de-
velopment as a playwright?

You learn from having your plays done, working with good actors and good
directors. I had written this scene that went on and on. I liked the lines.
Sandra Archer said, "Don't give me words, give me verbs. Give me an action
I can play." Revelation! I hadn't known why that scene didn't work. I learned
how few words are necessary and how paramount action is. And you learn
from failure. Every time you sit with an audience, watching a scene you wrote
go slack, you know what you have to cut. Anybody who can learn to be a
playwright without being produced is some kind of natural genius. I've learned
everything by doing it.

Has there been a change in the way you've written for the Troupe over the
years?

Different shows I write in different ways. Some are much more collaborative.
Sometimes somebody else has the brilliant idea and I write it. But in every
case, it's collaborative in the sense that everybody talks about it—a whole
lot, when there's time. Whoever has the idea has to sell it.

I suppose that I've developed a method of sorts, but that's as much from
teaching. Aristotle says that if you can't tell the plot in two sentences, you
don't really have a plot. But you don't always find the plot first. I spend a lot
of time trying to tell the story to the company. It's much harder than you
think. The advantage of having an ensemble is that sometimes people can fill
in holes for you.

The plays originate in different ways. The worst way is from a topic.
I've been trapped in that many times. You don't have an idea for a play until
you have an action. The Spanish Civil War is not an idea for a play. The best
way is the flash when it all comes in one piece. The last play, *Mozamgola*,
came that way. I read an article in *The Nation* called "Betting on the Wrong
Horse," about the U.S. supporting Unita in Angola. And bingo, I came up
with the basic situation: the harassed socialist president, the contra leader—
his ex-comrade in arms—and the girl they were rivals for back when they
were exchange students in the United States, who's now a CIA agent. Two
other people wrote it up with me. It's often been Sharon Lockwood who's

had that bingo idea. Audrey Smith, an actor with the company, came up with the idea of a superhero of clarification, who became Factperson and then Factwino. It's great having people around you with ideas.

With some plays, we tell the story to each other and decide, "You write that scene, I'll write this one." Usually I end up doing the final pass. With some, other people's participation is just in talking. Every few years I do one that's really mine. I get the idea and I do all the writing.

Which are those?

False Promises, Huahuatenango, Mozamgola, The Independent Female, Steeltown. Factwino became mine although several other writers worked with me.

Do you rely much on the Troupe's improvisations?

No. It's really a text-based company. Words and movement are precisely coordinated. But since rehearsals usually begin as soon as the first scene is written, there's enormous interplay between rehearsal and writing. The first time I hear a scene read, I learn a tremendous amount—what's too long, what's not there. I have occasionally used improvisations if I'm stuck on a scene. We once tried to do a show from improvisation but we only had a month and it didn't end up being done that way.

Then you work very differently from the way, say, the Wooster Group works.

It's the opposite. Our method is conditioned by necessity. We have to have a new show every year in the parks. That's a very demanding audience. And since we've also been performing indoors in San Francisco, we've been doing two shows a year for about eight years now. That is too much, so we're backing down to one again. This year we're reviving *The Dragon Lady's Revenge*— but after all, the last time we did it was 1973.

We make a piece like TV does, except that we get to fix it. Typically, we open an embarrassingly raw sketch of what we're going to do in the parks and work on it all summer. Then the show goes out on tour and we make the final changes. About a year and a half into it, it's finished. The actors make contributions in rehearsal, and more in performance. That's when the fine work really happens, when it's running, or when it's being remounted.

Because it's the interplay between actors and audience that's crucial?

Absolutely. Right away it's clear some stuff won't work, but other material you've got to run for an audience. From seeing it I learn where it needs more of a peak.

Is a show always cast before you start writing?

I usually know who I'm writing it for. And yes, that is a huge influence. I believe that actors are types. A good actor can play anything, if called on, but really there's a certain place where they excel, wider or narrower depending on how great they are. For some parts, I see the actor in front of me. But sometimes the director disagrees with me and casts somebody else. It always works. But the character is influenced by the voice I hear; by the energy, the movement I see.

When you revive a piece like **The Dragon Lady's Revenge,** *do you do much rewriting?*

At this distance, no. Actually I learned not to on *Dragon Lady* originally because we kept revising it every week to keep up with the headlines. And it didn't necessarily make it better. *Dragon Lady* is so old that if you change one thing, you have to change all the references. I am going to change the framing speech and bring that up-to-date. And there's a scene I want to rewrite, but rehearsals begin in two weeks and I notice I haven't started yet. When something has been down for six months and we put it on again, I always revise, until some magic point when it feels like it's finished. *Hotel Universe* we've revived seven times by now—it's our play for foreign touring because we can do it bilingually, in French or Spanish. I finally fixed something that had been bothering me for years.

Do you usually attend rehearsals?

Mostly I'm home writing. I wouldn't be there all the time anyway. That's crowding. I always go a couple of times a week, sometimes more, depending on where we are. I've learned—although my comrades would disagree—that beyond a certain point in rehearsal, you should leave it alone. Like about three days before opening [laughs]. And the first couple of weeks you should leave it alone, unless it's an easy change and will solve a big obstacle that's in their way. Sometimes they keep learning a new version and it keeps not working. That's the worst.

Are your plays at all autobiographical?

Yes, but not by intention. I've put my mother and my husband in some. With *The Independent Female*, I didn't realize I would do this when I started but I soon knew where I was drawing from. Although no one ever seems to recognize this. People or things I'm angry at I put in plays. I'm surprised that some people haven't recognized themselves [laughs]. But what I think is most autobiographical is that for the last ten years or so, I've been writing about people who are on the verge of giving up, about people trying very hard to stay in the struggle, to keep doing the right thing. Factwino—nobody wants to hear his message. If he could only make people think. It's the experience of the radical in America. I wrote a long essay once called "Comedy and Revolution," about comedy as the ideal revolutionary form. I can't remember which neoclassical theorist says comedy is always conservative, restoring social values. I don't think so—it's subversive, it often explodes social values.

I'm a retiring person. I would never write about myself directly. In *Annie Hall* Woody Allen says comedy is a screen that you put between yourself and pain. I had a miserable experience with *Spain* last year. I flopped at the Los Angeles Theatre Center, which is not the place to flop. The script wasn't ready. It wouldn't have been ready for a year but I thought I could pull it together. I put everybody through a great deal of pain. I couldn't talk about the experience for about three months, then I started to tell funny stories about it. You put your pain in a place where you can control it. You never expose yourself or if you do, it's only for a fleeting moment. Of course it's true that all of my characters are myself, some aspect of myself—as many other writers have said in many interviews. But nobody has ever said to me, "That's you, isn't it?"

Does the autobiography of the Troupe, the development of the ensemble, ever surface in the writing?

Everyone in the Mime Troupe would deny that we've ever done anything about ourselves. We deal with public issues of the utmost importance [laughs]. When you find patterns arising and clusters of characters being repeated, you figure out that there's something going on. But it's not conscious. People play the same kind of parts but often they don't mirror their roles in the group. The group autobiography *is* consciously in the fact that our plays don't have such happy endings as they used to. We no longer think that the revolution's just around the corner. This has been a very dark period. We're in the fifties again [laughs]. And these hard times definitely come out in the plays. Actually *Spain* was much more consciously about the group than anything else, in the debate between the anarchists and the communists. All the questions the characters faced in the play were questions I could find analogies for in our own experience.

Your work is a response to social problems.

Our plays come from the headlines. The subject is always on the national agenda, what demands to be spoken of this year. Now we want to do the contra-CIA-cocaine connection, so we're reviving *Dragon Lady*. The next thing we'll ask ourselves is what stance to take on the next election. In 1980 and 1984 we did "Stop Reagan" plays. We had been looking for a way to do South Africa when we hit upon *Mozamgola*. We all read the left press. We don't just get our news from the daily papers. And the analysis in our plays is definitely formed by the independent left: what do the radical economists say about plant closures? The idea is always to elucidate the issue. Not just how much does it hurt people to lose a job, but why have they lost jobs? Anger and hope are the two things we want to arouse. We want to make people angry and at the same time make them feel they can win. It's in their power to change the world. They've done it before.

And the first stage in that process is understanding?

But understanding can't be detached and intellectual. It has to be visceral. It has to be combined with anger. Anger's a much more socially and historically useful emotion than despair.

Which is why Factperson and Factwino, the characters who help people understand what's happening to them, are so central.

But it's no accident that Factwino is such a victim, that he's down and out, that nobody listens to him. Then the spirit of information comes down and gives him the power. It's wish-fulfillment, the radical dream.

How do your audiences respond to the work?

We have a lot of different audiences. The thousand people that come to our openings in the park are people like us, the graduates of the sixties. I'm a little old-fashioned for the current generation. We play for a lot of people who have been seeing our shows since they were in the student movement of the 1960s. *Factwino* was an immense success. I've never seen such a phenomenon. They were swarming all over him to get his autograph. Factperson, the first incarnation, was a *shlemiel* waitress who couldn't stand bullshit. We never planned a sequel but the response engendered it. Then Andrea Snow got pregnant and we had to change the character. I was looking for Fact-what? Then I was told, "Shabaka does this fantastic wino character." Some of our plays have somehow so tapped the group psyche that they develop a huge mass following.

You get different laughs in New York than in west Texas. I saw *Mozamgola* one night on campus in Ann Arbor and the whole left was there. All the political jokes, every subtle reference, got huge laughs. The next day, I saw it in a woman's prison, 90 percent black—the political jokes, nothing, but the love story really played. They loved the bad-girl heroine. The piece worked on an altogether different level. I have my classical source for that,

too. Dante said that there should be something for the people, for the bour-
geoisie and for the clerics. That's what my theatre is. It has to work on the
level of mass myth so that someone with no information can enjoy it. It has
to have a degree of art to entice the more sophisticated theatregoer. It has
to have a level of argument that intellectuals can be challenged by.

A lot of people in our audience don't go to plays. That's a big problem
when we go indoors because they don't follow. They want to see us in the
parks. It's a life-affirming ritual for them, like going to church. I constantly
have to answer to the charge, "You're preaching to the people." The converted
deserve to be preached to. They need revivals. But because we do musical
comedy, the good pieces will play for any audience—this is our national art
form. People may put it down, but for most Americans, it's like baseball.

The use of pop forms is instinctive with the Troupe. When we translated
commedia dell'arte, we looked for the American equivalent. We first found
it in melodrama. I stole the idea for my first melodrama, *The Independent
Female*. Arthur had told me about a play he saw in England, a melodrama in
which the labor organizer was the villain—but really, of course, he was the
hero, and all the terms of the melodrama were inverted. I thought that was
a great idea for a play about women's liberation. I found out melodrama was
the American *commedia* when I started writing. I also found that those radio
serials I'd been listening to since I was five years old stick in our pores. That
stuff works on people, even though they laugh at it. When sophisticated
theatres do melodrama, they spoof it so that it's gutless. You have to play it
with belief. The laughter will take care of itself.

How does a more conservative audience respond to your work?

When we play for wealthy people who subscribe to the Caltech arts series,
they aren't very responsive. The intellectual level they reject completely. But
they admire the artistry. It's a trick of sophistication: if you do it in a naive
way, people put it down. If it's sophisticated enough, they don't have to be
embarrassed to like it. They may reject the message but comedy disarms
people. They go out muttering, "What do they want me to do, lower my
rents?" [laughs]. A typical review from a conservative reviewer is, "Despite
its embarrassingly over-political message, the performance was actually quite
enjoyable." But you offend people sometimes. Fundamentalist Christians
walked out of *Factwino*.

Do you read the critics?

Sure, I have to read the critics. For business reasons, you gotta know. I love
it when I get good reviews. And I hate it when I get bad ones. Sometimes,
I know they're right. There's a certain kind of critic who hates political theatre

but doesn't cop to that fact, who's out to trash you. That kind of snake in the grass I hate. There is a guy who even trashes us when he reviews other people.

When I first started with the Mime Troupe, San Francisco critics never reviewed anything south of Market. *L'Amant* was reviewed in the London *Times* without ever having been reviewed in San Francisco. *Dragon Lady* won an Obie before it was reviewed in San Francisco. There was a rave in the *New York Times* that we did business on for three or four months. For a long time we didn't depend on the critics. Our audience in the parks doesn't pay attention to them, but indoors it's sink or swim.

How do you see the American theatre today?

Regional theatre is in an awful state. People have the best intentions. But the same plays are done all over the country, on the same circuit, and every theatre has the same structure, following the blueprints of TCG and the NEA. It's almost like traveling on an interstate. I think Berkeley Rep is an exception.

There's always interesting experimental work. Every year there are one or two people you never heard of who do something amazing. One group dies and another is born. I don't know if Broadway—selling for fifty dollars a ticket—is even theatre anymore. I go to New York and there's a line of people around the block and all the theatres are full. It's wonderful. But something needs to happen to the regional theatres pretty quick.

They have to rely so heavily on their subscribers.

I've changed my mind about subsidy. I swore for years—we all did—that we would never accept a dollar from the federal government. "We won't do your commercials because we don't dig your product"—that was our motto. Now we are beneficiaries of the NEA Ongoing Ensemble Grant. My trip to England had a big influence on me. Look at all the playwrights who came out of groups that wouldn't have existed in the seventies without the Arts Council: Caryl Churchill, David Edgar, David Hare. I think everyone should get a 50 percent operating subsidy. Really, after attaining a certain level of quality, it should all be much simpler. Subsidy is difficult to accept in our culture, not only for a radical. We're all Horatio Algers, right? You believe if it's really good, it'll make it on its own. But the theatre's too expensive. We need a subsidy system with a much broader vision, one that doesn't impose so many requirements, so much anxiety, so many blueprints. The proliferation of the two-character play is an awful thing. Everyone should write one, but I can't think that anybody wants to do it all their life. They're doing it because it sells.

Another problem is the fear of politics and of content which has haunted the American theatre since the trauma of the fifties. People don't even know that their minds have been imprinted by McCarthyism. They were in short pants taking afternoon naps when it was happening, but it determined their education, their aesthetic, the culture they grew up in. No matter how establishment the Mime Troupe gets, how many grants we get—we actually make $231 a week now instead of $40—we'll always be outsiders. And this is a good thing, it's a very healthy place to be. We'll always be unacceptable and stick in people's throats because we're political, something that's taken for granted by European playwrights. Not to deal with the issues of the day is unthinkable for Europeans. Americans have their head up their ass.

McCarthyism totally disrupted the leftist tradition in America and seems to have eliminated the opportunity for real progressive change.

Even now. There is a New Left but there are many more left-wing academicians and intellectuals than artists. The purge was most thorough in the arts. Because I went to graduate school in English, I think I know why: the New Criticism divorced form from content. All my literature courses preached the same message—the content of the work of art was completely independent, completely unimportant. Its quality consisted of purely formal characteristics. In the fifties with the New Criticism, the greatest thing a work of art could be was ambiguous [laughs]. I took that seriously. I swallowed it whole. It was the seventies before I realized what that was about. For artists, it's still uncool and uncouth to be political. There was a brief moment in the late seventies when political theatre was in style. But it was rapidly eclipsed by performance art, which is totally formal in most cases. But that's not an accident, it's part of the back-to-the-fifties trend. We—I speak for all political writers—will never be fashionable, which probably in the long run is an advantage.

But it's distressing to be ignored when your work is geared toward effecting political change.

It's a good thing for the purity of the political artist. It's a very bad sign for the political life of this country. We're going to do the newest Dario Fo play and try to sell it to regional theatres. They're very wary. I think, to a large degree, the theatres are underestimating their subscribers. At a regional theatre I will not name, I saw a sold-out performance of *Uncle Vanya*—sleepwalking actors performing for a sleepwalking audience. They would love a political comedy but the management doesn't dare.

But if the problem is with the artistic directors, will subsidies help?

No. You're right. I was confusing problems. Let's go back. I think subsidy for theatres is only half of the issue. Part of the problem is that subsidy is usually project by project. Always having to invent a project that sounds good on grant applications leads to a certain level of bullshit and is a big waste of time. Another is that the NEA tends to impose an administrative blueprint —you must have an artistic director, a general manager, a board of directors—which leads to ossification because in many places it's not organic. Theatres have spent a lot of energy conforming to the blueprint and in the process losing what started them off.

On the other hand, the real disease of the American theatre is the narrowness of its concerns: nothing outside the living room is of interest. There are many more successful political movies. You'd think the theatre could learn from Hollywood. There are more political novels. There's even stuff done on TV that you won't see in theatres. A political play will never make it on the regional theatre circuit. It's screened out at the earliest read-ings. Why would theatre be most affected by this political paralysis? Why is theatre the art form that fears content the most? When a theatre's denying its civic function, it's denying the source of its thrill. That's where you connect with the audience on a primal level. Obviously the Greek plays did that. They had a civic function.

When we did *Dragon Lady* the first time in New York, when Kissinger carpet bombed Vietnam, the reaction in the audience was so primal because it was the thing on their conscience they couldn't do anything about. In 1984 we finally came out and said "Vote," which is a big step for the New Left. Tremendous response from the audience. Why? Because they'd been worried about whether they should vote. This kind of writing is unartistic to your graduate playwriting students and to most playwrights and theatres. But they're missing something really great. It's when you're speaking to the audience about what's on their mind that they roar.

How do you think political change can happen in this country?

By waking people up. Political change took place in the thirties, and in the fifties and eighties in the other direction. Something has to be unleashed in people. Now reaction has been unleashed. But there's an immobilizing de-spair. I think my life's work is combating despair. I know there's an immense power that's latent in the American people. There have been times when it was awake, but now it's asleep, anesthetized.

It seems to me the great victory of the right has been the destruction of working-class consciousness.

It's despair that allows consciousness to be eliminated. That's what scares me. People don't want to know. When I take my daughter to school we pass an evangelical church housed in an old movie theatre. On the marquee it says,

"I'd rather know the truth than hear the facts." Meditate on that for a while. When you've lost your job three times, you don't want to know anything else. This country is in such a precipitate decline that people close their minds. Suburbs and television are great instruments of social atomization, the most brilliant inventions of the ruling class in the twentieth century.

So even before understanding, the first step must be to instill hope.

How do you dissipate despair? Sometimes with a blinding light, the fact that you can't deny. I think hope and enlightenment are all in one bundle. You have to deliver them together in the hope that it all works. You can't get hope without understanding. But understanding without hope, without energy, doesn't go anywhere.

What do you think of the work of other political playwrights, like Maria Irene Fornes?

The only one of her plays I've seen is *The Danube* and I liked it. But I never think of her as a political writer. I think of her as edgy and really smart, like Caryl Churchill, but less clearly political. But I don't know her well enough really to talk about her. This is far away from New York. It's a big problem. I'm really insulated.

What other political writers do you admire?

I love Doctorow. I love John Nichols. A lot of playwrights cop topicality without taking a political stand, which I don't consider to be political writing. I didn't think Emily Mann's *Execution of Justice* was a political play.

Why not?

Because it took no stand—let the audience decide. It was clear what the truth was. Dan White was not prosecuted. And the play didn't say that. I completely sympathize with writers' desires to explore political topics but I think a distinction has to be made between a political topic and a political play. A political play makes a political statement, has a political intention. And a political intention is to change history. I don't see many playwrights that come from that place. Caryl Churchill does. Dario Fo does. Brecht did. The others present the topic, they explore...

But ambiguously.

They have that celebrated virtue. Luis Valdez's political intention is to put the Chicano experience on the stage, which is itself a political act. A lot of

Asian-American writers aren't dealing with overtly political topics but have a political intention. I like Charles Fuller a lot. I thought *A Soldier's Play* was great. I know black people who said it was an assimilationist play, which I think is bullshit. I think *The Colored Museum* is great. That's really daring. It's not about politics but it's political. There is no black comic theatre and for George Wolfe to challenge the shibboleths and put them out there is really brave. I hope it signals a new trend, giving more black writers permission to be funny.

Is there any play of yours that you're particularly fond of?

I have a bunch of favorites, actually. *Factwino*, because it was such a good idea. It was not a great play but there was something in it that was totally right. The comic-book elements worked sweetly and connected. And it was fun. *The Independent Female* because it was a liberating experience to write it. It was the first original play I wrote. It remains so real for me because of things I expressed in it. *Steeltown* and *False Promises* for artistic reasons. I felt I achieved something new in them.

What are your goals for the future?

Steeltown and *False Promises* are both history plays. I want to do more. The challenge in writing history is to find a comic way of doing tragedy. Because the history you want to do is all tragic: wrong turns. I haven't yet found a way to make my style hold all the content that I want to deal with. I don't want to go to realism. So I have to find a comic-epic style of doing history.

That's another symptom of theatre's disease. Nobody writes history. Everybody bemoans the family drama but nobody writes anything else. There's quite a lot of material outside the living room. When I'm very old, I would like to look back on a cycle of history plays. I'm not interested in becoming more personal but in being able to bring big pieces of history to the stage. I'm interested in the macrocosm. I'd like to spend a year reading Shakespeare's histories. Since my talent seems to be for farce and comedy, when I try to write tragedy, it's pathetic. I have to find a language that doesn't trivialize things, that lets you step back and see the arc, the big movement of history, and the reasons things happened. I'm drawn to things like the Spanish-American War that seem to be turning points. Or the choice the labor movement made right after World War II. The problem is how to put that event on stage. I haven't gotten away from "The Meeting Scene" in which the people decide their future and make the wrong choice. There must be another way than that [laughs].

How do you feel about the next generation of playwrights, the ones you're training?

If I were in charge of the curriculum for MFA programs around the country, I would assign genres. From what I've seen, playwriting programs encourage imitation of successful models. They don't force students to do anything they aren't naturally inclined to do and don't try to teach them anything they don't already know. I would make them write history plays. I would make them write agitprop, not in the hope that they'd become agitpropagandists, but that their minds would be open to the compatibility of politics and art.

DAVID HWANG

G rowing up in San Gabriel, California, a star debater in high school and the son of first generation Chinese-Americans, David Hwang was expected to pursue a career in business, following in his father's footsteps. He decided instead to go to Stanford University because it didn't offer a degree in business. He majored in English and in his senior year, 1979, directed the first production of *FOB* in the lounge of the Okada House dorm. The play, like most of his works, is based on a real incident, in this case autobiographical: a double date with Hwang's cousin, Grace, accompanied by a young man newly arrived from Hong Kong, who brought along a limousine. They piled in, went driving through Westwood and saw a movie. Onto this incident, a confrontation between a second generation Chinese-American (Dale) and one "Fresh Off the Boat" (Steve), is grafted another struggle, between the girl, Fa Mu Lan, from Maxine Hong Kingston's *The Woman Warrior* (impersonated by Grace) and Gwan Gung, the adopted god of the first Chinese-Americans (impersonated by Steve).

    FOB, like all of Hwang's succeeding plays—*The Dance and the Railroad* and *Family Devotions* (1981), *The Sound of a Voice* and *The House of Sleeping Beauties* (1983), *Rich Relations* (1986) and *M. Butterfly* (1988)—is centered

117

on diametrically opposed characters. In *Family Devotions* the main conflict is between two Americanized Chinese matriarchs and their brother visiting from the People's Republic of China; in *M. Butterfly*, between a French diplomat and the Chinese actor with whom he is in love. Characteristically, the conflict builds to a climactic confrontation at which point he who appeared most vulnerable becomes, through an ironic reversal usually brought about by the revelation of withheld information, the victor.

In all of Hwang's plays a great deal is at stake in the conflict between characters and ideologies. Most crucial is self-identity, as defined by one's relationship to one's family and heritage. *Family Devotions* opposes an assimilated, affluent and Christian Chinese-American family, led by Ama and Popo, against the latter's brother, Di-Gou, who realizes that the family's history long predates the arrival of white missionaries in China. In a pivotal moment he turns to his grandnephew. "Look here," he says, "the shape of your face is the shape of faces back many generations—across an ocean, in another soil. You must become one with your family before you can hope to live away from it." Di-Gou triumphs (it is a Pyrrhic victory) by destroying the illusions of Ama and Popo and revealing the truth about the first convert to Christianity. Only by forging a bond with the past, the play suggests, can one discover one's authenticity and fight the debasement of modern culture. Hwang has elsewhere explained the process: "By confronting our ethnicity, we are simply confronting the roots of our humanity. The denial of this truth creates a bizarre world."

Hwang's most ambitious play, *M. Butterfly*, is based on a true story about a French diplomat, Rene Bouriscot, who conducted a twenty-year affair with a Chinese actor and spy, Shi Peipu, all the while believing him to be a woman. It focuses on the interrelationship between sexist, racist and imperialist adventure—in the bedroom, on stage and in the arena of world politics—expressing it in a fluid passage between the styles of Western realism and of opera, both Chinese and Italian. The mythological fulcrum of the play is Puccini's *Madame Butterfly*, whose action Bouriscot attempts to live out in his relationship with Shi, casting himself as the "cruel white man," Pinkerton, and Shi as his "perfect woman," the naive, helpless and all-forgiving Butterfly. When hauled before the French court Shi makes it clear that he has not been duped: "You expect the East to submit, and you definitely expect the women of the East to be submissive. That's why you believe they make the best wives." He knew his only chance to conquer was to become female and acquiescent. "I am an Oriental. And being an Oriental, I cannot be completely a man." In his final confrontation with Bouriscot the reversal is completed: Bouriscot is revealed as the gulled Butterfly and Shi as the manipulating

Pinkerton. Female has become male, helpless Madame transformed into the fatefully equivocal M.

Although most of Hwang's plays deal with the collision between East and West, his work is perhaps best understood in terms of questions that have long haunted American drama: how, in a land of immigrants, does one deal with one's heritage and construct a sense of identity? To consider Hwang simply a spokesperson for a particular ethnic theatre is to misunderstand American culture. As he has pointed out, that which passes for universal is simply the portrayal of "a relatively homogeneous society, with white males as the centers and prime movers"—in other words, the theatre of a particular ethnic group. The term "ethnic theatre" is really a misnomer. "There are simply the ethnics that have had access to an audience amd those that have not. As Asian-American theatre artists, we are claiming our audience."

■ ■ ■

MAY 5, 1987—ROYAL PACIFIC MOTOR INN, SAN FRANCISCO

What were your early experiences in theatre?

I don't come from a theatre background so it was surprising that I ended up a playwright. I was brought up as a musician, in Los Angeles. My earliest experiences in the theatre were playing in pit orchestras for musicals. The only thing that was strange was that I liked to stay after rehearsal and listen to the director give notes. But I put that aside and went to Stanford, and for some reason, in my sophomore year, decided playwriting was something I probably could do. I'd seen some work in San Francisco, at ACT, and the idea of creating a world and then seeing it come to life seemed very appealing. So I started writing plays without any knowledge of theatre. Stanford doesn't have a playwriting program per se but the novelist John l'Heureux was a great help to me—he told me that I was writing these lousy plays because I was working in a vacuum. I still think the best education for a playwright is to see and read all the plays you can.

The summer before my senior year in college, in '78, I went to the first Padua Hills Playwrights' Festival. I was in Los Angeles, home for the summer, and I saw an ad in the *L.A. Times* that said, "Study with Sam Shepard." Because it was the first year, only two applied, so we both got in. I worked with Shepard—he's a good teacher—and with Maria Irene Fornes, who's one of the best playwriting teachers on earth. Basically I learned to access my subconscious and from that—combined with reading and seeing a lot of plays—something gelled in my head. That summer I started a play that eventually became *FOB*.

At Stanford all the dorms put on plays, so in the spring I directed *FOB* as the dorm play. At the same time I sent a copy to the O'Neill Theater Center. The play was accepted and my director at the O'Neill was Robert Alan Ackerman. Bob brought the play to the attention of Joseph Papp, who produced it at the Public Theater in June 1980. The reviews were good and so after that I had a career.

Didn't you also go to Yale?

I entered Yale in September 1980 and stayed until the spring of '81. It's not that I didn't like the program. But I went to Yale for two reasons: to buy time and to get a firmer grasp of theatre history. In the playwriting program, you get your academics out of the way your first year and spend your next two doing workshops. But at that point, I was already getting workshops in New York. While I was at Yale, *Dance and the Railroad* opened Off-Off Broadway and then moved to the Public. I also had *Family Devotions* coming up at the Public in the fall. I hated living in New Haven, so it seemed reasonable to move to New York. Teaching has never been a goal of mine so I didn't feel I needed the degree.

During that period what playwrights had an impact on your work?

Sam Shepard, because of the way he juxtaposes reality and myth. He's very conscious that there are links to our past and that we, as a country, have a collective history. He attempts to make those connections in his plays. Also, in his preface to *Angel City*, Shepard talks about character in a different way, in terms of jazz improvisation rather than developing the character's arc in the traditional fashion. You see almost a collage effect, bits and pieces of the character at different points, butting up against one another. That's always interested me. *FOB* goes from one thing to another without any explicit reason. Even in *M. Butterfly* American slang butts up against a more classical language.

I was also influenced by Ntozake Shange's *For Colored Girls*, which I saw seven or eight times, partly because she gives voice to a particular concern that then becomes universal because it's stated well and fully. Also, because it was written as poetry, as staged by Oz Scott there was a real freeform theatricality to the work—the actresses on a bare stage, going from one location to the next with great rapidity, with nothing physically on stage holding them back. Among the modern playwrights I like, Pinter has the most craft. He always has great control over what he's doing and he's very deliberate about what he wants to achieve. That's something I would like to get better at.

You don't play with subtext.

No, not the same way. I admire Chekhov a lot but I can't create great emotional momentum from small events and well-observed details like he does.

What about Brecht?

I was very interested in Brecht at one point. But I admire the theory sometimes more than the execution. I don't think he's too skilled as a playwright. Although I understand you have to read him in German to understand what he's doing with the language. But if you read him in English, he doesn't seem to be doing anything subtle with character. I feel that what he's doing instead is creating an extremely interesting structure. In a way, I think that's what I do too. I'm not very interested in subtext or subtleties. I'm more interested in creating interesting layers of a structure that have reverberations, one upon the other. Maybe I'm less interested in Brecht because I've assimilated a certain amount of what he does, and I'm more interested in Chekhov or Pinter because they do things that I don't feel I have any grasp of.

M. Butterfly *strikes me as your most Brechtian, in technique and in political content.*

There's an argument being advanced in *Butterfly*. I guess when I talk about Brecht creating an interesting structure, that's what I mean, that he's able to bring conclusions together in the mind of the viewer which evoke a political response.

What about the traditional Asian theatre?

Asian theatre is an influence that I stumbled upon with *FOB*. I didn't initially intend *FOB* to be done in a Chinese-opera style. When I directed the original production at Stanford the ritualized part was much more an American avant-garde thing. But as soon as Bob Ackerman read it at the O'Neill and Mako and Joe Papp read it for the Public, they felt it should be done in the style of Chinese opera. So Mako cast John Lone, who has a background in Chinese opera, and I learned a lot about the form through John. It was incorporated into *FOB*. Then I consciously set out to write a play that would combine Western and Asian theatre forms—*The Dance and the Railroad*.

It always seemed to me, intellectually, that a blend of Asian and Western theatre would be interesting. I didn't know how to go about it and I managed to find people to help me figure it out. It's not like I'm the first Asian-American writer to come along, there have been lots of others before me. But they had been trying to create some sort of Asian-American synthesis in terms of the ideas advanced—political notions, or even polemics. I thought it was much more interesting to deal with that question in terms of form. It seemed to me if you took forms and merged them, you'd be making your political statement in a much more theatrical fashion. After *The Dance and the Railroad* I felt that I'd done that and since then I haven't been too conscious of the influence of Asian theatre. Some would argue that the Japanese plays—*The Sound of a Voice* and *The House of Sleeping Beauties*—are influenced by Asian theatre. To my mind, they're more influenced by Japanese literature. Or Japanese movies.

I had an interesting discussion the other day with the Japanese designer Eiko Ishioka, who's designing *Butterfly*. She was talking about how in Tokyo the vanguard of designers and artists are working with the notion of making some fusion of East and West. As Japan becomes more outwardly focused, there are more and more Western influences. She said that for them it's an intellectual concept but for us—Asian-Americans—it's in our bodies. I thought that was very good. I've never been to China and I've been to Singapore, Hong Kong, Japan only briefly. If what I write about Asia rings true, then either people don't know what is true and accept what I say because I have a Chinese face, or something got absorbed from my family that I use without being aware of it.

It seems, though, that the idea of how an Asian-American—or anyone, for that matter—uses his heritage is central to your work.

That's true. Let me explain. *FOB*, *Dance and the Railroad* and *Family Devotions* were produced in '81. They were all well received and there was a lot of press and attention. In '82 we premiered *FOB* in Singapore and I was working on a film script with a Hong Kong director. In '83 we did the two Japanese plays at the Public, but already I was starting not to work, not to write. In retrospect, I see that a lot of contradictions came up in me regarding my success in New York. First was the fact of age. If you're a rock musician, it's not such a big deal to be twenty-four. But as a playwright, it's pretty rare. I don't know that I was prepared to deal with it. And I didn't feel comfortable with the role that I was being asked to assume, as some sort of spokesperson for Asian America. I know that, to some degree, it's inevitable. But I didn't like it.

All of us who are minorities—or whatever you call it in this country— have some sort of conflict about our backgrounds. To some degree, you're very proud of being, say, Chinese and to some degree, the assimilationist thing is very strong and you don't like your ethnic background being brought up all the time. You like being a human being, too. My press was so focused on my being Asian, which is understandable because the work is Asian. But it called up this very conflicted emotion in me and, I think, caused me to go into a period when I didn't want to work. I didn't see the point in what I was doing. So I spent a couple of years not really writing. Then I broke out of that cycle by writing *Rich Relations*, which was done in New York last year and generally loathed. It's an autobiographical play in which I didn't want to deal with the ethnic issue. I wanted to talk about family matters, some of the spiritual issues in *Family Devotions*, but in terms of a family that can be any color. So we cast it Caucasian and it was extremely successful when we read it. Then a lot happened in production—we lost an actor, that kind of thing. When it was not well received that was a blow, because it was a very personal play, about my coming out of this period of inactivity. But you can't have a hit every time out.

How do you start a play?

I'm always aware of a structure, or some interesting formal question, when I begin, but my knowledge of where I'm going has changed a lot in the past ten years. With *FOB* I was really influenced by Maxine Hong Kingston's work and my basic notion was, what would happen if these two gods met in Torrance, California? When I began it, I had no idea what the next word would be. I just went through the woods by myself. I'm still really fond of *FOB*— it may be my favorite play simply because it was written so much out of instinct, before I acquired any so-called tools. As I've gotten older, I've become more aware of where I'm going from scene to scene, but I still don't plot things out or do a treatment. In *Butterfly*, I was aware what the arc of each scene was going to be before I started it. I don't know if, as a process, that's better or worse.

So in your recent work, a carefully worked-out plot is primary?

I've gotten a lot more interested in plot. One reason is that I've moved back to Los Angeles and I do some work in film and television. Whether this is a good or a bad thing in the long run, I don't know. But in *Butterfly* I'm interested in story. On the other hand, you have to say that the material in *Butterfly* lends itself to being about story. Who's to say what the next play will be? I can only trace the process in retrospect.

Structurally, all your plays build rather traditionally to a final confrontation, a stand-off—

A cathartic moment—

Which is then usually quickly resolved.

I've always had an innate sense for building a plot. If I try to account for that, the only thing I come up with is that I did a lot of work as a jazz musician in college and for a few years after. In music you become very aware of form and the fact that you have to be going someplace all the time. I do have a tendency to want to bang out the climax and go away because that, ideally, leaves the audience with a certain tingle. The play ends and you haven't totally figured it out yet. It gives you something to take home with you.

Can you explain how you've learned to access your subconscious?

This exercise is, I think, Irene Fornes's, which I use every time I do play-writing workshops. You start the students writing a scene, whatever they want, for about fifteen minutes. Then you tell them to draw a line across the page and start again, and at intervals you call out random words which they have to incorporate. In nine cases out of ten, the second half of the exercise is more interesting than the first. It recapitulates the process of when you're writing and an impulse comes into your head, and you have to decide whether you're going to follow it or not. When you're writing, you have to be open to things coming in from left field, so to speak.

That exercise makes you aware that exerting a great deal of conscious control over your work is sometimes the best way to strangle the life out of it. It was wonderful at Padua just being around writers who weren't afraid of *not* making sense. I have a need to make my work all make sense on some level. But I find it more interesting to go out on a limb, to allow impulses to come in which I don't understand, and then tie them together. What's interesting about the subconscious is that there's usually some way the impulses do tie together and make the piece richer.

Do you do a lot of reworking before rehearsals?

It varies from play to play. With almost all the plays there's been a period of substantial rewrites before rehearsals. But some more than others. I'm always open to rewriting during rehearsal, too, and sometimes have rewritten great chunks. But that's tricky. On the one hand, although the theatrical experience comes from the text, once you start seeing the play on its feet, the text doesn't actually take precedence over the experience. If the text looks good but the experience isn't working, you fiddle with the direction, but if it still doesn't work, it's really the responsibility of the words. On the other hand, in some ways rehearsal is the worst time to rewrite because you're under a lot of time pressure. If you've spent a year with the play, there's something absurd about rewriting the whole thing in four weeks.

How much did you rewrite Family Devotions?

The original play was three acts and had a couple more characters. It was rewritten extensively over a period of about a year, and then rewritten extensively again in rehearsal. A lot of things were cut. I think the rewriting was successful in giving the play a certain amount of sense, a more traditional structure. I think it was unsuccessful in that it robbed the original of some heart. As you can imagine, *Family Devotions* is an expensive play to put on. So it had to succeed if it was going to be produced again. Its reception was only so-so in New York. The *New York Times* liked it but a lot of the other papers were mixed. The audiences seemed a little confused by it. Consequently, it was not done again until this year in San Francisco.

It's always been important to me to get that play right because it has a special place in my heart. So I rewrote about half of it for this production. It was only a few months ago so I can't be too objective, but I think it went very well. Audiences responded to it better, they weren't as confused as they were by the New York production. I guess the moral of that story is that though you can't tinker with a play forever, sometimes you get a chance to give it a second life and that's nice.

Of all your plays, it seems to be the most highly comic and to have the most disturbing ending. In the recent rewrite, did you attenuate the comedy at all?

Family Devotions is basically autobiographical and I found that in the six years between when it was originally staged and when I rewrote it, I'd gotten all this extra material about my family. It turned out to be a funnier play, and also more cohesive. To some degree, the second half has to come as a shock, but there's a fine line to walk to make it a shock that seems sensible in retrospect.

How is the play autobiographical?

Family Devotions is about an upper-middle-class Chinese-American family and I come from that background. My father's a banker and my mother's a pianist. My mother's family converted to Christianity several generations ago back in China and we have a lot of pastors in the family. They're essentially what's known as born-again Christians. For a long time I went to church and subscribed to those beliefs on some level.

Family Devotions comes from one incident. I had just had *FOB* performed in New York and I was coming back to California. My extended family had a get-together at my uncle's house in Belair, with the tennis court in back, and we had visiting my granduncle from the People's Republic of China who had not seen our family in twenty years. We decided that it was important

125

to have a family devotion ceremony and confront him with his past, to see if he could be brought back to God. It seemed really odd, if I put myself in this guy's shoes, that he'd be coming out of the PRC after twenty years and end up in Belair with a bunch of Chinese-Americans playing tennis and trying to convert him to Christianity.

In both autobiographical and dramatic terms, then, Chester's deciphering of Di-Gou's recollection is the play's crux, his coming to terms with his heritage.

Chester's link-up with Di-Gou, who represents an alternative history from the one that he was brought up with, allows him to reconcile himself to his past. It's a history he feels more comfortable with. Actually in the rewrite the speaking in tongues is done very differently and the family secret is different. I knew I was going to rewrite the play when my extended family got together last Thanksgiving and were having family devotions. One of my granduncles who's a pastor told this story. His mother had had two girls and wanted a son and then she had six more girls and drowned them all in the well in back. The ghosts of these six women came back to haunt her and she went to all the exorcists, but it didn't work until finally she met a Christian missionary who successfully exorcised the ghosts, at which point my great-grandaunt became a Christian and subsequently gave birth to my granduncle. As a family secret, this seemed central to what the play was trying to be about: to what degree can you cut yourself off from guilt or your responsibilities to the past, simply because you've adopted a Western religion or come to a Western country? So that event is a proper metaphor.

America's a country that's extremely present-oriented. It really has no history to speak of. I come from a part of America that's even worse than that. I come from Los Angeles and I like it though I know it's totally tacky and quite superficial. In Los Angeles something is old if it was built in 1920. I think part of my fascination with Los Angeles is just the flip side of my desire to be tied into something larger, some sort of history.

It seems there's a certain spiritual bankruptcy in this country which comes from an unwillingness to recognize the past. It manifests itself in a lot of ways, like not having respect for old people, or discarding consumer goods as soon as the next ones come out. I do that as much as anybody else but I'm fascinated by the way it seems to indicate a deficiency in this culture. Theatre throughout the world comes from ritual or a gathering of people to celebrate a commonality. The fact that you get a group in one space looking at their own people doing things implies that. In this country, in this age, the way to create spiritually in the theatre is to forge a link to something further back. That's one way to deal with, to fight the religion of the present in America. That's how I've chosen to attack it in my work.

126

Which is why so many of your plays are about mythology.

For me it's really the impulse to reclaim my heritage. It's scary not to have a sense of past because it implies not having a sense of future. Since for the past thirty or forty years we've had the ability to control the future of the world, it's scary to think that we have no sense of future.

In this country there's very little understanding of our cultural heritage, but also of history generally.

We don't even remember what happened in Watergate, and that was fifteen years ago. Certainly we don't remember the Civil Rights movement. That's appalling to me.

Both Dance and the Railroad *and* Butterfly *are history plays.*

Dance and the Railroad is definitely a history play. *Butterfly* is about very recent history.

But you strongly historicize the personal story, comparing various imperialist ventures, like Vietnam, with Bouriscot's sexual imperialism.

What I was trying to do in *Butterfly*—I didn't really know this except in retrospect—was to link imperialism, racism and sexism. It necessitates a certain historical perspective.

And a look at the mythologies created to justify them.

Particularly Puccini's *Madame Butterfly*.

So the play is really focused on two systems of domination, the cultural and the sexual.

Cultural superiority is essentially economic. Whatever country dominates the world economically determines what culture is, for a while. There's a lag, because the country gets to determine the culture even after somebody else takes over economically. It still has the mystique of being the old culture, whether it's Britain or the United States. Probably the next world power is going to be Japan. You can't deal with cultural mystique unless you deal with political mystique, political power.

I was interested in how you handled the fact that Bouriscot's mistress, Shi Peipu, is really a man. That makes for the reversal at the end, the fact that Shi turns out to be Pinkerton.

That's the axis on which the play turns. Insofar as this is possible, I would like to seduce the audience during the first act into believing that Shi is a woman. We're so conditioned to think in certain ways about Oriental women and the relationship of the West to the East, that I think it would be fun to get into the audience's head in the first act, in a very reactionary way, and then blow it out later. I don't know to what degree that's possible because anyone who goes to see this play, especially if it runs any length of time, will probably know what it's about. But I still think it can work on some level.

So you want Shi played by a man?

Definitely. You have to create the illusion for the audience, you have to trick them. It's dirty pool if you give them a woman and say, this is a woman, and later, when he appears as a man, you give them a man. You have to play by the rules. If you're saying that Bouriscot was seduced by a man, then you have to seduce the audience with a man. *Butterfly* runs the risk of indulging the sin it condemns, like violent movies that are supposedly antiviolence. If you cast a woman in that role, you'd condemn the oppression of women by oppressing a woman in a very attractive way on the stage. If you oppress a woman who actually is a man, it's much more interesting.

The play also allows you to explore another collision between Western and Asian-style theatre.

I'm actually not too interested in exploring that issue, that form, right now. It's just that in Japanese or Chinese theatre (or in Shakespearean theatre) men play women's roles. In Kabuki the theory is that a man plays a woman better than a woman does because the man can be the idealization of a woman. That's essentially what the play is about: that the idealization of a woman is false to its core, even to the point of the woman being a man. So it happened that I ended up using this form again.

And you have the Western operatic style as well.

You can do opera and then you can do a kind of sitcom.

But your work is not about integrating the styles, it's more about collision.

It's about finding a relationship between them rather than fusing them into an amalgam.

Have you always chosen your director?

I've either chosen or else had veto power over the director. So effectively, yes.

Any production you're particularly fond of?

John Lone, Tzi Ma and I worked very closely on *The Dance and the Railroad*. They made suggestions about the text and I had input in the production.

Because they were acting and John was also directing, I was able to sit back and give notes as a director. We really worked as a unit. While I don't agree with many people that *Dance and the Railroad* is the strongest work of mine textually, I do think it came off the best because there was a complete integration of text, movement and direction.

Other than Family Devotions, *have you done much rewriting after first productions?*

No. After you have what you decide is the definitive first production, which is usually in New York, you have to let the play go into the world and make its own way.

Do you read the critics?

Yes. Individual critics are useful mainly from a commercial standpoint. If you get a good review you can use it on an ad. Therefore, they're important to your career. But in terms of influencing the work, I think the only way they can be useful is if you read a whole bunch at one time, when you have a certain amount of distance on the play, because it's the closest thing you get to going out and taking a poll of the audience. If there are things they all agree on that they didn't like, then you have to believe that something went wrong. I tend not to read a critic when someone tells me in advance that it's going to be particularly difficult to swallow, that it's sarcastic or mean. With *Rich Relations*, the Frank Rich and John Simon reviews were not positive but they made their points in an articulate fashion, so that's okay. Clive Barnes and Doug Watt seemed pretty upset, so I didn't read them. I don't particularly like to be sniped at in print.

How do you see the American theatre today?

I don't go to theatre too much anymore. But I don't think it's because the work being done now is worse than the work I saw five or six years ago.

But unquestionably money has gotten tighter.

I'm having the experience now of working in the commercial theatre for the first time, preparing *M. Butterfly* for Broadway. And I have to say I like it —though maybe by the time this book comes out, I'll have decided that I hate it. When we say that Broadway's dead, or the commercial theatre is dead, I wonder if we're not making a self-fulfilling prophecy. Because we say there are no outlets for young playwrights on Broadway, it never occurred to me to seek out a commercial producer. I thought you had to go to a nonprofit theatre and hope that if the play's a hit, a commercial producer picks it up. We're contributing to the decline of Broadway by censoring ourselves before we even attempt it. On the other hand, if Broadway is going to die, I don't feel too bad about it. I don't have any particular love for institutions per se. If the institution of Broadway dies, then I figure something will come up to take its place, like the Off-Broadway movement, or Off-Off in the early sixties. It's not really a problem.

There are some things, however, about working in the theatre that are not too pleasant. Theatre—particularly nonprofit—is still a poverty art, especially in this country, where it's not well subsidized and the audience still needs to be developed. That has certain adverse psychological effects. In the nonprofit theatre there's the attitude, stated or unstated, that somebody owes me something because I'm not being paid what I'm worth. When you get people working together who feel that on any level, it creates an atmosphere that's ripe for tension and pettiness. I don't know what the answer is except for the government to fund the theatre more properly. I hate to make it sound that so much human behavior is dependent on economics, but I feel it's inevitable, particularly in this country where our economic place has a bearing on our psychological self-image.

Can you suggest other reasons for theatre's present problems?

It's not a very interesting time for ideas in general. The eighties, the Reagan years, are just boring intellectually. I've always believed there are times when ideas are in the air and different people pick them up in varied places. If you believe that, you have to believe that there are times when there are no ideas in the air.

Theatre demands an application of intellect and is a good forum for new ideas. To some degree, a form like film can survive a period like this even though I don't think there have been many interesting films in the eighties —film has the ability to appeal to something else. Because good theatre appeals to the mind, interesting ideas are a prerequisite. Since there are no interesting ideas in the air, the popular theatre has concentrated on spectacle. That's been the expensive substitute for ideas. But I think it's starting to change. Maybe we're already starting to come out of the Reagan years. Even the film industry is beginning to reflect the notion that films should deal with ideas.

So then, for you, theatre is a forum in which a culture or society debates with itself?

At least in my own work, I perceive it as a forum for a society to confront itself. In a good play that confrontation should be total, which means that it's not only political, or spiritual, or intellectual, but combines all these elements.

When you confront someone totally, you're also confronting them on an emotional level.

What are your plans for the future?

Butterfly is supposed to go to Broadway next spring. In London we're doing some version of *House of Sleeping Beauties* with Laurence Olivier and Jean Simmons for television. We're still trying to figure out who the American distributor is going to be. I'm doing an adaptation of H.G. Wells' *War of the Worlds* with Philip Glass. It's not quite an opera, it's more a ninety-minute Glass piece which includes a narration read by an actor. A designer named Jerome Serlin who works in multitextured designs and then projects things on them is doing a visual show to go along with it. This is going to open in Vienna in May of '88 and tour Europe and Australia and then come to the States. Then I have some film projects which I like a lot but which may never see the light of day.

What are your longer-range goals?

When I came out of the period of not writing, I knew I was going to be a writer for the rest of my life. Despite all the things that had taken place before, I was never sure how strong my commitment to the craft was.

I like the environment I'm in now because I'm able to work in different media. That's healthy because I have different ideas and have to find the proper home for each. We all know there are things a film can do that the stage can't do, and vice versa. Aside from that, it's hard to make long-term plans. I find that the work determines itself, to a large degree. You have a certain amount of influence over it, but you can't force yourself to write something. And what you can write evolves and changes. So the only thing I can say about the future is that I will be a writer and that I would like to work in many different forms.

DAVID MAMET

D avid Mamet is the American theatre's foremost warrior-philologist. He traces his awareness of the music of language to years of piano lessons and his father's passion for semantics; his ear for the combative power of language he ascribes to his family. "In the days prior to television," he recalls, "we liked to while away the evenings by making ourselves miserable solely based on our ability to speak the language viciously."

As a teenager Mamet worked as a busboy at Chicago's Second City. His first play, *Camel*, a semisatirical revue, was written during his years at Goddard College in Vermont. For eighteen months he studied acting in New York at the Neighborhood Playhouse, but soon gave up trying to find work on the strawhat trail because he was "terrible." After a year teaching and writing *Lakeboat*, he returned to Chicago in 1969 and worked as a cabdriver, short-order cook and high-pressure salesman for a real estate firm that sold "worthless" land in Arizona and Florida. In 1971 he took a job as drama teacher at Goddard and founded the St. Nicholas Company to stage his own works and such classics as *Anna Christie*. Back in Chicago in 1972 he wrote *Duck Variations*, which was first performed that year, and *Sexual Perversity in Chicago*, which gathered considerable attention two years later. These have

132

been followed by a string of major plays: *American Buffalo* (1975), *A Life in the Theatre* (1976), *The Water Engine* and *The Woods* (1977), *Edmond* (1982) and *Glengarry Glen Ross* (1983), for which he was awarded the Pulitzer Prize.

Although Mamet has written many different kinds of plays (and screenplays), his most vigorous project and the one about which he has been most eloquent is the demystification of the American Dream. "It was basically raping and pillage," he explains. Mamet sees that "this capitalistic dream of wealth" has led to a dead end: "We are finally reaching a point where there is nothing left to exploit....The dream has nowhere to go so it has to start turning in on itself." All of Mamet's plays, to varying degrees, explore this process of self-destruction and the extraordinary inequities and hypocrisies that flourish in a society in its death throes.

Mamet's focus—psychologically, socially and technically—is on estrangement. His plays not only probe the alienation of the individual from himself and his society, they use alienation as a technical device (in a way totally different from Brecht). To see Mamet as simply a realist is to neglect the fact that realism is only one pole of his work—one in which a character's psychology and his deeds are in alignment—and is always opposed to a more "esoteric" force driving psychology and deed apart. To varying degrees, all of his plays introduce a schism between character and action, between what an individual says and what he does. They generate tension in the clash of motives, justificatory discourse and action. A Mamet character can never fully account for what he does; there's always a horrifying unknown, slipping beyond the grasp of language. "There's a schizophrenia in my writing. On the one hand, I like to write very esoteric stuff," he explains. "I also like to write Neo-Realist plays like *American Buffalo*. My true metier lies somewhere in between. I'm really into language as poetry."

In *Edmond*, perhaps the most "poetic" of his "in-between" plays, the central problem lies in the title character's attempt to use a wholly inadequate language as an intermediary between his desires and the world. The play charts the gradual descent of an American urban, white, middle-class Everyman who, educated and articulate, is totally unable to connect with a world that doesn't play according to his rules. A rage and madness are unleashed in him and he becomes utterly estranged from his actions. Only when Edmond acknowledges the breakdown between the narrowness of his language and the depth of his desires does he begin to apprehend himself as whole and to forge a link with others and with his environment.

In most of Mamet's plays, the social construct he uses to focus his critique is business. Both *American Buffalo* and *Glengarry Glen Ross* are explorations of a systematic process of brutalization; both enact Mamet's realization that in a capitalist economy all relations are, to some degree, commercial relations;

both acknowledge the arbitrariness of the demarcation between personal and mercantile. "There's really no difference between the *Lumpenproletariat* and...the lackeys of business," Mamet notes. "Part of the American myth is that a difference exists, that at a certain point vicious behavior becomes laudable." Perhaps the most fascinating aspect of Mamet's examination is the connection he draws between commercial and ontological terrorism. At the end of *Glengarry* the mystery is apparently solved, the thief apprehended. And yet niggling doubts remain: Is anyone else involved? How deep and extensive is the conspiracy? Is anyone *not* guilty? Certainty is no longer possible in this world and a kind of existential vertigo sets in. Is capitalism the cause? Or the effect of something even deeper?

Mamet has noted that as a result of the failure of the American Dream, "the people it has sustained—the white males—are going nuts." Certainly he is not the first American playwright to notice this madness; both O'Neill and Miller addressed it, as have a number of Mamet's male contemporaries. His work is distinguished from theirs less by the causes suggested than by the tonality of the analysis. Mamet's is without nostalgia, without a sentimental attachment to a time when white men—and the mythology created to justify their hegemony—ruled the world. His work unmasks that mythology, but without being didactic or narrowly prescriptive. If theatre's function is, as he maintains, to celebrate, his own does so less by reveling than solemnizing, performing a rite simultaneously mythic and political (can the two not be connected?). "Theatre is a place of recognition," he says. "It's where we show ethical interchange." It is, from its origins, a place where society can debate its future.

■   ■   ■

FEBRUARY 11, 1987—STUDIO C, WEST 54TH STREET, NEW YORK CITY

What led you to become a playwright?

I was an actor, and I started directing actors. Then I was teaching and directing students and I started writing, really, to illustrate the points that I was talking about as a teacher. I started a theatre company and we didn't have any money to pay royalties. And that's how I started playwriting.

Before that, what got you interested in theatre?

There was a community theatre in Chicago and I spent a lot of time hanging out at Second City. At that time in Chicago, it was just in the air.

During that period, what playwrights particularly influenced you?

Lanford Wilson was a big influence on me—the collections of his early plays, like *Rimers of Eldritch* and *The Madness of Lady Bright*. There was also a book from the New American Library—I think it was called *New Voices from the American Theatre*—that was a major influence on all of us who were young in the sixties. It included *Mrs. Dalley Has a Lover* and *Upstairs Sleeping* and a play by Murray Schisgal. *Waiting for Godot* was the most influential play. A lot of the plays from Grove Press in the sixties—Pinter's *A Night Out* and *Revue Sketches* and Ionesco's *Rhinoceros*—were a great antidote to all those wretched British series of modern European theatre with their bad translations of mediocre plays.

In Godot Beckett places the main action in the traditional sense—Pozzo's blinding—offstage. That's a strategy you use a lot as well, placing the conventionally dramatic event between the scenes, as in Glengarry or The Shawl.

A very good rule of dramaturgy is that you can't show the unshowable. You can't dramatize "They waited for a long time" better than by having a cut. If the event in *Glengarry* is not the robbery, but rather something closer to the through-line of the protagonists, a condition rather than a dramatic action, the robbery doesn't have to be shown. You can just cut past it. That's a lesson we all learned from cinema.

And this has the effect, as Beckett and Pinter have taught us, of redefining dramatic action.

Well, maybe. I don't know. Take a play like *Betrayal*, a brilliant play that just puts everything backwards. But Pinter curiously doesn't redefine the dramatic action. He uses the dynamic between the traditional dramatic structure and the audience's perception of it to create, almost in a cinematic way, a third reality. But the rules of dramatic structure, redefine them how you will, are based on the rules of human perception. That's what enables deviation from them to work. That's what enables so-called performance art to function. There's really nothing there other than randomness, in a lot of instances, but it works because the human mind will always impose order.

What about Tennessee Williams? You refer to him in Writing in Restaurants.

He had a great impact on me but not until later. In the sixties his work was viewed, at least in my community, as classic rather than contemporary. Although of course he was a contemporary writer. I became very interested in the work of Tennessee and also Arthur Miller. I started working my way backward through dramatic history.

What about Miller?

I think he has a very different view of writing from mine. He sees writing as a tool of conscience. His stuff is informed by the driving idea that theatre is a tool for the betterment of social conditions.

How does that differ from what you do?

I just write plays. I don't think that my plays are going to change anybody's social conditions. I think Mr. Miller's always thought, and it's a great thought, that his plays might alter people's feelings about real contemporary events. My view is very, very different because we're different people from different generations. I think the purpose of theatre, as Stanislavski said, is to bring to the stage the life of the soul. That may or may not make people more in touch with what's happening around them and may or may not make them better citizens.

So it might indirectly have a political impact by making people more aware?

Yes. I wished that I could write that kind of play. I tried it once in a while. *Edmond* is an example.

What about Brecht?

He influenced me a great deal. *Edmond*, again, is a good example of that. I used to teach the works of Brecht and was fascinated by him. All that nonsense he wrote about his writing I think is balderdash, a direct contradiction of the writing itself—which is the most wonderful, charming, involving, quintessentially dramatic writing. It's wonderfully whacky.

To some extent, Brecht the theorist wanted to deny what Brecht the playwright was doing.

All of the comics like me always want to be tragedians. I think the same was true of Brecht. Historically, his plays fall under the wide aegis of comedy. His stuff is brilliant.

Did your training in New York under Sanford Meisner have a greater effect on you than any other work?

Absolutely. The most important thing I learned at the Neighborhood Playhouse was the idea of a through-line, which was Aristotle filtered through Stanislavski and Boleslavsky. That idea is a couple of thousand years old. Also the idea from Stanislavski of the subjugation of all aspects of the production

—not just the script, but the acting and the plastic elements—to the through-line of the play. That has stood me in very, very good stead in film directing.

In your plays the through-line is so strong that the characters can be saying things that are very, very different from what is really being communicated in the subtext.

That's why theatre's like life, don't you think? No one really says what they mean, but they always mean what they mean.

And the subtext is always about power, buying and selling.

Why not? Lately I've developed a real love of Thackeray. The thought occurred to me that almost every English novel I know, whether it's *Vanity Fair* or *Pendennis* or *Howard's End* or Orwell, is all about the guy trying to raise the money to get his bowler hat out of hock so he won't be embarrassed when he goes to the party. They're all about people being embarrassed about their lack of money. And I guess most American literature—the American literature that I love, that I grew up on—is about business. That's what America is about.

Also, in acting, subtext is usually defined as a power dynamic.

I've been teaching acting for about twenty years now, and I love it. It's all about two people who want something different. If the two people don't want something different, what the hell is the scene about? Stay home. The same is true for writing. If two people don't want something from each other, then why are you having the scene? Throw the goddam scene out—which might seem like an overly strict lesson to be learned in a schoolroom but is awfully helpful in the theatre. If the two people don't want something different, the audience is going to go to sleep. Power, that's another way of putting it.

All of us are trying all the time to create the best setting and the best expression we can, not to communicate our wishes to each other, but to *achieve* our wishes *from* each other. I think awareness of this is the difference between good and bad playwriting. Whether it's a politician trying to get votes or a guy trying to go to bed with a girl or somebody trying to get a good table at a restaurant, the point is not to speak the desire but to speak that which is most likely to bring about the desire.

How do you write a play? What do you start with—character, dialogue, plot?

Well, there's an old cowboy's trick. The herd is coming through fast and one cowboy asks another how you estimate the number of cows so quickly. The other cowboy says: "It's very easy. You just count up the number of hooves and divide by four." That's how you write a play. You do a lot of writing to figure out what the hell the play's about and throw out three-quarters of it and write it again and look at it and find out what *that* play's about and throw out three-quarters of it and write it again.

Most playwrights have spoken of the importance of letting the unconscious material out first and then going back and working on what has been released. Is that a fair description of your process?

I think so. I have my processes of writing a play. But technique is training to break down the barriers between the unconscious and the conscious mind. That's true whether you're playing Ping-Pong or writing. After a number of years, one attains a certain amount of technique which enables the unconscious to respond, in the case of tennis, faster, or in the case of playwriting, perhaps better, than the conscious mind could. The bad side is that you tend to do things in the same way. That's called habit.

Do you ever work from an outline?

Sure. When I write movies, I always work from an outline. When I write plays, at some point I work from an outline. I may have several thousand pages of dialogue before I decide it's time to write an outline.

You've generally chosen your director for a first production?

Yes.

You've worked with Gregory Mosher a great deal.

We did a bunch of plays at the Goodman from '75 to '85. We're doing a new play next February at Lincoln Center, *Speed-the-Plow.*

Do you always attend rehearsals for first productions?

It varies. There have been plays with Gregory where I was there every day. We had conferences deep into the night. For example, *American Buffalo.* And then there were plays where I went to the first rehearsal and said hello to the cast and showed up at the opening. For example, *Edmond.* That was the most brilliant production I've ever seen on any stage. The whole thing was done with two or three chairs and a table. It was devastating.

Is there some quality in a good production of your work which you would identify as a David Mamet style?

No, I don't think so. I think that, as Vakhtangov told us, we shouldn't rush to scenic solutions—they should follow the essential solution which comes out of a consideration of what the play is about and what the character is doing to get what he wants. What I want in my productions—or in any production—is honesty, simplicity and directness.

When you attend rehearsals, do you do much rewriting?

Sure. If the audience beats you to the point, take it out. If they don't understand, put it in. If the structure's wrong, fix it.

What about after first productions?

Sometimes you don't get it right and you're never going to get it right and it's useless to kill yourself over it. It's better, past a certain point, to learn a lesson for the next play rather than give yourself the luxury—if indeed it is that—of working something forever. Sometimes I've got to say, "There's an answer to this problem but I don't know it."

Any other favorite productions, besides **Edmond?**

John Dillon's production of *Lakeboat* at Milwaukee Repertory Theater with Larry Shue. Wonderful, beautiful, unforgettable. I go to the theatre to enjoy myself, just like anybody else.

How do you feel when you go to see theatre that's more confrontational?

Like what?

Like **Aunt Dan and Lemon.**

I feel confronted. You seem to have the notion that in my estimation there must be a right way and a wrong way to do things. But I don't think that that's true. There are as many different kinds of theatre as there are playwrights. I went to see Jackie Mason last night—a brilliant, brilliant evening. I felt very confronted at times. That's the point. It's nice that ABC Television is having all this brouhaha about *Amerika*. I want to see that. I hope I feel very confronted.

Your plays are confrontational only indirectly, insofar as they're about asking questions rather than providing answers or delineating a mystery.

In *Writing in Restaurants* I say that the purpose of the theatre is to deal with things that can't be dealt with rationally. If they can be dealt with rationally, they probably don't belong in my theatre. There are other people who feel differently and who work that way brilliantly. One of them is Arthur Miller. *Incident at Vichy, The Crucible*, also his new play, *Clara*. Or Wally Shawn, in *Aunt Dan and Lemon*. Or Fugard, for example.

Do you read the critics?

Once in a while.

Do you take them seriously?

There are good critics and bad critics, well-meaning and depraved critics. I'm like anybody else in the world—I'd rather be praised than criticized. There are some people who may write about my work and make very, very good points about it, but I'll be goddamned if I'm going to pay any attention to it. They don't speak in a kindly and respectful fashion, the way that I would speak about them if it were my job to criticize them. So fuck 'em, in short. And that, I think, sums up my feelings about critics.

Many of the playwrights I've spoken to have commented on the sorry state of the American theatre.

America is in a sorry state. We're at a very difficult time. Our culture has just fallen apart and is going to have to die off before something else takes its place. So whether you say American theatre, or American car production, or the American standard of living, they're all in the same boat. Theatre is not an aspect of our civilization to be separated out. It's part of the body politic.

Broadway has become like Las Vegas. It's very rare that a serious play is able to run there.

I don't think it will ever happen again. It's just life. If someone went to Provincetown in 1920, he could have seen some great theatre on the wharf, had a moonlight stroll down the beach, had some magnificently fresh and inexpensive seafood, and breathed the clean air. If that person came back to Provincetown today, he would say, "Wait a second. What happened to this beautiful community? Why are there so many people here? Why is everything so expensive? What happened to that theatre?" What happened is that the world changed. Theatre went someplace else. Cheap seafood went someplace else. Good air went someplace else. The same is true of Broadway.

What about the regional theatres?

I don't know anything about them. I got a lot of bang for my buck out of regional theatres in the seventies, had some great times working at the Goodman, and Actors Theatre of Louisville, The Empty Space, Yale Rep, Milwaukee Rep. I don't know what's happening with them now.

In your essay, "Decay: Some Thoughts for Actors," I was surprised to read your statement that "The problems of the world...are, finally, no more solvable than the problems of a tree which has borne fruit." I find that a rather despairing attitude—an attitude I don't get from your plays.

I didn't feel in despair when I wrote that. I felt despair *before* I wrote it— like a lot of people today, I felt frightened and confused, and very anxious. Looking around and saying, "Well, this is what's happening," I felt, *after* I wrote that essay, rather calm—somewhere between hopeful and resigned.

Do you have any idea, or any guess, as to how change will take place?

If you read the paper, you see that the world is trying to determine which of the many alternatives for decay and dissolution will work. One is a plague. Another is a nuclear accident or a war. Another is economic catastrophe. I think it's going to be something rather surprising. I was talking to Greg Mosher about it just the other day and he says that he's kind of looking forward to it. I think a lot of people are.

Your plays often draw a connection between a brutal social network and a particular economic framework. Glengarry *is perhaps the purest example. Do you think it's possible that a change in the economic structure would lead to a radical change in society?*

I don't hold to that view. Of course that's a very Marxian view. I think that the economic system is not susceptible to change, but that it is an outgrowth of the intrinsic soul of the culture. You can't change the economic system. They changed it in Russia and sixty years later they're back where they started.

When you say "soul of the culture," do you really mean "human nature"?

Not human nature. Because I think that human nature is altered by certain essential aspects of life in a given place, at a given time. For example, the same people live in California and Vermont, but the human nature is conditioned by such factors as the different flow of the seasons, the difficulties of earning a living from the soil. So although human nature remains the same, it's tempered by different climates and different locales. The economic system is an outgrowth of this conditioning.

Do you think it possible to create an economic system that isn't brutal?

Sure. I think it's been done in the past. At various times in history there was a sufficient stasis, a sufficient equilibrium between that which people possessed and that which they desired. It's kind of an anarchistic view, in that

141

these people I'm thinking of lived in small communities and were capable of making their own ad hoc, logical rules and regulations. I live in a small town in Vermont where people can do business by giving their word, leaving a check at the post office, calling up the bank and saying, "Will you send me this money?" One reason they can do this is common sense. If you live in a community where you're dependent on the same people day in and day out, then it's common sense that those people would deal honestly with each other.

And isn't that what it comes down to, this sense of community? That's the message in **The Water Engine.**

"All people are connected." The other view of the theatre is that it's really a great time to go in and kick some ass because people are so starved. As I said, I saw Jackie Mason last night. I hadn't realized how long it's been since we've all sat in the theatre and laughed because we shared the same values.

You say that, as a writer, you don't have a political agenda. Then what effect do you want to have on your audience?

When I write a play, what I'm trying to do is write that play. As for the effect...it's not that it doesn't interest me, but it's really not my job to manipulate the audience, whether for a political motive or to get them to "like" my play. My job with the play succeeds according to its own logical syllogism. If this, then that. That's the difference between a playwright and a writer of advertising. The writer of advertising should be concerned, as Mr. Ogilvy tells us, solely with the effect it's going to have on the reader or the viewer, to persuade to buy the product or service advertised. If the writer of advertising is worried about the awards that he or she is going to win, or the esteem that he or she is going to win in the advertising community, or even the aesthetic beauty of the ad—absent its ability to influence the viewer—that person is not doing his or her job. Playwriting is exactly the opposite. Somebody said that if everybody likes everything you do, then you're doing something wrong.

How do you see the relationship between your work for stage and screen?

Hollywood people are very, very cruel and also very, very cunning. One of the things that they will say to me and to other writers, if they don't understand something or if it's not bad enough for them, is, "It's very theatrical. It's too theatrical." That is used as a curse word. Also as an irrefutable statement. What are you going to say? "It's not theatrical"? I try to write the best I can for whatever medium I'm engaged in. We all know that we should stay away from Hollywood, but we don't. I try to do the best job I can, because in addition to my own love of the work, I'm getting paid for it as a working man.

When you direct your own work on the stage or the screen, do you work on it any differently than you would someone else's?

No, not at all. You ask the same questions, reduce it to a through-line: What does the protagonist want? What does he or she do to get it? What does the play mean? That's all. Someone else might know different questions to ask, but I don't. Whether I direct them myself or whether they're directed by, say, Greg, a lot of my productions tend to be incredibly austere. Which I like. Which I love, as a matter of fact. Other people may have a more pronounced visual sense. The questions that I ask in terms of the plastic elements are: Where does this take place? What does it mean to the play?

So everything is determined by the life on stage.

Greg did a play of mine called *The Disappearance of the Jews*, which takes place in a hotel room. It was designed by Michael Merritt, who's designed many of my plays and movies. We kicked around what the hotel room would look like and finally I said the scenic element essential to the dramatic thrust of the play—why this room rather than another room?—is that this is a place where these two guys can be alone and be intimate with each other. That's what we came down to. So we said, well, what if we take everything away except for the two chairs and a little cigarette table between them. Then Greg said, "If we really want to say that's all it means, and we don't want to overcharacterize, let's reupholster the chairs in white muslin so that we take away the distracting element of the particular choice of fabric." So we aren't asking, what kind of hotel is it? The important thing is, it's a hotel. It was a brilliant set. I think Merritt's sets for the Miller plays which Greg directed are absolutely brilliant.

Is there any theatre you've seen recently that you particularly admire?

I haven't gone to the theatre much over the last year. I've been working on *House of Games*. I admire Greg's work on the Miller plays at Lincoln Center. I admired *Platoon* and *A Room with a View* and *Crocodile Dundee*. I liked *Radio Days* very much.

What is Speed-the-Plow *about?*

It's a play about my experiences in Hollywood—two producers and a secretary. I also may be directing a new movie that I wrote with Shel Silverstein.

Where do you think the hope for the future of theatre lies?

I think it's a great time to be a young person in the theatre. All bets are off, as in such times of social upheaval as the twenties in Germany, the sixties in

Chicago, the period from 1898 to 1920 in Russia. Traditionally, these are times when new theatrical forms arise. That's what all this garbage about performance art is about, to a large extent—it's young people in the culture experimenting, casting about for a new form.

Certainly the political scene has become increasingly polarized over the past six years and I think that holds true for cultural products as a whole.

I think the lines will become more and more sharply divided. I think we're going to start putting people in jail again for what they write. People have been subconsciously afraid of expressing themselves because the times are so tenuous. And the reality will follow that feeling. So that will be exciting.

And frightening.

And very frightening, sure.

And you don't see a gentle way out of this state of polarization? You believe there will be a radical change?

It's like the weather. People get oppressed by the heat and humidity, it's got to rain before it's going to clear up. There are ebbs and flows in any civilization. Nothing lasts forever. We had a good time. We had Tennessee Williams. We had the hula hoop. We had the Edsel. All kinds of good stuff. The Constitution. To name but a few. Shelley Winters. Now you've got to pay the piper. Big deal.

EMILY MANN

S tudying piano, flute and recorder while she was growing up, Emily Mann was determined to become a musician and composer. During her junior year in high school, however, she got involved with theatre and decided on a different career. She trained as a director, at Harvard University and the Guthrie Theater in Minneapolis, and wrote and directed her first play during her five-year tenure at the Guthrie. *Annulla, An Autobiography* (1977, revised 1985) is a documentary drama based on an interview she and a friend conducted as part of an oral history of her friend's family, many of them survivors of the Holocaust. This was followed in 1980 by a second documentary, *Still Life*, about a Vietnam veteran, his wife and his mistress, whose New York production the next year won six Obie awards. In 1984 she premiered *Execution of Justice*, an examination of the San Francisco trial of Dan White, which two years later was presented on Broadway. Her most recent work is *Betsey Brown*, a rhythm-and-blues opera based on the novel of the same name by Ntozake Shange.

In her plays Mann has evolved a distinctive and powerful dramatic form that combines her interest in oral history and journalism, her prowess as a theatre director and her understanding of musical architecture and counterpoint. In each, she illuminates a particular circumstance by running historical fact against a number of interwoven voices that describe the feeling of an event from the inside. Through this counterpoint of objective and subjective, documentary evidence and real speech, she draws a complex portrait of a particular society. The interplay of perspectives clarifies the network of individual motives and provides insight into the larger social matrix of which they are a part.

Because Mann understands the intricacies of theatrical and musical form, she offers deeply dramatic portraits, structuring documentary material by subjecting it to ironic juxtaposition. Within each play as a whole, she orchestrates a carefully supervised irony which, by the end, assiduously and often violently reverses the spectator's initial assumptions. This strategy forces the spectator to confront his or her own attitudes and beliefs and, without offering a facile solution, encourages reevaluation of deeply troubling issues.

Still Life is a fugue for the theatre that examines the operation of violence in American culture by interweaving the monologues of Mark, a traumatized ex-marine who fought and killed in Vietnam; Cheryl, his pregnant and terrified wife; and Nadine, his exuberant mistress. The play is less about Vietnam than about how and why both men and women resort to violence when they are unable to deal with anger and guilt. It carefully diagrams chains of violence —spouses brutalizing each other and parents abusing their children—to show how violence is fostered within the family and passed on from one generation to the next. By setting the examination of domestic violence next to Mark's memories of the Vietnam War, Mann draws a distressing and ineluctable connection between imperialist forays abroad and brutality at home.

While addressing the relation between public and private violence, Mann's plays analyze the transmission of brutality by focusing on inheritance not as a *fait accompli* but as a process. In all four a parent-child relation is pivotal. In *Annulla*, in the midst of the title character's stories and observations, the authorial Voice recalls giving birth to her own son and thinking, much to her dismay, that Annulla is wrong, that "women are just as capable of brutality and murder as men." In *Still Life* the horror of Mark's confession that he killed three children, a mother and a father in cold blood is redoubled by his fear for his own son: "He's going to die for what I've done." In *Execution of Justice* the Young Woman asks the play's crucial question immediately after the announcement of the jury's verdict: "What are we teaching our sons?" In *Betsey Brown* the development of a young black woman's attitudes and self-image is the center of the play, as Betsey is torn between her mother's insistence that she think and behave like a white person and Carrie's demand that she celebrate her heritage and her uniqueness.

In her work Mann has introduced a new political sophistication to the

American theatre. Unlike the writers of agitprop, she is not interested in effecting a clear separation between victim and victimizer, the exploited individual and an oppressive social and economic system. Having come of age both politically and theatrically in the late 1960s, she realizes that contemporary American culture—a society of the sixty-second spot, of the decontextualizing "Six O'Clock News"—does not provide people with a way of understanding the larger forces at work. Indeed, quite the opposite could be said: the ruling social and economic powers have created the society of the disembodied and disconnected image precisely to prevent people from understanding what they are part of. Addressing this situation directly, Mann uses documentary material to provide a more comprehensive picture that illuminates the origin and means of perpetuation of violence in American society. Her plays dramatize the realization that there is no moral high ground, that all are implicated in the workings of brutality, and that there is no easy escape from violence, coercion and decay.

■   ■   ■

JULY 16, 1987—EMILY MANN'S HOUSE, GRANDVIEW-ON-HUDSON, NEW YORK

How did you get interested in theatre?

I was in high school, at the University of Chicago Laboratory School, in 1966 and things in my neighborhood were heating up. The Hyde Park area was a seat of political ferment: the Weathermen and SDS, the Panthers ten blocks away. Elijah Muhammèd lived three doors down, drugs were coming in, people were getting heavily politicized. When we arrived in 1966 the neighborhood was integrated and absolutely for integration. By '68, with Black Power, the separatist movement had taken hold and there was a lot of heartbreak for everyone.

I was always interested in music, writing, art and literature, and the theatre became a place where these came together in a very exciting way. You worked in a collaborative fashion and made something beautiful, something positive or critical—but still in a positive way—to say to a community. It felt much better to me than being one in a mass of people marching—not that I didn't march, but I have always distrusted crowds. I don't like that anonymity, being part of a group that can get whipped up. I'm sure it's all my training about Nazi Germany [laughs]. This rather brilliant guy at the Laboratory high school, Robert Keil, took a lot of emotionally churned up, smart, excited and excitable young people and turned all that energy into an artistic endeavor, making theatre.

I hadn't really had much interest in theatre before that. I remember my first Broadway show was *Fiorello!*, about the mayor of New York. We were invited to go because my father, who's a historian, had just written the biography of LaGuardia. I was very excited—I was seven, I think—and I got to go backstage and meet Tom Bosley. But theatre never occurred to me as something you actually did, as a serious person in the world [laughs].

What work did you do with that group?

We did Anouilh's *Antigone*, Megan Terry's *Viet Rock* and one of her improv pieces, a Jules Feiffer cartoon piece, *The Tempest*, *The Crucible*—very eclectic group. We did Capek's *Insect Comedy*, which was brilliant. I started out first with visual stuff, doing props, makeup and design, and then I started to act. Then the director said, "You should try your hand at directing." And that put everything together for me—writing, visual arts, music. I was sixteen when I directed my first play. I did two plays and then went to Harvard and I knew that's what I wanted to do. My first year I took a playwriting seminar with William Alfred and wrote my first play. He subsequently became my tutor. And I acted. But it wasn't until my sophomore year at Harvard that I really started to direct, and then that's all I did. I stopped writing for three years, except for academic writing, which is too bad.

Then I got the Bush Fellowship in directing to go to the Guthrie. You did a year at the University of Minnesota and a year at the Guthrie and at the end you got an MFA. I was lucky, Guthrie Two had just been started up again. The directors there saw my first school project and gave me the opportunity to direct. Before that, however, during my senior year in college, I thought I wanted to get out of theatre and go into journalism. I was going to turn down the fellowship. I was completely disenchanted, thinking theatre was a useless thing to do in the world, and embarked on a journey with my best friend. We had gotten a grant to study her family history in Europe.

That's what Annulla *came out of.*

Yes. I had an incredible transcript and because I didn't want it to be a book—I wanted it to be a play—I said, "What the hell, I'll go to Minnesota. If I don't like it, I'll go to New York." I had a lot of friends in journalism in New York and Washington. I thought I could write a book or do some oral history that made some sense. I remember sitting at the Guthrie, I think it was a production of *Tartuffe*, and Barbara Bryne made an entrance and she *was* Annulla. I thought, "Oh my God, I'm going to stay here, I'm going to work with this woman." She was the great star of the Guthrie and I finally got the guts to show her the huge transcript backstage: "This is going to be a play. Would you like to look at it?" She laughed and said, "Well...sure." She read it and two days later said, "This is fantastic, I've got to do it." So I wrote it for her and that's what kept me going there. It hooked me back into theatre.

So the text of Annulla *is all taken from the transcript, with the addition of the Voice.*

It's all taken from the transcript or from memory. Her activity was my directing but the real Annulla actually was chopping carrots and making chicken soup.

I find the question of violence there particularly interesting—it reminds me of Still Life. Annulla *criticizes violence but she treats her sister in a rather brutal way.*

That's hilarious [laughs]. She's brutal and yet she can't live without her. And she talks about how the one really destructive relationship in her life was with her mother and how she adored her father and always wanted his approval. She hated Indira Gandhi. She's not exactly consistent in her political theory [laughs]. That's one of the things I love about her.

Reading that play confirmed for me what I believe to be your basic project: examining what happens when oppression is internalized.

Absolutely right. I've never heard it put that way.

It's internalized as a lot of different things—as blindness, as self-hatred. Often it's passed on and others are treated brutally. That's what Still Life *is about.*

It's also what *Execution* is about.

What fascinates me about Still Life *is that it's so ambiguous morally.*

You don't feel that way about *Execution*?

There the miscarriage of justice is so obvious.

But on so many levels.

And the play needs White's suicide. I saw it at Center Stage before he died.

It's like waiting for the other shoe to drop. I wasn't surprised by the suicide. Most people who knew the story intimately weren't. His best friend, Falzon, was clear about that. He thought he should have done it that day. Either justice would be done in a court of law or he'd have to do what was right. So that always interested me. Plus, *Execution* is really the liberal's conundrum.

How so?

My father once joked—I'm not so sure that he was joking, but he said it jokingly—that one of the things he loved about the play was that it could make his liberal friends support the death penalty. Now, I'm against the death penalty in this society so I was appalled to hear this. But the kind of rage the trial brought out in gentle people, or people who considered themselves gentle, is astonishing. It's like the Eichmann trial. "I would like to tear his arms and his legs and his head from his body. Maybe then he'd feel the kind of pain...." The kind of ugliness that people felt justified in feeling for the war criminals, I heard in San Francisco. So when watching the play, when it's done with full force, you're torn in half, between rage and a political sensibility that doesn't allow these feelings of revenge to come out. The ironies abound—Moscone and Milk being against the death penalty, and White being for it. He got off under the liberal system and then he had to take his own life. Often against one's will one can find real sympathy for White, which is very disturbing. And often he'll make you face the prejudice that you hoped you'd be free of. So in that way, it's like *Still Life*. That's what makes people so mad at the play. The most virulent attack is always, "She wasn't clear enough!" All the anger that they're feeling is not really against the play, I think it's often against themselves and the emotional and political confusion that it brings up.

After all the years, I feel very clear about where I stand and where justice was done and wasn't done and how things have to change to ensure justice is done. And about what the cost of prejudice is in this society. We see a complex picture emerge of the homosexual community in San Francisco. It's a varied group and people were politically at odds with each other, until the AIDS crisis. People who share a sexual preference can be as far apart politically, emotionally, aesthetically, as can be. There is no such thing as "the gay community." Or "the black community"—what is that? It's varied and complex. The plays are conundrums. A lot of people think *Still Life* is a play about a Vietnam veteran.

What impact did Brecht have on you?

Oddly enough, I had a different take on Brecht from a lot of people. He first hit me because he got rid of romantic artifice and tried to tell the truth directly. There's a coolness and a reality that I really like. Most stage acting and writing embarrassed me because I didn't believe it.

Do you mean realistic theatre specifically?

I even thought that about acting in Shakespeare. I hate phoniness. Or I'd listen to new plays and say, "I don't believe this. I don't care about this. There's no muscle. This isn't how people I know talk." I came from a very interesting neighborhood that had a lot of clashes of different cultures and I loved the sounds and the rhythms. But I never heard that on stage.

How was your interest in documentary sparked?

I remember coming home my senior year in college when my father was head of the American Jewish Committee's oral history project on the survivors. I read some of the transcripts and was blown out. In one a mother, a Czech woman, was interviewed by her daughter and she talked about a recurring dream she'd had while in the camp—of a ballerina all in white. She'd seen her as a child but couldn't remember the ballet or the dancer. But whenever she pictured her, she knew life was worth living. I remember coming downstairs, my face washed with tears, saying, "This can't just stay in an archive for historians of the Jewish experience to look at." My father said, "Unfortunately, this interview belongs to the mother and daughter and there's nothing we can do about it." At that point I thought, "I have to talk to people, I have to get it down, to have it in their own words," because you could hear, from the page, the cadences and rhythms of the Czech woman, as opposed to those of her daughter who was American born. And both of them reaching toward each other across a language barrier, as well as an experiential barrier. It was extraordinary. That spurred me on in my whole quest with family documentary. I started with *Annulla*.

So Brecht was crucial in those early years.

Because he tore down all the artifice. Certainly, it was great to be freed of naturalism. Beckett, for the same reason. Shakespeare for language and rhythm and scope, breadth of ideas, the ability to have fifteen hundred ideas on stage rather than one.

What about Franz Xaver Kroetz?

Oh, God, I love him! But that came later.

You directed **Through the Leaves.**

Yes. And I'm dying to do *Mensch Meier*. I understand that play! I wish I were more articulate today. You can see how much I'm feeling, but I just can't get it into words.

That's just what Kroetz is about.

Yes [laughs]. What's amazing is his ability to speak so eloquently through inarticulate people. His people earn every syllable. There's not an ounce of sentimentality. He just tells the truth. It's down to the bone, very raw. He went on from where Brecht left off. I read Kroetz after I wrote *Still Life* and felt a kindred soul. That's how I feel about Mamet.

You're all working to redefine the relationship between text and subtext. In Kroetz there can be a chasm between the two.

That's right. When he says, "Wait twenty-five beats," he means it. You need that. Structurally Kroetz does something that I like to do too—he'll take raw fragments of conversation and distill them down to a set of combustible elements. That's the building block for him. It might be a speech, it might be three interchanges. But that's it. Each scene is an explosion.

Like that of Brecht and Kroetz, your work is confrontational.

I'm surprised I didn't say that first off about Brecht. It's all about making direct contact. I guess I don't like the word confrontational because it makes me think of people recoiling and protecting themselves. Brecht is having a conversation with the audience all the time. Directly. It's part of taking away the bullshit, saying, "We're in a room. We don't pretend we're someplace else. And we're all dealing with this event that has something to do with us." That recognition freed me the most. I love performance and I love concert. In a lot of ways, *Still Life* is like a concert. And I love courtrooms.

So did Brecht. Think of how many of his plays end with courtroom scenes. He uses the same strategy you use in Execution, *making the audience the jury.*

In *Still Life* as well. We are the judge and the jury. I haven't seen it recently, since we have started revising history and dealing with Vietnam, but in the late seventies, early eighties, Americans sitting and dealing with *Still Life* was intense. It's very interesting to see *Still Life* in other countries. In France, there was a brilliant production that has run for two-and-a-half years and has just been on French television. It's very stylish and heavy, with rock music and a lot of Algerian undercurrents. It's like us watching a Fugard play: "Oh, isn't it awful about apartheid." We have racism, so we sort of understand, but it's all about *them.* In France they were freer to look at *Still Life* as a play, or a poem. They looked at it like a Beckett play. They talked about the language, the rhythm and the images, and it was about war and love and death [laughs], very French, right? When Barney Simon did it in South Africa at the Market Theatre, he put "No More Genocide" on at the end. He put up the names of everyone who had died in the resistance movement in the past ten years. He brought it into a South African context. In this country, it's a different experience doing the play in a VFW hall and in a theatre. It changes with the audience.

This play gets people crazy. My friend who is a brain specialist said, "My God, no wonder people go psychotic after seeing this, if you're making those connections. You don't want to put those thoughts together." The nightmares come together, the synapses, it's crossing wires.

Any other recent work that's had a great impact on you?

Mamet's *Edmond* and *Glengarry*. I'm hooked into his work. But I'm really more affected by art, a lot by music, and by listening in restaurants and in cabs, talking to people. People come up to me and tell me their stories. I'm more affected by particular encounters with people or groups or events, of people coming into my life and turning it upside down.

Caryl Churchill had a great effect on me, *Top Girls* especially. Ntozake Shange, with *For Colored Girls*. Greg Mosher directed a production of *Sizwe Bansi* at Goodman Stage Two—I've known Greg since I was nineteen, we were assistant directors together—and he did it, as I recall, with a bare light bulb and a table and two chairs. And these two brilliant actors. I don't think I was ever unable to walk out of a theatre before that. And I felt that way after seeing *Woza Albert!*.

It's hard to talk about what's affected me in terms of what's on the page or even what I've seen. It's been travel and event.

Will you describe the making of Still Life?

It started with the real Nadine coming to see *Annulla* and saying she had a friend she wanted me to meet who had a war story to tell. I said, "Thank you very much but I don't want to deal with another war story." And she said, "You must, he's so brilliant and amazing and the gentlest man I've ever met." She was the best friend of my best friend in Minneapolis so I said yes. I decided to meet this man at the Guthrie, in a conference room, because that seemed to be neutral ground and I had no idea whom I was going to meet. All I knew was that he was an ex-marine and a Vietnam vet and "the gentlest man" she'd ever known. We went into a room and he could barely look at me. For over three-and-a-half hours he spoke in a monotone about war atrocities and what he saw over there. When I walked out I was shell-shocked. He just wanted to talk. All I said was, "And then what happened?" I couldn't even steer him in other directions.

I called up the real Nadine and said, "I can't do this. I was against the war. The war split our family apart and the war split me apart. I haven't even now dealt with how I feel about it." I said, "I think he should talk to someone at the V.A. He really needs to get it out but I'm not sure I'm the person. I'm not a trained psychiatrist, I'm not a priest." The next thing I knew, he called me and asked, "Will you meet my wife? I think you're wonderful and you know how to listen and she really is another casualty of the war. I think it would be good for her." I have a very hard time saying no [laughs], so he arrived at my apartment with her. He had not told me that she was pregnant. She was only six months but she was very, very big and when she came up those stairs, she could barely walk. She sat down in the rocking chair and he said, "I think I should leave you two alone so you can really talk."

As soon as he left the room she said, "If I thought about this too much, I'd go crazy, so I don't think about it"—her first line in the play. "I'm not too good with the past. Now, *he* remembers, that's his problem." And the next thing she said was, "You know, every day I fear for my life with him." I asked, "Why don't you leave him?" She said, "I'll never leave." So I thought—and this is the craziness in me—"My God, here's one woman who says, 'This is the gentlest man I've ever known,' the other woman's afraid he's going to kill her. This is a play! [laughs]." We started to talk and she and I connected on a very deep level. I met with her only three times but each was epic. Maybe twenty hours in three meetings. We just couldn't stop.

Then I met with him over a period of months. Nadine was the woman he was having an affair with, but I didn't know that when I first met his wife. [Laughs] He was twenty-eight, Nadine was forty-three, I think. Different worlds completely. I didn't put it together. The way they were together seemed very natural and easy and friendly. So I missed all the signs. I figured it out after a couple of times with her. He would never talk about it. I ended up with about 140 hours of tape. I was shattered by what I had learned and I didn't know what to do with it. So I found student volunteers at the Guthrie, who loved *Annulla*, and because I was broke, I asked them if they'd help me out. And we transcribed. Then I put it aside. I couldn't handle it at all.

Almost nine months later I was feeling an incredible responsibility to these people. They'd given me their story and it was important to tell. So I tried to face it again. When I did, I found a theatrical voice for each person, distilling each down to its own rhythm and poetry. That took a long time. When I got it down to a three-hour set of highly ordered monologues I had a reading. Everyone thought it was brilliant and I hated it. I thought it was dead as a doornail.

Then my husband Gerry Bamman asked me, "Why did you put the monologues in that order?" I said, "Can't you see? This thing relates to that, and that thing relates to this." He literally handed me scissors and tape and said, "Why don't you put them closer together?" I started to do that and it was like I was on speed or I was tripping, I couldn't stop. I stayed up for two straight nights with clippings all over the room. It took two weeks of insanity to do. I really thought I was going crazy, because there were all these wild images—there was a reason why I put those things together. I had the cellophane mess of the pages, all Scotch-taped. I just Xeroxed them and invited friends over to read it to. And it went off like a shot, it was like being in the middle of a music machine—you had to play these notes and if you did, you started to gyrate.

The next step was refining that. I knew there were some sections that didn't electrify. Sometimes it was a matter of making it less cut up. I just kept having it read to me. I had to hear it. One night after a reading, I had gotten drunk and I called Greg Mosher at 3:00 A.M. and said, "You have to do this." He laughed and said okay [laughs] and, in fact, he did.

Did any of the three real people come see it?

Cheryl did not come, she wanted to pretend it never happened. Nadine came to the Chicago opening as sort of a star and then realized she was going to be judged in a different way. She felt that Mark should be played by a movie star but that we got the wife right. She was very proud of it...in a very odd way. It was pretty hard on her. Mark came to New York with a lot of his friends, but his friends were very upset because they had thought it was a play about him being a hero. He liked it. He's an artist, a photographer, and he said, "You got this. This is right." Sometimes we had veterans in the audience who'd go up to John Spencer afterwards and ask, "What unit were you in?" He said, "I'm just an actor." They said, "You are not. That's not fair" [laughs].

It seems to me that as a documentary writer, your main goal is to provide perspective. Which is why the plays are so elaborately framed, textually and visually. The Voice in Annulla, *the slides working in the other two plays, allow us to see.*

I think what gives you perspective in *Still Life* is that rigorous form, the limitation of the actors not being able to look at each other except where specified. Having to keep it going, except where the pauses occur. That, in a way, frames it even more than the slides do. Often the slides wake you up because you're getting into this whole language riff and they're a shot of reality.

You use real images to provide a distance on the staged action.

In *Execution* they're information: here's what you need to know now.

And there are all the different voices.

Which provide a lot of different perspectives. *Execution*'s a mean play, in many ways. It took so much out of me. It's the impossible play to write. It breaks every rule. It puts a man at the center of the play who you don't want to be at the center. The play's about the community, about the impact of this man's actions and of the legal system's response on that community. It's like what's happening with Ollie North. You keep seeing that sweet face: "Yes, I lied to Congress. Yes, I shredded documents." We go through the litany of crimes against his fellow Americans and he still talks about himself as a patriot, as a man who did no wrong, and there are "Ollie North for President" stickers. Norman Lear said that television loves moisture, the sweaty upper lip and the moist eyes.

I was playing with how media made Dan White. If you just read the transcripts, you go, "What?" You see that man go through it on stage, and his little, sweet wife, like Betsy North, sitting there—the perfect all-American couple—and you see how it happened. So it's tricky because the courtroom and the theatre are almost identical. So many good actors and good playwrights know that the first way to hit an audience is emotionally. Secondly, if you're lucky, you'll get to the intellect. That's what they were doing in the court. What I came to understand writing and directing *Execution* was the power of the courtroom as theatre. You put the defendant in a blue suit and people like him, you put him in a brown suit, they don't. Ollie North's costume is brilliant. And his lawyer was wearing the perfect defense-lawyer costume, the blue suit with the colored tie. They're dressing for the camera. Same thing with the White trial.

That's why you use all the different media in the performance.

Exactly. The media is so incredibly irresponsible with the North hearing, I can't believe it. Aren't there any ethics in journalism anymore?

Reagan's greatest success has been to set the level of political dialogue. He's still setting it.

There's so much information every day—"Give me twenty minutes and I'll give you the world"?—I mean the chutzpa of that is unbelievable! They announce that the President lied to the American people and in the next breath they describe so-and-so's slash murder up in Harlem. It's one horror story after another and I don't think the brain processes it. Everything's given equal weight. Americans are bombarded with information but it's become meaningless. One thing doesn't connect with another. No one's saying, "For twenty minutes we will now consider the following question." In *Still Life* everything's juxtaposed for a point. And it keeps narrowing it down.

Still Life takes you step by step to the final slide. Do you always know the end point you're moving toward?

I knew the end of *Still Life* and *Annulla*. I didn't know the end of *Execution*. I kept being unable to end the play. And then, boy, it ended. He ended it.

It wasn't until the last day I met with Mark that he made his confession.

I didn't know how I'd get from the confession to "I'm alive, my friends aren't. This is a still life." But I knew it wouldn't take a long time. I knew on some level that the women had heard the confession.

Cheryl resists the truth as long as she can. She keeps on trying to keep him from telling it. And then she has to deal with it being out there. Nadine sort of knew he would confess. She could then put her own perspective on that. All three of them are trying to put it in perspective. But it's so awful and there's almost nothing you can say, except, "Now that I know this, how can I live my life?" They each have their own survival covering.

How does Emily Mann, the director, work with Emily Mann, the playwright?

I really do change hats. I like to remove myself entirely and look at a play as a director and see how I'm stimulated by it. I like to work with the actors so that I know immediately if it's an acting problem, a directing problem or a writing problem. If it's a writing problem, I can fix it. I don't have to take the playwright to dinner and say, "Look, I know you don't want to touch a word of your perfect script, but this isn't working." If I can't come up with a solution and I know it's a writing problem, somebody will often say something—it could be the janitor—to give me insight into it. I find that I direct my work best when I actually trust the script and say, "This is a good text," as I do with Ibsen or Chekhov or Mamet.

What happens in developmental programs is that after a day or two of rehearsals someone will say, "This doesn't work. This needs to be cut. This doesn't relate to that." I can just see *Still Life* at a developmental conference: "Why aren't these people *talking* to each other?" [Laughs] They assume that you have to be taught how to write.

When I'm writing, I don't see every moment. *Still Life* is a form I'd never seen in my life. I didn't know how I was going to stage it. But I had to write it. My great friend and collaborator Tom Lynch figured out the table. I have to do a whole lot of work as the director before I start to work on my own play. It's a totally different mindset. In some ways, I'm more daring as a writer.

Trying to find the form that fits the content for a piece of work on stage, starting almost from ground zero, is what I do as a writer. All this stuff comes up that I'm absorbing and learning about. It may be in the form of documents, or confrontations, or memories of those confrontations. It may be in notebooks, tapes and transcripts. Then I distill a mound of material that will cover this entire table into a text that's playable. That means playing with form. It comes from knowing the theatre. Also from watching new music and jazz and rock. Mostly black artists—a lot of church music. I love gospel. I love charismatic religions.

Despite your distrust of crowds?

I love the energy that happens rhythmically and emotionally in a crowd. I love the possibility that they can start to fly in an event that is benign. I'm also terrified by that power. I think anything you put on a stage is a great responsibility because you may have the power to move and change. You can get people marching in goose step. You've got to take complete responsibility for both the statements you make and the effect you have on a crowd. A lot of people argue with me about that. But that's one thing I'm absolutely sure of. Intention is all important.

Do you read the critics?

I wish I didn't. But I do. When it comes to my friends' work, I skim them to see if it's going to help or hurt. If it's going to help, I often read slower. If it's ugly or vicious or negative, I skim it just long enough to know there's no hope and throw it out. I don't want to have anybody else's bad phrases about the work of people I admire in my mind. When it comes to my work, I'm quite the opposite. If it's a good review, I'll skim it and go, "Whew, that won't hurt us." When it comes to the bad ones [laughs], it's terrible, I do read it. Now I couldn't tell you what some of my most devastating reviews were because I blocked them out. I couldn't write if I kept them in my brain. I remember that sock in the gut with the *Still Life* reviews, and I remember where I was and what I was doing.

If we were not in an economic climate where the reviews actually mattered—how long the work will survive and what the next piece can do—I don't think I would read the critics. I love getting letters from people I know and don't know. There are about five people in my life to whom I really listen. They may not always be right, but they know what I'm trying to do. And if I reach them, I'm doing it. It means a great deal to me when they write it down. After an opening it's incredibly useful. Then, whichever way the critical establishment goes, you have a way of deciphering the critical code. The point is, you have to survive your critics. Outlive them.

The economic problems with the commercial theatre and the real estate in New York and all the other economic factors are making it an unlivable city for everyone, not just artists. There's a meanness in this town right now that's killing its young and its old.

Don't you think, though, that the critics' activity is just a part of what the mainstream press is doing, suppressing any political challenge? Like the newspapers in which they appear, critics' opinions are dictated by business—in this case, the business of theatre.

As entertainment. I'm not against it, in fact, I love it, and there's a lot of entertainment in [laughs] my work. But I went into the theatre because it was a forum for ideas and stories, a way for members of a community to get together and face each other.

What about the regional theatre?

It's been my salvation. I used to be on the road most of the year but I have a marriage and a child now and I just can't do it. I felt fragmented, drained. One year I worked every day and I ended up below the poverty line. Then I was too angry to work, so I decided to take a rest. But I believe in the nonprofit movement. I think the national theatre in this country is the regional theatre. And that includes the nonprofit theatres in New York. As we can see now, our important work is starting and often ending in the nonprofit theatre. The regional theatre has allowed me to make my plays, direct new plays and do a great array of classical work. And break the rules and stretch myself artistically in every direction.

What scares me is that so many of my colleagues are saying, "We can cut this process short. We don't have it right, we don't have what we want, but we can get away with that." What?! You can never get away with anything! When you say that, *you* know it's not what you want. Are you getting away with anything when you're cheating yourself and the work?

That seems particularly true in New York.

Have you noticed that there's no classical work in New York City—except for Shakespeare in the Park? New Yorkers are the oddest audience because they don't have a theatre background. They think they know theatre. But they don't know Shakespeare, or Molière, or Restoration drama. They don't have any theatre history to speak of. Whereas at the Guthrie, when we did *Execution*, they had that season seen Liviu's *Midsummer Night's Dream* and *The Tempest, Hedda Gabler* and *The Importance of Being Earnest*. So they had an incredible context to put it in. You come to New York and you're on another planet.

What are your plans for the future?

Betsey Brown, which I'm creating with Ntozake Shange and Baikida Carroll, goes into a workshop next month. And suddenly, out of the blue, people are coming to me with documentary ideas. But I need to find out what my next piece is after *Betsey*. I'm gathering lots of material but I don't know what it is yet. Lots of things are hitting home.

I do separate my film work from my theatre work. TV and film projects fund my work in the theatre. Right now I have been asked to write *The Story of Winnie Mandela* for NBC and Camille Cosky. I go to South Africa in October. But it's hard for me—because I'm not a facile writer I become connected to what I write no matter what medium I use. I'm doing a lot of highly technical work so my writing craft is getting sharper. It also sharpens my directorial eye—often you have to visualize film and television work on the page almost to the gesture. I'm glad I'm doing all that work. But the next theatre piece keeps eluding me. I don't know if it will stay in documentary form or not. Everything starts there for me, but I may actually take off now into something else.

RICHARD NELSON

A s a child, Richard Nelson was always encouraged in his love for the theatre (his mother had been a dancer before she married). He grew up on Broadway musicals, seeing his first, *Destry Rides Again*, when he was seven. Since 1975 he has had twenty plays produced, both original scripts and adaptations of works by authors ranging from Beaumarchais to Dario Fo (he has served as dramaturg and translator for several major repertory theatres). As Nelson explains, his original works fall into three periods. In the first, the result of his experience as a newspaper reporter, he explores real events and the relationship between events and their reporting. The plays in this series include *The Killing of Yablonski* (1975), *Conjuring an Event* (1976), *Jungle Coup* (1978) and *The Vienna Notes* (1978). After adapting several classic plays, Nelson began what he describes as his classical period, with *Bal* (1979), *Rip Van Winkle or "The Works"* (1981), *The Return of Pinocchio* (1982) and *An American Comedy* (1983), using mythological figures to elucidate the workings of American society. His evolution is continued in his most recent plays, *Between East and West* (1984) and *Principia Scriptoriae* (1986), which frame events and artfully juxtapose them to reveal the complex correlation between interpersonal relations and social context.

Despite changes in his style and subject matter, Nelson has striven relentlessly to uncover the political and moral implications of personal choice. He eschews political dogmatism, however, by combining his social project with an epistemological one. In the process of examining political activity (in the broadest sense), he questions the accuracy of those instruments that would fix its meaning. He understands that individual thought and action are constantly being limited and defined by an ideology and a political economy over which one has little control. He writes, therefore, not about political certainty but about equivocation and doubt, looking beyond the well-meaning individual to the complex and corruptive system of which he is a part and which he can never fully know.

In *The Vienna Notes* Nelson studies the construction of political discourse by looking at the disparity between live event and its subsequent translation into writing (a movement which, of course, is reversed in staging a dramatic text). The play, in effect, presents two lines of action simultaneously: the attempted kidnapping of Senator Stubbs by terrorists in a farmhouse outside of Vienna, and the senator's uninterrupted narration of the same event as he dictates his memoirs to his secretary. The audience's attention is directed less toward wondering what will happen during the siege than noting the difference between the senator's descriptions, his instant replay of events, and the real emotions evoked—particularly those of Georgia, the senator's hostess, who has just discovered the body of her murdered husband. By the end of the play the primacy of action in relation to a written narrative has been subverted as the retelling of the event demonically gains a permanence and truth-value that the event itself lacks. At the same time, the play illuminates the sinister moral implications of this process: not only does Stubbs *do* nothing to help Georgia; his discourse, albeit unintentionally, mocks her suffering. The play demonstrates how the modern political leader has lost his connection to experience and real human need and has become instead concerned only with the fabrication of image, posture and rhetoric.

Nelson's investigation of the debasement of American politics is continued in *The Return of Pinocchio*, a play about the greed and viciousness concealed behind a genial personality. Set at the end of World War II, the action chronicles the return of the rich, successful and totally Americanized Pinocchio to his impoverished Italian hometown. Confronted there with people willing to do almost anything to survive, he is totally unable to understand what his former countrymen feel. His idea of assistance is to throw money and American cigarettes at their misery. In rhetoric unmistakably like Ronald Reagan's, Pinocchio defends free enterprise as "a beautiful yet fragile organism," and, having been fleeced of his money, he insists on mopping the cafe floor to pay off his debt. "It's not out of any moral sense of responsibility," he explains, but "to keep the free enterprise system from crumbling and to keep the world from the Reds." In the end, Pinocchio learns nothing and his belief system stands revealed as a tissue of lies founded upon brutality and murder.

In his most recent plays Nelson is shuffling temporal sequence and using allusive scene titles, a fragmentary scenic form and a more naturalistic style. These innovations create a more contrapuntal dramatic texture in which, as Nelson explains, he is able to track simultaneously a number of thematic and imagistic threads, variously personal and political. The plays themselves are about the decay of friendship, love, a country, a goal. They dramatize displacement and exile, peopled by characters in the wrong place at the wrong time, alienated from themselves and each other and incapable of making a connection with their environment. These men and women, as fragmented as the dramatic form itself, are clearly Nelson's image of Americans today, haunted by loss, isolated and disoriented. But his plays reflect more than frustration. They also dramatize the desire to connect with one's environment and construct a different future. In the words of Chekhov, screamed forth by Erna in *Between East and West*, "I long to go home."

■　　■　　■

DECEMBER 1, 1986—TCG OFFICES, NEW YORK CITY

What interested you in theatre?

When I was about ten, I fell in love with the theatre. From the time I was about thirteen to fifteen, my family lived outside of New York in a town called Elmsford and I used to come in and see many, many musicals. Then we lived in Detroit and I would go to the Fisher Theatre, the Broadway tryout house there.

Why did you gravitate toward playwriting?

I had humiliating experiences acting when I was young. Directing wasn't a possibility, so writing became one. I'd written stories and poems and I started writing plays when I was about fifteen. I had a reading in my high school. At Hamilton College I won the playwriting contest each year. I had the encouragement of a couple of professors and in four years of college I had maybe fourteen plays done, many of which I produced myself in various spaces, from lecture halls to the chapel to outdoors. It was a very intense time of writing and experimentation. I did a piece called *A Reading of King Lear* in which I broke down the play into image patterns. Three actors were each given a pattern and so read only fragments of the play, different characters' lines.

163

On graduation I received a travel grant which gave me enough money to live anywhere in the world I wanted for a year and do anything I wanted —there were no restrictions. That gave me the opportunity to write full time for a year—I had wondered whether I could get up in the morning and write every day. When I wrote in college, it was always in chunks. So I went to Manchester, England for a year and wrote, and saw a great number of plays.

Why Manchester?

My wife had one more year of school and she got into the University of Manchester as an exchange student. I really didn't want to be in London because there my days and evenings could be totally occupied by theatregoing.

Coming back to the States in '73, I asked a couple of friends from college who were living in Boston if they wanted to form a theatre company. We chose to move to Philadelphia. I don't remember why—none of us had ever been there. We hooked up with the Public Radio station, WHYY, and did a monthly two-hour show for a year, producing a number of plays. We became an experimental radio drama company, on the cutting edge of something that didn't even exist.

I began to be very interested in real events. I wrote a play called *Watergate: An Event* while Watergate was unraveling, a play about Hank Aaron's 715th home run, a play about the fall of Agnew. A few years before this time, Jock Yablonski, his wife and daughter were murdered outside Pittsburgh. A series of trials had finally brought the head of the United Mine Workers, Tony Boyle, to trial in Media, quite near where we were living. Through an alternative newspaper, *The Drummer*, I got a press pass and covered the trial. But what I was interested in was the notion of an event, the notion of history and the relationship between the reporter and the fact. Out of that series of articles came two plays, one of which was *The Killing of Yablonski*. That was the first play of mine done professionally, at the Mark Taper Forum lab in 1975.

Gordon Davidson had been doing stuff like *The Trial of the Catonsville Nine*, so my unsolicited manuscript was picked out of the slush pile. The Taper's literary department found *Yablonski* very funny and ironic—the first part is about a guy who can't get rid of his stomach gas. So I began a short relationship with the Taper. We lived in Los Angeles for about six months and the next year they did *Conjuring an Event*. Then my plays about reporters and their relationship to events were done in New York—*The Killing of Yablonski* at the PAF Playhouse, *Conjuring an Event* at the American Place and *Jungle Coup*, the third of the group, at Playwrights Horizons.

What were your influences at this time?

Sam Shepard was really important and exciting for me—*The Tooth of Crime, The Geography of a Horse Dreamer, Action,* his earlier plays. I started to recognize the obvious, that I'm interested in nonnaturalistic theatre and that the history of world theatre is basically nonnaturalistic. In America there's so little sense of world culture or even our own, and there's almost no chance of exposing oneself to classical work. So I hit on the idea of writing translations and adaptations of classical plays for two reasons. I wanted the opportunity to give myself an education in a writerly as opposed to a scholarly way. And I recognized very clearly that this could help me make a living in the American theatre. Whereas my plays were being done in 300-seat theatres, adaptations of classical plays were being done in 900-seat theatres. Since you're paid a percentage, it's a huge difference.

So I talked to theatres and people asked, "What languages do you know?" I said I have a reading knowledge of French and that's it, but it doesn't matter. I wanted to follow the English example of Edward Bond, Howard Brenton and Christopher Hampton, who commission a literal, word-for-word translation and then work off that. This is very threatening to many people in academia because I'm saying, given the choice between someone who knows the language and someone who knows the theatre, choose the theatre. Certainly the best thing is to know both. But that is very, very rare. Michael Frayn is one of the few playwrights I know who's fluent in the language that he translates, Russian, and a scholar as well.

I got my opportunity when David Chambers became Acting Artistic Director of Arena Stage. Liviu Ciulei was going to direct Molière's *Don Juan* and David asked me to do a scene on spec. I did and he liked it. Liviu was in Rumania at the time so they showed me his notes about his concept. I went to work on a translation and then pushed it into an adaptation. I was very happy. The theatre was very happy. Liviu arrived and clearly he didn't like it. We spent two days arguing about the first page. Our disagreement centered on a phrase, *il faut que,* about Don Juan burning in Hell. One could translate it either "It is necessary that Don Juan burns in Hell," or "It's bound to happen that Don Juan burns in Hell." How you translate that is a moral decision. "It's bound to"—it's fact. "It's necessary"—it's a drive, a political activity. I had made the political choice. Liviu was much more interested in the cosmological viewpoint. Once I recognized that, I said okay and rewrote it for him. I worked with him in rehearsal and we became close friends. I wanted even more involvement in classical theatre and David Jones of the Royal Shakespeare Company, who had founded the BAM Theatre Company, asked me to be his literary manager. So I was doing translations and adaptations for the Goodman, for Liviu, and for David Jones. And all of this was starting to feed my work.

The plays influenced by my classical work were *Bal*, done at the Goodman; *Rip Van Winkle*, done at Yale Repertory Theatre; and *The Return of Pinocchio*, done at The Empty Space and this year in New York. These are about mythological figures, about trying to get a simple picture for a complicated society. They're political examinations of how a society works. Those plays were fed by translating Don Juan, Goldoni's *Il Campiello*, Brecht's *The Wedding* and *Jungle of Cities* and Erdman's *The Suicide*. The last play of that group, *An American Comedy*, attempts to forge a mythological style which, unfortunately, none of the critics in Los Angeles seemed to understand. It's a very ironic play which critically was treated as straight-on serious. The Mark Taper production was quite good.

Now I've started a new group—*Between East and West, Principia Scriptoriae* and two others: a cycle of one-acts which I've been writing for a long time, called *Fear and Misery of a Generation*; and a new play called *Sensibility and Sense*, which I think will be done in London. This group is where, I believe, I'll be for a long time, because it seems extremely rich and brings together a lot. Again, there's the influence of adaptations and translations. I did a translation of *The Three Sisters* at the Guthrie and being inside of Chekhov's head was really exciting.

What was it about Chekhov?

There's an amazing thing at the beginning of *Three Sisters*. The women are sitting, talking about how sad things are, and from the next room we hear someone say—basically—"Bullshit." That's so wonderful. I had not realized that Chekhov is such a great ironic writer. The scene is about conflict, watching the two things hit. I was tremendously energized by this understanding.

What I'm trying to do right now is create a new form of narrative theatre in which I use the elements of realism and frame them and talk about them. It's as if we're walking along and I say, "Let's look in this keyhole." You hear a conversation start in mid-sentence and they talk and then I close it and say, "That's what's happening." Or I'll make a joke about it. I've been working with scene titles. It started with *Pinocchio* and *Rip Van Winkle* but now they are, I hope, complex comments and conversations. The way those signs are presented is very important to me because they're a voice, a character in the play. What I want to do is take a chunk of real and another chunk of real, and comment by putting them against each other. My ambition is to have someone say across a table, "Do you want sugar in your coffee?" and when the other person answers, "No," it means everything about that relationship and everything about society. It means what we are doing in Nicaragua and it means the complexity of dealing with Russia and it means an image of the twentieth century as a world of displacement. All of those things should come out of the real, the moment.

It seems, in your use of titles, that you're doing almost the opposite of Brecht. Brecht used them so we'd know what was going to happen, to reduce suspense. Your titles create suspense. We know the scene will have something to do with the title, but we don't know what. When I saw Principia, *I was trying to figure out the relationship between the formal device and what was happening in the lives of these people. What you have there is a metaphor for the relationship between society and the individual.*

It's also a metaphor for the relationship between your heart and your mind, between the emotion and trying to find its meaning. If someone is crying on stage and then you pop back and see a title, you think, how does that relate? I've got you thinking about someone crying. That was Brecht's concern as well. If you're just watching someone cry, what's the point? I want tears, I want emotion and passion on my stage because I think that's part of life, and yet I don't want it to dribble away into a kind of pleasure for the audience. It's the difference between relating individually and socially to a situation.

There's a kind of double determinism in this. On the one hand, the characters and emotions function within the playwright's frame, and on the other, the playwright is subject to the force of society as a whole.

Yes. And that's both good and bad. Because at the moment my work...I don't think it ends up cynical. I think it ends up in despair at the inevitability of loss.

What else has influenced your writing?

William Faulkner has sat on my back since I was sixteen. I've never quite known how to use his sense of structure and storytelling. *The Wild Palms* has two novellas in it—"Wild Palms" and "The Old Man"—that don't relate. Both are incredibly passionate stories, and he tells them in alternating chapters. Why did he do that? You start to get sucked in and he pulls you away. It's a true image of the world, of our kind of world: you get passionate and you're pulled back and you look at something, and then you get passionate again and you pull back again. You're following two things and the thinking that's required is part of the point.

I find now that in plays like *Between East and West* and *Principia* I'm writing about a class of people we should have a positive name for, but don't. The word we have is "intellectual." I'm looking for a word that means someone who thinks and attempts to relate to the world and to relate his or her thinking to the world. I talk about their displacement, not only in space but in time. The new play, *Sensibility and Sense*, goes back and forth between 1937 and 1986 and is about two women and a man, quite leftist in the late thirties, who are now in their seventies. One has written memoirs and the other is suing for libel, sort of like Lillian Hellman and Mary McCarthy. This battle, in the age of Reagan, between degrees of left-wingedness is humorous and sad and courageous. In the second act of *Principia* all the writers are good and smart people. Their goals seem very simple. And yet they mess it all up. By the end, they don't really know what they can do. It gets worse and worse and worse. That's been my writing journey, from involvement in events to worlds in despair over the confusion of involving oneself in a society like America's.

Anything more to say about Brecht?

Brecht's a great influence. I think he's the best twentieth-century playwright. He makes me believe that theatre can be what we often call it in this country: a forum, an arena, a place—theatre can be a public as opposed to a private, voyeuristic act. He always reminds me that theatre can be about something. He has a good sense of irony and a very interesting sense of structure, a cleanness. He tells a story straight. If he's interested in a parable, he's going to tell the parable. He's not going to hide it. I've not seen too many Brecht plays for the simple reason that I live in the United States, where it's very hard to see Brecht plays done in a full way. His alienation effect is simply what we've been talking about: it engages the mind. But we've learned to understand alienation as being put off. So people say, "That can't have been a Brecht production because I wasn't put off."

But in most North American productions you are put off. They're so horribly dry and academic and boring. So few directors know how to have fun with Brecht.

We did *Jungle of Cities* at BAM and learned just how funny he can be. He has that pixieish quality of distortion, and of playing with you. In ways, Edward Bond has influenced me as much. Bond brought a kind of grotesque passion to the world of Brecht. Bond's *Lear* is one of the great plays of our time. I think he's about the best craftsman in the English-speaking theatre, able to write what he wants—large scenes, small scenes. There aren't many playwrights who even aspire toward that kind of craft.

I just saw the Berliner Ensemble in Toronto and it was a revelation, in part because it was so much fun. I'd always read Brecht's work as angry, I thought effective political theatre had to issue from anger. What amazed me was its lack. The social criticism came not from a position of doubt but of certainty. And it created an extraordinary sense of poise and equilibrium and clarity.

I did an adaptation of Beaumarchais' *The Marriage of Figaro* for Serban. I said, "There are two ways of doing *Figaro*, one where you're playing to the masters, one where you're playing to the servants. If you're playing to the masters, you're angry. If you're playing to the servants, it's joyous." It's like going behind the woodshed during slavery to make fun. It's a release, it states the obvious condition. Stating the obvious in an entertaining way, as Frank Rich does not understand, is a worthwhile function of the theatre.

That's also **The Return of Pinocchio.**

Yes. A *Saint Joan of the Stockyards* or an *Arturo Ui* can be so much fun that it's not going to change anybody's beliefs. Theatre can make one feel not so alone. It doesn't necessarily have to change one's life.

How do you start a play? What do you start with—plot, characters, idea?

It has changed. Right now I keep a notebook, making notes on the train, wherever. I began collecting play ideas with *Principia*. One was "Latin American literature." One was "Shaw and the intelligent American woman." One was "Agog in a conservative time." There was Woodrow Wilson, Amnesty International, Ezra Pound and Pisa, the death of Lorca. Clearly I was hunting for something. *Principia* answers about four or five of those. And it ends up that "Ezra Pound in Pisa" is one line in the play. Yesterday I was taking notes on an idea for a play when I realized that that was only a scene in another play that I was thinking about. I want to write a play about Americans in London, academics on sabbatical. Right there is my world—a world of displaced intellectuals, of Americans in confusion. It can give me a sense of where America is. I'm hunting for images that allow me to continue to understand and explore what interests me.

Then there are elements of one's personal life. Within a very short time, I had my first child and my mother died—an illness at the same time as the pregnancy. To learn to be a father and a son at exactly the same time was so extraordinary. I started to see the world somewhat differently. Time became very interesting to me—getting old, being pure.

I wait to start writing until I'm going to have a clear run at a draft, somewhere between two and four months. I get halfway through and then start again, halfway through and start again. When I have a draft I show it to a couple of people. Then I make another draft. What I've learned from *Principia* and this new play is to let it sit for about four months and then rewrite it. The other thing I've learned—which, I guess, makes me a little academic—is to put together a small library for plays. I'm very much interested in South Africa right now, so I'm reading and getting books together. When I'm writing, my shelf of books reminds me what I'm doing, gives me little touchstones.

With *Principia* and *Between East and West*, there was very little rewriting in rehearsal—a change for me. With *American Comedy* I made numerous changes, probably every page. For *Principia* I did rewrite the last scene—I heard the first read-through and didn't like it.

Do you usually attend rehearsals for first productions?

Yes, definitely for first productions and larger productions after that as well.

How closely do you work with directors, designers?

Very closely with the director. But it's the director's show so my being involved with the designers depends on him. I would never deal with the designers independently. I think it's useful to be invited into a design situation, especially for the signs. Sometimes designers read them and don't quite understand what I'm doing—especially when I insist, as in *Between East and West* and *Principia*, that they stay on for the whole scene.

With some directors there's a period of time—a week or ten days—when they don't want a writer around observing their foolish mistakes. It can be a little intimidating to think that the person behind you, the playwright, has all the answers. One doesn't want the playwright to become the internal critic, a judge, and therefore not a part of that company. If you don't have a good relationship with the actors and director, it's hard, in the last stages of production, to push toward absolute clarity of intention, saying "No, that's too long," or "That line isn't working."

It's necessary for a younger playwright to be there because the theatre is a very difficult form and it's the way to learn what you're doing. I read a lot of scripts and I'm amazed that people write long stage directions and don't know what can be done, how to communicate and what an actor needs. You can't write a line and then a stage direction like "he turns and sips his coffee loudly and looks away sadly."

Was there any production experience that was particularly happy for you, and why?

The production of *Principia* in London was the happiest time I've ever had in theatre. That's not to disparage the production at the Manhattan Theatre Club, which was very, very good. London was just one of those times when everything came together. David Jones directed and his interests in the world are exactly my interests. He lives with one foot in America and one foot in

England. The Royal Shakespeare Company actors were really, really happy to be in the play.

There's something both good and bad about English actors, but it turned out to be very good in my case: there's an agreed-upon way of working, an unspoken knowledge of what is being attempted. In the States, because of the Method and other acting notions, people are sometimes in the rehearsal room with other agendas. They're there for themselves, there's no sense of continuity, there's no company, so there are all kinds of tensions and problems: "Am I going to lose my job?" In London, it was a totally smooth process of people uncovering the play. And then the reaction to the play was so extraordinary for me. I've said that for years I was trying to make an interesting orange, a nice orange, and the critics would come up to me and say, "What an ugly apple." Finally someone said, "That is an orange." And I felt I was not insane. It was that much of a release for me. The kind of work that is called confusing here was called ambiguous there.

Do you usually read the critics?

I start. There are a lot of reviews I never finish reading. But yes, I do, and it hurts me. Initially, I feel quite vulnerable because my work is based on self-questioning, taking on my beliefs and twisting and questioning them. If someone finds fault with the work, my immediate response is "Maybe they're right." By and large the canon of my reviews is pretty awful. But you just keep going. You find people who support and encourage you, and try not to doubt them. You try to be clear.

With many, many plays of mine, what I was trying to communicate and what was talked about in the press did not mesh at all. For *Pinocchio* this year, the *New York Times* criticized me for changing the Disney original from a whale to a shark. But in the original Italian, it's a shark. The response to *American Comedy* was so bad that it's very difficult for me to work at the Taper, though they've produced four of my plays. In Seattle, The Empty Space seemed like a wonderful place to work—they did *Pinocchio* and sold out their previews just on word of mouth. And then the two critics, one a former sportswriter, just devastated it. But I get my plays done and I get them published and I get support from foundations and organizations like TCG.

Your work is clearly threatening to a lot of critics. It's interesting, though, that they can appreciate British political writers like David Hare and Caryl Churchill.

Frank Rich represents a whole political world in America now. He writes well, he's a very smart man, I grant him that. But he does reflect the audience

171

that came out of the sixties and is fed up with politics. It's disgusting cynicism. And yet, carrying the liberal mantle, they're interested in black politics, British socialism, maybe feminist politics. But if you're a male like them and you try to write about things that matter to you—which may, indeed, reflect back on them—then they're not very happy to hear it.

They represent the bankruptcy of liberalism in America.

I agree. That was the basis, really, for *Principia*. I was interested in figuring out what happened. If I wanted to make a comment, it was "Okay, I recognize we can't go back to the sixties. We were naive, we were young, we were silly, but there was also something good there—belief in change. The heart was there and now it's been cut out. Let's not lose the heart. Let's recognize that the world is complicated. Let's recognize that things are ugly and we may have to compromise, but let's remember that things are possible."

The production of *The Front Page* at Lincoln Center is really disturbing. I'm a big fan of Jerry Zaks, the director, and Gregory Mosher is a good friend, and I haven't talked to either about this. I was really distraught. *The Front Page* is a play full of moral questions. It's a play whose cynicism is focused on racism and on grotesque, ugly political manipulations. But it was treated as "Ha ha, isn't it funny the way the world is?" Questions of morality were not addressed in that production.

Can you say more about how you see the American theatre and your position in it?

I see a part of my career now moving overseas. Some of the regional theatres have done wonderful things and built a real profile. A lot are not able to do that. And so the nonprofit resident theatre movement is not the success that one hoped it would be. There are only a handful of theatres out in the country that I find really interesting. But that's a handful more than we had thirty years ago. I find that making a living is difficult. I've been one of the few over the past five years to make a living from the theatre and from grants. But I get very scared. I see my opportunities drying up. I see the theatre reflecting a society in which we are not articulating moral concerns and in which the only goal appreciated by our peers is success.

There was a time when we agreed that theatre had to be about something, when we had to find out what it should be about. In New York you once had theatres like the Chelsea, doing European plays, and the Phoenix. Now we're down to the Public Theater, which is terrific, and the Manhattan Theatre Club, and Playwrights Horizons—although I find the work they produce is in a specific direction, by and large (they did do a Keith Reddin play). The opportunities here are less and less and less. It's indicative that six years ago David Jones was hired to create a classical repertory company at BAM and a month ago there was an article in the *New York Times* Magazine about BAM and fundraising. Theatre has become about fundraising.

I have received a number of grants but they are what you would call start-up grants. Once you get going, people feel, you shouldn't need them anymore. Again, that's the notion of success. I'm now being rejected for grants I've never had. It's because I've had so many. And yet I've also produced from those grants. I'm looking down the road and asking, "How do you continue your career?" It's hard to figure out. I'm at a watershed, with the success and attention and comfort in England, and a somewhat hostile critical and financial environment here. Ask me in a year, then I'll know.

*Many of your plays—*Vienna Notes, American Comedy*—are deconstructive. They're about plot-making. We see the writer, in the play or outside of it, trying to find a plot.*

A hidden agenda in all of my work is that it is about art—its value, purpose and function. Just as you see someone creating in *Vienna Notes*, struggling in *American Comedy*, you have people retreating in *Principia*, sitting there mutilated and reading the translation of *The Seafarer* or *Canterbury Tales*. In *Between East and West* the climax of the play is Gregor trying to correct the pronunciation of Erna's *Three Sisters*. I played jokes for myself, like in *Jungle Coup* and in *Vienna Notes*: the names of the characters are based on artists—Georgia, Stubbs and Rivers. That's another skin of the onion. The plays are efforts at being involved in society and at questioning values. What am I doing? How am I making things matter or not matter?

Stubbs' incessant reflection is a way of avoiding dealing with what is happening around him.

That's right. In *Conjuring an Event* I look at it in a different way. What one creates is all there is. That's what the *New York Times* didn't understand when they called it a series of atrocities against reporters, simply because a reporter says, "I am everything. Everything goes through me so I am everything." They took that as a wild, crazed attack on the freedom of the press, when in fact I was dealing with the nature of watching. I hadn't really thought of *American Comedy* like that, but it's very much the case. The whole play is about looking for a story.

In fact, much of it is spent literally looking for a manuscript. Do you have any favorites among your plays?

I don't really. Some are more successful, more fully realized efforts. I wrote *Bal* for me and never expected to have it done. I'd been writing with a typewriter for years but I put it away and took a little pencil and a little piece of paper and wrote really small and wrote a play. And that changed me. So I have fond thoughts of that play. I chose to write *Rip Van Winkle* to be free to say, "So it lasts four hours and has sixty characters. I'm not even going to worry. I'm going to have a war on stage and I'm going to do whatever I want." The writing of the *Three Sisters* scene in *Between East and West*, knowing I'd gotten something right, was great. I once spent five months working on a play about the homeless—a farce in which I had six sets of twins. Six actors, each playing two characters—so you'd have endless goings-on, actors having offstage conversations with themselves. Some of it is very, very funny, but it's very hard to resolve. And *American Comedy*: yes, the plot is the process of writing the play. Because I didn't have a plot, it became about the pleasure of discovering the story.

I want to return to your comment about **The Marriage of Figaro.** *I accept your distinction in regard to the class being addressed. The only problem is that there is no class consciousness in this country. The division between social classes is growing but most people aren't aware of it. So people in the underclass identify their interests with those of the ruling class.*

There was a time when I hoped that I could do plays for a socially varied audience. But I don't know where that audience is or how to reach it. I made a choice a while ago...there's a lot of very interesting people who go to the theatre. They may be upper middle class, college educated—doctors, lawyers, aeronautical engineers—but if you sit down in a room with these people, they're really smart. And so I want to engage them.

This brings up one of the more complicated efforts I've made, which was a big, big disaster—the adaptation of Dario Fo's *Accidental Death of an Anarchist*. It was a disaster because the *New York Times* hated it. I made a political choice. I looked at Dario Fo's play and said, "This is not going to change the world. This is a funny play, saying quite obvious things about police brutality and social corruption." What's the strength of it? Fo wrote it as a celebration of what everybody knew. He would play it for a thousand union members. Now it's silly for me to think, in adapting it, that suddenly a thousand blue-collar workers are going to march to Arena Stage to see it. So I had a choice. I could lie to myself, I could disengage myself from my audience and do an easy, mean-spirited, "we're political and tough" show; or we could have a fun celebration of the obvious corruption. But to do this I needed to bring in my audience, even my Republican audience. So, at the very beginning, I increased the number of doctor jokes. I added some lawyer jokes, put in a few more bureaucrat jokes. It would be a free-for-all but it was not going to change the world. This was going to be servant-to-servant but I was raising the level of servant quite high. And it was very successful. People loved it.

Coming to New York, I hit an expectation problem: Dario Fo was not being allowed into the country and that must mean he's a terrorist or a revolutionary and therefore his play must spit in the face of the bourgeois Broadway audience. On the other hand, it ran for two years in the West End. So we came in with the expectation of a commercial hit that was going to spit in the face of Broadway. And I couldn't achieve that. Nor does the play. I was criticized for trying to be honest to the play and to engage an audience in a direct way with their concerns, not to lie and say, "You're a working-class audience."

So much traditional left-wing discourse is totally unacceptable to an American audience.

As it should be, because I think the concerns are different. I don't think it's liberalism versus a new conservatism. Because of television, because of what's happening in our political system, we are basically fighting the battle of engagement, period. When after six years of Reagan you see that smiling and being good on television matters so much, it's incredibly depressing. A vast majority of people are saying, "I don't want to think. I don't want the tough questions."

There's a quote I keep over my desk. It's from Plutarch and it's the whole context for my work, in a way. He said, "Politics is not like an ocean voyage, something to be gotten over with. It is a way of life." That's what we miss. The liberal movement fell apart because it said that if we do this, then we'll get that result. And when it didn't happen, everything crumbled. What needs to be infused is the sense that it matters daily what we do—politically, morally, socially. We matter.

In telling that message, you're running counter to what we're being told by the media, politicians, Hollywood. I was very disappointed in the New York production of The Return of Pinocchio. *I see it as a kind of grotesque but very funny clown show. But the production here was so heavy and psychological. There was no fun in it at all.*

It's a tricky one to do. We don't have what I would call a selective style, where you choose and everything you do matters.

Which I think the British do have.

They're happy using their technique. For my plays I've found it quite good. I don't mean to disparage American actors. When you get the emotional commitment that an American actor can give you, matched with technique,

175

it's really quite amazing. That's why you find British actors so interested in American acting.

You were talking before about the fatalism in some of your work. I can see that in **Between East and West** *but less so in the other works. When I spoke to Irene Fornes a few weeks ago, she distinguished between teaching by example and teaching by demonstration. She has chosen the latter, like Brecht, and it seems that you have too, in plays like* **Vienna Notes** *and* **Return of Pinocchio.** *I don't find that a fatalistic choice at all.*

Bal is a character who's totally grotesque, but hopefully the play is saying, "You take what we're seeing to the extreme and this is what you get." It's not fatalistic because it is engaging an audience with the assumption that one can actually change.

I'm not sure how in depicting a bad situation one leads the spectator to believe he can change rather than leading him to believe he's trapped.

You want to keep a realm of truth and you want to be realistic. Years ago I was interested in being a minister. I think there's a definite Calvinism in my work. As I understand it, the bottom line of Calvinism is: God can be doing awful things to you, good things to you, all kinds of things. You have no control, or any real understanding of why things are being done. You plow your fields eighteen hours a day, not to be rewarded by having a great thing happen, but as an act of faith. One's belief is in one's deeds, without the expectation of rewards. And so you end up with the process, the activity, the exploration, as an end in itself.

The philosophy of language and linguistics have interested me for a long time. After J.L. Austin died, a series of his lectures was put out called *How to Do Things with Words.* He had the notion that there are speech acts in life, where the act of saying something is, in fact, doing it. Saying "I do" in a marriage ceremony is more than words. It's a fact. "I promise" is more than a description, it is the act of promising. I've found that theatre is very much a speech act, it's about speaking and doing and how they become one. That's in *Vienna Notes*—that notion, that search. Art can become a speech act. One reads certain poetry not because of what it's saying but because it's beautiful, it's good, and reading it is an act. The Plutarch quote and the Calvinistic idea are two sides of the same coin. They are not goal- or reward-oriented. They are action-oriented—being involved with politics for the rest of your life. Don't expect all the poor people to become rich. But that doesn't mean you ignore the poor people. In the search for writing, in the search for understanding and communicating your world, it means that the effort is enough.

Acting out commitment.

Acting out *is* a commitment. That's a tricky philosophical base on which to build a whole life, a whole way of thinking, but I think it ends up being very generous and very human. And then, how disturbing rampant materialism will appear.

Commitment, ultimately, is an act of faith.

You can't look for proof because that's self-defeating. That's what happened to liberalism. It wasn't an act of faith, it was an act directed toward a result.

Noam Chomsky's career greatly interests me. He got into computers very early, in the fifties, trying to reconstruct language with computers. After some years of work, he hit upon a point of recognizing certain deep structures in language which are inherent in human beings, and which are not computerizable. He found proof that man is not a blank slate and that there are deep truths in him. He made the jump of saying that there are also inherent moral truths. Therefore one had not only a right but an obligation to become engaged in social causes, not for oneself, but for the race, for the world. He found a religious truth within the study of language.

And a political truth.

A study of language can lead you in a straight line to protesting the Vietnam War. That's an extraordinary idea. The world is a mass of things that interrelate and politics is one of them. Politics is a truth. Social involvement is a fact. It is there, whether one denies it or not, and must be dealt with. That's why I think it's mistaken to talk about the purity of one's politics—that doesn't exist. You're talking about your life and the elements of your life include politics. When you deny an element, you're killing yourself.

MARSHA NORMAN

B orn and raised in the suburbs of Louisville, Marsha Norman spent her childhood as a loner. Her mother, a Methodist fundamentalist, did not consider the neighborhood children "good enough" to play with her daughter. So Norman passed the time playing the piano, reading, writing and playing with her imaginary friend Bettering. An honor student in high school, she majored in philosophy at Agnes Scott College in Atlanta and then returned to Louisville to work with disturbed adolescents. Her first play, *Getting Out*, created a sensation when performed in 1977 at Actors Theatre of Louisville. The next year it played in Los Angeles and New York and in 1979 opened Off Broadway, running for eight months. Norman then wrote two more plays for ATL: *Third and Oak* (1978), comprised of two interlocking one-acts—*The Laundromat*, a comic, wistful meeting between two lonely women, and *The Pool Hall*, about the son of a famous pool shark—and *Circus Valentine* (1979), about the attempt of a woman aerialist to save her family's circus. These were followed by *The Holdup* (1983), which subtly transforms the mythology of the old West to dramatize its passing; the Pulitzer Prize-winning *'night, Mother* (1983); and *Traveler in the Dark* (1984), about the crisis of faith suffered by a guilt-ridden surgeon.

Norman's sweepingly psychological work focuses on an oppressed and divided protagonist unable to comprehend how he or she is being destroyed. Although Norman relies heavily on the audience's empathic response to this dominant figure, her drama is not simply character-driven. It is highly structured work, firmly rooted in the conventions of the well-made play, using realistic dramatic texture and character development. The protagonists of *Getting Out* and *'night, Mother*, Arlene and Jessie, are drawn with careful attention to psychological details and are in similar positions. Both struggle for emotional wholeness and control over their lives, against virtually impossible odds. Both are estranged from their sons and tended by mothers who don't understand them. Both are victims of a society they cannot fathom and both are forced into a final and lethal confrontation which kills either a part or the whole of the self.

The title *Getting Out* is ironic—Arlene, though released from prison, clearly has not escaped. Not only is her former prison cell part of the play's setting, but her apartment itself "must seem imprisoned," with bars on its single window. Furthermore, Arlene brings the past with her in the person of her rude and violent self, Arlie, who shares the stage space. The two don't explicitly interact; instead Norman interweaves the past and the present, the plights of the two heroines, while retaining naturalistic dialogue and scenic conventions. The play documents the attempt at reconciliation between the two selves, which can be accomplished only by the sublimation of Arlie's violence and rebelliousness. The two selves cannot easily coexist; because Arlie's rebellion is without social or political dimension, she cannot give Arlene the strength she needs to make an independent life. If Arlene is to survive outside, however, she must deal with that part of herself she killed to get out of prison.

In *'night, Mother* far more is at stake than a part of the self. At the beginning of the play Jessie announces that she has decided to kill herself and at the end she does so. In the intervening ninety minutes, she and her mother fight for her life. As they do, they illuminate their crushingly prosaic lives, as well as the many personal problems that have driven Jessie to make her final choice. After years of unhappiness and frustration, Jessie has finally reached the point where she refuses to be taken for granted, degraded by her family or objectified, whether as epileptic or dutiful daughter. She will no longer allow herself to be dispossessed and wrests herself from her mother in the only way she believes she can. Her mother loses and the quality of that loss is signaled less by the fatal gunshot than by Mama's final anguished realization, "I thought you were mine."

Many of Norman's characters rebel against the strictures of middle-class life (and she describes herself as a "natural rebel"). Inevitably, however, their rebellion has greater impact on their own psyches than on the society around them. The plight of the divided protagonists of *Getting Out* and *'night, Mother* gives them an almost uncanny resemblance to the suffering heroine of nineteenth-century drama. But Norman has made a crucial difference by expunging the villain who, in the past, was the one to be confronted and destroyed. In both plays, the villain has been internalized and the protagonist divided against herself. The heroine of *Getting Out* is literally split in two.

Norman's crippled characters never rebel successfully and all are driven to attempt some form of suicide. Arlie stabs herself repeatedly with a fork and Jessie shoots herself. The connection between rebellion and self-destruction testifies horrifyingly to the success of an oppressive culture in destroying the individual's understanding of how he or she is being crushed. The characters of *Getting Out* and *'night, Mother* cannot look beyond their personal grief or envision a different society. However, just because they don't, it does not follow that the spectator cannot. For many, the great emotional impact of Norman's plays lies in their power to warn the spectator of the fatal consequences of blindness and to impel him or her to make different choices, those which will not allow the individual to be dispossessed.

■ ■ ■

JULY 9, 1987—MARSHA NORMAN'S HOUSE, NEW YORK CITY

What got you interested in theatre? And what particularly drew you to playwriting?

I was fortunate enough to grow up in a house where television was forbidden and, though radios weren't actually forbidden, they just weren't there. And movies were taboo. So I lived in a world of books, which was wonderful. Mother, quite simply, did not know the dangers of books because she didn't read. So inadvertently she put me in touch with the most dangerous things of all. As well as theatre. She did believe in sending in the four dollars so that I could go to every elementary school event there was. There was a lot of children's theatre in Louisville. Also both groups that would later unite to become Actors Theatre of Louisville were founded when I was in the seventh grade or so. So I saw first-rate professional work. I can remember going up this little dark stairway with a light bulb hanging down and seeing *Glass Menagerie* in a tiny theatre. It's really critical for theatre writers to see theatre as young as possible.

Then in college I happened into a hotbed of theatrical activity in Atlanta, with Pocket Theatre and Theatre Atlanta. The Met was even still stopping when I was there in school. I always felt more alive in the theatre, more in contact with other people like me. I always felt that I belonged there, that it was something I could do. I even had the perverse feeling occasionally of knowing that I could do better than what was on the stage.

I remember seeing really violent early work of Peter Shaffer, things like *Royal Hunt of the Sun*, and also *J.B.*, *Macbird*, pieces that have a wild-haired theatricality. They were the ones that really moved me. Particularly those about people in search of unseeable parts of themselves. I realize now that it's no accident that *Getting Out* is about an attempted reconciliation between an earlier, violent self and a current passive, withdrawn self. It seemed to me that the theatre was the place to examine that isolation which was the primary quality of my life. It was mine not only by birth and early childhood, but it's something that I have sought to maintain, not in an arrogant way, but because it seems that I belong off by myself.

I never considered writing a viable possibility and always imagined that I'd have to work for a living. So when I graduated from college, I went to work in a mental hospital, and after that, for the state arts commission. Ultimately, I got involved with a children's newspaper and children's TV in Louisville, where there was this extraordinary theatre. So I had virtually twenty years of training in the theatre before I ever started to write. You can really see it when writers' work is part of a continuing dialogue. It's really a shame that the audience is no longer in touch with that dialogue.

You mean with the past, with a tradition?

Yes. They haven't a clue. You can't write out of a tradition that the audience knows—unless you write TV plays.

When did you first get involved with Actors Theatre of Louisville?

I was writing full-time and Jon Jory called me in and offered to commission a play from me. I was to go around with a tape recorder and interview people in the community about busing and then we'd put it all together in some kind of show. I got home and thought, "How can I turn him down? I've always wanted to write a play, and here's somebody offering to pay me five thousand dollars to write one." But I didn't want to write about busing. So I went back and said, "I really thank you but, no, that's not what I want to write about." Jon and I proceeded to have three lunches at which he went over, fairly quickly and in an entertaining fashion, the unbreakable rules of the theatre. The last discussion we had was about good subjects for plays. Jon urged me to go back and try to find some moment when I had been frightened physically, in real danger.

Right away I thought of Arlie, this kid I had known at Central State Hospital ten years before, a kid who terrified everybody, who had absolutely no sense of consequence. She could not be coerced into anything because she was not afraid of what you would do to her. And she was thirteen. I had kept up with her in the years since then and knew that she was in federal prison serving time for murder, after a somewhat notorious career in the Kentucky penal system. So I decided to write about her and immediately thought, "I don't want to write about murders, or about what she did." I knew the one thing she had always counted on was that she could run away. I wondered what would happen to somebody like that when she was put in a place where she could not run away, could not get out. What then? I told Jon and he said, "Great, why don't you write ten pages?" I did and he said, "Oh well, it does appear that you can write dialogue. You just write dialogue like mad. Why don't you finish this." Jon went to Switzerland for the summer and when he came back in August the play was finished. In September *Getting Out* won the Great American Play Contest and in November it was on stage and the rest, as they say, is history.

That was exactly ten years ago, so it's not been an awfully long time. I wrote *Third and Oak* almost immediately after that, and then *Circus Valentine*. Then ensued one of those great theatrical fights—Jon and I didn't speak for four or five years—followed by a wonderful theatrical reconciliation. Now we're fast friends. I'm writing another play for Jon.

Would you describe the style so identified with Actors Theatre of Louisville that you helped forge as a kind of lyrical realism?

I don't think it's so lyrical. That's what Circle Rep does, or Lanford Wilson. There's a much grittier, much harder edge to the realism of Louisville and I think that's why it's come to an end. We've seen the last of the trailer-park plays. I did not write any of them, but that's where the work that I started ended up, with people hitting each other over the head with frying pans in trailers. It turned into ultimate confinement and domestic violence, so bizarre and brutal that audiences just said no thanks.

Jon has been particularly sensitive—because of my influence, I think —to strong women characters. That's a really important contribution; on the whole the American theatre, dominated by men, does not perceive women fighting for their lives as a central issue.

Structurally, your plays are very traditional.

Wildly traditional. I'm a purist about structure. Plays are like plane rides. You buy the ticket and you have to get where the ticket takes you. Or else you've been had. In plays you have eight minutes at the beginning in which to let the audience know what's at stake, who this is about and when they can go home. I think audiences get real nervous if you don't do that. And then you have to take them where you said you were going. Plays are pieces of machinery in that way, ski-lifts—you get in, and you want to go straight to the top and get out and look at the view. You don't want to be caught halfway, dangling in the air, and realize where you are. The theatre is a world of illusion. You cannot break that illusion by being dull, by taking side trips, by diverting the audience's attention.

I really believe that plays can only be about one person. I've tried and lots of other people have tried to break this rule and make plays about two people or about groups. The audience will subvert this every time. Consider if *The Big Chill* were a play. It purports to be about a group, but as you watch, you're desperate to find one person to hang on to, to hook up with. Two hours is the kind of time that you can devote to one person who, for the moment, represents you, on some level.

How do you feel about Chekhov then? His strategy is quite different.

People talk about Masha in *Three Sisters*; it's about her, as far as everybody is concerned.

What about Tennessee Williams? Has his work had a big impact on you?

There's that power of southern writers' work, not only on the world, but on each other. We share the notion that you cannot escape your family. You can't escape where you were born, who you were born to and what you've inherited. This is a southern version of fate [laughs]. I think that northern, urban writers have the notion—a quite legitimate one—that you can sort of make up the past as you go along, you can find new family. Southern writers know better than this. Your family's going to hunt you down. Just when you think you've gotten away, you'll get a call and one of them will have done something so unconscionably loony that you have to go and straighten it out. And once you're there, you will find that you're hopelessly mired in this and that everybody looks at you and knows exactly who you are. Whatever you have done since you left does not matter to them. Our writing is absolutely linked to this problem of how do you change when the perceptions of the people around you don't change. How do you know who you are when you are made up of these people that you *despise*? How do you move at all with all these people hanging onto you?

So you see family and the past as a situation you can't get out of?

It's worth trying. But I don't think family's really escapable.

Not many of your characters get away. But Archie in **The Holdup** *does.*

He's wonderful. I just love him. There's a possibility of a production of that play this year. It's very strange, the work of mine that's primarily funny has not been received well at all. It's so clear to me that the press is saying, "We want you to be the Lillian Hellman of your generation. We want you to write intense family drama and always be well dressed." It's just absurd. Even *'night, Mother*, which *is* intense family drama, is wildly funny and nobody ever talks about that. *Traveler in the Dark* is about a very smart man who comes upon a day when his intelligence is not enough. This is a pretty funny situation. Suddenly he has to figure out what else will work. It's like being on a picnic with a bottle of wine and no corkscrew.

I'm sorry, but it's really very pleasant to laugh. It's one of the primary methods of dealing with pain. These plays are not simple entertainments. I despise the American critical community right now, particularly for the entrapment of contemporary writers. There is a smug, superior attitude on the part of critics and they have no sense of humor—there's not a funny one in the bunch. The only saving grace is that nobody is going to remember who they are. So all the rest of us have to do [laughs], is to stay alive long enough to get our work written.

Finally I think I'm old enough to defy everyone and say, "If I feel like writing another comedy, I'm going to." The comedies are no less difficult to write and infinitely more difficult to produce and yet it's a real pleasure to stand in the back of the theatre and hear an audience just convulsed. Laughter is rare in the world. People mainly sit in front of their televisions and listen to laughter without ever joining in.

Are you conscious of working in a different mode when you're writing a comedy?

No, it's a question of how weighty the issue is. Archie, the center of *The Holdup*, is not threatening to kill himself, he's simply threatening to grow up. It's a simple matter of what is at stake.

Although there's a murder in **The Holdup.**

Of course there is. It's just the excuse for a very funny funeral. I love that funeral.

It's also a step in Archie's liberation.

The Holdup was such an important play for me to write because it was the first play in which I contained the action. In that way, it was a technical exercise. These people are going camping and we're drawing a circle around them and nobody can get in or out, and what happens happens because of who these people are. There aren't any doors to open or phones to ring. It's no accident that *'night, Mother* came next because once you learn how to do it, you can set a play in the middle of the living room and tell the set designer not to put the doors in. You can have a telephone and explain why it's not ringing—it's Saturday night— and everybody in the audience buys it, world-wide. The critics don't understand that when they attack a play like *The Holdup*, what is at stake, in effect, is *'night, Mother.*

How do you begin a play? With an outline, a character, a line of dialogue?

There are two beginnings. There's the beginning of the thinking, when you know that you have something that will make a play. And then there's the beginning of the actual writing. The beginning of the thinking—I think of it as the moment when there's an amazing conjunction of form and content. You've been thinking about someone you remember from a long time ago and you can't figure out why you keep thinking about this person. Suddenly at dinner parties you're telling stories about this person. And you hear yourself doing this because, if you're a writer, you're also observing yourself. You become aware that this person has arrived for consideration, so the content's basically there. But if you can get the story told at dinner, you should not write a play.

What you need is a form that will contain that story. With *Getting Out*, for example, I knew I wanted to write about this woman who'd just gotten out of prison, but I realized that it's not enough just to write about her, you have to know who she was. Well, as soon as you say that sentence, you have the form: put the other person on stage. So you have this amazingly stable little triangle with the two of them and the point of reconciliation. This thing will stand up forever. The same thing is true in *'night, Mother*—you have Mama and Jessie and the door behind them. The piece I'm working on now has six people in it but three have exactly that kind of relationship. There is an amazing feeling dealing with a triangle, which people have known for thousands and thousands of years. The trouble with contemporary life is that people don't take advantage of ancient principles that have continued to be true. Pythagorean, that's what it is.

With *'night, Mother* I knew I wanted to tell the story of this woman who kills herself, but I didn't have any idea how. At the time, in '81, there were a number of other plays on the subject. But I kept saying that these plays—particularly *Whose Life Is It Anyway?*—are tantrums. I wanted to put somebody in the room with this woman, somebody who cares deeply, wildly, madly, who will fight this person to the death to save her own life. This is a gladiator contest where the point is to keep the other person alive. And once

I had that, I had all these parallels—gladiators and world heavyweight boxing championships—and I understood immediately how this has to work. You have to have a closed ring, nobody can get out or in, you can have only two people.

I knew going into *'night, Mother* that it was going to be the most treacherous act of my writing life. So I went to the world of music. I was in a mad Glenn Gould state at the time—I've spent my life at the piano. Okay, I thought, what if I do a little sonata form, a three-act play with no intermission? You can actually feel the moment when the orchestra stops and the conductor raises his hands and Jessie says, "You talked to Agnes today," and the second movement starts. The second movement ends when Jessie goes in to get the box of presents, Mama just having said, "Don't leave me, Jessie." The actors would come on stage knowing, "We don't have to go all the way to the end. We just have to get to the Agnes section." And then you start in on Agnes and think, "Great, I'll just get to 'Don't leave me, Jessie,' then I can take a breath"—this is from Mama's point of view—"and get down and wash the floor." And then all they have to do is go to the end. *'Night, Mother* would be undoable if it weren't for that. People would fall out of it all the time. But they don't. So I think that if you don't have structure, you might as well not have anything to put in it. If you don't have the bookshelves, you don't have the books.

I have a great trick during that period of thinking about the play. I say, "I'm not writing until I absolutely have to, till I can no longer contain it." I build up the piece in a pressure cooker, as it were. All that time I'm writing myself notes in the form of questions. What did Daddy do? How long ago did he die? Where did he die? What did he ever do for Jessie? Those kinds of questions. Curiously enough, you'll find that just from asking the questions, you'll get all the answers during the next weeks. It's internal research into the lives of these people. From those questions will come lines of dialogue —you begin to hear the voicing, what they can talk about, what they think is funny. The first line of dialogue I wrote for *'night, Mother* was Jessie's line, "We got any old towels?" As soon as I wrote it down, I understood that it was a ritual piece, that Jessie was coming in to celebrate this requiem mass, that she has these stacks of towels: here are the witnesses, the household objects. She comes in as though she is the altar boy.

I wait until I cannot avoid it anymore and by that time, I already know what the beginning is, because of all this scribbling down. Then it's really very easy. I keep two kinds of notebooks, one that has structure and information in it and the other that has my own thoughts—"Can we really have this? What about that? What would happen if this?" I have a wonderful piece of paper upstairs that says, "Have I written something that anybody will want

186

to see? Have I written something that will last? Have I written something that will humiliate me?" This comes from a pretty grim moment in the writing of *'night, Mother.* I thought, "What is this that I've written?" Humiliation is easily a possibility.

Do you usually attend rehearsals for first productions?

I usually go although I find it difficult and don't enjoy it at all. I go more or less out of self-protection. I'm beginning to think it would be ideal to have the first production done by people you really trusted but who were far away. You'd simply get on a plane and go see it. Then there would be an awful lot you would know immediately. One of the problems with the current style of play development is that writers get too involved in the casting and rehearsals. Their judgment gets clouded by their personal investment in the production. The only thing that you should really be invested in is the script. I really think we could do with a period of cooling away and saying, "You guys solve this problem. You do what you think needs to be done. Don't cut anything and don't add any lines. Just do it."

Writers have been so involved because critics are unable to tell who did what. If you are alive, you're going to take the rap for everything that is done. You're going to take the directing rap, the acting rap, you're going to be blamed for everything. Credit, strangely enough, sometimes gets given to people other than you. So you go to protect yourself. If this actor is going to make you look like a fool, maybe you can get him fired, or maybe you can get him calmed down.

Is there any production of a play of yours that you feel was particularly fine?

The Broadway production of *'night, Mother* was perfect. My favorite performance was the closing one, strangely enough, because it finally didn't matter what the audience thought, whether they laughed, how they were going to get through it. I have had an inordinate and painful concern for the audience in my writing career. I get to the theatre and think, "Oh my God, these poor people, now they have to go through this." And so it's always hard for me to watch the audience. I want them to have a good time, I want them to have such a strong experience. I wish I didn't care so much. But I do.

Susan Kingsley's performance in *Getting Out* was magnificent. A particularly memorable performance was one given at the Manhattan Federal Prison. The prison life happening on the other side of the play became another backdrop. Phones would ring in the prison and guards would walk through the middle of the play to answer—all very, very surreal. That particular audience did not want to know how hard it was going to be to get out. So their reactions to the play virtually turned it inside out. They rooted for all the wrong people. They had no sympathy for all the right people. They ended up terrifying the cast.

What is the European reaction to 'night, Mother?

'*Night, Mother* is done all over the world. Any list that New Guinea is on is a long list. It's still running in Spain, four-and-a-half years later, with all of the jokes taken out. Curiously enough, my work has always been popular in Eastern Europe. But this time I've caught the Mediterranean crowd. What strikes you as you watch it in a foreign country, in another language, is that the play seems to contain this other culture. In Italy you get enormous "Mama mia" Mamas, and the Jessies are always Ariels, little sprites. In Scandinavian countries it's quite the opposite. The mothers are really small, like the old woman who lived in the shoe, and the daughters are Valkyries, towering over these little Mamas. In the Latin American countries Mama and Jessie look like sisters.

The great thing about watching the play in another language, particularly one you don't understand, is that you get it all. You can even tell if it's a good translation or not. Edward Albee told me that years ago and I didn't believe it. How can you tell if this is a good translation into Finnish? I promise you, you can. You're so aware of what you can expect from the audience, you know what the trip is like, you know what the scenery is like. So if people don't gasp at the right time you think, "Gee, something happened."

Do you always read the critics?

Oh sure. I read the good reviews because it's fun. I get people to tell me if there are bad ones, to tell me where they are so I'm not surprised. One of the most horrible things that can happen to you is when somebody comes up and says, "Weren't you just furious when you read that *Saturday Review* article?" You feel so humiliated by this person who's gloating about how you've been stepped on once again. So you have to protect yourself from these people who will make it a point to come up and console you.

Critics today are reviewing plays, not writing criticism. Those of us who have been around long enough know that. And we all are now aware that there is a whole generation of young writers, people like William Finn and Peter Parnell, who are gone. They were like fireworks, and when they did their second play the critics dismissed them and they went away. We have all been saying that what the critics are doing is dangerous, but now there's proof that they're literally destroying the theatre, pulling the writers right out. Why should Peter Parnell write for the theatre?

What else do you hold responsible for the current state of theatre?

A real problem is that the development of a play can take four years. I used to say two years. It now takes four, simply because of all the activity in the play world, all the play contests that have scared a lot of people out of the woodwork. More scheduled slots are already filled. I think a play a year is about right. Neil Simon is the only playwright in America who's been able to afford to write a play a year. Consequently he has seven or eight good ones and fifteen or sixteen entertaining ones. Now seven or eight terrific plays is really a wonderful accomplishment. You have to write thirty to get seven. But people are not writing the thirty plays. I wrote a play in '77, '78, '79, '80, *'night, Mother* in '81. I wrote *Traveler in the Dark* in '83. Now it's '87 and I've not written another play. Nobody's getting to do enough work in the theatre. Broadway is virtually closed for serious drama. August Wilson will probably have the same experience I and David Mamet had, the ten-and-a-half-month run.

Do you think of your work as teaching? Irene Fornes spoke about how her plays teach by holding unfortunate situations up for the spectator to examine.

I do think there's a quality in my work which says, "Look at this, I know you haven't seen this before. You've been walking right by this person." Calling attention to previously unnoticed things, people, situations is not really my intent, it's simply part of the power to take the attention of a group of people and focus it in one place. It's kind of a magnifying-glass trick. You capture sunlight and focus it and burn the hole right through. I've always perceived that as part of the gift, that I was interested in things that were perfectly common and obvious, but nobody saw them.

Are you referring principally to personal issues or social ones?

I'm thinking of the plights of single people. Here is a person representing a particular life who has to make a particular decision. I find myself in considerable awe of these people's courage. These people have captured me and I'm able to call everybody else over and say, "Look at this." But teaching, no, I don't think so.

Has the women's movement had an impact on your writing?

Women have been writing about women since women have been writing. But the world has not always been willing to pay attention. Fortunately I was born at a time when my work was going to be taken seriously. Living in another age, I could very easily have been ignored, or because of the conditions of my life, not have had the mobility that's required for a life in the theatre.

How do you respond to criticism of 'night, Mother *from feminists?*

I haven't read it. I know that in general I'm regularly attacked by women who say, "She's making us look bad." Or "Because she's a woman, she should be doing this or that." I would assume there's been talk about mother-hating, which is a gross misunderstanding of what *'night, Mother* is.

Some people criticize 'night, Mother *for ignoring outside forces, focusing on personal issues rather than societal ones.*

There isn't any society, as far as Mama and Jessie are concerned. I don't think Americans think of themselves as a society. People say, "I'm *an* American," not "I'm American." We have no national society. We are all, at this moment, in a terrible state of despair about even being associated with certain people who are also Americans. People are just out there wildly and desperately alone, trying to figure out where they are from, who they are, does anybody matter.

Getting Out, *too, is peopled by characters without social or political consciousness. Arlie is a very curious rebel. She's not indicting or even really criticizing society. She doesn't understand it.*

Not a clue. I think that Americans in general function out of a family context. The violence is all domestic, by and large. And I think that plays written by Americans are generally a child's view of what happens in that child's house. Unfortunately, most American dramatists don't write long enough to begin to write about anything else—say, to get fully into an adult's view of adultery. Now Sam Shepard, with *Fool for Love*, is finally doing that. That's great. This is the first of his plays that is not written from the little-boy perspective. I don't mean to be denigrating, I just mean adults are real big and God help us, they're going to come crashing down. It will be wonderful if enough of us survive into writing about adultery. It's clear from looking at the English, who manage to keep their playwrights alive and working, that this is what happens next. Everybody writes about their marriages.

It's very, very difficult to write a play. How long has it been since Sam wrote one? It's staggering that all of us have been silenced for so long, but encouraging, as I saw at the Dramatists Guild yesterday, that many of us are writing again. Maybe we've figured out how to support ourselves in some other way, to gain the freedom to be able to write for the theatre, to consider it a kind of hobby. You cannot be dependent on the theatre financially, emotionally, artistically—you simply cannot be at its mercy when you're writing. We're returning to the theatre now with a sense that this is simply a private pleasure. I derive some satisfaction from it, like snorkeling. So I have to figure out how to live my life so I can spend a month snorkeling every year. It's almost that way.

Where do you think the hope lies in the theatre? In the regional theatres?

I'm tempted to say it lies in libraries and publishing. It's up to this generation of writers, my generation, to complete our bodies of work before we die and to try to protect the later work from the bitterness that sets in. It's as if the critics are sitting there with rolls of masking tape and first they wrap up your hands and then they wrap up your feet and pretty soon you're a mummy. And then they ask, "Why isn't he writing anymore?" Tennessee Williams is the perfect example. Only on the morning after he dies does the *New York Times* give him what would have kept him alive, recognition of his rightful place. I think the hope is for people like me to complete the plays that we have in us, to carry our particular vision forward into the later stages of life. Americans are increasingly having to deal with the ends of their lives. The end is lasting longer than it did. It's people like me who need to write about that.

I'm very concerned that we don't seem to be producing young writers. English playwrights say the same thing. Writers have one play done and then they disappear and they're writing for TV or doing whatever. Theatre's truly an old, shady business and you have to have it in your blood. It has to be something you can't live without. We're not addicting enough young people to the theatre. We make it impossible for them to go see plays. We saturate their minds with all other forms of entertainment, largely disposable. So they don't get the mythology, they don't get hooked.

Can you tell me anything about your new play?

It's quite a theatrical piece, wildly theatrical, back to *Getting Out*. It uses all the old tricks.

You can never know what you'll be writing about because you never know what's going to be there when you begin to investigate that part of your memory that is still holding the effects from ten years ago. Two years from now, when I start to consider my next play, who knows what that will be? I would like to keep writing for the theatre. I have no illusions about what good can come to me as a result of it, I'm not counting on it to bring me anything. What I hope is that it doesn't kill me. But I don't feel entirely sure about that. I know the world expects an awful lot from me and yet seems to be doing everything it can to prevent me from doing the work.

Do you have a favorite among your plays?

No, I don't. There are things that I love desperately in all of them. I'm inordinately fond of quoting my work. I will tell the jokes, and won't even credit the work. Probably *Traveler in the Dark* and *Circus Valentine* have the most gorgeous writing. That's the poetry that nobody's ever wanted to hear from me. But I'm free to do what I want, if I'm willing to take the consequences. I'm glad to be talking now instead of a year ago. To answer the question about hope for the theatre, I would have said there isn't any. And, in fact, there may not be any. But for me there is a way to work without having to decide about hope. I can write and think, "I have pleasure in writing and if this is all that ever happens, if this is the best that it ever is, that's fine."

DAVID RABE

G rowing up in Dubuque, Iowa, David Rabe wanted to become a professional football player. He decided instead to study acting, then writing, and finally left Dubuque to pursue graduate training in theatre at Villanova, before dropping out and getting drafted. He spent 1966 in Vietnam, assigned to a hospital support unit at Long Binh, serving as guard, clerk, driver and construction worker. He tried to keep a journal but soon gave up because "it resulted in a kind of double vision that made everything too intense." Returning to the States, he was shocked to discover that Americans were not interested in what was happening in Vietnam. "Everybody seemed totally removed from the war," he explains. "People were interested in simplifications, in the *debate* about the war rather than in the experience of the war itself." In a series of four plays—*The Basic Training of Pavlo Hummel* (1971), *Sticks and Bones* (1971), *The Orphan* (1973) and *Streamers* (1976)—David Rabe provided that much-needed insight into the experience of the American soldier, doing battle both in a foreign jungle and on the home front.

Rabe's Vietnam War plays explore issues far broader than the label might suggest and, in fact, are best understood as part of a wider cultural examination that uses distinctly American anomalies, either characters or institutions, as points of departure. His other plays widen the inquiry, exploring a go-go dancer's decline (*In the Boom Boom Room*, 1973), the murderous rivalry of petty jewel thieves (*Goose and Tomtom*, 1982), and betrayal and self-destruction among Hollywood writers, actors and casting directors (*Hurlyburly*, 1984). Eschewing simplistic answers to complex personal and social problems, each of Rabe's plays plumbs the experience of the well-meaning but shortsighted individual caught within a deranged and destructive society. His Vietnam plays are not narrowly antiwar; they do not argue a political point so much as chart the dynamics of the disparate but interrelated pathologies that produce a situation like Vietnam: male violence, racism, xenophobia and misogyny.

In *Sticks and Bones*, his most fiercely surrealistic play, Rabe models his four protagonists on the characters from *The Adventures of Ozzie and Harriet*, the popular television comedy and paean to the middle-class American family. Into this blandly idyllic environment, David returns from Vietnam, blinded and disoriented. Ozzie, Harriet and Ricky, unnerved by David groping his way through the house like a demented fury, answer his pain first with platitudes, then with obscenity and violence. Finally they help him commit suicide. For this family, unacquainted with anxiety and death, valuing people only according to how much they possess, there can be no common ground with David, as he realizes: "We make signs in the dark. You know yours. I understand my own. We share...coffee!" The disparity between the emotional force of the action and the dispassion of Rabe's plot summary provides a gauge of the play's savage irony: "At the start, the family is happy and orderly, and then David comes home and he is unhappy. As the play progresses, he becomes happier and they become unhappier. Then, at the end, they are happy."

Rabe's most naturalistic and violent play, *Streamers*, takes place in an army barracks outside Washington, D.C. in 1965 and brings into conflict four very different young recruits, alternately black and white, gay and straight. The tension steadily builds among them and is finally detonated when Richie and Carlyle prepare for a sexual liaison and Billy, the play's representative of middle-class, middle-American values, refuses to permit it. Billy is fatally stabbed, but not before Rabe exposes the racism and homophobia that underlie his liberal affability. He dies a scapegoat for all those, both on stage and in the audience, who had tacitly supported him. The unifying metaphor in the play is that of a parachute that fails to open, streaming uselessly above a soldier as he plunges to his death. By the play's end, it has become a disquietingly apt description of the fate of every man, whether killed in action or senselessly cut down before even being given a chance to die in Vietnam.

In *Hurlyburly* Rabe continues his exploration of male rivalry and violence in a very different milieu, the battlefields of Hollywood. Peopled by the not-quite rich and famous, the play is filled with baroque and scurrilous descriptions of their world-weary debaucheries. The action focuses on Eddie's ruthless and unthinking betrayal of his friend Phil, and the latter's death in an automobile accident several days later. Only at the end of the play does Eddie realize that Phil was a suicide and, racked with remorse and self-doubt, begin to reexamine his way of life and the choices he's made.

In *Hurlyburly*, as in his other plays, Rabe uses an unlikely hero— morally problematic at best, selfish, violent and blind at worst—to question the workings of a pernicious society. Having set up this dubious hero, Rabe carefully and shrewdly works to turn the spectator's empathy and understanding toward him. Well before the final curtain, however, Rabe breaks the spell; and the spectator, newly aware of his complicity, is forced to question the values he has been seduced into supporting. This dramatic strategy (which has striking similarities to that used by more conventional tragedians) is used in concert with a highly theatrical realism to provoke a double confrontation, of self and society. As he makes clear in the interview, Rabe aims explicitly at personal rather than social confrontation, in the hope that the subjugated individual will develop the insight, skill and power to realize himself and change his world.

■   ■   ■

DECEMBER 30, 1986—THE APARTMENT OF DAVID RABE'S AGENT, ELLEN NEUWALD, NEW YORK CITY

What were your early experiences in theatre that led you to become a playwright?

I didn't really have any. My interest in writing started when I was eighteen. I had some success in writing in general, but not playwriting, no ambition or sense that that's what I would do. I lived in a very provincial town, there was no real theatre of any kind.

Where did you grow up?

Dubuque, Iowa. I went to a lot of movies. But the first artistic experience I had was sophomore year in high school when I saw James Dean. This was the first time I understood that you could take these things inside you and make something out of them, rather than trying to get rid of them or pretending they didn't exist, which was the basic lesson taught by the world I grew up in. So I thought maybe acting was it and I did some in college. Although I did write a couple of plays in college, I tended to write short stories. But I was inclined to theatre, so it was a curious split. The struggle went on through the following years. At Villanova I continued to write prose and act. Then I quit graduate school and got drafted.

When was this?

I quit in '64, was drafted in '65. A year after I was out of the service, I went back to graduate school, tried acting one more time and hated it. So I quit and started to focus on writing plays. Over the next two or three years I wrote the first two, *Pavlo Hummel* and *Sticks and Bones*.

Where were you working then?

I lived in Philadelphia and then I moved to New Haven, where I worked on a newspaper and continued to write, from 1968 to '71, developing the Vietnam plays. By '71 *Pavlo* was sort of finished and *Sticks and Bones* was sort of finished. There was a draft of *Orphan*, a fragment of *Streamers*. By then I was back at Villanova, teaching. And that's when *Pavlo Hummel* first got picked up by Joe Papp. Those plays had been rejected everywhere, at a lot of the regional theatres and in New York.

Why, do you think?

I think in a strange way they were too complex. They didn't quite sit right ideologically. They weren't blatantly, simple-mindedly antiwar, and they certainly weren't for it. People with a strong liberal point of view—which is sort of where my politics sat at the time—didn't know quite how to take them. Even when *Sticks and Bones* was done, I think people didn't know. It caused a strange reaction. They wanted the Vietnam vet to be more likable. I think the play succeeds in that it provokes even the most liberal of audience members to want to do something to that guy [laughs], and so when it happens, they're complicit in something they don't want to be complicit in.

The same thing happens in Streamers *when you lead the audience to sympathize with Billy because he seems like a nice, regular guy. And then, just before he's killed, the venom that comes out of his mouth makes the audience think about who they've supported.*

It's not just Billy. The same is true of all the characters in *Streamers*. Even Carlyle is likable in a peculiar way up to a point, and then he goes over. But David in *Sticks and Bones* was so unrelentingly aggressive, not sympathetic in a conventional way. The liberals wanted desperately to sympathize with him and his plight. They just wanted him to be a little bit more polite about it [laughs]. The writing is outrageous.

Back in those years, what theatre influenced your writing?

There's a difference between what you consciously admire and what you see that has an effect on you. I feel Arthur Miller has been a long-term influence. But I was far more consciously influenced by Ionesco, the Open Theatre production of *The Serpent, The Entertainer*. I tried to be influenced by Pinter but couldn't be. I really don't see eye-to-eye with Pinter about anything and yet I tried to graft certain things on because he was popular and his techniques are very seductive. Ionesco was probably more important than anybody, for his linguistic flights. Maybe Genet too, a little bit. In a funny way, you incorporate all these things. You put them together with Arthur Miller and it's a very strange amalgam. I saw things at La Mama that I can't even remember now. I tried to be influenced by certain writers because I couldn't get my plays on. I would go to things and try to understand the rules for getting a play produced. But those didn't sit well and now I look back and think that the people who really influenced me are the ones I've named.

I've never thought of you as part of the Off-Off Broadway movement.

I didn't fit anywhere. Finally Joe did my work because he wanted new American political plays. But *Pavlo* confused him. Pavlo's not a conventionally sympathetic, straightforward character.

I see a point of contact with Miller in the problematic hero.

The plays of his I really like are his less successful ones. *After the Fall* is a great play. Technique, construction—I don't think there's a connection. But there's a kind of moral complexity, an ethical crossover that we share. *View from the Bridge* I like.

What about Brecht?

No. Maybe I've never seen him done well. But he never aroused me the way these others did. The schematic nature of his plays, at least as I've experienced them, didn't intrigue me. He had a point to make before he started writing and he makes it throughout.

What do you feel was the most important part of your training? Villanova? Working with Joe Papp?

When I was in college, a professor, George Herman, at the girls' school where I did most of my theatre work, was very encouraging. And there was a priest, Father Ray Roseliep, who taught creative writing—not playwriting—at the college, who was also encouraging. The lessons he taught me somehow stick more than anything else. That embrace and encouragement is more mean-ingful than any technical training. I read a lot of books on playwriting, and I guess they're worth reading, but I think you just have to hang in there and peel away that stuff and let your own inner impulse toward construction emerge. You need encouragement and opportunities. There's an abundance of critics—people saying "That's not the way to do it."

When I taught playwriting I always tried to see what the writers were doing dramatically on the most rudimentary level. If they had one page that worked, I would try to see what they were doing that made it work and tried to make them conscious of how that happened, how to make that work on more pages than one.

When you write a play, how do you start?

With an impulse or a situation or sometimes just a fragment of dialogue that begins to expand once you work on it. Something sticks in my mind—it could be a real person or a real exchange of dialogue or a fragment that just pops into my head. It doesn't have to have any historical basis. I'll decide to work on it and it'll either expand or it won't. It's just a feeling I have, when it's going well. I do best if I don't get too conscious too soon. Usually the best things happen when they develop in ways you hadn't anticipated. So I try to work in a way that will allow that to happen, which isn't easy—your mind is always jumping ahead. Some people work from an outline or notes but I find them more of a block that stops me from following these impulses when they show up.

How long does it take you to write a play?

I've had very different experiences. I wrote the first draft of *Hurlyburly* in two or three months of concentrated work. I had made a few notes for it about five years earlier, just the opening eight or nine lines of dialogue.

Streamers has a most unusual history. When I came back from the army and started to write, maybe nine or ten months later, I wrote a one-act play, a kind of mood piece, which is essentially the movement of the first act. I wrote it in about three hours. It was very intense and almost effortless writing, almost what the final work is. It didn't have the beginning wrist-cutting scene and it didn't have the sergeants. Carlyle was just a minor character who came in and was very worried, while everybody else was stoic. He was upset and wondered why everybody else wasn't. I put it away and wrote the other Vietnam plays. About three years later I worked on it again and it expanded into a fifty-page one-act play. It now included the stabbing.

There was a producer who wanted to do it in New York. It could have been my first production but I said, "It's not finished." There was just the killing, basically. There was no metaphor in it. There was no streamer in it, no sergeants. It was powerful but it just didn't seem like a play to me. I put it away and another three or four years went by. The other plays had been done and I went to work on it again, in about 1973, and this time it came very quickly. I put the beginning and ending on it and the sergeants came in. Then I had a play. If you took the actual writing time for each version and added it up, you would have only about a day—but a day over a seven- or eight-year period. The other plays tend to be more linear in their development.

Do you generally choose the director for your first productions?

I have, up to a point. Mel Shapiro was supposed to do the first production of *Pavlo*, but he had to go to Washington so Joe introduced me to Jeff Bleckner and we worked very well together. He did a beautiful job. His production of *Sticks and Bones* was good, but I don't think the play was quite right for him. Maybe nobody during that period could have made it work the way I think it should. I think it should be made really, really funny—grotesque and funny in an aggressive way. At the time, audience and actors wanted to participate in the moral issues and so the theatrical nature of the piece couldn't quite emerge. The cartoonish, grotesque and poetic have to collide in a theatrical way. But everyone was always trying to make transitions, make them blend together. Since then I have seen a couple of productions done in high style, almost as farce, with this guy walking through it being overly poetic. The poetry finally is madness and they have to kill him. You can't get from "Hi, Mom, hi, Dad" to the poetry in a transition.

The first play was tough and aggressive. I really understood *Pavlo*. I was a little more confused about *Sticks and Bones* and almost overwhelmed by it. *Hurlyburly* had a renowned director with tremendous ability, Mike Nichols, but he wanted to make the play mean almost the opposite of what it ought to mean. I didn't quite know how to deal with the fact that I didn't really understand the play rationally. Things would happen in rehearsal and my gut response would be, "That's not it." And they'd ask, "Well what is it?" and I'd say, "I don't know." And I didn't. So they'd say, "It might be this or this or this." And I said, "It might be but I don't think so."

Now that I look back on it, I can see that Mike was trying to change the tone of the play, and to some extent succeeded. Lines were cut as if the length of the play were the issue when, in fact, the length had never been tested. And the meaning of the play had never been established. I can see now that his conscious or unconscious intention was different from mine. When I did catch on, I dug my heels in and wouldn't cut or change any more. It was only then that I began to grasp what the play meant and what he was doing. So the end result was something that was neither his nor mine and thus, I think, it didn't make a lot of sense at certain points, particularly in the third act.

Mike blocked the play so that his story was different from the story of the text. And his story, his blocking, was so clear that the text couldn't come through it. He needed to make cuts because certain scenes made his story impossible. The third act, because I wouldn't cut anymore, became a no-man's-land.

Can you be more specific about the differences between your views of the play?

Eddie is living in Hollywood—metaphorically, in this business-corrupt world. The representatives of that world, the people who are succeeding, are Artie and Mickey. Eddie thinks he wants to be part of that. Eddie thinks he would like to be Mickey. He'd like to be cool and smart and sophisticated and not have these feelings bothering him all the time. On the other hand, he has Phil because Phil makes him feel alive and offers him a feeling of passion and vitality.

The way the play works—and the way it seemed to work at Trinity Rep in Providence—is that Eddie betrays Phil because he takes Mickey's advice in the most simple way. Mickey is forever hot-shotting and making Eddie feel that the reasons he has Phil in his life are not the best. Eddie gets mixed up and sort of becomes Mickey briefly, attacking Phil in the second act. In other words, he's a guy who says, "Either I'm going to be Phil or I'm going to be Mickey." But in the end, he becomes himself. So the third act is the rejection of Mickey. The play is the story of a guy who is searching and dissatisfied and worried and vulnerable and crazy—all those things Mickey pretends don't exist. When it works right, the whole anagram business is there to provoke Mickey to reveal how fucking cold and cynical he is. When Eddie experiences that, he sees it for the first time. And he faces the fact that he has allowed himself to be taken in. There are no speeches in which the character says what I'm saying, but that's really what's going on.

When Eddie breaks down at the end.

Yes, through his exchange with this little girl who doesn't know what she's talking about either. She's just trying to get off the street. But inadvertently they arrive at a moment that both changes him and testifies to this change.

Mike made a play that put Eddie in the Mickey role. He cut everything about Phil that could make him interesting or complex or vulnerable and tried to turn him into a total creep—though with Harvey Keitel's performance he couldn't succeed. He tried to make the relationship between Eddie and Phil what Mickey says it is. Rather than appearing as a character's insidious maneuvering, Mickey's observations were made to be the ones with which the audience could identify. Now if the first two acts evolve that way, then by the third, you're not going to care about either Phil or Eddie.

And there were blocking things with the women throughout—how much of this was conscious on Mike's part, I have no idea. In the second act Bonnie arrives as a blind date for Phil. Mike blocked it so that as Eddie said, "It's a blind date," he was putting cocaine in her nose. In rehearsal I said, "No, that can't be because he looks like a pimp. That's not what this is." Then when Bonnie comes back and she's a mess, Eddie was blocked just to sit unmoving on the floor, as if he didn't hear her. He looked like the worst prick ever born. Up in Providence, in David Wheeler's production, Eddie tried to take care of Bonnie, gave her a towel. He's still saying the things he's saying, they still have the argument they have, but everything is changed. Eddie has at least a leg to stand on. At least there's a dialectic. Then they can have a dramatic scene. The other way, it's just an open-and-shut case. The dialogue becomes meaningless. I don't understand this directorial strategy except as a personal statement Mike wanted to make. It doesn't make any dramatic sense to take a complex character who has all these moral concerns and to block him in such a way that the audience is going to have no interest in him.

Once you're in rehearsal in the big time, there are pressures to which you'll fall victim—unless you can be impervious to them. To the extent that your concerns about success, career, reviews, your next play influence you, you're compromised. I think that goes for everybody in the business. As you rise into what is thought of as the top, you meet more and more talented people. But they're all compromised so that they're not functioning at their full power. You're compromised in ways you don't even know. You don't experience it as compromise unless you're really astute about yourself.

Once you get to Broadway, the forces that determine the success of a work have almost nothing to do with excellence.

Yes, and I don't ever know what to do about it. You can become very conscious of it, but they're forces, they're really there and they really affect you. And when the audience marches in, it too is affected by this force. It produces judgments that have no basis. It would be like marching in to your dentist's and saying, "I'm going to tell you what to do." The audience comes in and tells the people who spend their lives doing theatre, "No, we don't want that."

Do you feel that you've been better served in recent years by the regional theatres?

I feel I've been lucky in that I've written plays that have been done professionally and I'm able to make a living, either from the plays themselves or from other writing I've done, for movies, for which the pay was based partly on the reputation I have as a playwright. But I'm at a point now where I'm trying to figure out how best to live and work over the next twenty years, or however many I'll have. I'm trying to be realistic and evaluate what's happened over the years and how it really works, not how I would like it to work. I always used to feel that a good play would convert the people around to it, that the vision of the play would draw people in. But it's very difficult to make that happen in professional theatre. The pull is toward everyone's next job, the reviews, reputations. I'm not trying to put all of that down—they're all real and painful considerations.

I don't have a lot of experience with regional theatre, so working in Providence on *Hurlyburly* was new and very interesting. I worked with David Wheeler once before—he did the *Pavlo Hummel* with Al Pacino. He's very good and very open and he'll let you really work. He let me step in and say whatever I had to say. The production needed that extra nudge which I was able to give it, having struggled with the play for so long. In publishing it, I put whole scenes that had been cut from the New York production back in. Providence was my first chance to see one of them—one very important scene had never even been rehearsed in New York.

Walter Kerr described an infuriated audience in New Haven when* Streamers *was first done. What do you remember of that?

It's interesting when you're doing a play like that in New Haven and there are no reviews. It's not been stamped with any kind of approval. The audience just comes in. Mike Nichols directed it, so I don't know what they were expecting. *Streamers*—they could have expected a party. You get a very raw reaction because they don't have any preconceptions. The first reactions were sometimes quite extreme. Some of it had to do with us not yet having the production quite under control. Plus the Carlyle up there, Joe Fields, who didn't come to New York because it was felt that he was too old to be a recruit, is a primeval actor, a beautiful and powerful actor, and a wild-looking man. I really think they thought he was going to get them next.

One time a whole busload of people walked out. They probably just thought the bus was going to leave. I laugh about it now, but it was very hard to take. *Sticks and Bones* was not dissimilar. The actors in *Sticks and Bones* used to say they needed combat pay to go on stage, because the audience's emotions were so confused and hostile to some of what went on, particularly at the end of the play. When we got *Streamers* into New York, we got it more under control. But there were always people walking out, fainting. It's funny, because my reaction when such things happen is to get very upset, and yet I continue to try to stir the audience's emotions so that they have to confront what they are feeling.

Do you read reviews?

When I first started, I read everything. Now I skim or ask to be told. Reviewers don't have time or space to do anything very meaningful so I've stopped looking for that. Finally, it's only about good or bad business. Up in Providence, they had money to hire local writers, scholars, to write a little article about each of the plays. There was a pamphlet by three different people, not all theatre people, about aspects of the play. This kind of work is not being done in the newspapers.

If reviews are good, they're never quite good enough, because they're not complex enough. If they're bad, they're just discouraging. A lot of the reviews of *Hurlyburly* spotted things but they couldn't possibly interpret them correctly because they didn't know what was cut, they didn't know about the blocking. They tended to blame the play but there's nothing else they could have done.

Most of your plays have dark endings, with a situation and characters in worse shape than they were at the beginning. And yet, I don't get a sense of despair. Perhaps because you concentrate on social process, you seem to offer, if only by implication, the possibility of an alternative vision.

I do feel that people can alter themselves. The world may be falling apart, but whether it does or not, you're going to be separated from it, and therefore its fate ultimately is not your concern. Your own development, your own soul is your concern. I would never say that the world's *not* going to fall apart. But you can work on your life within it. Perhaps if enough people did that, it would change society. If you decide that you'll change only if the world changes, you're going to be in big trouble.

I really hadn't thought too much about what you were talking about. But I know you're right. It's like what I said about *Streamers*—when it didn't have the sergeants, it was just this ugly killing in a room, without the funny little growth and the ignorant development that Cokes has. He doesn't even know his friend's dead. But he has developed a touch of compassion for people and life, for himself and everybody. It's almost always by accident, I believe. In a funny way, it's fate. In other words, it doesn't matter. They're the same thing.

Like Phil's note.

Right. It's something I'm becoming more conscious of, exploring consciously.

In Eddie's transformation.

I see now that's the theme of the play. All these little accidents, until finally there's the accident of the girl coming in as Eddie's about to do God knows what to himself. In Providence I worked to make it clearer that he's got pills and he's liable to be dead if she doesn't come in. So there is a sense of alternative. But it's subjective. You have to be in the world you're in—the society, the family—and deal with it from there.

The earlier plays seem to be directed more at changing society.

But they really never were. In the introduction to the Viking edition I said that I didn't consider them antiwar plays because antiwar plays are conceived with the idea that they can affect the fate of a war. I don't think plays can do that. Even though the plays were part of a political movement, in them I was trying to express what I thought. I was saying: You can do what you want about the war. But don't lie about it. Don't pretend that it's good, or it becomes uglier than it is. Don't pretend it's heroic. Don't pretend that everybody who goes over there is a monster or a hero. Most of the kids didn't know anything about what was going on. Some of them loved it, some hated it. There was in those plays a social consciousness of some kind. But as I look back, I think the plays refuse to be as simple as the social necessities would dictate. I guess I don't think that David Mamet would be any bleaker in his view of social development than I am.

So your plays are focused more on that moment of individual realization.

I think so. That's what I see. Eddie gets it. Even Pavlo gets it, in a funny way. He's dead but...[laughs]. Both Pavlo and Chrissy in *Boom Boom Room* are people who go right up to it and then miss it, they go right by it because what it asks is too terrifying. But they do get up to it—Chrissy with her books and her charts. When she actually goes home and asks the question, she accepts her parents' lie.

What can you say about your use of language? In Hurlyburly *the characters use language to shield themselves from reality.*

I feel that in life and particularly in drama, language is something people use to create realities, to create truth and systems and inflict them on other people, or try to coerce others into agreeing with their reality or submitting to it. That's what happens in the world. It happens in our own minds, with the words we think. The words create reality, rather than reflecting it. We attach ourselves to a particular invention or way of thinking and conflict can develop with someone who has an opposing allegiance.

If you take the religions of the world and you break them down, you see that they have essentially the same beliefs. If you took the subjective experiences of people with different religions, they would occupy similar emotional terrain. But we name them differently. If I say God is Yahweh and you say God is Allah, we may in fact have the same inner view of that experience but we'll kill each other over which name to use. For me, the plays are language. There's really nothing else theatre can offer to compete with movies except a language which, in a peculiar way, can stimulate the mind. Language can be very evocative and rich and send people on journeys of the word. The traditional theatre has always been rich in language.

The period of realism is aberrant. If you look at it historically, you see it came into being as the world anticipated the motion picture. Naturalism. Belasco, marching elephants around the stage.

That was contemporary with the early years of photography.

It's all tied together. Philosophically, it reflected science and the invalidity of subjectivity, the idea that only the objective is valid. Then movies came along. Theatre can't compete visually. It's difficult to break out. It isn't just a matter of being extreme or anarchic. There must be a way of being visionary in the theatre.

In *Sticks and Bones* the fundamental conflict is about how to talk about experience. The family wants to use cliches. David wants to use poetry. The cliches are reductive and poetry is expansive. So there's an immediate conflict. I think that that runs through all the plays, some more than others. *Hurlyburly* was the most fun. I had no idea they were going to talk that way. The poetic use of jargon—the way they put it in the wrong place, or take it from one field and put it in another—just came and was very exciting. That's something used by Mamet, Shepard, in their different ways. For a different purpose, perhaps.

Is there a favorite among your plays?

I was going to say *Hurlyburly* but finally, in the last month, it's been realized for me. For a long time I thought it was *Goose and Tomtom*. I find the play that I like is the one that I think has not had a fair shot yet. After we did *Goose and Tomtom* at Lincoln Center in a little workshop, I saw that the play could work and how it could work. So I felt good about it and it ceased to be my favorite.

205

How do you see the American theatre today?

I think it's pretty desolate, really, but I'm going to continue working in it. I love the theatre. But the economics are such that it's very difficult for theatre to remain vital. A play has to be an unbelievable success, like A *Lie of the Mind* revving up all this machinery, people calling it the greatest play, Shepard the greatest writer. Or in my case, you have to have seven movie stars. Then there isn't any theatre, really. There are just these events. There are not enough plays on the boards for a real theatrical environment, for a play to be okay and run for a while. It's not just Broadway, it's everywhere.

Although theatres like the Public, the Manhattan Theatre Club and Second Stage are able to run some good plays as part of their seasons.

Those places always do interesting things, whether it's a new play or a Che-khov. *Coastal Disturbances* is a good play and it's getting nice responses but it's in a hundred-seat house. Maybe it'll move. Joe's theatres have at least three hundred seats. But the community still doesn't exist. Broadway's another world and it's so difficult to get there. Once you're there, you're into a realm of compromise, which is inevitable since there's that much money. I think, though, there are ways through it. Whether I'll succeed or not, I don't know. Maybe, after all of these experiences, I know whom to work with. These pressures are insidious. They affect your nervous system, not your thoughts or your ideals. It's in your body. It's a demand, like the wind.

What are you working on now?

I'm working on a novel, mainly, but I have half a play written and a lot of pages for some other plays. And a lot of notes for still others. I've worked on this novel on and off for a number of years and it's been haunting me, so I've decided to bear down and stay with it until I finish it. I'm not going to leave it until I get at least a first draft. Then I'll work on one of the plays.

WALLACE SHAWN

A t fifteen his hero was Dostoevsky, at seventeen, Henry Kissinger. In the span of those two years Wallace Shawn turned his back on literature, considering it too self-indulgent, and decided to become a diplomat, civil servant or politician. He studied history at Harvard and then spent a year in India teaching English. Enrolled in Oxford to study politics, philosophy and economics, one day in 1967 Shawn saw an announcement of a playwriting contest. He entered the contest and lost. But from that moment on, he knew what he wanted to do.

Shawn's first play to be produced was *Our Late Night* in 1975, followed by *A Thought in Three Parts* (1977), *Marie and Bruce* (1979), *The Hotel Play* (1981) and *Aunt Dan and Lemon* (1985). He also cowrote and starred in the Louis Malle film *My Dinner with Andre* (1981). More, perhaps, than any of his contemporaries, Shawn eschews conventional dramatic devices and techniques. His plays, described by the author as "intense, extreme, even maniacal," neither rely upon straightforward linear plots, nor develop character by gradually revealing inner truth. Instead, they juxtapose narrative description against short dramatic scenes, peopled by characters that resist psychological analysis. In a modification of Brechtian procedure, Shawn thereby provokes the spectator to a direct confrontation of the material presented. Although the confrontation is multifold, its essence is perhaps best conveyed by Shawn's description of an important realization in his life. Having been raised in a secure, liberal environment, he was shocked when he first went to summer camp. "The counselors were very tough and occasionally sadistic," he explains. "Once, when they were annoyed with a boy, they actually suggested that we beat him up! The whole world turned out to be like that camp. I still can't get over it, and writing, for me, is a way of trying to make sense of this world I'm surprised to find myself in."

Shawn's most fully realized and successful plays, *Marie and Bruce* and *Aunt Dan and Lemon*, explore man's seemingly boundless capacity for brutality. Both play psychosexual pathology off a variety of social crimes, ranging from the subtle squelching of one's humanity to American carpet bombing of the Vietnamese countryside. *Marie and Bruce*, while documenting a day in the sadomasochistic relationship between the title characters, is far more than psychological exploration. In its central section, set at a friend's party, Shawn runs the disintegration of their relationship against the all-too-familiar little murders committed in casual conversation. By so comparing different forms of cruelty, Shawn details both private and social neuroses, the complex patterns of desire and disgust, anger and acquiescence, impotence and self-hatred. His dramatic strategy relies on repetition rather than development. Characters do not change but constantly repeat themselves—like Marie in her abusive and savagely comic harangues—becoming more and more desperate as they proceed. What changes is the spectator's response, which passes from amusement to disgust to understanding—insofar as the enigma of human cruelty can be understood.

Aunt Dan and Lemon is more ambitious in relating private brutality to political crime. Most of the play is narrative, consisting of the stories of Lemon or her Aunt Dan, the idolized best friend of her parents. Shrewd, charismatic and hedonistic, Aunt Dan indoctrinates the eleven-year-old Lemon into the mysteries of her misanthropy, warning Lemon, for example, that she must always treat serving people humanely, not because they deserve it, but lest they rebel. Dan's most fanatical homily, however, is her defense of Henry Kissinger against the ineffectual criticism of Lemon's liberal mother. "The whole purpose of government is to use force. So we don't have to," Aunt Dan explains. "*Other* people use force, so we can sit here in this garden and be incredibly nice." In counterpoint against the political dispute Shawn runs a personal and sexual plot-line—Dan's recollections of Mindy, her permissive and murderous friend. At the end of the play Shawn brings all of the strands together. Lemon, who has long been fascinated with the Nazis, tells the audience that what distinguishes them from the countless other mass murderers is not their "killing human beings to create a certain way of life," but their candor. Then, in the play's most disturbing and confrontational gesture, she questions the very existence of compassion, assuring the spectators that she has never felt it, and begging them to express their gratitude toward those—the Nazis, by implication Kissinger and the current Cold Warriors— "willing to take the job of killing on their own backs."

More explicitly than any other play of recent years, *Aunt Dan and Lemon* exhumes and scrutinizes the assumptions on which the American political and economic system is based. It points out the behavioral and ideological threads that run from personal contempt to genocide, with the aim of confronting the audience with its complicity in the maintenance of a murderous status quo. To the dismay of some spectators, Shawn does not give any character in the play an effective rebuttal against the realpolitik of Dan and Lemon but rather impels the spectator to refute Lemon's argument—if he or she can—outside the theatre's walls.

■　　■　　■

DECEMBER 31, 1986—TCG OFFICES, NEW YORK CITY, THEN THE IBIZA
RESTAURANT NEXT DOOR

Can you talk about your early experiences in the theatre and, specifically, what drew you to playwriting?

Well, my experience is the same as everybody's. In other words, it's not very interesting. When I was in the fourth grade, I was in a play. People thought I was quite funny and so that was a good experience. In the fifth grade I had a teacher who encouraged me first of all to totally change my approach to life and secondly, to write a play and act in it. It was on the serious and philosophical side, on the tragic side. It was an enormous experience for me to write a play and be in it. People were quite moved by this play and looked at me in a different way. I don't think it would take Sigmund Freud to figure out that this was positive reinforcement, a pleasant, even wonderful experience, and I'm sure the rest of my life has been an attempt to crawl along behind that experience and repeat it. But this is psychological speculation which is of absolutely no interest or importance.

I wrote more plays in the seventh and eighth grades. My brother and I did certain things of a theatrical nature in the privacy of our own home. It's really rather pathetic when you think that as a child I imagined that there was a grown-up equivalent to these rather profound experiences that I had at school and at home in connection with theatre. The illusion was compounded by thrilling theatrical experiences. In the seventh grade I saw *The*

Iceman Cometh with Jason Robards, Jose Quintero's production at Circle in the Square. The next year I saw *The Chairs* and *The Lesson* of Ionesco at the Theatre de Lys. The next year, I believe, I saw *Endgame* at the Cherry Lane and Ionesco's *Bald Soprano* and *Jack* with Salome Jens. In the eighth grade I saw *Long Day's Journey into Night* twice. So I had these incredible expectations of a real theatre, a professional theatre that would be of enormous importance somehow. It's really pathetic when you think of that because that just isn't true.

When did you first have a play done professionally?

The first rehearsal of the play was in September of 1972. The first performance of the play in a workshop version was in the spring of '74. But then it was not performed in its final version until January of '75. I'd be very surprised if you were able to turn up a longer rehearsal period in the history of theatre. The play was called *Our Late Night*. It was done by Andre Gregory's company, the Manhattan Project.

Looking back at your work of the seventies, are you conscious of any major influences? You've mentioned a number of plays you saw.

It's embarrassing to admit but I am not really what you would call a theatre buff. I'm humiliated when I visit the homes of other playwrights and I see the thousands of plays that are on their bookshelves and their incredible knowledge of theatre. I have generally found some of the other arts more of an inspiration. As I said, I was overwhelmingly inspired by those productions that I saw between the ages of twelve and fourteen. And then, occasionally, I had some big experiences in reading plays. For example, I was quite blown away by reading Racine and Molière at a time when, for some reason, I thought that I knew French.

I was a school teacher at one time and spent a year in which I did almost nothing but prepare a production of *The Tempest* with students from the ages of, say, ten to thirteen. That was a big experience of immersion in a script. Ibsen is someone I have loved. But I think that plays are generally quite hard to read and it would be humiliating to admit the number of masterpieces of theatre that I've never seen or read. If you define inspiration as a feeling of encountering some work of art and then thinking, "Oh my God, I would like to create something exactly like this," or even, "This puts me in the mood to go and try to do something," then I would have to say that it didn't happen to me so much in relation to theatre. Much more, for instance, in relation to looking at painting. There was a period, around the time of *Our Late Night*, when I used to see the New York City Ballet a lot. That was very inspiring to me. Opera and other music is inspiring to me.

What about Brecht?

I wish I could claim to have been an unbelievable expert on Brecht but even now I wouldn't describe myself as one. I did play the violin in England in a student production of *Mahagonny*, which was a thrilling experience.

I'm interested to hear you talk about the impact of painting and dance because I've noticed that your plays don't really make use of dramatic development in the traditional sense. You use blocks of text, short scenes, juxtaposing these different elements. And it seems that your plays depend less on a dialectical development to a climax than the presentation—or gradual revelation—of a consciousness, or a psyche, or a psychosis almost, not just in the psychological sense, but in the social sense as well.

Mmm, mm.

Almost the way a painter would use blocks of color or forms in a still life, say.

It's laughable, in a way, that someone who has no sense of character or plot would become a playwright. It's possible that this happened only because I went to such encouraging, friendly schools and generally had a very supportive—or overly supportive—childhood background. I came to believe, like many other people from my class, that a person could do anything he wanted to do in life. When I meet people from different backgrounds and they describe their childhoods, often there will be an episode in which, for example, the child does a drawing and shows it to a teacher and the teacher says, "Well, dear, you don't have much talent for drawing," or "That isn't the way that a person's arm is connected to his body. You'd better do that over again." Or the child shows a poem to the English teacher and the English teacher says, "You obviously have a problem writing poetry." It never occurred to me that I needed to have certain qualifications in order to write plays. It never crossed my mind. No one ever said, "You have certain talents but you should avoid this field because you lack a sense of drama and that's what theatre is all about," or "You don't know what a character is or what plot is and you never will know. And that's the motor of theatre."

I thought, when I was a child, that you could do anything in theatre. My brother and I sometimes presented fairy tales that had stories of a more conventional kind but then—and these were all operas, they had music as well—I remember we did one on the subject of dynastic decline in China.

211

It had a story of some kind but it was really an exploration of this theme. On another occasion we did something about Wittgenstein which had a little bit of a plot but also had these philosophical passages drawn from his writings— this was when we were a little older, you understand.

I've always had to invent some kind of form for my plays that will take the place of the form that plays usually have. I know for a fact that the only reason one watches something for more than fifteen or twenty minutes is because it has a plot and you're curious to know what happens next. But having no talent for the regular type of plot development, I have had to struggle to invent an equivalent that would be equally gripping. Maybe that is why I've found inspiration in these odd places. When I've seen a painting that has overwhelmed me, I've thought, "Oh my God, maybe there's some- thing in this that will give me a clue to how to organize my plays."

Marie and Bruce *seems almost Cubist in the way it offers different perspec- tives. It's not the unfolding of a plot, of an action, that holds our interest but the gradual revelation of an extremely complex situation whose implications change.*

When I was in England from '66 to '68, I saw some wonderful productions, including Olivier's *Three Sisters*, which was incredibly beautiful. When I came back to America, the two productions that meant the most to me, in totally different ways, were Albee's *All Over*, which I saw twice during its extremely short run, and the Manhattan Project's production of *Alice in Won- derland*.

Did you have any formal training in theatre?

I studied acting at the HB Studio for a year in 1970, because it was sort of a cliche that a playwright should know about acting. But in school I didn't study English or theatre. I had no intention of going into this line. The whole joke is quite possibly on me. I mean, if I'm a bad writer, everything falls into place. The whole story makes a lot of sense, without any paradoxes, if it is all a mistake. But that can't be totally determined yet and it's not my problem to worry about it—well, I do sometimes worry about it. If it were a certainty that my writing just fulfilled some purely private fantasy, if it were a known, provable fact that it had no value, then I would worry because I don't believe that that would be a proper way to channel all of the money that has been poured into my upbringing and education.

When you write a play what do you start with? *Say, with* **Aunt Dan and Lemon.**

That kind of question treads on my private process, which is too delicate for me to invite other people in on. It's not as if I were Thomas Mann, who just sat down at the typewriter every day and tossed off these great works. I'm sure that he could have told you all about his life as a writer and it wouldn't have prevented him from doing exactly the same thing the next day. In the course of my life, I've occasionally had a good idea for something that I could write. It's happened a limited number of times and by describing the process publicly I would think it might diminish the chance that I would ever be able to do it again.

When Aunt Dan and Lemon *first went into rehearsal in London, was it complete?*

It was a little more than complete because the director had suggested that I add certain things to what I originally gave him. The things that I added were not too good so almost all of them were gone by the time the play opened.

Do you normally work closely with a director?

For all of the plays that I've had done in New York, I've been at the rehearsals. I've missed very few, for better or worse. I don't say that that's a good idea. It's just a historical fact.

Do you provide much input as a production takes shape?

My feeling is that the production takes the shape that the director gives it. That's determined by the director's own taste. The actors will respond with great sensitivity not just to what he says or even to what he thinks he wants, but to what his taste actually is, inside. So it isn't possible for the writer or anyone else to have a big influence on the production—though there are certain specific decisions that a writer can fight. But if what the audience sees is a painting, basically painted by the director, it's a little bit absurd for the writer to try to influence small parts of the design. He may mar the effect that the director would otherwise be able to achieve. It's by far the best policy, really, to trust the director. But it's impossible to do that if you're sitting there and the director is doing something that violates your most profound beliefs about the play. And also, actors, and even directors, must be free to experiment and try things out.

The nervousness of the author who sits in the room and sees something that seems to him to be going in the wrong direction is not usually a positive contribution. On the other hand, if the writer doesn't attend the rehearsals, he may be totally shocked at what has been made of his play. And of course the audience only has one experience. They will go to their grave believing that that was the way the author intended it. So it's a difficult dilemma.

213

There's a tremendous temptation to go to the rehearsals because you're thrilled at the wonderful opportunity of seeing the actors do your material. You don't want to miss a single minute of it. I've been very fortunate in having wonderful actors do my plays, and wonderful directors.

Is there any production of yours that you're particularly pleased with?

Well, that wouldn't be fair to say. Most of the productions of my work that I've seen have contained some things that have given me enormous pleasure.

What then is it about these productions that you've liked? What qualities are particularly important for you?

A production never has anything to do with what you picture when you're writing the play. It's just as if a person meets someone and says, "Why don't we get together this evening?" They each have some picture of what might happen in the course of the evening. But then if those two people actually end up making love that evening, the experience would be in a different category from any earlier two-dimensional imagining. Similarly, as a playwright you have a picture in your head, but it would be impossible for any production to have much to do with that picture. It seems to me that if you like theatre, you like the fact that actors bring something unique and unexpected to a script. The thrilling experience for the writer is that they do something that you never could have imagined.

Now obviously, in your mind, the play is interesting. You have the fantasy that people watching it, including yourself, will be gripped and fascinated. If the play is performed and people are unbelievably bored and restless, and you yourself are unable to keep your attention on it, then one of your most important expectations is unfulfilled. So it's gratifying if you have prepared the recipe and then, when someone follows it, the result is something delicious, rather than garbage. If it is garbage then there's a desperate debate. Human psychology being what it is, it's likely that the director will say, "This recipe, if correctly followed, creates poison," and the writer will reply, "No, it's only because you haven't followed it faithfully enough that the result is bad."

Did you do much rewriting of **Aunt Dan and Lemon** *during rehearsals?*

Unfortunately I'm not very good at that. First of all, I'm very, very vain and stubborn and believe that what I've done the first time around is perfect and that I've thought of every possible change that could be made and rejected it for very good reasons. So I'm reluctant even to try to change anything and I put up a big fight because I always feel that great acting and great directing will make the things work. I'm very, very, very difficult to deal with in that way—it's not fun for the director. What's even worse is that I literally don't have the talent to write quickly or to fulfill a particular purpose that comes up in rehearsal. It may be absolutely clear that if only there were a line at a certain point that expressed vaguely a certain thought, it would clarify the play enormously. I am very, very bad at coming up with such things because when I'm actually writing the play, each line serves much more than one purpose and is usually written before I have any sense that it has a purpose.

Usually, things have come originally from my unconscious mind and then when I've worked on the play, I have perhaps seen that a line I've written has a purpose. But if I think about it from that point of view, it has not just one purpose but five and they're all interwoven in a certain way. By the time the director sees the play, I've been working for months on it in its later stages, so that each element has been integrated with the others. For many months, I might not have added anything new. I would just have been stirring up the potful of things that are already there. So if I suddenly leap in and write one line that's supposed to serve only one purpose, I usually write a line that is so crude and bad and superficial it stands out. The whole audience would imagine that the original writer has died and some terrible hack has been brought in to throw in this line.

I have had a few good moments when I've been able to toss in a few good things. Although I'm stubborn, there does come a time when I might see that this moment does not work, at least not in this production. By which I mean that it is totally boring, that it conveys nothing to the audience. There's no point in making hundreds of people sit still and watch something that means nothing. Then you feel, "This section must be removed from the play or changed. Even if I write some third-rate garbage."

I was interested in the controversy surrounding **Aunt Dan and Lemon.** *More than any other play I've seen in the past six years, it described for me the experience of Reagan's America—fascism with a smile. I was amazed by how squarely the play addresses that. And I was further amazed that some of the more progressive critics—like Joel Schechter—gave the play such a damning review. For me, it wasn't difficult to process because I'm used to a kind of confrontational theatre which forces an audience to deal directly with a problem. It makes the audience respond. I understand that some audience members did stand up and talk to Lemon during her last speech. Did that happen often?*

I suppose compared with other plays, there were more vocal responses from the audience. When I was acting in it, there was certainly a feeling that at any moment someone might speak out during the last speech. But for better or worse, I don't think there was much real controversy.

The fact that certain people totally misunderstood the play is not the same thing as a controversy. There were members of the audience who had no idea what was going on, who made no sense of the totality of the play and simply saw a meaningless series of unrelated episodes, the final one being a speech in praise of Hitler. Those people were left thinking they'd seen a kind of vaudeville show, and they were very upset, not exactly by the play, but by that final speech. These people, for the most part, were not very sophisticated—they had not had too much experience with far-out art forms in which there is a peculiar device such as a narrator who is not to be trusted and doesn't speak for the writer or the producer. Even though I'm joking about it today, with the distance of time, in fact it was a painful and awful experience. Some of the people who didn't understand the play went through a lot of real suffering. Some people who saw it had been personally victimized by Hitler or had family members killed by Hitler and genuinely believed that they were sitting in a theatre and hearing the return of Hitler. So that was quite shattering.

Then there were a couple of extremely sophisticated people who didn't get it. Even Robert Brustein, for some reason, didn't get the main drift of the play. Brustein felt it was, in some way, an attempt to torture or provoke liberals, and Schechter more or less took the whole thing absolutely straight, without quite seeing that you weren't supposed to take it straight. He thought it was a right-wing play, although I don't really see how you could think about it for too long and come to that conclusion. What would be the point of it then? A playwright who wanted to defend Reaganism wouldn't in a million years go about it that way. It just doesn't make sense. I speak with such arrogance about this only because there were so many people who did understand it. So I feel that Brustein and Schechter somehow missed the boat.

I've written some things that very few people have seen the way that I thought they would be seen. You begin to feel a bit foolish saying, "Well, three hundred people saw this and they all misunderstood it." Then you have to realize that you might not have made it clear. But in this case, if the play isn't an extreme questioning of right-wing views and of America and of ourselves, I don't know what it could possibly be. It doesn't make sense in any other way.

It deprives the spectator of a safe, detached liberal perspective and makes him deal directly with incredibly loaded material, without someone editorializing on the sidelines. That's where the power of the play comes from. So there must be the risk of misinterpretation.

I suppose if I thought about it, I would have guessed that a certain percentage of the people would not know where I, the writer, was coming from. During the play the audience is not told where the writer stands or what they're supposed to think. And anybody who actually thinks about the questions raised in the play is going to get upset, with the exception of a handful of right-wing people who simply accept the fact that we want to be on top and we don't mind doing whatever needs to be done to stay on top. And a handful of people on the left who sincerely believe that they know exactly what must be done to change the way the world works and who sincerely believe that they are already—except for the two hours spent in the play—devoting all of their time and effort to making those necessary changes. But most people on the left are not so sure that they've figured out the perfect formula for change or that they are living in the most appropriate and morally justifiable way.

Most of the reviews looked almost exclusively at the framing story, not the Mindy episodes. I thought of the Mindy scenes as the center of the play. The setting had a lot to do with that—the dark interior, the space for personal, sexual relations. Did you structure the play to examine the interrelation between public and private life?

One of the disturbing points raised in the play is the fact that Aunt Dan, who has these brutal views, is attractive and charismatic. She has an appetite for life and is, to a great extent, free of guilt. Her tough-minded attitude makes her in many ways more attractive than the guilt-ridden liberal. There's something about Lemon's suburban English world that is sexually inert and lifeless. The stories of a lively and sexy and glamorous life in London exert a great charm over her. To me it seems very natural that the same woman who admires Kissinger's skill as a high-stakes player in the international sphere would also admire Mindy, who skillfully swindles the drunken tourist out of sixty thousand pounds through the use of her wits. And Aunt Dan is a sexually lively woman. This is part of her appeal in contrast to the drab parents.

The play frankly raises the question, "Do right-wing people have more fun? Are they frank about themselves in a way that is not true of liberals?" It's an issue that we should think about. Why does Aunt Dan have so much vitality? Why are such people charming and attractive when the liberals seem somehow pitiful? Why is it that Lemon despises her mother and idolizes Aunt Dan? We may think she's made the wrong choice but it happens to be the choice that an awful lot of people have made. In the election that preceded the writing of this play, why were so many people attracted to Reagan, finding Carter weak? In '84—I was already pretty well finished with the play by that time—a lot of people said of Mondale, "He's so weak." This is something to worry about.

I was interested that you chose to make the two protagonists female. Aunt Dan watches the exercise of power from afar. She's not directly involved in wielding political power. Hers is a different kind of power, a curious and disturbing ability to nurture. Being female distances her from world politics. She observes it with a certain dispassion.

The play suggests, fairly or unfairly, the vicarious enjoyment we get out of violence committed by world leaders. It is about people reading about the exercise of power, rather than being personally involved. Although, of course, as citizens of a democracy, we actually do wield power, whether we're aware of it or not.

But the play does show Dan as an actor in the psychosexual drama, in the manipulation of power there.

Yes, it does. A passage that was cut from the New York production largely because of length, but which is in the printed text, shows Dan being involved in another love affair. She describes it to Lemon. It shows Aunt Dan herself involved in a little bit of trickery and manipulation and lying. As for why the two characters are women, you might just as well ask, why was Hamlet a prince rather than an ice-cream salesman? It's just the way it came to me originally. It wasn't that they were men and I made a choice to turn them into women or that they were neuter and I made a choice to make them women. They were women.

Do you read the critics?

I always have. I grew up in New York and read the *New York Times* from an early age—that's a part of the normal world to me. I used to be so, well, thrilled with the experience of having one of my plays put on that I didn't want to miss any moment of that. It would be inconceivable to be written about in the newspaper and not read it.

How seriously do you take them?

I've read one or two things about myself that were reasonably devastating, that made me more deeply aware of the possibility that my life is a hollow mockery of some kind, that I'm an idiotic person, totally self-deluded. In the particular case of *Aunt Dan and Lemon*, I feel I've benefited enormously from the critics. I don't just mean that I got a good break from them, which I certainly did for the most part, but also that they genuinely performed a leadership role and helped audiences to understand the play, sent them into the theatre in the right frame of mind. But if I were going to pick twelve people to be my mentors, I don't think these would be the ones I would come up with.

With my previous plays, it was heartwarming and encouraging each time I got one or two good reviews, even one or two that showed real understanding. For the most part, before *Aunt Dan and Lemon*, most of my reviews were negative—in some cases, hate-filled diatribes. I got a few of those for *Aunt Dan and Lemon* as well.

I think the truth is that most people misunderstand what you do. I think it would be quite shocking if each member of the audience wrote a few hundred words about your play. I don't think that the average critic is necessarily farther off the mark than the average audience member.

Reviews come out all at once so it can be a shattering experience if you feel that you've poured the best of yourself into something and twelve people in a row, in print, with thousands of copies out on the street, say, "No, your life is meaningless. What you have done is bad." It's humiliating because your friends and relatives read it and, of course, there's also the fact that if the reviews are bad, the play will close and not many people will see it. There have been a number of critics over the years who seem to have an almost personal loathing of me and that can be upsetting. In general, I try to look at the critics as ten or fifteen people who, for one reason or another, have been hired for this job and who, instead of giving their opinion to the person sitting next to them, write it down and it's printed. That's all it is, really. Some of the people you respect to some degree; some, perhaps, you don't respect at all. There have been a few people in my life whom I have really idolized and, on a couple of occasions, I've had to withstand the shock of learning that they didn't respect my writing. That is much worse than reading a review by someone who doesn't happen to respect you.

Many of the playwrights I've spoken to have commented on the sorry condition of the theatre. How do you see the state of the American theatre?

You might ask, "What is the state of bingo in America today?" I would say, "Well, it's fine. It is what it is. Certain people spend one or two nights a week playing bingo in some gathering place and they enjoy it and that's all there is to say about it. It doesn't hurt anybody and it's not harmful to the world and if something happened and bingo became illegal and no one could play it anymore, that would be a shame for those people but it wouldn't be very important." You might ask, "What is the role of striped shirts in America today?" I would say, "Some people wear them. They enjoy them. It really doesn't matter very much whether striped shirts are manufactured or not. People wouldn't be exposed to the elements if suddenly there were no more striped shirts, they would wear something else."

America is the most powerful country in the world. The ruling class of America is the most powerful group of people in the world. There are different entertainments available for the ruling class. The more sophisticated members of the class these days tend to go in for something like skiing or luxuriously prepared food. An older, less sophisticated and less wealthy segment of the ruling class would go in for theatre. Theatre is not one of the most brilliant and scintillating forms of diversion available. There's a quality of glamour and excitement in connection with new restaurants, very occasionally with a new film, sometimes with the art scene, maybe occasionally with dance or performance art. Lively young people are attracted to those forms. Most people who go to theatre formed a habit of theatregoing in their youth. Or they are people for whom the newer forms of diversion are just too far-out, too sexy, too fast-moving. Theatre is slow, it is unsexy, it's quiet.

I have a sympathy with the members of the ruling class because I am a member of that class myself and I know that these people suffer and are sad and miserable and deserve entertainment like anyone else. I suppose that they have a desire to be soothed and diverted. Now I never particularly wanted to fulfill that role. My personal ambitions were always much greater than that.

I believe that in order for the world to change, there must be people who devote themselves to assessing the situation that we're in, to thinking and to writing. The world can never change unless there are people who are trying to understand it and express their understanding. You might think that our theatre could be a place in which both that type of analysis and a dialogue about the way the world is run are attempted. It could be part of a thinking process going on in our society. In London I have often felt that theatre was an important way in which members of society communicated with each other about the way things were going, and about very specific issues such as the problem of Northern Ireland or of corruption in the London police department. Very intelligent people write plays on those subjects and people go to see them. Discussion is furthered about these issues and what might be done about them.

But here, quite honestly, I think it would be ludicrous to think that the theatre has that kind of role because most people interested in the way the world is going don't go to theatre. They wouldn't think of it. Most of the people who go to the theatre are simply looking for a certain kind of soothing experience that will take their mind off their troubles. So if that's why a person has come to the theatre, I feel like an idiot grabbing him by the throat and trying to get him to worry about the things that are bothering me. My style as a human being is to indulge people who need to escape. Yet I insist on confronting them as a playwright. It's quite embarrassing, it's quite unpleasant, it's quite awkward.

There are occasionally in New York theatrical events that are incredibly intelligent and thought-provoking. It's just that there aren't enough of them to create an audience that regularly goes to theatre hoping to find such things. A really intelligent play has to run for a very long period before it begins to attract the people who would be most interested in it.

Of course there's a category of entertainment that people call "disturbing" or "thought-provoking." They don't literally mean that a person would be disturbed in the sense that he would think, "My God, there is a problem with the life I'm living." They don't literally mean that someone would actually think, "My God, things are wrong. Things are bad, they should be changed." They mean you'll have the experience of saying, "Oh, dearie me." Just another form of entertainment.

Quite frankly, I feel that my life would be better spent if I were an entertainer or a clown. But it isn't my dream to be the guy who sings in the beer hall to entertain the Nazi generals. There are other groups that need entertainment more. There's a question as to whether the people in power should be entertained because it's really more important that they examine how they're using their power. If a retired dentist comes to see a play, I don't begrudge him his moment of diversion, but in general I think that the class to which I belong should have their attention focused on reality.

So you think theatre can be an effective political tool?

Theatre could have a political function in a very indirect way. It could have an artistic function that, I think, has political importance in that good works of art sharpen the awareness. That's part of what turns people into honest and sensitive observers of the world rather than complete fools. All we are, really, is the sum of the things that have influenced us: our friends and family and people we've known and books we've read and experiences—including artistic experiences—that we've had. Theoretically, a play can influence people for the better just by sharpening their sensibilities.

I've had a frustrating time in theatre in America because I feel that most of the people sitting in the theatres are not really getting much out of the plays that I've written. But obviously, even on a night when most people have been totally alienated from the play, there may have been one or two in the audience who derived great value from it. Maybe that justifies the whole thing, in some way.

There are low artistic standards in theatre, in my humble opinion. That alienates a lot of potential audience members who have high standards. Everybody knows that a bad evening at the theatre is much worse than a bad evening at the movies or in any other art form because there's the embarrassment of sharing the horrible experience with the live actors. There are an awful lot of people whom I admire who not only don't have the habit of going to theatre but whom it would be almost impossible to convince to go, because the experiences they have had have been so embarrassing and awful. I do think there's an unbelievable amount of wonderful acting talent—that's where I think New York is very strong.

Do you have a favorite among your plays?

Aunt Dan and Lemon is the one I'm proudest of. But I have an affection for many that have never been done and probably never will be done.

What are your plans for the future?

I've had the good fortune to be able to think of a few good ideas. If I were to have another good idea someday, then maybe I would be able to write another play. But I don't think of myself as a...obviously the fact that I'm talking to you is an indication that my feelings are hurt when there is a list of American playwrights and I'm not on it. On the other hand, I actually don't quite accept the label *playwright*, because I don't actually follow...I'm not someone who....I think the analogy for playwright is *wheelwright*. The basic idea is that you sit at your lathe and turn these things out one after another. I don't do that. I find it wonderful to be able to write anything. And I would be pleased to write more, pleased if it were to turn out in the form of a play. I know my way around theatre a little bit so there's always a feeling that it would be a shame just to throw that away and try to start again in a totally different form. But honestly, I'd be delighted if I ever wrote anything in any form. One has absolutely no choice about those things—at least I don't. I'll do whatever I'm able to do.

STEPHEN
SONDHEIM

S tephen Sondheim was a precocious child, picking out tunes on the piano
at age four, reading through the *New York Times* in first grade. When he
was ten he moved with his mother to Pennsylvania and quickly became a
protégé of a family friend, Oscar Hammerstein, just as the lyricist was preparing *Oklahoma!* for Broadway. At fifteen, Sondheim wrote his first show,
By George, which he brought to Hammerstein for criticism. "He taught me
how to structure a song like a one-act play," Sondheim recalls, "how to
introduce character, how to make songs relate to character, how to tell a
story." Unsure whether to pursue music or mathematics, he went to Williams
College, decided on music and upon graduation in 1950 continued his studies
in New York with composer Milton Babbitt. "What I learned from Milton,"
Sondheim explains, was "basic"—albeit "sophisticated"—grammar. "It was a
language, whereas what I learned from Oscar was what to do with language."
After a short stint in Hollywood as coscriptwriter of the comedy series *Topper*,
Sondheim returned to New York in 1953 and began work on his first com-
mercial show, *Saturday Night*, only to have it collapse with the death of its

producer, Lemuel Ayers. A few years later he was hired to write lyrics for *West Side Story*, followed, in 1959, by *Gypsy*. Finally, in 1962, the first musical for which he wrote both music and lyrics opened. *A Funny Thing Happened on the Way to the Forum* has been followed by ten musicals in which Sondheim has almost single-handedly transformed the Broadway musical into an incisive, intellectually sophisticated and at times disturbing dramatic form: *Anyone Can Whistle* (1964); *Company* (1970), directed by Harold Prince, his longtime collaborator; *Follies* (1971); *A Little Night Music* (1973); *The Frogs* (1974); *Pacific Overtures* (1976); *Sweeney Todd* (1979); *Merrily We Roll Along* (1981); the Pulitzer Prize-winning *Sunday in the Park with George* (1984) and *Into the Woods* (1987).

Unlike the songs of most Broadway tunesmiths, which dramatize an unambiguous dramatic moment or psychological state, Sondheim's are filled with tension, both dramatic and harmonic. As acknowledged, they are each structured like a one-act play, each with its own turning point: a moment of recognition, decision or psychological exposure. Sondheim is acutely aware of the complexities of character ("I like neurotic people," he has said) and he keeps a separate folder for each song with detailed notes on character psychology, background, dress. Although he writes using what he describes as a "free-association process," he remains extremely attentive to rhythmic structure (which usually comes to him first) and musical atmosphere as well as lyric rhyme and alliteration schemes. He always works from the specific dramatic situation, staging each song in his head as he's writing it, knowing that it must carry the dramatic action forward.

In twenty-five years Sondheim has collaborated with librettists and directors with widely varied interests and styles, and has based his work on divergent sources ranging from Plautus, the brothers Grimm and Ingmar Bergman to Kabuki and Grand Guignol. Despite this diversity, Sondheim's work remains obsessed with mutability and the passage of time, his stage peopled by doubles, either those with multiple perspectives on an event (*Company, Pacific Overtures*) or a single character at different points in his or her life (*Follies, Pacific Overtures, Merrily*). In his musicals the pivotal moments are almost always characters' confrontations of the past, of choices made and not made, of a present that just manages to elude their control. Sondheim dramatizes this inner conflict not just lyrically but by creating a complex musical structure based on the tension between a rhythmically regular but usually highly chromatic accompaniment and a heavily syncopated or irregular melody built on an uncommon intervallic pattern.

Follies, with a book by James Goldman, is Sondheim's most intricately ironic piece, offering an analysis of self-destructive personalities and relationships, using the vernacular of musical comedy to critique its conventions and form. *Follies* is about estrangement—from the past, from one's desires, from the results of one's choices—dramatized by using two levels of action and two sets of protagonists, the men and women assembled for the Follies reunion and their younger selves. When the older group recalls the past, it is there before them, both what they would like to relive and what they would forget. To dramatize the characters' pain and their deep sense of loss, Sondheim has written two kinds of songs: straight book songs that further the plot, and pastiche, purely presentational Follies numbers. While the book songs present the deeply conflicted emotions and situations of the characters directly, the pastiche numbers work in counterpoint against the plot, concretizing the romantic dreams of the protagonists and subtly and powerfully transforming the language of Gershwin, Porter, Kern and others. They capitalize on the audience's archetypal responses to vaudeville and old musical comedy and at the same time, by mobilizing unexpected dissonances in both harmony and character, they unmask the formal and ideological bases for these popular entertainments.

In his more recent work Sondheim has become interested in bringing to Broadway the complexity of opera without abandoning the musical comedy form, which mixes spoken dialogue and songs. In developing this strategy, Sondheim continues in the tradition he inherited from Hammerstein, using all the devices that have made musical comedy the quintessentially American theatrical form: great melodies, elaborate song and dance, snappy comic dialogue and happy endings. Simultaneously, he uses these devices to comment on the tradition, and in doing so, he holds a mirror up to American culture. "Who's That Woman" from *Follies* is an extraordinary example, central not just to that show but to his entire body of work. In Michael Bennett's staging, the young, beautiful and innocent chorus girls of the past sing and dance upstage while below them, their older, disillusioned selves reflect upon their lives:

> Who's that woman?
> I mean I've seen that woman
> Who's joking but choking
> Back tears.
> All those glittering years
> She thought that
> Love was a matter of "Hi there,"
> "Kiss me!" "Bye there."
> Who's that woman,
> That cheery, weary woman
> Who's dressing for yet one

More spree?
The vision's getting blurred,
Isn't that absurd?
Lord, Lord, Lord!
That woman is me!

■　　■　　■

FEBRUARY 17, 1987—STEPHEN SONDHEIM'S TOWNHOUSE, NEW YORK CITY

What interested you in writing for the stage?

I got into the theatre because of Oscar Hammerstein, who was a surrogate father for me during my teens. I had taken piano lessons and I had some interest in music. I started writing shows when I was in prep school and then continued under his tutelage over a period of years, through college, until he died. I've often said that if he had been a geologist, I probably would have become a geologist.

What shows had a great impact on you?

Hammerstein took me out of prep school on my birthday to go to the tryout of *Carousel* in New Haven. But what most influenced me was the period when I was his gofer, assistant, typist, et cetera, on *Allegro*, the third Rodgers and Hammerstein show. That was the summer preceding my second year in college. And I was an apprentice at Westport County Playhouse the summer after I graduated. I learned how the professional theatre works from *Allegro*, and I got some hands-on stage-managing experience at Westport.

During that period, what writers influenced your work?

I suppose I was influenced by Rodgers simply because I was influenced by Hammerstein. Obviously, the bug got me and I started to enjoy theatre. I listened to lots of songs from the preceding era and was writing a lot.

What were your early pieces like? I know Saturday Night *was one of the first.*

Saturday Night was the first "professional" show. That came about by chance. I was an usher at a wedding and one of the other ushers was the producer and set designer Lemuel Ayers, who had optioned an unproduced play called *Front Porch in Flatbush* and had tried to get Frank Loesser to do the score. Loesser had turned him down so he was looking for somebody else and I was recommended to him by the groom. Ayers commissioned me to write three songs on spec. I did and he liked them. That was my first professional experience as a theatre writer.

By that time I had gone through this—what shall I call it?—syllabus that Oscar had outlined for me of writing four shows: the first, based on a well-formed play; the second, based on a not-so-well-formed play; the third, based on a nondramatic work; and the fourth, an original. I had also written two shows in college. So by the time *Saturday Night* rolled around, I had done my apprentice work, though I was only twenty-three. It's pretty naive but it's a professional score.

Were there any themes or ideas that reappear in your later work?

None at all. I just picked plays I liked. The first one, what I considered a well-formed play, was *Beggar on Horseback*, which we actually did in college. We had permission from George Kaufman and Marc Connelly, its authors. The second was *High Tor*, my choice for a not-well-formed play, which I couldn't get permission for. The third was *Mary Poppins*, which I never completed, and then came the original.

With the older generation of songwriters—the Gershwins, Cole Porter, Rodgers and Hart, Rodgers and Hammerstein—the song was often an externalization of an inner state.

Yes, if you take it that seriously, but I don't think those writers were thinking of them that way. They were just writing songs for the most part—*Porgy and Bess* is an exception. Rodgers and Hammerstein, though, don't belong on that list. They were really trying to write, naive as it may seem now, songs as an extension of character and situation—which Oscar had been doing since *Showboat*, really. The others were just writing songs to go between jokes. The songs could be moved from show to show because they weren't too specific. All that nonsense about *Pal Joey* being a thoroughly integrated show—they weren't interested in that.

It was a shock to me when I was writing *Forum*, when Burt Shevelove said to me, "You know, this is the old way of writing songs, the way that Cole Porter and others wrote them. You take a moment and you savor it." It hadn't occurred to me before to do that. Essentially, *Forum* was a reversion to pre-Rodgers and Hammerstein principles of American songwriting. The plot was complicated and much more well formed than those of the earlier shows, but nevertheless the songs were respites, the way they were in Plautus' time and in musicals of the twenties and thirties.

So was Anyone Can Whistle *the first show where you tried to use the songs in a different way?*

Well, no, *Forum* does that too. *Whistle* was an attempt to use the vernacular of the musical theatre in an ironic way, as commentary. But it's used only for one character, the mayoress, to show her venality, single-mindedness, greed. I used the language of the musical theatre, essentially empty of content but full of invention and delight, to contrast with the book characters, the main characters with whom my sympathies lay. I treated her in that brash, show-business way, and gave her a glittery shallowness. I used pastiche methods to make her a cartoon character. The rest of it is straightforward book/song-writing.

Is there any one piece you consider a watershed?

Forum was an experimental show—something most people don't recognize. A one-set, one-costume show hadn't been done, at least in my lifetime. *West Side Story* attempted an integration of song and dance and dialogue to make a kind of cinematic seamlessness. *Gypsy* was traditional. I can't say *Whistle* was a watershed, but it certainly was my first attempt to use musical-comedy vernacular to make a comment or a point.

What about Kurt Weill and Bertolt Brecht?

They distorted popular forms to make their point—they didn't write the vernacular so much as interpret it. I don't like Brecht. At that time my exposure to him was minimal. When *Threepenny Opera* succeeded Off Broadway, a producer asked me to do a translation of *Mahagonny*. I read it through and didn't like it at all. I'm not a Brecht-Weill fan. I'm one of those heretics who likes Weill's Broadway music better. I do like *Threepenny Opera* very much, though. I can't tell about the lyrics because they're all translations and it seems to me that they miss the point. Judging from what little I was able to make of *Mahagonny*, the whole idea of Brecht is a parable-like simplicity of writing which is very hard to translate. In fact, I don't believe in translations. But I do like the music in *Threepenny*. The rest of their work strikes me as repetition of the same stuff. But then I've never seen Brecht done on native soil by the Berliner Ensemble. Also, the whole idea of *lehrstuck*—I understand it intellectually, but the idea of theatre as a political or didactic force is not familiar to me so I feel slightly hesitant about it.

I'm surprised to hear that you don't like Brecht because I've always thought of Sweeney Todd *as being Brechtian.*

Many people say that and I'll tell you why. You get the lower classes walking up and singing at you so you say, "Aha." Then, there's the line about "man eating man." But you must understand that it is sung by an insane man at the peak of his insanity. It's not the author's point of view at all. Brecht constantly alienates you from the story by having characters turn front and make points. *Sweeney* is entirely a plot piece which has a ballad motif running through as if there were a narrator. Brecht doesn't have a narrator. If anything, *Sweeney*'s closer to *Allegro*, which also had a chorus. *Sweeney Todd* is based on Greek principles, with a chorus commenting specifically and directly. They tell the story. Everybody else just acts within the scenes. "Man devouring man" is sung to another character, not to us. The show isn't Brechtian; it's a straightforward operetta with narration by the chorus.

I regard Brecht as far less "alienating" than you've described him. What I find most Brechtian about Sweeney Todd *is the connection made between the economic and political framework and the characters' motives.*

The social implications are in the setting—there's very little of that in the text. That's Hal Prince's overlay. Although the division of the economic classes is implicit—and on occasion explicit—in Chris Bond's original, it is not the major emphasis. It's a melodrama, a horror show, that's all it's meant to be. It's supposed to scare you. It has a theme, of course. It's got to be about something. But we are not making a comment on society.

What about opera?

I've never liked opera and I've never understood it. Most opera doesn't make theatrical sense to me. Things go on forever. I'm not a huge fan of the human voice. I like song, dramatic song. I like music and lyrics together, telling a story. I am not particularly attracted to performers per se. It seems to me that opera's like rock, or pop: you have to be interested in the performer, not the song. When I studied with Milton Babbitt he said I had to get into opera. Knowing that I was a Strauss fan, he first sent me to *Rosenkavalier* and I left after one act. I thought it was endlessly boring. I'd heard a lot of opera on record and I liked some of Puccini's music, so I then went to the Met to see *Bohème*. The curtain went up and there were a lot of starving artists in a hundred-foot studio with a 900-foot roof and I thought, "What is this?" They were all forty-five years old. When I was in Salzburg with Hal Prince and his wife, I saw *Bohème* in a 700-seat theatre and cried for two-and-a-half hours straight. That's my idea of opera. I still think *Bohème* is long-winded but it attempts to tell a story and to characterize musically. I like *Carmen*, I like *Bohème*, I like some of *Tosca*. Puccini generally I like best. And the first act of *Peter Grimes*, and *Porgy and Bess*, and *Wozzeck*. That about does it.

I realize you've worked with many different collaborators over the years, but can you explain how a work takes shape?

Except for *Sweeney Todd*, I've generally gone to writers and asked them if they had any ideas. Or I'll sit with a writer and invent ideas. Occasionally, as with *Pacific Overtures*, the idea has been brought to me. Then I have to find out, first, why it should be sung, as opposed to spoken. How can music not only enhance but fulfill the work? Once that's decided, it's a matter of breaking it down—as with every other kind of art—then bit by bit putting it together. I never make general notes until the librettist actually writes a couple of scenes so I can get into the literary style, get to know the diction of the characters. I'm a very good mimic. I'm very good at enhancing and fulfilling and filling out and inventing within the style. We usually discuss where songs will occur. With the librettists who work from outlines, it's like spotting music cues in a movie.

The major thing is to be sure that you're all writing the same show, which is not as simple as it sounds. With *Forum*, which we worked on for four years, it wasn't until a month before rehearsals that I realized something was peculiar about it. I felt uneasy. I thought maybe it was just because it was my first score for a Broadway show. But I had Jim Goldman read the book and listen to the score. He liked both, but he said, "They don't go together." I had been writing a sort of salon score, and Shevelove and Gelbart had been writing this very elegant low comedy. And indeed, that's what's wrong with it. It's a wonderful show and I like the score very much but too often the songs are not on the same plane as the book. So you've got to decide on things like that and you've got to decide how, why and where the music's going to function. Those are ineffable things. You can't make a general rule for yourself.

I try to use song in unexpected ways. I like surprise, because I think that's the essence of theatre. Over a period of years, I've tried to learn how not to write the expected. Often I will take a scene from a librettist and not write the song that seems to be called for simply because I don't want the audience ahead of me. A lot of audiences feel uncomfortable with that. But I don't want to see a song coming a mile off.

What do you think is a particularly good example of that?

Sweeney's full of them. "Pretty Women": you're expecting a murder and you get a love song instead. That's an extreme example. In *Whistle* all of the mayoress's numbers come in unexpected ways. In *Company* none of the songs are inside the scenes, all are from the outside. That's partly because George Furth didn't write dialogue that you can musicalize. His style simply doesn't allow it. I tried to write songs in the style of George's scenes, but I couldn't do it. So you're in the middle of a scene and suddenly a character comes out and comments on it. Now that's a Brechtian approach. That's the alienation effect. You're asked to view the scene rather than to be in it.

When you're writing, do the lyrics come before the music?

No, they come together. The germinal material is either an accompaniment, a harmonic progression or a lyric line or two. Generally, I work for musical atmosphere. Harmony is very atmospheric, I find—it can set the mood or the tone of a scene or a song. Musicals can't really be through-composed, but I try to make the most out of the least, which is a lesson I learned from Milton Babbitt: to reduce it to simplicities. A Bach fugue is an enormous cathedral based on four notes. I try to collect a few themes which are resonant and utilize them in various ways in the course of the evening, to build from there.

Like the repeated motifs in Sunday in the Park.

Yes. *Pacific Overtures* was where I really started it. But there are not only repeated motifs, there are sometimes repeated, hidden harmonic progressions, all kinds of compositional techniques I learned from Milton, that are not often used in musicals because they're not through-composed. It's the same principle as movie music. A good movie score is based on two or three themes which play in various ways and constantly awaken emotions that are identified with either the characters or the situations. I've used that in every show from *Pacific Overtures* on. But I like to experiment in different ways. Sometimes I associate motifs with ideas, sometimes with characters. For me it's a little obvious always to associate them with characters—that's *real* movie music. In *Merrily* I used motifs in modular ways. Instead of developing a theme, I was just moving blocks of furniture. *Sweeney Todd* and *Sunday* were more developmental.

So in writing you're as concerned with the subliminal effect as the explicit content.

Absolutely. That's one of the things music can do. And lyrics, too. *Sunday*'s full of such lyrical attempts. I got that a lot from Jim Lapine because he writes that way. I'd never used word and phrase motifs so extensively—a score can become very self-conscious if you overdo that. In musical theatre there's so much recitative now that songs have disappeared. That's because recitative is easy to write and composers don't understand that the real point of song-writing is to write a song. It's important to hold things together with either refrains or resonances. But the idea is still to make songs.

So many of your songs dramatize a contradictory emotional state.

That's true of heavily ironic shows like *Anyone Can Whistle* and *Company*. Not so true of *Pacific Overtures*. It's true once or twice in *Sweeney Todd*.

It's not true at all, I think, in *Sunday in the Park*. It depends on the characters. Contradictory states are true in certain stories, but not in others. The first time I tried it was with *Anyone Can Whistle*, talking about a famine in musical comedy terms. All drama is based on contradictory states. That's what subtext is. There's something going on on the surface and something going on underneath it. That's what a Chekhov play is about. You have to be careful not to spell it out too much musically.

Subtext distinguishes your work from that of your predecessors.

It's true, but don't forget, they were not interested in drama. They were interested in a song per se. Their musicals were not about situations and people. They were about entertainment, a comedy scene for its own sake, a song for its own sake. Generally, they were about performers, too. Most of those musicals were written when Broadway was full of performers like Ethel Merman, before movies and television took them over. You see "subtext" in a very naive way in rock shows, which are constantly using "pastiche" to make sarcastic points. People spell things out too much nowadays. It's like getting punched in the ribs. You have to have something there to intrigue the audience. Of course, it also sometimes leaves them in a state of bafflement.

Your use of contradiction between the sentiments of the lyrics and the music is often subtle, as in "Every Day a Little Death."

The funny thing about that song is that it was originally the release of another song sung by the Countess. Hal Prince didn't like the rest of the song but he liked the release, so I expanded it. And it was his idea to put it in that scene where they're having tea. It never would have occurred to me since it was so against what seemed to be going on in the scene. It's very effective that way.

Do you usually attend rehearsal?

No, I'm usually home writing. I rarely finish the score before rehearsals. Directors don't particularly want you around the first week, when they're starting to stage the show and the performers are learning the songs. So I come in the second week to work with the actors on the songs. Then there's an enormous amount of rewriting that goes on during rehearsals, if for nothing else than to reset keys. And there are other songs to write. But I'm around rehearsals a lot the third and fourth weeks.

I know in the past you've often done a lot of rewriting.

There have been a lot of small changes during rehearsals. As I said, I'm usually finishing a score then because it's very useful to write when you see the cast.

Ideally, one should have the show cast and then write it. With *Sweeney*, after I'd written two songs for Mrs. Lovett, Angela Lansbury agreed to do it. Then I was able to write not for Mrs. Lovett but for Mrs. Lovett played by Angela Lansbury. Elaine Stritch was cast before some of *Company* was written so I wrote for Elaine Stritch as Joanne. Len Cariou was cast early in *Sweeney*.

A delay in finishing a score may be partly due to procrastination, too, or fear—more fear, perhaps. And I'm slow. In any event, what goes on during rehearsal period is mostly writing, not rewriting. I wrote about seven songs during the rehearsal period for *Night Music*. I wrote the whole Follies sequence except "Losing My Mind" during rehearsals. In contrast, with *Into the Woods* I wrote only two songs during rehearsals. *Sweeney Todd* was finished before rehearsals except for the last fifteen minutes, and I knew what I was going to do with them.

The truth is that I don't like rehearsals. I get embarrassed hearing my own work. I assume that the cast is embarrassed to sing the stuff. I recognize this as a neurotic reaction, a foolish and unfounded reaction, but nevertheless it is my reaction. So, I write a lot during rehearsals.

Have you done much rewriting after first productions?

We're rewriting *Follies* now, but it's a new show. Jim Goldman wanted to rewrite it entirely. So it requires new songs. We did a new version of *Merrily* out on the Coast two years ago—rewriting which was much for the best also required new songs.

Can you describe the change in working with Hal Prince to collaborating with James Lapine?

Hal's a director and Jim's a writer. So there's no comparison. Jim has both hats on at once, but primarily we work together as writers. So the comparison would be with other librettists, not with other directors. Hal is really the only director, outside of Jerry Robbins, that I've had a close experience with. Jim services the writing. That's what he's interested in. And he's visual—he started as a photographer.

Broadway musicals are a highly formalized kind of theatre and must appeal to a larger audience than your average Off-Broadway play. Have you ever felt that you had to compromise in order to please an audience?

No. Never once. Hal didn't like "Happily Ever After" because he thought it was negative. I changed it to "Being Alive" not because of the audience but because of my collaborator. And I don't think he was doing it for the audience. It made him dissatisfied. Now maybe he was fooling himself. Maybe he was thinking of the audience but that's not the way it was presented to me. He thought it was wrong.

Musicals are very presentational. People face front and ask for applause. And certainly I believe that all theatre utilizes the audience as a collaborator, be it Shakespeare, Chekhov, or musicals. But musicals seduce audiences more directly. Therefore, I always write with an audience in mind. This is not to say that I write thinking of how to make the show popular.

Once I choose to tell a story, I tell it the best I can for my enjoyment when I stand at the back of the theatre. Will this make me laugh, will this make me cry? Then, if I stand at the back of the theatre and the audience isn't laughing, I try to analyze it. I think, "Why is that line not getting a laugh? Have I put too many words in it? Is there not a pause in the music? Is it not a good joke? Oh—they didn't understand that that's the girl's father." And then I fix it. That's not my idea of a compromise. That's my idea of a collaboration with the audience. Jim Lapine, as serious a fellow as I've ever worked with, says he doesn't start to enjoy his work as a director until there's an audience there. Once he knows who he's communicating to he can start to fix things.

Actually, I get terrified in front of an audience because I'm so used to them walking out and hissing and following me up the aisle to tell me how terrible the show is. I never change anything to *please* an audience. I change it to make them have a good time. I want them to have the same good time that I have. The horror of movies is that they're always the same—they never acknowledge the audience reaction. What keeps theatre alive is that each experience is unique. Each audience does affect the material, it affects the way the actors perform. Clarity is particularly important to me. I want the audience at least to understand what I'm doing. And then if they don't like it, they don't like it.

Why do you think some people have such a strong negative response to your work?

I think people are threatened by intelligence, particularly in the musical. I think a lot of them resent it, too. Walter Kerr has actually said that he wants musicals to be strictly for relaxation. He doesn't believe that they should carry any weight or make any kind of comment. I'm all for fun but I can't write that way. And I've never seen a musical I liked that was just fun, including *Guys and Dolls.*

Do you read the critics?

Oh, sure, I'm masochistic, I read them all. Although with *Sunday in the Park,* I held off until a couple of weeks after we'd opened and then I read them and was appalled. I got much worse reviews for *Sunday* than for the earlier pieces. Most everybody hated it. As time went by I thought I'd be accepted more and more, but it turns out I get worse reviews. The only review I read with any real interest is the *New York Times*, because that controls business. But I can virtually predict what the others are saying. I know the ones that sort of like me and at least are trying to understand what I'm doing and the ones that hate me before they go into the theatre. And since none of them count at the box office, I don't give a damn.

Do you have any favorite productions?

No, I like them all. The only production that was a disaster, really, was *Merrily*. The casting, the idea of doing it with kids was a mistake, Hal's and mine. And Hal has freely admitted that the physical production was a mistake. But the others have been very good. *Sweeney* was always conceived as a small piece but Hal wanted to do it large and I wanted Hal to direct it. It's a little horror play, but Hal was influenced by Meyerhold. He likes opera. He likes bigness. I like huge theatre too, but I also like small theatre. If we had done it small, nobody would have said it was Brechtian. But I thought the production was wonderful.

Do you sense a shift in your work now, with James Lapine?

No, I just like working with him. It's wonderful because he's thinking as a writer and director at once. I like his sensibility. He comes from a generation much freer theatrically than mine. So it's fun to write with him, to work with someone who is not Rodgers and Hammerstein. He's less linear and I've always been interested in nonlinear theatre at the same time that I believe in strong stories.

That's why I pursued the question on Brecht, because he was so important in developing a kind of nonlinear musical theatre.

The thing about Brecht is that I don't see anything going on in the way of character and that's what I'm interested in. I believe that action is character. I'm just not interested in Brecht's kind of political writing. And yet *Pacific Overtures* is quite Brechtian—it's absolutely a show of ideas. Though there's character in it, it primarily illustrates points of view toward a cataclysmic political upheaval that has resonance today all over the Western world. That's why it interested Hal. Hal's a much more political animal than I. That's why he did *Sweeney* in that sociopolitical way.

Do you think of your writing as political at all?

Not in the least. I'm interested in storytelling and character. That's what I grew up on. And except for *Pacific Overtures*, that's what I've always written.

Of course, there's a social comment to be made about everything. You tell me what happened to you on the bus and I can tell you its social implications. But what makes stories really work for me is character, and that includes Shakespeare. As Wilson Mizner said, people beat scenery.

It has often been remarked that your musicals are about characters confronting themselves, coming to deal with their emotional truth.

That's what every play is about. Musicals are not considered the same animal, but in fact the kind I like are. It's what you learn in English 1: protagonist and antagonist. The protagonist makes a journey and discovers that he's killed his father and married his mother. Catharsis. Curtain. That's exactly what it should be. All the way through both *Sunday in the Park* and *Into the Woods* Jim Lapine and I kept asking, what are we saying at the end? What does it all add up to? Where's the catharsis? We end with a show, the Seurat show, that baffled a lot of people. They didn't get the second act at all.

With Sunday in the Park, *though, I detected a shift in your methods. Dot is the character who carries the real emotional thrust of the piece.*

Dot is the antagonist and George is the protagonist. It's the old classical principle: she makes him change. He takes the trip. It's all about how he connects with the past and with the continuum of humanity. The spirit of Dot in the painting is exactly what makes him do it. But he's the one who comes to a recognition at the end. If you don't connect with the past, you can't go on. People who say the second act's not necessary misunderstand the play. The second act is what it's about. The first act's the set-up.

It seemed to me that George's rejection of Dot was never properly atoned for. I didn't feel that he made the same inner emotional connection that many of your earlier characters make.

Well, what can I say? Surely you must see, whether it affected you or not, that the whole last fifteen minutes is about that connection. If you didn't feel it, you didn't feel it. The attempt is not to get you to contact Dot but to make you understand his contact with Dot, his connection with his past, which is the past of all of us. Every artist is connected to everybody who's ever painted a picture. If you don't understand that as an artist, you're lost.

I was very disturbed by George's rejection of Dot in the first act and what that suggests about how artists work.

That's the classic triangle which I believe is universally true. He's got his "wife" and his "mistress"—his art. One of the triumphs of the show, as far as I'm concerned, is that Jim made it seem not like a cliche. George doesn't really choose to reject Dot. He wants both. There are, of course, people who put up with somebody who has an obsessive interest. Plenty of artists' wives are happy and fulfilled. And plenty are not.

The more we read about Seurat, the more I realized that he's not a man I would want to have dinner with. He was obsessive. There's little that is known about him so we had to expand the story. But the eyewitness reports indicate that he was very shy and timid until the subject of art came up. Then he was fanatic, aggressive, argumentative and absolutely inflexible—a man with a mission.

Because I saw him presented as the Artist, with a capital A, I thought the show suggested that it was perfectly acceptable for an artist to reject emotionality in his personal life.

We thought about that, but we were dealing with a very individual artist. Renoir wasn't like that. Seurat was. When you think about it, what kind of a fellow paints dots on a canvas over and over again? Do you want to have dinner with someone who's painted five million dots? That's not for me, thank you. That's not Renoir and the Impressionists saying "light, light," and painting all over the canvas. It's interesting that you think of him as representing a lot of artists.

But George is the only real artist we see on that stage, carefully differentiated from Jules.

That's also true. But artists are all different personalities. Picasso, with his seventy-four mistresses and eighty-seven wives and sixty-four children, lived a gregarious and rich life. But he was out there working obsessively over his canvases every single day of his life. We were not trying to make a statement about the Artist. I don't believe in generalized statements. *Pacific Overtures* is not a generalized statement about gunboat diplomacy. It's about a specific incident between Japan and the United States. We're not trying to imply anything about other kinds of imperialist adventures. This is American imperialism in 1853. If you want to draw resonances and conclusions from that, that's fine. But that's not what we're saying. Brecht is constantly telling you: this is the way everything works. No, this is the way certain capitalisms work. That's what I object to.

I do believe that George's problem—my art or my life—is common to a lot of people. But what we were writing about was what an interesting man this must have been. Actually, we didn't even start to write about the man, we started to write about the painting. One evening Jim Lapine and I were talking and the painting came up. It looks like a stage set. Why are those people not looking at each other? Jim said to me, "The main character's missing. That's the artist." Once he said that, we had a play. It never would have occurred to me, as a writer, to bring the artist into it—I would have written about what all those people were doing, why they were all in the park on that day.

How concerned are you with history? Many of your musicals have been period shows.

The curious thing is that I'm not the least bit interested in history. In college I never took history courses. The shows are other people's ideas. I get interested in the stories and a lot of them take place in period. The fun for me about *Pacific Overtures* was the style—I'm very into style. But you can explore that with contemporary material too—take *Company.* That's also history, a socioeconomic situation, a specific kind of society within a society. It's urban America. I believe that in the specific lies the universal. I think it's Fitzgerald who observed that if you start with the specific, you end with the universal, but if you start with the universal, you end with nothing.

What is your view of the American theatre today? So many of the playwrights have commented on how bad the situation is.

They're talking about the commercial theatre. I don't think the noncommercial theatre is in such bad shape—it's in better shape than it's ever been. The commercial theatre's in terrible shape.

Why?

Three other entertainment media have come along—movies, television and records—so a whole generation and a half has grown up without the theatregoing habit. Tickets have become so expensive, a luxury. Much of the middle class that used to support the theatre can't afford it anymore. If you're going to spend forty-five dollars for a ticket it had better be something worth forty-five dollars which means it's got to be a spectacle. On the other hand, regional theatre is thriving, at least for now. I tend to think that live entertainment will never die, but I may be wrong. In Truffaut's *Fahrenheit 451,* a woman riding a monorail passes her hand over her clothes because she's losing contact with the live experience. Maybe we'll all be sitting in front of boxes, getting everything secondhand. I like to think that the need for live storytelling will stay alive. But the need for commercial theatre, absolutely not. People can go see the Statue of Liberty.

What are your own plans?

Into the Woods should open in October. The new version of *Follies* will open in London in July. The English National Opera's going to do *Pacific Overtures* in the fall. They've already had two workshops of it which were very encouraging—indeed, thrilling. That's the show that belongs on an opera stage, not *Sweeney Todd*. *Sunday in the Park* is supposed to be done in London in the fall. But *Into the Woods* has my concentration now. We ran for six weeks in San Diego and it turned out very well.

Any longer-range goals?

No. I go from show to show. I never look ahead, I never have anything planned. I'd like to write with Jim. What I want to do is write shows and get them performed.

MEGAN TERRY

T he work of no other contemporary American playwright can boast the
extraordinary scope of that of Megan Terry. In the course of over thirty
years her collected plays have become a virtual compendium of the styles of
modern drama, ranging from collaborative ensemble work to performance art
to naturalism. After training at the Seattle Repertory Playhouse, the University of Alberta and Yale University, she moved to New York, where in 1963
she became a cofounder of the Open Theater. During the next ten years,
working closely with Joseph Chaikin, she was instrumental in effecting the
Open Theater's break with psychological realism and in developing their
distinctive and influential ensemble work. In 1966 she wrote *Viet Rock*, the
first rock musical, which premiered at La Mama, has been performed world-
wide, and was presented again in New York in 1987. During the late sixties
and early seventies she continued to write for the Open Theater and became
a founding member of the New York Theatre Strategy. In 1974 she moved
to Omaha, where she lives today, as playwright-in-residence at the Omaha
Magic Theatre. In recent years she has continued to develop and refine the
style of her early work while experimenting with ever more diverse forms
and techniques.

Despite the eclecticism of Terry's work, it remains unified by a particular dramatic technique—the rapid transformation of one character into another —and a deep political commitment. Her early transformational plays—including *Calm Down Mother*, for three women, and *Keep Tightly Closed in a Cool, Dry Place*, for three men (both written for the Open Theater, 1965)— examine the operation of sex roles, both psychologically and sociologically. Both are comprised of a series of linked sketches that gives the audience the opportunity to observe the connection between a succession of female and male roles and situations. Both provide actors the chance to explore a number of different characters, theatrical styles and kinds of social interaction.

In her transformational plays Terry challenges the hegemony of the consciousness of the intractable individual that had so dominated American drama in the 1950s. Instead, her work insistently throws the spectator's focus onto society and the way it maintains oppressive roles and attitudes. Her more recent plays continue the investigation, using multiple series of transformations and focusing more urgently on the origin of exploitative formations. These include *Babes in the Bighouse* (1974), which explores the symbiotic relationships between prisoners, guards and wardens in a woman's prison; *American King's English for Queens* (1978), which examines language's crucial role in the development of sexist attitudes and stereotypes; and *Goona Goona* (1979), which uses a Grand Guignol style to investigate American family violence.

Another important facet of Terry's work has been the study of strong women from history whom she holds up as an inspiration for modern Americans. In *Approaching Simone* (1970) she dramatizes the life of the French philosopher, theologian and educator Simone Weil, using a style closer to that of a Christian Passion play than to her early transformational work. She strings together scenes from Simone's life to document the development of her political and spiritual beliefs and to create, in opposition to the patriarchal Judeo-Christian mythology on which Simone was raised, a kind of counter-mythology—female, pacifist, nurturing and strong. In *Mollie Bailey's Traveling Family Circus: Featuring Scenes from the Life of Mother Jones* (1985) Terry juxtaposes the extraordinary generosity of Mollie Bailey as circus manager, wife and mother against the struggle of Mother Jones for mine workers' rights. Structured upon these two parallel and interwoven stories, the play demonstrates that women have—and can still—become successful without sacrificing themselves to competitiveness and greed.

As Terry explains in the interview, she is less interested in a carefully developed unbroken plot than in associative connections, in multiple actions, in brief scenes linked together and peopled by a panoply of characters. Despite this, however, she has written naturalistic, highly plotted work, most notably her 1974 play *Hothouse*. In it she focuses on the process of emotional growth by portraying three generations of women living in one house and their relationships with various husbands and lovers. Although Terry uses elements of the well-made play (the release of withheld information is particularly important), the final resolution depends less on the characters' revelations about the past than on the three women's understanding of their likeness and community and their recognition that the flowering of the individual must be based on self-reliance and love.

With more than sixty plays to her credit, Megan Terry remains a key figure in the development of the American alternative theatre. Beginning with her earliest work, she has devised a politically and socially activist theatre, using a diversity of nonrealistic forms to challenge a culture which has systematically disparaged nonlinear drama. She has introduced contentious subject matter into the American musical. She has written documentary dramas on important and troubling issues. And more, arguably, than any of her contemporaries—and during a period when it has no longer been fashionable —she has kept alive the techniques of the theatre of the 1960s, renovating the spirit of that turbulent decade: "Live your life as if the revolution had been a success!"

■　　■　　■

JULY 14, 1987—J.W. MARRIOTT HOTEL, WASHINGTON, D.C.

What drew you to theatre when you were young?

My family's so theatrical, a huge Irish family. I grew up being an audience for all these incredibly talented people. My mother was a great singer and performer, and my grandmother a marvelous storyteller. My aunt was a stage director, my uncle was a concert pianist, my cousin was a pioneer in the field of creative dramatics for children.

And we lived three blocks from the Seattle Repertory Playhouse. When I was a teenager, I scratched at the door until they let me in. I did everything at the theatre—I wanted to be a designer. Maybe through the mists of time it seems so grand to me, but I haven't since then seen a group of people who knew each other so well. They had worked together for twenty years and ranged in age from thirty-five to sixty-five. For American and European naturalism they were superb. The director had studied with Stanislavski and was a Jeffersonian idealist and a woman, Florence James—her husband was the leading actor. In my family the Irish oral tradition was all just roly-poly fun; these Seattle Rep people gave me a classical grounding.

What productions were particularly important for you?

Pygmalion. I got to play Clara Eynsford Hill and Burton James, the leading actor, was a great theoretician about comedy and tragedy. My attitude was originally tragic. He said, "If you take another attitude, you'll do something different to the audience and you'll enhance the play and the character." One night I made an adjustment and I got laughs. Clara is a very small part, but I got a hand on my exit. The light bulbs went off in my head and I began to understand that I could make the audience laugh at will, just by attitude.

I was fascinated by Shaw and his arguments and read all of his work. I got a chance to act in *A Midsummer Night's Dream* and to play Kate in *Taming of the Shrew.* Then, when I was working backstage, Mr. James would read to me from the Greeks. The Jameses had some severe problems with the House Un-American Activities Committee—one of the things brought up at their trial was that they had done an all-black production of *Lysistrata.* I became very impressed with Aristophanes and read his work on my own. It led me to an appreciation of all the Greek writers.

Also, for punishment in high school—before I met the Jameses—they would put us in the library and I discovered Chekhov. I was into comic books at the time and I ran out of things to read and reached over and picked this thing off the shelf and couldn't put it down, it was a total revelation to me.

What specifically excited you about Chekhov?

The way he could handle so many people and give you the sense of a world. I felt like I could live there and that I knew those people, even though I could never pronounce their names properly. The states of deep feeling in Chekhov, with the comic attitude on top, helped me begin to see how things are layered and that the subtext is so important. Mrs. James would have us write biographies of what we were doing offstage—dialogue—so when I was playing Irina, I wrote down all of the things she was thinking and saying before her entrance. That's one of the things that got me into writing. When I came to New York and was performing in plays of lesser writers, I began to think I could really be a playwright, because the things that I was writing, that were being said offstage, were more interesting than the lines I had to say onstage.

But I was writing back in Seattle. The Jameses also asked us to write personal biographies—how we got into the theatre, what our deep feelings were, both personal and political. They tried to give us a global view. Mr. James used to say, "This country politically is in kindergarten." He was afraid he'd never live to see the adolescence of America politically. (Maybe we're just dawning into that now.) Both of the Jameses believed that the playwright was a supreme creature and that to aspire to be a playwright was the highest, most civilized calling.

The House Un-American Activities Committee succeeded in closing down the theatre. The University of Washington took it over. But the fact that they sent all these people from Washington to stop a theatre impressed me a great deal.

When did you get involved in the Open Theater?

1963. Joe Chaikin saw a play of mine at the Cherry Lane Theatre, *Ex-Miss Copper Queen on a Set of Pills*. It was produced by the Playwright's Unit—Edward Albee, Richard Barr and Clinton Wilder—on a double bill with Terrence McNally's play *The Other Side of the Door*, starring Estelle Parsons. John Strasberg and I had a very good production going and then this Actors Studio director came in on opening night to break down the actors. The Studio had this theory, which they said they got from Freud, of breaking down the arrogance of the actor and getting to the real whatever. This fool came in one hour before curtain and turned our leading woman into a piece of protoplasm. He so destroyed her self-confidence that she forgot all her lines.

I thought, "If this is New York theatre, forget it." I was shocked and appalled. Joe Chaikin and Michael Smith were in the audience. Smith was a critic for the *Village Voice*—the kind of critic who was a partner with the artists. He loved the theatre as much as we did. He let people know where to come and what was happening. When there was a breakthrough, he would be the first to proclaim it. After the show I got a note that Joe wanted to meet me—I didn't know who he was. He said, "Hated the production. We're thinking of starting a theatre and we're looking for writers and would you be interested?" After what I'd just been through I said, "Absolutely." I could see no future in the so-called commercial theatre if this was the way people were treated.

We all got together with the idea that the actors would be cocreators with the writer and the director and that they should have equal status as human beings [laughs]. We did not like this notion of the director as analyst who could read your mind and know what is best for you, this paternalistic attitude. It's coercive and manipulative. We wanted to find another way to do theatre. We had dreams about the spiritual qualities of acting that we didn't think were being revealed in the commercial theatre.

What was the work situation like with the Open Theater?

We started with what we knew and what we'd done, and went on from there. We made some incredible discoveries about acting—or rediscoveries. When

I first looked at the New York theatre—except for one production, O'Neill's *A Moon for the Misbegotten* with Wendy Hiller, Franchot Tone and Cyril Cusack, which was staggeringly beautifully acted—all the things I saw were what I considered acting from the neck up: marvelously trained voices, beautiful gestures. It was theatre of upward mobility—about going to the theatre to learn how to behave like a WASP. You would go to parties in New York and see people lighting their cigarettes like they saw it done on stage. That wasn't what we were in the theatre for. We were interested in the possibility of growing as human beings, being aligned with a great spiritual consciousness—not theatre as entertainment, although I enjoy that aspect of it.

Chaikin was enamored of Brecht and some of the modern Europeans. I was more crazy about Strindberg and Ionesco and Sartre. I was also fond of *Peer Gynt*, of Ibsen's more poetic plays. I started writing transformation plays because most plays are about one person—one person gets to show three or four aspects of the personality, while all the other people have supporting roles and usually are stereotypes. What if you could see all of the aspects of all of the people? Most three-act plays spend two acts building to a climax, with a short denouement, and that's it. What if there were plays with ten climaxes?

People are very well educated, from films, radio, television—we know all the stories now. It seems to me that you can speak to people in a new kind of shorthand, by the use of dramatic clues. It's like Gestalt psychology —connect the dots, the incomplete completes itself. At the Open Theater I was watching young people grow and develop, and many things were coming together in my mind. I had seen in Mrs. James's workshop the incredible joy of improvisation. I started writing them down because I saw the actors often couldn't repeat them. I was trying, even in Seattle, to relieve them of the playwriting problem.

I got so interested in the idea: What if there were ten stories in the span of an hour? And in making a play almost like a game. Plot is not what is interesting to me about the theatre—it's the theatre itself, the fact that we are all alive at the same time. And that anyone who comes to the theatre has an incredible amount of information in his or her head. I love the idea of play, playing with the elements of theatre. That's what I try to do. My early plays were actually presents for the actors and wonderful games for the audiences. That's how I saw them, at least.

What else influenced your development of transformations?

A lot of it comes from analyzing movies, commercials, prints, advertising, jump cuts, dissolves, fades. You get a new kind of comedy by constantly changing the situation. And you get the laugh when the audience recognizes the reference or makes the leap. They laugh because of the fun that happens in their heads.

Unlike most of the drama of the fifties, your transformational work breaks down that predominance of the individual's subjectivity.

The audience can supply it.

But in the early sixties it was quite a radical technique.

A lot of people got very angry with me. I was shocked at the anger.

Why were they angry?

[Dramatically] "I want to wallow in my neurotic state of being." I saw so many actors doing that and I wanted to pluck them out of that. I didn't realize that they loved being there.

Spectators, too.

It's "The Movie of the Week." The Actors Studio trains you to play neurotics and losers—and play them very well! Their directors went into film and took the actors with them. We're still living with it. And some of it is glorious, but it isn't exactly taking us forward. It doesn't show the healthy, spiritual possibilities of the actor. It's too narrow a vision—although it's one actors need to know about so that they can play it. They should be able to call it up at will. It shouldn't be painful, it should be joyous.

What you're describing has certain similarities with Brechtian acting, when the actor does not become a character but holds it up.

You can still become the character, but then you can drop it. Our actors were trained to do that. It takes Actors Studio actors half an hour to drop it. We used to have this exercise called the transformation of the styles. You take the same dialogue and do it as Molière, as Shakespeare, as *The Days of Our Lives*, as Noel Coward, as Tennessee Williams. The actors were able to do that, without pain. I get worried when I see actors going through pain. I don't believe in masochism in theatre.

In those first ten years or so, were there any other major influences?

Gertrude Stein. That's the first and last book I ever stole—*Last Operas and Plays*. I stole it when I was seventeen from a library in Canada—I must give it back to them someday. Her work is so fresh! So funny! The whole thing is to read it out loud. People get confused about Gertrude Stein because they try to keep it on the page. It's full of transformation. In my teenage years I was also interested in the Cubists and the Impressionists. In her word portraits Stein would try to write like the Cubists—it all came together for me, I could see exactly what she was doing. *The Mother of Us All* reads like it was written this morning, and it's so relevant and funny and marvelous. I used to do the short-story sections at cocktail parties and have people falling all over the floor laughing. They would ask, "Who wrote that?" And I'd say, "Gertrude Stein," and they wouldn't believe me.

Other influences: stand-up comics and impressionists, cartoons—Bugs Bunny, Tom & Jerry. They all deal in transformations. That's how fast my transformations should be. When they are, they provoke incredible laughter from the audience. When people try to show the transition, they fall into the morass. Transitions should be as pure and quick as those of a child playing —with total commitment each time.

Which is why there are so many children in your plays.

Right. [Laughs] I taught play school in Canada for two years. Ninety children. That was something else, let me tell you. I learned a lot from them.

How did you get involved with the Omaha Magic Theatre?

Jo Ann Schmidman started the Magic Theatre in 1968, when she was a soph-omore in college. She had a director in the winter who kept it going when she was away. Jo Ann had read all about the work we had been doing in New York. She is a very idealistic and spiritual person, and she wanted to make a strong theatre in the Midwest for the people who lived there. When Chaikin saw her in *Approaching Simone*, he put her right into the Open Theater, which was unusual. People used to have to go through horrendous probation to be allowed into the Open Theater. Since we worked only four to six months of the year, Jo Ann was able to keep the theatre running in Omaha.

So when the Open Theater closed Jo Ann still had the Magic. It was lucky for me. Ellen Stewart of La Mama had been very hospitable to me and still is. She put on *Viet Rock* and gave me space to do a play a month there right up until *Viet Rock*. That was how I was able to learn so fast—with audiences. But then La Mama became so popular that you were lucky if you got a slot every two years, and I was developing so fast, writing so much. I wanted to be able to work more than once every two years.

In recent years how do you start a play?

There's really no one way I write. I may write a play because I want to work out some neurotic state. Or I may write a play because all the children of our audience have grown up to a certain age and say, "We want to be in a play." So I'll write *Fifteen Million Fifteen-Year-Olds* for them. Or I'm so upset about something that I have to say something—for instance, *Viet Rock*. Then I'll spend all my time researching and interviewing and checking my feelings, working that out. I may want to write about someone in my family I love very much and want to memorialize. I may see someone walking down the street in a certain way. I'll imagine a whole life for that person and go home and write a play about this person who interested me because of the walk. Or I may be in a supermarket and hear a phrase. Or I may take a visual cue. For instance, I'm writing a play now called *Accordion* that's jagged and triangular. It has absolutely no plot, but you squeeze the form and these things happen in an accordion shape.

There are so many stimuli around that sometimes I have to put myself in a dark room to calm down. I wish I were more than one person. There's just so much to do and so many exciting things going on. At the Omaha Magic Theatre Jo Ann has been able to attract some fine painters and people who sculpt not only with bronze and wood but with light, and four or five composers. We just had a meeting last week about a new piece we're working on. The working title is *Pro-jec-tiles*. We'll all be pulling this together—writing it, building it—and everything is progressing at the same time. Jo Ann is writing some of it, I'm writing some of it. It's very stimulating having these fully mature artists from other fields to work with.

We did a big piece last year, *A Sea of Forms*, which was total bliss—living in a sculptural environment for five months and writing text to go into it, music coming in every day, and Jo Ann working with the actors. Ten minutes after the play was over the audience wanted to buy the script. Many people came back to see it again and again. There was no more value placed on the human beings than on the sculpture. I cried when we had to take it all down. But we're going further in this next piece.

How did you get the idea to bring Mollie Bailey together with Mother Jones?

Everyone was bitching, "Men won't let me do this, our culture won't let me do that." Some friends doing research on circus people were down in Texas and ran across a memoir of a circus family. It's an incredible story of a woman with a huge family, which I could relate to. Mollie Bailey believed that you can grow through disciplined work—which I believe in, too. That's why I love theatre. The discipline of theatre is extraordinary—the whole idea of rehearsal as a structured life. Mollie Bailey was incredibly successful financially and ran this circus for her husband. She was not only able to feed her family of nine children plus all the extended relatives, she also provided jobs for many people.

Another friend said, "Why don't you write a play about Mother Jones?" And I thought, why not put them together? Here's a politically committed woman, her own family destroyed by yellow fever. But instead of lying down in the gutter or retreating to crime or killing herself, she takes all of her nurturing feeling and uses it for the mine workers. She adopts miners and their families so that they become her extended family. She turns a negative into a positive. She lives to be a hundred through walking. She walked the length and breadth of America, not once, but many, many times. She learned eight or nine languages so she could teach the children of the miners. She birthed a thousand babies and didn't lose one of them. And I thought, "Mother Jones reminds me so much of my grandmothers." I put Mother Jones and Mollie Bailey together to show other women and men that you can do something if you have a dream and believe in yourself. You can make your way through commitment, belief, determination, reaching out, communication—and you can do it in America.

I got to travel all over the world with the Open Theater and I saw very clearly that as a woman I would never have developed to the degree that I have in any other country. I would never have been able to learn, to have autonomy, to have the exciting life that I have. And it was possible to do it in the last century, too. I was so sick of all the neurotic plays, and all the defeats—you know what our dramatic literature is like. Let's put up a few successes and see how they did it. Let's celebrate it.

Both are love stories. Mollie's for her circus and her husband and children, Mother Jones's for the workers. Love is the basis for her social action.

It's true. Love is transferable, it doesn't have to stay in the nuclear family. Mother Jones organized the United Mine Workers and she was a great speaker, ran many successful strikes. She was instrumental in bringing about the eight-hour day and the repeal of the child labor laws because she was able to project the love she had for her immediate family, which she lost, onto a wider group of people. I think it's good to remind ourselves that that is possible. What an incredible engine love is. Anger is another.

Can you give an example of a play that is written out of anger?

Viet Rock. I felt anger at the destruction and the confusion, and turned that anger into an examination and discussion and catalyst. One of the best things *Viet Rock* did was bring a lot of very bright people into the theatre. I meet people everywhere I go who say, "I was in *Viet Rock* when I was in college and I decided to dedicate my life to theatre because of the experience of the ensemble." Some of my plays use the best of what many young people have to give. A play like *Viet Rock* doesn't push them beyond what they can do. It shows them in their beauty and strength.

So in a fundamental way, what you're doing is fostering a sense of community.

I hope so. And letting young people know that sensibility is a valuable thing to have. They shouldn't swallow it. But it needs to be let out in a disciplined, organized framework.

What inspired American King's English?

So many things. Mainly listening to how people talk to their children in supermarkets. It's terrifying. English can be used like bullets. The way people speak to their young determines how they think about themselves—it becomes internalized. English is very confusing because we don't have masculine and feminine, like French. So for little girls growing up everything is "he," and women have to double-think, triple-think. I had a lot of fun with that. I like to use humor to show things to people.

When you go into rehearsal do you always have a finished script?

No. For *Family Talk*, which is now called *Dinner Is in the Blender*, I didn't have a final scene and I was getting worried. Sometimes there isn't enough time. I run the front of the house and sell tickets and help write grants, besides trying to write plays. But I'm used to being up against the wall. My improvisation training has certainly helped me at the typewriter.

Do you write a lot in rehearsal?

Yes. For *Babes in the Bighouse* I made the set first and started writing scenes after I built the jail. Jo Ann learned that in prisons the way people walk is significant. So we worked for weeks on how the prisoners walked, the guards, the visitors. The play's performed walking in place and is about one person imposing his or her will on another—the guard on the prisoner, the head of the prison on the guard, one guard on another guard, one prisoner on another prisoner. As we worked on walking—I often do what the actors do in the early stages—I was writing. We also noticed that the men in our company wanted to examine what it would be like to be a woman in that situation. So we studied not only being a prisoner but also being a woman.

So some of the women's parts were played by men?

Yes. This got us into a lot of trouble with the feminist separatists, but it was a revelation to the males in our audiences. Men came to us after that production and said, "For the first time I understand what the feminists are talking about." They identified with the men being women in subordinate situations where they had no power unless they complied with someone else's will.

When we did *King's English* at a prep school for boys, I realized that young boys don't listen to anything women say. They didn't laugh at one thing any actress said. They all laughed when the males spoke or did something funny. The educational system has to be totally overhauled. People are making noises in that direction, but under the present administration it looks like just more blood and guts in Nicaragua.

I think one reason for all this militarism is that some of the supermacho males have been alarmed at the power of the women's movement and its implications. They need to be seen as the protectors. Listen to and analyze the dialogue coming out of the Iran-contra hearings, the fear they're laying on the American people about how the Sandinistas are going to come pouring across the borders. They need to create demons so they'll have a job.

There's no reason for the largest arms build-up in history unless you have an enemy.

Today Reagan asked for $140 million for the contras, which is what we get for *all* of the arts in America.

What can be done?

The budget is policy. We have to keep saying it so that people get it through their heads. I say to the feminists: If you are serious, why aren't you making a shadow cabinet as they do in England? Be ready to take over. What if these fools collapse? Do you have any ideas? How would you run the country? Study economics. In Omaha you watch the collapse of the breadbasket of America. You see small towns going under, people leaving the farms—middle-aged people, bewildered, having to be retrained. You would never know it on either coast. When are they going to wake up? It's collapsing in the middle. How long before it gets to the coast?

So your political work is far more than feminist.

Oh yes. We're living there in the community. I write one play a year which I think is giving voice to community concerns. And then I write my personal plays, my fun plays on the side.

One line of Simone Weil's from Approaching Simone *seems to encapsulate your work: "I am against totalitarism in all its forms"—understanding that it takes infinitely many forms.*

Yes it does. It may even take a feminist form. They wanted me to be accountable to their party line. I said forget it. I am interested in freedom. That's why I love this country so much, and our Constitution. I have the freedom to develop in any direction I want. And I want that for everybody else. Theatre is a great social forum. It's a terrific catalyst. It can bring people together for meaningful discussion and moving forward, or even just mind-expansion. It's a legal high, and we don't have too many of those.

Is Hothouse *a more personal play?*

Right. It's also an antiwar play and a history play. For some things I want to get across to people the best form is American naturalism, because I want to capture certain moments in American history. I find when I'm teaching that if people know anything before Elvis Presley, it's a miracle. They don't know how we got to where we are. They don't understand the progression of history. They aren't aware of some of the intense experiences the people of the last two generations have had to live through.

I think the sixties was the greatest flowering since the beginning of this country. We had a huge group of incredibly gifted people in the sixties. The plan of the people now in power, trying to put down the sixties, to rewrite history, has got to be stopped. We who lived through it have plenty to say about that. It's like a beacon, a shining era, a time of freedom. It got perverted and messed up, but while it was pure, it was incredible.

Have you written a play about the sixties?

Viet Rock was of the moment. But I'm going to write one in retrospect, before they get all those history books printed and start brainwashing the kids.

Do you have any favorites among your plays?

I love *Approaching Simone*. Simone Weil is another beacon. She developed on her own. She's totally opposite from me. She's all mind. I'm all feeling. She was born with this incredibly developed mind. I'm in awe of that. The way I'm constructed, I have to get to my intellect through my feelings, so it takes longer. I used to meet priests out walking and they would have her books. The books would be in shreds, they had read them so many times. She's unsettling to a lot of people—Catholics and Jews—because she refused to be baptised. "I will point to the church, but I won't go into the water." [Laughs] That's what Simone implied. The idea of a visitation from Christ is hard for people in modern culture to accept. She said she had to believe it because she wasn't looking for it. She got into Christian prayer through listening to Bach. An amazing journey—and such a young person. Her life parallels Christ's. Simone and the masculine Christ—yin and yang. A giant female brain to balance the brain of Christ.

In *The Gloaming, Oh My Darling* I was trying to catch the language of my grandparents and great-grandparents. The family stories and the lusty attitudes. World War II sent all the men to war and the women to work so

I got to be with my grandparents and learn from them. I'm sorry for the kids raised now. Because of the automobile we have this incredible mobile culture and children don't know who their grandparents were. I was really lucky— I had four generations. It's important always to have that strength to call upon.

A lot of people like *Goona Goona*, but it was so painful for me to write that play. And I had to see it every night and take notes on it. It's about child and spouse abuse.

Do you read the critics?

No, I have someone read them for me. And if there's something to be learned from them or if they would give me a lift then I read them. But I have total recall and in the early days the critics just drove me nuts. I don't want to be sitting around when I'm ninety remembering some of that garbage [laughs].

On the other hand, there was Michael Smith—it depends on whether they're in it with you or they're using it to make their own career. But I don't blame them because we have it better than they do. We have a chance to live forever and they don't, so they're out to kill us. That's just the way it is. They go out with the garbage tomorrow. They have to make their mark immediately so they have a different attitude toward what they're doing.

I really regret that the critics were too stupid to record the incredible thing that went on in the American theatre in the sixties, the development in acting and staging. They had the chance to do it while it was happening and they didn't. Unfortunately they were obstructionists every inch of the way.

The sixties was a lot of fun. I thought it was so American. I wanted to put a lot of different kinds of Americans on the stage. There were no parts for women—that's why I wrote *Calm Down Mother*. There was nothing to celebrate theatre as sport. I'm a big fan of team sports. I love baseball. The greatest thrill of my life was when our theatre company was invited to go to the 1980 Olympics and play *Running Gag*, and I saw the Chinese and the Swedish athletes embrace our actors and identify with them. (They run on stage for the whole show.)

Because of all the work done by the painters and French writers, the Existentialists, and our American film, the time was right. I said to myself, "Everybody knows all the stories so I can throw out exposition," which has always bored me. Some people say that form is organic or that women write in different ways from men, but it just seemed to me that we all had a common frame of reference. I see many Americas now, but at that time you could speak to the community and they knew what you were talking about quickly. The mind works very fast.

I always had this idea that I could construct models in which people could walk around and play—intellectual models. That's how I thought of the transformation plays. My grandfather taught me to build things, to build houses. I was trained as a designer and I think of playmaking in that way. I built stage sets and I had facility with tools.

The next step is to see more than three dimensions—I see many more than three dimensions in the models of my plays in my head. They are architectural and emotional and intellectual structures that the audience can enter and kick around and play in. They can see what's in this room, what's in that room. One thing I used to say to actors I directed was, "Now you own the play. Start kicking it around so that it doesn't become frozen. Take possession of it, it's your house now, you live here, decorate it any way you want to. And the walls are not rigid, they bend like plastic." A plastic man in a plastic house.

The older I get, the more possibilities I see in the brain. I feel like I'm about ten years behind myself in what I'm able to get down on paper. That's my only regret. It has taken me a while technically to catch up with what's happening inside. It's amazing when you start feeling and seeing it from the inside. Sometimes I just lie back and watch my mind playing and leading me. I think it's there for everyone—you just have to open yourself up to the possibilities of your own brain. The collective unconscious. The individual experience. There's a lot of fun in that and that's what I was trying to do in these tiny ways with those tiny plays in the sixties, to show that possibility.

How do you see the American theatre?

Well, there are so many of them. And there are so many Americas. That's why there can't be one playwright to speak for America like there used to be. There are so many groups of people who won't hear. They won't clue into it. In the Midwest we're playing to people who are essentially independent individuals. They give you a break, they'll give you the benefit of the doubt. They will hear you out but they'll argue with you all night. But they respect you because they know what hard work is. I love playing to that audience because they have an independence of spirit, a sense of humor, and they know what it is to be up against a wall.

Different writers speak to different groups. The yuppies in their condominiums will find their own writer, right? There's a big revival of the classics going on because they think they can't get into too much trouble with a play that has lived for four hundred years. I see what is going on across America because of the cutback in money from the federal funding agencies. And there's a cutback in money from private funding agencies for the arts. There is so much to take care of in health and welfare that some of the big foundations that were giving a lot of money to the arts are now having to provide money for the basic necessities, to keep body and soul together. The result is small-cast plays, millions of *I Do, I Dos,* many three-person shows. If you have seven people on stage now that's a big cast. The regional theatres are not doing what they had hoped to do. The movement looked in the seventies like it was really going strong. The regional theatres were growing, the NEA was able to establish grants for ensembles.

People have to go out and get involved in the political process, just as if they were sitting around the kitchen table and saying, "Okay, honey, how are we going to spend the money this year? Are we going to burn it up on bullets or are we going to spend it on people who create things out of thin air, like artists?" I am thrilled about the Iran-contra hearings because I hope that this will be the beginning of a national public debate on how we are going to spend the money of the richest country in the world. Are we going to tear up more homes and families like we did in Vietnam? It's always the women and children who are the biggest casualties in modern wars. In the old days when just the men went out to fight, it looked like Mother Nature's birth control. But now it's "I've got more technology than you have."

We have huge talent in this country. I am astounded by the people who walk through our doors every day. The people graduating from theatre schools in the Midwest are now coming to us. They used to go to either coast. They can't afford to go to New York anymore. They go to Chicago, Atlanta, Minneapolis, Seattle, Miami—these places have burgeoning theatre scenes. The energy won't be in New York if the young people can't afford to live there.

What made the sixties so terrific was playing "Can you top this?" with one another. All of the theatres were within walking distance so we could really see what each was doing. There has got to be a way to share the work faster. In England all the best writers are on radio or TV all the time. We could be doing the same thing. It makes me furious. And we're losing whole generations of actors because they have no way to develop. What this country spends its money on! The people in the Open Theater were brilliant, beautiful actors. I get really angry. But I just do what I can do.

What are your own plans for the future?

I can't possibly live long enough to fulfill all of my ideas. I just want to keep working at the Omaha Magic, to help develop the young people. We have a lot of writers showing up. We can't possibly produce them all so I think we'll do readings of all the ones we like. We'll let the people in the Midwest know what the new writing is. We're doing a series, what we think is the best of the new writing, and we're also going to bring out the plays of the sixties that we think our people should know about.

I wish more people would start their own theatres and stop waiting for the phone to ring. I helped start three or four theatres. Stop bitching and get to work! There are good writers around—and people who are really interested in good writing. There's competition again, and it's great. I just wish that more money would be turned loose to support these people and I wish we had a national vehicle to help get this stuff up. With our fragmented culture, television could be put to some unifying use: Look at yourselves, here are our artists—we have so many—take pride. In the fifties they put one play after another on TV. What's the problem now? Those wimps that run TV are so wound up with technology that they won't take any more chances.

Plus there's the conservative tenor of the times. I don't care what anyone says, it all comes down from the top. Get out and vote, get involved in the political process! Getting artists to vote is really hard. At the last election I offered to have an all-night party and drive everyone to the polls. They said, "Oh it won't make any difference." They woke up the next morning and there was a big difference. They couldn't believe the difference, especially when all the funding started getting cut. So there is a lot of work to do.

LUIS VALDEZ

O ne month into the 1965 Delano grape strike, which solidified the power of the United Farm Workers, Luis Valdez met with a group of union volunteers and devised a short comic skit to help persuade reluctant workers to join the strike. He hung signs reading *Huelgista* (striker) on two men and *Esquirol* (scab) on a third. The two *Huelgistas* starting yelling at the *Esquirol* and the audience laughed. Thus began Valdez's career as founder and director of El Teatro Campesino and author of a diverse and yet deeply interconnected collection of plays.

For two years the Teatro remained actively involved in the union's struggle, performing in meeting halls, fields and strike camps. Drawing on *commedia dell'arte* and elements of Mexican folk culture, Valdez created *actos* (acts), short comic sketches designed to raise political awareness and inspire action. *Los Vendidos* (*The Sellouts*, 1967), for example, attacks the stereotyping of Chicanos and government-sanctioned tokenism. A Chicano secretary from Governor Reagan's office goes to Honest Sancho's Used Mexican Lot to buy "a Mexican type" for the front office. She examines several models—a farm worker, a young *pachuco* (swaggering street kid), a *revolucionario* and finally a Mexican-American in a business suit who sings "God Bless America" and drinks dry martinis. As soon as she buys the last, he malfunctions and begins shouting *"Viva la huelga,"* while the others chase her away and divide the money.

At the same time that he was writing and performing agitprop for the Farm Workers, Valdez turned to examine his pre-Columbian heritage, the sophisticated religion and culture of the ancient Mayans. The Teatro settled in two houses in San Juan Bautista in 1971, where they farmed according to Mayan practices and Valdez developed the second of his dramatic forms, the *mito* (myth), which characteristically takes the form of a parable based on Indian ritual. For Valdez the *mito* is an attempt to integrate political activism and religious ritual—to tie "the cause of social justice" to "the cause of everything else in our universe." *Bernabe* (1970) is a parable about the prostitution of the land. It opposes the pure, mystical love for La Tierra (the Earth) by the mentally retarded *campesino* of the title against its simple possession by landowners and banks. At the play's end Bernabe is visited by La Luna (the Moon), dressed as a 1942 *pachuco*; La Tierra; and El Sol (the Sun), in the guise of Tonatiuh, the Aztec sun god. In a final apotheosis, the "cosmic idiot" is made whole and united with La Tierra, at last revealed to be Coatlicue, the Aztec goddess of life, death and rebirth.

In the 1970s Valdez developed a third dramatic form, the *corrido* (ballad), which, like the *mito*, is intended to claim a cultural heritage rather than inspire political revolution. The *corrido* is Valdez's reinvention of the musical, based on Mexican-American folk ballads telling tales of love, death and heroism. *Zoot Suit* (1978) is perhaps his best known *corrido* and was the first Hispanic play to reach Broadway, after a long and successful run in Los Angeles. Mixing narrative, action, song and dance, it is the story of members of a zoot suit-clad *pachuco* gang of the forties, their wrongful conviction for murder and the "Zoot Suit Riots" that followed. His 1983 piece, *Corridos*, featuring songs in Spanish and dialogue in English, has been videotaped for Public Television.

Valdez's most recent play is the comedy *I Don't Have to Show You No Stinking Badges*, which has been acclaimed in Los Angeles and San Diego. A play about the political and existential implications of acting, both in theatre and society, it takes place in a television studio in which is set the suburban southern California home of Buddy and Connie Villa, two assimilated, middle-class Chicanos, "the silent bit king and queen of Hollywood." Their son, Sonny, who has just dropped out of Harvard Law School and has returned home with his Asian-American girlfriend, tries to find work in Hollywood, but despairs at having to become one of the many "actors faking our roles to fit into the great American success story." With Pirandellian sleight of hand, Valdez uses a director to interrupt the scene (which it turns out is an episode of a new sitcom, *Badges!*) in order to debate the social function of art. "This isn't reality," Sonny protests. But the director assures him, "Frankly, reality's a big boring pain in the ass. We're in the entertainment business. Laughs, Sonny, that's more important than reality."

Although closer to mainstream comedy than mystery play, Valdez's exploration of role-playing represents more a development of than a break with the technique of his early *mitos*. Both *Bernabe* and *Badges* eschew naturalism in favor of a more theatrically bold style, the earlier play drawing upon a naive formal model and the later a sophisticated one. *Bernabe,* in keeping with the conventions of religious drama, opts for a simple, mystical ending, while *Badges* refuses the pat resolution of television sitcom by offering several alternative endings. Both examine the spiritual implications of material choices; both are celebratory despite their socially critical vision. This continuity over a fifteen-year period attests to the clarity of Valdez's intention: to put the Chicano experience on stage in all of its political, cultural and religious complexity; and to examine the interrelationship between the political and the metaphysical, between historically determined oppressive structures and man's transhistorical desire for faith and freedom.

■   ■   ■

MAY 6, 1987—LUIS VALDEZ'S OFFICE IN EL TEATRO CAMPESINO,
SAN JUAN BAUTISTA, CALIFORNIA

How did you get interested in theatre?

There's a story that's almost apocryphal, I've repeated it so many times now. It's nevertheless true. I got hooked on the theatre when I was six. I was born into a family of migrant farm workers and shortly after World War II we were in a cotton camp in the San Joaquin valley. The season was over, it was starting to rain, but we were still there because my dad's little Ford pickup truck had broken down and was up on blocks and there was no way for us to get out. Life was pretty meager then and we survived by fishing in a river and sharing staples like beans, rice and flour. And the bus from the local school used to come in from a place called Stratford—irony of ironies, except it was on the San Joaquin River [laughs].

I took my lunch to school in a little brown paper bag—which was a valuable commodity because there were still paper shortages in 1946. One day as school let out and the kids were rushing toward the bus, I found my bag missing and went around in a panic looking for it. The teacher saw me and said, "Are you looking for your bag?" and I said, "Yes." She said, "Come here," and she took me in the little back room and there, on a table, were some things laid out that completely changed my perception of the universe.

She'd torn the bag up and placed it in water. I was horrified. But then she showed me the next bowl. It was a paste. She was making papier-mâché. A little farther down the line, she'd taken the paper and put it on a clay mold of a face of a monkey, and finally there was a finished product, unpainted but nevertheless definitely a monkey. And she said, "I'm making masks."

I was amazed, shocked in an exhilarating way, that she could do this with paper and paste. As it turned out, she was making masks for the school play. I didn't know what a play was, but she explained and said, "We're having tryouts." I came back the next week all enthused and auditioned for a part and got a leading role as a monkey. The play was about Christmas in the jungle. I was measured for a costume that was better than the clothes I was wearing at the time, certainly more colorful. The next few weeks were some of the most exciting in my short life. After seeing the stage transformed into a jungle and after all the excitement of the preparations—I doubt that it was as elaborate as my mind remembers it now—my dad got the truck fixed and a week before the show was to go on, we moved away. So I never got to be in the Christmas play.

That left an unfillable gap, a vacuum that I've been pouring myself into for the last forty-one years. From then on, it was just a question of evolution. Later I got into puppets. I was a ventriloquist, believe it or not. In 1956 when I was in high school, I became a regular on a local television program. I was still living in a *barrio* with my family, a place in San Jose called Sal Si Puedes—Get Out if You Can. It was one of those places with dirt streets and chuckholes, a terrible place. But I was on television, right? [laughs], and I wrote my own stuff and it established me in high school.

By the time I graduated, I had pretty well decided that writing was my consuming passion. Coming from my background, I didn't feel right about going to my parents and saying, "I want to be a playwright." So I started college majoring in math and physics. Then one day late in my freshman year I walked to the drama department and decided, "The hell with it, I'm going to go with this." I changed majors to English, with an emphasis on playwriting, and that's what I did for the rest of my college days.

In 1964 I wrote and directed my first full-length play, *The Shrunken Head of Pancho Villa*. People saw it and gave me a lot of encouragement. I joined the San Francisco Mime Troupe the following year, and then in '65 joined the Farm Workers Union and essentially started El Teatro Campesino. The evolution has been continuous since then, both of the company and of my styles of playwriting.

During that period, what was your most important theatre training—college, the Mime Troupe?

It's all important. It's a question of layering. I love to layer things, I think they achieve a certain richness—I'm speaking now about "the work." But life essentially evolves that way, too. Those years of studying theatre history were extremely important. I connected with a number of ancient playwrights in a very direct way. Plautus was a revelation, he spoke directly to me. I took four years of Latin so I was able to read him in Latin. There are clever turns of phrases that I grew to appreciate and, in my own way, was able almost to reproduce in Spanish. The central figure of the wily servant in classical Roman drama—Greek also—became a standard feature of my work with El Teatro Campesino. The striker was basically a wily servant. I'd also been exposed to *commedia dell'arte* through the San Francisco Mime Troupe, with its stock characters, the Brighellas, Arlecchinos and Pantalones. I saw a direct link between these *commedia* types and the types I had to work with in order to put together a Farm Workers' theatre. I chose to do an outdoor, robust theatre of types. I figured it hit the reality.

My second phase was the raw, elemental education I got, performing under the most primitive conditions in the farm labor camps and on flatbed trucks. In doing so, I dealt with the basic elements of drama: structure, language, music, movement. The first education was literary, the second practical. We used to put on stuff every week, under all kinds of circumstances: outdoors, indoors, under the threat of violence. There was a period during the grape strike in '67 when we had become an effective weapon within the Farm Workers and were considered enough of a threat that a rumor flashed across the strike camp that somebody was after me with a high-powered rifle. We went out to the labor camp anyway, but I was really sweating it. I don't think I've sweated any performance since then. It changed my perspective on what I was doing. Was this really worth it? Was it a life-and-death issue? Of course it was for me at the time, and still is. But I learned that in a very direct and practical way. I was beaten and kicked and jailed, also in the sixties, essentially for doing theatre. I knew the kind of theatre we were doing was a political act, it was art and politics. At least I hope I wasn't being kicked for the art [laughs].

What other playwrights had a major impact on you in those days?

Brecht looms huge in my orientation. I discovered Brecht in college, from an intellectual perspective. That was really the only way—no one was doing Brecht back in 1961. When Esslin's book *Brecht: The Man and His Work*, came out in 1960, I was working in the library, so I had first dibs on all the new books. Brecht to me had been only a name. But this book opened up Brecht and I started reading all his plays and his theories, which I subscribed to immediately. I continue to use his alienation effect to this day. I don't think audiences like it too much, but I like it because it seems to me an essential feature of the experience of theatre.

Theatre should reflect an audience back on itself. You should think as well as feel. Still, there's no underestimating the power of emotional impact—I understand better now how ideas are conveyed and exchanged on a beam of emotion. I think Brecht began to discover that in his later works and integrated it. I've integrated a lot of feeling into my works, but I still love ideas. I still love communicating a concept, an abstraction. That's the mathematician in me.

How has your way of writing changed over the years?

What has changed over the years is an approach and a technique. The first few years with the Teatro Campesino were largely improvisational. I wrote outlines. I sketched out a dramatic structure, sometimes on a single page, and used that as my guide to direct the actors. Later on, I began to write very simple scripts that were sometimes born out of improvisations. During the first ten years, from '65 to '75, the collective process became more complicated and more sophisticated within the company—we were creating longer pieces, full-length pieces, but they'd take forever to complete using the collective process.

By 1975, I'd taken the collective process as far as I could. I enjoyed working with people. I didn't have to deal with the loneliness of writing. My problem was that I was so much part of the collective that I couldn't leave for even a month without the group having serious problems. By 1975 we were stable enough as a company for me to begin to take a month, two months, six months, eventually a year. I turned a corner and was ready to start writing plays again.

In 1975 I took a month off and wrote a play. We did a piece called *El Fin del Mundo (The End of the World)* from 1974 through 1980, a different version every year. The '75 version was a play I sat down and wrote. I started with a lot of abstract notions—the mathematician sometimes gets in the way—but eventually I plugged into characters born of my experience. Those characters are still alive for me. Someday I'll finish all of that as a play or else it will be poured into a screenplay for a "major motion picture" [laughs].

Shortly after that, in 1977, I was invited by the Mark Taper Forum to write a play for their New Theatre for Now series. We agreed on the Zoot Suit Riots as a subject. *Zoot Suit* firmly reestablished my self-identity as a playwright. Essentially I've been writing nonstop since '75. That's not to say I didn't write anything between '65 and '75. *Soldado Razo*, which is probably my most performed play around the world, was written in 1970, as was *Bernabe. The Dark Root of a Scream* was written in 1967. These are all one-acts. I used to work on them with a sense of longing, wanting more time to be able to sit down and write.

Now I'm firmly back in touch with myself as a playwright. When I begin, I allow myself at least a month of free association with notes. I can start anywhere. I can start with an abstract notion, a character…it's rarely dialogue or anything specific like that. More often than not, it's just an amorphous bunch of ideas, impressions and feelings. I allow myself to tumble in this ball of thoughts and impressions, knowing that I'm heading toward a play and that eventually I've got to begin dealing with character and then structure.

Because of the dearth of Hispanic playwrights—or even American playwrights, for that matter—I felt it necessary to explore the territory, to cover the range of theatre as widely as I could. Political theatre with the Farm Workers was sometimes minimal scale, a small group of workers gathered in some dusty little corner in a labor camp, and sometimes immense—huge crowds, ten thousand, fifteen thousand, with banners flying. But the political theatre extends beyond the farm worker into the whole Chicano experience. We've dealt with a lot of issues: racism, education, immigration—and that took us, again, through many circles.

We evolved three separate forms: the *acto* was the political act, the short form, fifteen minutes; the *mito* was the mythic, religious play; and the *corrido* was the ballad. I just finished a full-length video program called *Corridos*. So the form has evolved into another medium. I do political plays, musicals, historical dramas, religious dramas. We still do our religious plays at the Mission here every year. They're nurturing, they feed the spirit. Peter Brook's response when he saw our Virgin play, years ago, was that it was like something out of the Middle Ages. It's religion for many of the people who come see it, not just entertainment. And of course we've gone on to do serious plays and comedies like *I Don't Have to Show You No Stinking Badges*.

It seems that a play like Bernabe *aligns the* acto *and the* mito, *politics and the myth. It uses religious mysticism to point out the difference between simply owning the land and loving it. The political point is made by appeal to mystical process.*

The spiritual aspect of the political struggle has been part of the work from the beginning. Some of that is through Cesar Chavez, who is a spiritual-political leader. Some people—say, the political types—have had trouble dealing with the spiritual. They say, "It's a distortion. Religion is the opium of the masses." But it seems to me that the spiritual is very much part of everyday life. There's no way to exclude it…we are spirit. We're a manifestation of something, of an energy.

The whole fusion between the spiritual and the material is for me the paradox of human existence. That's why I connected with Peter Brook when he was here in '73—his question was, "How do you make the invisible visible?" To me myth is not something that's fake or not real. On the contrary, it's so real that it's just below the surface—it's the supporting structure of our everyday reality. That makes me a lot more Jungian than Freudian. And it distinguishes me, I think, from a lot of other playwrights. A lot of modern playwrights go to psychoanalysis to work out their problems. I can't stop there, that's just the beginning for me. I've had to go to the root of my own existence in order to effect my own salvation, if you will. The search for meaning took me into religion and science, and into mythology.

I had to sound out these things in myself. Someone pointed out to me the evolution a couple of years ago. *The Shrunken Head of Pancho Villa* is theatre of the absurd. One of the characters, the oldest brother, is a disembodied head, huge, oversized. He eats all of the food that the family can produce. So they stay poor. He has lice that turn out to be tiny cockroaches that grow and cover the walls. He sings "La Cucaracha" but cannot talk. And he can't move. He's just kind of there. In a metaphorical sense, that was me back in the early sixties. That's the way I felt—that I had no legs, no arms. By 1970, when I got to *Bernabe*, I was the idiot, but I'd gotten in contact with the sun and the moon and earth. Fortunately, out of these grotesque self-portraits, my characters have attained a greater and greater degree of humanity.

I've always had difficulty with naturalism in the theatre. Consequently, a lot of people have looked at my work and said, "Maybe he just can't write naturalism. His is the theatre of types, of simplistic little stick figures." What I needed was a medium in which to be able to do naturalism, so I came to film. *La Bamba* is naturalism, as well as of the spirit. There I wanted the dirt, so I got the dirt. I wanted intimate realistic scenes between two real people. I can write that stuff for the stage too, but it just doesn't interest me. The stage for me—that box, that flat floor—holds other potentials, it's a means to explore other things.

As much a ritual space as anything else.

Most definitely. It seems to me that the essence of the human being is to act, to move through space in patterns that give his life meaning. We adorn ourselves with symbolic objects that give that movement even more meaning. Then we come out with sounds. And then somewhere along the line we begin to call that reality—but it's a self-created reality. The whole of civilization is a dance. I think the theatre celebrates that.

So religion functions in your work as a connection with the past, with one's heritage and one's bond to all men.

Sounding out those elemental drums, going back into the basics. I was doing this as a Chicano but I was also doing it as someone who inhabits the twentieth century. I think we need to reconnect. The word religion means "a tying back."

The vacuum I thought I was born into turned out to be full of all kinds of mystery and power. The strange things that were going on in the *barrio* —the Mexican things, the ethnic things—seemed like superstition, but on another level there was a lot of psychic activity. There's a lot of psychic activity in Mexican culture that is actually political at times.

Zoot Suit is another extremely spiritual, political play. And it was never understood. People thought it was about juvenile delinquents and that I was putting the Pachuco on the stage just to be snide. But the young man, Henry Reyna, achieves his own liberation by coming into contact with this internal authority. The Pachuco is the Jungian self-image, the superego if you will, the power inside every individual that's greater than any human institution. The Pachuco says, "It'll take more than the U.S. Navy to beat me down," referring to the navy and marines stripping zoot suiters in the 1940s. "I don't give a fuck what you do to me, you can't take this from me. And I reassert myself, in this guise." The fact that critics couldn't accept that guise was too bad, but it doesn't change the nature of what the play's about. It deals with self-salvation. And you can follow the playwright through the story—I was also those two dudes. With *Zoot Suit* I was finally able to transcend social conditions, and the way I did it on stage was to give the Pachuco absolute power, as the master of ceremonies. He could snap his fingers and stop the action. It was a Brechtian device that allowed the plot to move forward, but psychically and symbolically, in the right way.

And Chicanos got off on it. That's why a half-million people came to see it in L.A. Because I had given a disenfranchised people their religion back. I dressed the Pachuco in the colors of Testatipoka, the Aztec god of education, the dean of the school of hard knocks. There's another god of culture, Quetzalcoatl, the feathered serpent, who's much kinder. He surfaces in *La Bamba* as the figure of Ritchie Valens. He's an artist and poet and is gentle and not at all fearful. When my audiences see *La Bamba*, they like that positive spirit. The Pachuco's a little harder to take. But these are evolutions. I use the metaphor of the serpent crawling out of its skin. There's that symbolism in *La Bamba*—it's pre-Columbian, but it's also very accurate in terms of the way that I view my own life. I've crawled through many of my own dead skins.

Although Badges *and* Bernabe *are very different, in both of them the met-aphysical is given a political dimension.*

I like to think there's a core that's constant. In one way, what I have to say is quite basic, quite human. In another way, it's specifically American, in a continental sense. I'm reaching back to pre-Columbian America and trying to share that. I feel and sense those rhythms within me. I'm not just a Mexican farm worker. I'm an American with roots in Mayan culture. I can resonate and unlock some of the mysteries of this land which reside in all of us. I've just been in the neighborhood a little bit longer. I'm a great believer in dreams. I've had some fantastic dreams. I dream when I'm standing up. I try to make my dreams come true.

What about the endings of your plays? Zoot Suit's *seems very Brechtian, a happy ending immediately called into question. Then you present three dif-ferent possible futures for the characters. And* Badges *is similar. You present what could happen, depending on the choices the characters make.*

Multiple endings—multiple beginnings, too—have started to evolve in my work. I don't think there's any single end. I firmly believe that we exist simultaneously on seven levels—you can call them *shakras* if you're so in-clined, or you can call them something else. In the Mayan sculptures, there's a vision of the universe in those ancient headdresses, in which you see the open mouths of birds with human heads coming through them, and then something else going in through the eyes and coming out again. That's a pulsating vision of the universe. It might have been born from the jungle but is, nevertheless, an accurate description of what is going on below the surface, at the nuclear level, in the way atomic particles are interacting. To me the universe is a huge, pulsating, enormously vital and *conscious* phenomenon. There is no end. There is no beginning. There's only an apparent end and an apparent beginning.

We're very emotional beings—tremendously gregarious creatures. We're very loving and caring for our mates. We're violent, there's no question about that. Tremendously cruel, intellectually cruel, unlike the animals. But even the cold-blooded murderers among us have emotion and sentiment. So it's good to end on a strong feeling. Sometimes, in the search for the right feeling, I have three or four endings.

We had an ending and beginning to *La Bamba*, which I had scripted and seemed right on paper. But our first preview audiences rejected them, so eventually we snipped them. What we had was not exactly a Brechtian turn, but it was a stepping back and looking at the fifties from the perspective of the eighties. Our audiences told us they didn't want to come back into the eighties. They wanted to stay in the fifties. I had been trying, on some level, to alleviate the pain of Ritchie Valens' death, but audiences told us, "Leave us with the pain." So that's where we left it.

Can you describe how you work as a director with your own material? When you start rehearsals, do you have a finished script?

These days, there's at least a first or second draft. I've also worked in the opposite way, with no script whatsoever. I believe in the reality of my process as a playwright, and sometimes the audience has to suffer through it, although I try not to force paying audiences to. But back in the late sixties, early seventies, our audiences didn't pay that much—in fact, many of our performances were free—so I felt I could take certain liberties. One time we were working on a new piece, on the road in L.A., and I got new ideas for some dialogue. I was talking to the actors all the way up until curtain time. During the show I was in the wings, making notes on scraps of paper and handing them to the actors as they went on stage [laughs]. And what's really ridiculous is that they did it.

Now this is not as crazy as it sounds. You can do precisely this in making a movie. You create new lines on the spot, the actor goes in front of the camera and delivers. I'm still rewriting *Badges*. This is our closing weekend coming up and I'm introducing a couple of new scenes in the second act. I feel that so far I've found only an apparent ending. The real ending is down the road someplace. I'm touring with this play across country, I want to get to New York with it, so I'm working on it.

As a director I switch gears. Writing is a solitary process—you're in there with the words and I love that. But I also love directing, getting out of myself and into other people. As a director—and this again comes from my experiences in the Farm Worker days—I have to know who I'm working with. And what they are like. If I have four actors, or a dozen actors, plus crew, my first job as a director is to get them to become one, to arouse a lot of enthusiasm.

More and more the first thing I want to establish in character development is the movement. You can't have a feeling, an emotion, without motion. You can pick up a lot from the associative school, referring back to your own experiences, but I think it's also possible to get people to laugh and cry through what they do to their bodies.

We talk a lot about the theatre of the sphere. I firmly believe that each of us exists within his or her own sphere. The actor must begin to move within it. Every part of him resolves itself in tiny spheres—a fist spinning on a wrist, joints, legs, arms. The body centers on the solar plexus and the gut, the pelvis. I insist the first element is to move your pelvis. That gets into very sexual kinds of movements and people sometimes get embarrassed. But out of them comes a lot of basic emotion. Freud is right. We are anal and sexual. Jung comes in with the idea that we trace a sphere. Once you get into the sphere, you find your connection with Mother Earth, with the sun, with the moon, with a drop of water, with the known universe. And when you begin to inhabit your own sphere as an actor, you finally begin to stretch its limits, to encompass and envelop other people, including an entire audience. You can project yourself.

You can't get away with "acting" on film. You have to cut it so close to the bone, you have to *be*, to get down-and-dirty. It's "the Method," to be sure. So you have to make it small, intense and real. On the stage, because you have to project, things sometimes get out of whack. And you have to switch to a new mentality. This is where ritual comes in. Performance on the stage is much more like dance than anything else. Dance is real. You can't fake dance. But somehow a lot of people start acting as if they're "acting," and think they're doing it right. In fact, acting is something totally different: it's a *real act*. Which gets back to politics, in that our first theatrical acts were real political acts. That's why that dude was out there with a high-powered rifle—he wasn't seeing theatre, but a threatening political act.

Now it seems that the political dimension has become sublimated, less explicit. You're no longer writing agitprop.

There is a time and place for all forms. It's twenty years down the road. But the political impact is still there. The only difference is that I'm being asked to run for governor now, which I'm not interested in doing. My purpose is still to impact socially, culturally and politically. I'm reaffirming some things that are very important to all of us as Americans, those things that we all believe to be essential to our society. What I hope is changing is a perception about the country as a whole. And the continent as well.

I'm just trying to kick my two cents into the pot. I still want El Teatro Campesino to perform on Broadway, because I think that's a political act. El Teatro Campesino is in Hollywood, and I don't think we've compromised any social statements. We started out in '65 doing these *actos* within the context of the United Farm Workers. Twenty-two years later, my next movie may be about the grape strike. My Vietnam was at home. I refused to go to Vietnam, but I encountered all the violence I needed on the home front: people were killed by the Farm Workers' strike.

Some critics have accused you of selling out.

I used to joke, "It's impossible for us to sell out because nobody wants to buy us." That doesn't bother me in the least. There's too much to do, to be socially conscious about. In some ways, it's just people sounding me out. I don't mind people referring back to what I have been. We're all like mirrors to each other. People help to keep you on course. I've strayed very little from my pronounced intentions. In '67 when we left United Farm Workers and started our own cultural center in Del Rey, we came out with a manifesto essentially stating that we were trying to put the tools of the artist in the hands of the humblest, the working people. But not just nineteenth-century tools, not clay and straw, or spit and masking tape, or felt pens. We were talking about video, film, recording studios. Now we're beginning to work in the best facilities that the industry has to offer. What we do with them is something else.

Do you read the critics?

Sure. I love listening to the public. They're the audience, who am I to argue with them? They either got it or they didn't. The critics are part of the process. I do have some strong feelings about the nature of American criticism—I don't think that it's deeply rooted enough in a knowledge of theatre history. Very often newspapers just assign reporters, Joe Blow off the street. Perhaps it would be too much for the public to have somebody who's overly informed—is that possible?—about the theatre. There's no overriding sense of what the theatre's about in America. There's more of that sense in Europe, and a deeper appreciation for change, direction and a body of work.

In this country we are still victims of our economic system. If you make a buck, you're interesting. So obviously the only solution is to make a buck, to show that you can. That doesn't bother me, if it's attached to reaching an audience. At first, we never thought much about charging. But the poor people saw us working. They said, "We feel funny about taking this without giving you something." Our entry into the professional theatre meant that there was an audience here willing to pay.

How do you see the American theatre today?

My overwhelming impression is that theatre's not nearly as interesting as it could be, that it's been stuck in its traces for many, many years. Broadway has not moved out of the twenties from what I can see. It might be because so many of the houses on Broadway are nineteenth-century playhouses. Much of the material that I see—and I don't see nearly enough—is too anemic for my tastes. I have trouble staying awake in the theatre, believe it or not [laughs]. I mean I can barely stay awake at my own plays.

I feel that the whole question of the human enterprise is up for grabs. I don't think this country has come to terms with its racial questions, obviously. And because of that, it has not really come to terms with the cultural question of what America is. There are two vast melting pots that must eventually come together. The Hispanic, after all, is really the product of a melting pot—there's no such thing as a Latin American race. The Hispanic melting pot melds all the races of the world, like the Anglo melting pot does; so one of these days, and probably in the United States, those two are going to be poured together—probably in a play, and it could be one of my own [laughs].

There's a connection with the Indian cultures that has to be established in American life. Before we can do that, however, we have to get beyond the national guilt over the genocide of the Indian. What's needed is expiation and forgiveness, and the only ones in a position to forgive are the Indian peoples. I'm a Yaqui Indian—Spanish blood, yes, but largely Yaqui. I'm in a position to be able to forgive white people. And why not? I think that's what we're here for, to forgive each other. Martin Luther King speaking in 1963 at the Lincoln Memorial was a beginning. It didn't reach nearly far enough. We're still wrestling with it. Deep fears, about miscegenation and the despoliation of the race, have to be dealt with. I'm here, through my work, to show that short, brown people are okay. We've got ideas, too, and we've got a song, and a dance or two. We know something about the world that we can share. I'm here to show that to other brown people who don't think very much of themselves, and there are a lot of those.

I wish there were more plays that dealt with the reality of this country. The racial issue is always just swept aside. It deserves to be swept aside only after it's been dealt with. We cannot begin to approach a real solution to our social ills—a solution like integration, for instance, or assimilation, without dealing with all our underlying feelings about each other. I'm trying to deal with my past, not just with respect to Anglos, but to blacks and Asians. I draw on the symbolism of the four roads: the black road, the white road, the red road and the yellow road. They all meet in the navel of the universe, the place where the upper road leads into the underworld—read consciousness and subconsciousness. I think that where they come home is in America.

What are your plans for the future? And goals.

I'm into a very active phase right now, as writer and director, but with writing as the base. I have a number of very central stories I want to tell—on film, on television and on the stage. I want to be working in the three media, on simultaneous projects that feed each other. I like the separation between film, television and theatre. It makes each a lot clearer for me. In theatre, there are a number of ritualistic pieces I want to do that explore the movement of bodies in space and the relation between movement and language. That sphere I can explore on film, too, or television. What film gives me is movement around the actor—I can explore from any viewpoint, any distance. But theatre's the only medium that gives me the sheer beauty, power and presence of bodies. Ritual, literally.

I've got a piece that I've been working on for many, many years, called *The Earthquake Sun*, about our time. All I can tell you is that it will be on the road one of these days. I have another play called *The Mummified Fetus*. It takes off from a real incident that happened a couple of years ago: an eighty-five-year-old woman was discovered with a mummified fetus in her womb. I have a couple of plays that the world has not seen, that we've only done here.

In television I have a number of projects. *Corridos* has begun to open up other possibilities. I talk about video as electronic theatre. I'm getting into the idea of doing theatre before cameras, but going for specifically theatrical moments as opposed to real cinematic moments. *Corridos* is an example of this. And film—I'm going after the proverbial three-picture deal. I want to make movies the way I do plays.

I hope a more workable touring network will develop in this country. The links between East and West must be solidified. I think it's great for companies to tour. We're very excited about the possibility of our company plugging into the resources of the regional theatres, as we've done with *Badges* in San Diego and at the Los Angeles Theatre Center, even with the Burt Reynolds Playhouse in Florida. We hope to be able to go from regional theatre to regional theatre all the way across the country, including New York. In that way, we'll be able to reach a national audience.

I still want to experience the dust and sweat occasionally. I'm trying to leave time open for that. This month we're going to celebrate the twenty-fifth anniversary of the United Farm Workers—we'll be back on a flatbed truck, doing some of the old *actos*. I don't want to lose any of our audience. I want worldwide audience. We had that—up until 1980 we were touring Europe and Latin America. I want to tour Asia with the Teatro Campesino. Essentially, I would like to see theatre develop the kind of mass audience— it's impossible of course—that the movies have. I wish we could generate that enthusiasm in young people and in audiences in general, get them out of their homes, away from their VCRs, to experience the theatre as the life-affirming, life-giving experience that it is.

MICHAEL WELLER

W hile an undergraduate music major at Brandeis, Michael Weller joined
a theatre group called Hi-Charlie that produced original musicals. He
wrote the score for one of their shows and then decided that he wanted to
sketch out the book for a second, as well as write the music. He wrote a draft
based on James Purdy's *Malcolm*, gave it to Hi-Charlie, and asked them to
find a "real playwright" to complete it. Much to Weller's chagrin, they liked
it as it was, refused to let him write the score and produced it in 1963.

For almost twenty years Weller has been hailed as the chronicler of a
generation, those who came of age in the 1960s. His first success, *Moonchildren*, about a group of college students, was produced in London in 1970.
Under the direction of Alan Schneider, who was long associated with Weller's
work, the play moved from Arena Stage to Broadway two years later. *Moonchildren* was followed by a series of plays which has brought Weller's history
of this generation up-to-date. These include *Fishing* (1975), *Loose Ends* (1979),
Split (1980) and *Ghost on Fire* (1985). In addition, Weller has written a play
about the old West, *The Ballad of Soapy Smith* (1984), and the screenplays
for two Milos Forman films, *Hair* and *Ragtime*.

Weller's drama tends to be driven by character rather than plot. The narrative is slowly accrued through the accumulation of details of interpersonal relations. All of his plays are closely attentive to group dynamics and tend to be dominated by several key figures whose interrelationship is foregrounded, rather than by one overruling protagonist. The personal development of the group is set in counterpoint against a background of lowering problems and social issues beyond the immediate control of any of the characters. *Moonchildren*, for example, depicts men and women making the transition from adolescence to adulthood, haunted by the Vietnam War, race riots, the draft and the burgeoning student protest movement. The action of the play consists of the interaction of plot-motifs ranging from the most whimsically comic to the most grave: lovers getting together, others breaking up, a cat having kittens, students threatening self-immolation, disappearing hamburgers, a mother's death. Out of these details a portrait is slowly constructed of a society in transit, struggling to come to terms with newly found freedom, idealism, social activism, loneliness and despair. Weller himself has described his characters' journey as taking place "across a desert strewn with patches of quicksand." Most find their way. A few get lost.

Loose Ends, a more tightly plotted piece, spans nine years in the relationship between Paul and Susan, from their first meeting to a reunion after their divorce. Each scene ends with a dramatic question mark: will they stay together or drift apart? The play dramatizes the interplay between their evolving relationship and the various outside pressures working on them. It traces their path through courtship, marriage, pregnancy, abortion and divorce, keeping the audience aware of the continually changing impact of family and friends, career pressures and their growing affluence. The development of the characters is a complex one. On the one hand, *Loose Ends* shows their gradual loss of ideals and increased materialism—in Paul's change from Peace Corps worker to film editor, in the movement of the setting from a moonlit Balinese beach to an apartment on Central Park West. At the same time, the play chronicles the emotional maturation of both Paul and Susan and their growing comfort with themselves and each other. The play ends with no resolution, the only certainty that their relationship will continue, an enduring series of loose ends.

Ghost on Fire is both more traditional than Weller's other plays, with its clearly defined ironic reversal, and more theatrically bold in its use of nonnaturalistic devices to break the texture of the action. It opposes death to rebirth, presenting the conversion of film director and teacher Dan Rittman through his love of and commitment to his old friend Neil, dying of a brain tumor. The pivotal moment for Dan, the one that gives him perspective and allows him to help his friend die, takes place when he and Neil meet an old black man who, sitting in a wrecked car in a South Carolina field, conducts them on a visit to heaven. There Nathan sees his dead children, telling them, as Neil and Dan film the scene, "It's how you live the time you've got, that's all that counts." At the end of the play, after Neil has peacefully expired and Dan has recognized and dealt with the failure of his marriage, Dan returns to work. "You go on. For whatever reason. For Neil, maybe." But most importantly, "*For other people*. You never know who you might touch one day."

Ghost on Fire testifies both to Weller's move toward more conventional dramatic form and to the increasingly theatrical and schematic nature of his recent work. His basic project, however, remains intact: the creation of a dramatic fabric that runs the evolution of a group of characters in counterpoint against the changing social backdrop. Despite the dual concerns, Weller's drama—and this may in part explain its singular pertinence for the sixties generation—remains firmly focused on the problems of individual consciousness, subordinating social problems to personal ones. For Weller recognition, self-confrontation and change are paramount and his plays remain testaments to the durability of hope and the potential for growth in the face of adversity.

■   ■   ■

FEBRUARY 9, 1987—MICHAEL WELLER'S OFFICE, EAST VILLAGE,
NEW YORK CITY

What were your early experiences in theatre?

I actually remember the first time I went to the theatre. I saw *Beauty and the Beast* in Las Vegas. I was deeply touched by it and I don't know why. The one thing I remember is how beautiful the beast's costume was. I've completely forgotten about Beauty [laughs]. In high school I was directed towards the theatre by a teacher.

Where was this?

At Stockbridge School, in Massachusetts. She was a genius at teaching and had worked out ways for drama to help kids figure out who they were. She did a lot of improvisation work and a lot of making up plays. She had taught Mike Nichols at one point. All year long we did drama. I remember clearly one improvisation where I was stunned at how my concentration made everybody do what my imagination dictated. I was normally very quiet. Suddenly I discovered that I had this incredible power when I improvised.

It was a big thing to get into the senior play. You got out of class, and you got to rehearse off-campus. We did a production of *Peer Gynt* that was directed by Arthur Lithgow, John Lithgow's father, who used to run the Great

Lakes Shakespeare Festival. I played the middle-aged Peer Gynt. My dad—I didn't know him too well at that point because he hadn't brought me up—said, "You have a real knack for that." That was praise he didn't need to give. He, of all my family, was the one most attached to the bigger world, the world that appears in magazines, the world where famous people live. So he had the weird authority of that world.

At Brandeis I got into Hi-Charlie, a group that did original musicals. I wrote the score to one of the pieces—*A Cool Million*, the Nathanael West piece. I enjoyed that but I looked at the piece and thought, "The book isn't good. I have to do something from the ground up. But how do you do that?" I'd never written anything before. I had no impulse in that direction. So I went out and got a book, *Playwriting Made Easy*, and studied it. I wrote what I thought was a rough draft of a book based on James Purdy's *Malcolm* and Hi-Charlie produced it just as it was.

Do you still compose?

A little bit, just for fun.

Any similarity between the two processes?

I don't compose seriously enough to say there's a process to it. Playwriting I do with a little more care and attention. A lot of the time, though, I write musically. I don't see the words, I hear them. For that reason, my spelling is awful. I'm not aware of the thing on the page, but as something that's going to be up there in front of people. The page is just a distracting, in-between step. My ear gives me a sense of when things have to be bigger, of the dynamic size of the piece. When I was in school I always loved the idea of writing a modern symphony. But I never got to the point where I could master the orchestra. I just loved the sheer size, the number of instruments, the bigness of an orchestra. As I become less concerned with making a living directly from playwriting, I find myself compelled in a symphonic direction in plays. I love plays on a big scale. I like watching them, rehearsing them, writing them.

If you're going to write on a big scale, you have to let the audience's mind follow a heavy, clear way through the middle, like those gyroscopes—you can't get it off balance too much. When I go to the theatre now, I get antsy at small plays. If I see there are three people in the cast, I go, "Oh, my Lord." What if I don't like them? There's no relief. I suppose what I'm saying is that the frivolous part of me enjoys all that frippery. In my way of looking at theatre, you don't get to anything deeper until all of the cheap stuff is satisfied—color, size, pretty people, all that nonsense.

When did you go to England?

I went there in '68 because of a drama teacher. When the musical was accepted for Hi-Charlie, I enrolled in a playwriting course. The teacher, John Matthews, was one of the most intelligent and unmystifying teachers I've ever had. He said, "I think you'll get much better habits as a theatre person if you go to England because it's a profession there and you will learn how to spend a life in the theatre. So give yourself a few years."

So I went to the University of Manchester, where I had Stephen Joseph for my teacher—Hermione Gingold's son by the publisher Michael Joseph. He died the next year. He used to collect a group of twelve people and issue a degree that he invented called a Diploma in Drama. I don't think it officially exists, but I've got one. He would choose people utterly at whim. He had no goal except to entertain himself enormously all year. And so he would bring together the wildest bunch of students. The theme that drew them all together was something inside of Stephen that we had to guess. He was one the world's great eccentrics. He took me in because it was evidently his plan to have one American homosexual in the group each year, and he was sure from my letter that I was gay. So for the first month and a half there was hell to pay because he saw me dating some of the girls in the school. Then it turned out that another American was gay and so he came around.

At the university there was a chapel with a theatre in the top and he would take you up there for a week and a half, teach you how to use all the technical stuff, teach you box office, administration, painting flats, everything. Then he would say, "It's yours. I don't want to see it empty all year. You don't have to come to me for permission to do anything. You figure out between you who gets to use it when. You invite me to see what you do. And you're all going to get A's, so you don't have to do a thing. But this is the last time you're going to get a free ride. If you work, I'll notice and help you." Those of us who were looking for this kind of opportunity leapt at the chance and were in that studio all the time, learning by being with our peers and arguing it out. We worked, ate and slept in the theatre. We ended up taking a play to a festival in England and to another in Parma, Italy. That year was amazing. Almost everybody's gone on into the theatre in some significant way. I think that would happen a lot more if theatre schools were run according to the whims of one great person who, forgetting all the normal qualifications, just says, "That person pleases me."

What influenced you during that period?

I was very much under the influence of British writers, in particular John Osborne, John Arden and John Whiting. At one point I wrote in a kind of fake British way. I wasn't really getting anywhere. Although when I look back, I can see there were places where I was already writing like me. But I didn't yet know what that was. So I was trying to use models. My most conscious one was John Whiting. The only other playwright I really connected with was Sean O'Casey. Later, when I started gaining more recognition, I kept being described as being like Chekhov but I'd never read his stuff and the little I'd seen, I hated. I thought it was the most boring, somber, dreary shit I'd ever seen. But that's because it was being done very badly. When I was in England somebody pointed out to me that Chekhov was really funny and that he saw action with a double focus. After a few years, he finally clicked for me. But he wasn't an influence and still isn't. I find that the big secret of what he's on to is something I wouldn't dare touch. I don't feel comfortable with his medical perception of the world.

The guy I was rooming with in England was a reader for the RSC. He started getting in plays that were being done Off Broadway—Lanford Wilson, Leonard Melfi, Sam Shepard. I read them and went, "Whoo, this is great." Because the only American play I'd ever really loved, incredibly loved, was *The Zoo Story.* I thought the writing was so stunning because it sounded like normal people thinking and talking, and no other plays did. The people were very natural in their behavior, but what was going on inside of them was so weird and subjective and free. I didn't know anyone else who wrote like that. So when I saw this group of writers who were really more a continuation of Albee than of anything before, I was very excited and I thought, "That's American. They're writing a new language that I haven't seen on stage." So I read anything I could get ahold of by these people. And then one day I sat down and the first play that sounds like me popped out. I knew my ear from home could guide my composition.

Did Tennessee Williams have any impact on you?

None at all. I find him amazing but alien. I don't find my world constantly illuminated by what he writes. I'm awed by his fluidity inside characters—tonally, he flows through them with such ease and surefootedness. The only time I felt a connection to him was when I saw an early version of *Orpheus Descending* at Circle in the Square. It was like social drama, a perfect portrait of a little southern town and all of its zanies.

What about Arthur Miller?

I just read *Clara* and *I Can't Remember Anything,* the two plays that are being done at Lincoln Center. Again, I admire the hell out of him but something doesn't fully click for me. I love the passion and the emotional bigness of it—he has an enormously important thing on his mind. But there's some-

277

thing about the way his plays are proofs of things which I find unsatisfying. So I have to ignore that part of his work and I don't think he'd want me to. I have to look for the power elsewhere. The first of the one-acts, with the old radical and his friend from down the road, is a wonderful play. And very uncharacteristic. It's just these two people who aren't quite arguing it out. They're just constantly getting on each other's nerves in a terrifically true way. You can guess everything you need to know about them. It's so impressive that he could find a new way to write. In the other one, he had something wonderful to say but uses such an old-fashioned, melodramatic device. It doesn't for a minute involve you.

How do you start a play?

Many different ways. I don't have a method at all. I take a lot of notes through the years but I'm not sure what they'll be for. Then suddenly a play will loom in the middle of that. I'll get a category for certain notes. I keep responding to things all the time until it becomes clear that a certain category suits a whole bunch of things I'm noticing. They all start to shape around an idea.

Writing is an enormously tricky business. I'm quite disciplined and I can sit and write if I have to. But it has to reverberate into something that's beyond what you can talk about. And you know when that's taking you over. You slowly realize that you're being haunted by this piece and that you have something major to work out in it. You subject yourself to incredibly rigid laws when that happens. You won't let anything go by because you know that what you're putting in the play is extremely important in a way that you don't know yet. If you're not honest about it, you're fucking with yourself in a bad way. You're not taking yourself seriously. So when that takes you over it's great, because suddenly you have something to do every day, something that involves very high standards of attention and craft. It's like those big glass jars that you can blow into to produce a deep bass sound...when it feels like that, then I know I'm doing it right.

And then you go back and work on it more consciously?

In a funny way, that's when you work with the least sense of having to make choices consciously. The craft part of you is always alert, but questions like "Now what happens?" tend to answer themselves when you're writing out of some deeper level. When you're totally conscious, it's always very technical —you know where it's going, how it has to be played, why you did it that way. It's important for me not just to slip into normal connections.

I like the surfaces of the play to look very familiar so an audience coming into the play would say, "Yeah, that's just folks." I never want them to be aware that they're being assaulted by something complicated. I want them to think "This is a nice meal." But when you analyze what's happening moment by moment, it's radically strange. Often at the beginning actors try to approach my stuff from a naturalistic point of view. And it doesn't work until they abandon questions like, "What's the superobjective?" They run into trouble until they realize that I'm doing paste-ups in the way that real emotions happen, and let it just come as it comes. One thing that I'm always conscious of is writing the emotions of a scene not so that it just plays through, but so that it's always twisting.

Which is why you're not writing well-made plays. You're more interested in development and growth than pat answers.

I use all the techniques of a well-made play. I just don't use them the way that a well-made play uses them. The characters do have objectives. They do have secrets. They are fooled on stage. There are scenes of recognition.

Although your plays don't hinge around the revelation of information about the past.

No, although lately I've used such revelations once or twice to explore how encounters with the past are part of how we live our lives or make decisions. In a certain category of well-made play the act of recognition changes your life. That was a fair and valid metaphor in that stage convention, but it's finally a lie. Sure, you have your big encounter and you say, "I'm sorry, I'll never do it again," and then you go right on and do it again. Even if it was a significant recognition about a significant event. Neurological man is a creature of conditioning and habit—but we're not machines. We invent ourselves in interesting ways. I'm trying to use a form that takes that perception seriously. You have to replace the superobjectives of the traditional plays with something else. So you work out your little games, as Chekhov did.

Near the beginning of Ghost on Fire *you set an end point, Neil's death.*

But that's not really the end point. What I'm setting up is how bad thinking about life results in bad actions. So you see a guy—Dan—with a very fucked-up love life misusing one of his students. Then at the end his life has worked out better and he uses the student as she ought to be used. You're watching a man who comes to the point where he has no defense against what he's done. He tried, as a lot of people do, to say "Who cares?" If you have a talent, the standard lie about it is that it belongs only to you. If you see things that way, you're condemning yourself to a terribly unrewarding life. You will shrivel inside, like a nut in a shell.

But if you realize that you're part of a social organism, in which each person is assigned a certain task, then you're always acting on behalf of both

279

what you were given and a community that you were given it for. You can toil with a little less self-consciousness and self-importance. You're doing what you do because that happens to be your gift. If you don't do it well, it's like an investment banker fucking your life up or like a brain surgeon not operating well. If, as an artist, you're not functioning well, you're fucking people's lives up because you're not telling the truth.

That's Dan's speech: "You go on for other people." Both for Neil and in service to others.

We've lost that idea, which is a Christian idea, perhaps in reaction to Roman decadence. In a period when you see a lot of people getting bound up with the pursuit of happiness in a bad way, you want to remind them where real happiness lies, in using what's unique in you to serve others. There's a wonderful quote from Kurt Vonnegut: "Americans are forever searching for love in forms it never takes, in places it can never be." Before whom do you expect to stand with the achievements of this life? How could Ivan Boesky stand up at Stanford and say, "You can really feel good about greed," and the students not attack him, assault him bodily? It was not that he could say that that astonishes me but that the students allowed him to live. Anyone who said that when I was in school would have been shredded. As artists, we had better point out that there are other things to devote yourself to.

So many people are choosing to ignore what's happening in this country.

Do you see that in your students?

A number of them seem to have blocked out anything that points beyond their immediate gratification.

That's also a post-Roman Empire point of view: let's set up monastic orders instead of watching while the Goths and Vandals take the empire apart. Out of an opulent time, out of a consumer time, you look for happiness in retreat. I can see that a religious person now could create a very appealing alternative life for these kids who have been driven to expect so much out of life, and yet don't know what it is. It's arrogant to speak on behalf of another generation but I know I've seen this happen on campuses in the last few years. Some kids are fascinated by doing things as a group. Others are just "Gimme, gimme, gimme, I want." If you ask "What do you want?" they say "Money," and if you ask "Why?" they say "Because I'll be happy." Then you ask, "Why will money make you happy?" They answer, "I can buy everything I want." And then you say, "Why do you think that that will make you happy? You've got everything now and you're not happy yet. What's going to change, buddy?"

So many don't understand the concept of community. But that's hardly limited to eighteen-year-olds.

They have to get their ideas from somewhere. I had an amazing weekend at a Jesuit college. The topic of the weekend was the sixties. They were showing *Hair* and doing a play of mine. To my astonishment, the state had demanded that, because the school invited me on special funds, they also have someone who held the opposite political opinions. Typically, when the state intervenes, they fuck themselves up. They had this complete idiot historian who became my best exhibit. In the public debate a kid asked, "Where did the hippies go?" And he said, "They all took too many drugs and they died. They're all dead." There was this wonderful uneasy tittering in the student body and I said [laughs], "Well, I can't speak for all of them, but I know a few who've survived."

Afterwards a group of us went to a wine bar—the avid students. One of them was a really interesting girl who was quite clearly overwrought and neurotic and living on the edge. She started asking me, "What would you do now if you were a student and you wanted to change something on campus?" When I asked what their problems were she got embarrassed and said, "Well, drinking on campus, we're not allowed to drink." So I said, "Don't apologize for it. That may seem small but if you feel that it's your right to drink, find the arguments for it and then draw attention to it. Go out and get cases of booze, sit down in the middle of the campus, tell the press—they're your best friends in all of this, they love a story. You can even hang up signs saying, 'We don't like alcohol but we should be free to make that choice'—if the issue is freedom of choice." She said, "Okay, but what if they arrest us?" I said, "You spend the night in jail. This is America. It's okay." And she said, "But what if they find out who was the ringleader of the group?" I said, "Who's going to tell?" She answered, "My friends." I said, "Why would they do that? They're your friends." And she said, "They want the same jobs I want." I said, "Do you really mean that you feel so suspicious of your fellow students?" And she said, "Well you guys grew up with Woodstock, you all get together and have a nice time. We grew up with Watergate. We know what it's all about. You stab your friends in the back and get away with anything you can." She thought that was a positive lesson about the world.

I often think, what will we remember about this very nice man in the White House? What is his poem of the decade? For me it is that America should be a place with an umbrella over it so no one can get in. Inside that umbrella, we're real tough and we'll get anyone who tries to touch us. So we never have to be flexible. We never have to respect an opposite opinion. This promotes the image of a deeply frightened country, always having to rattle its arms and hide. It has no gesture of going out and negotiating. It's like a time without sex, without the place to engage the other person.

This is the first time in history when everyone has been asked to take absolute responsibility for the future. If we fuck up, it's over. There are no terms to deal with that in. What's arisen in America is the idea that you don't have to worry about it. Not only are you not asked to take responsibility, you're asked to go out and play and feel fine because we're going to make this dome over you so they can't get you. We're simply not being taught to understand and accept responsibility.

Have you always chosen your directors?

I've always been very insistent on who directs my work, even to imperiling a production.

With first productions, do you always attend closely to the rehearsals?

Yes, and often for the second and third productions, until the play is what I mean it to be and there isn't any more major work to be done. If I don't like it at that point, I just have to write a new one. The Goodman production of *Ghost on Fire*, directed by Les Waters, was the second one but I treated it as the first because there was a whole side of the play that had as yet to be seen and I wanted to be there to cut or rewrite to make that emphasis work.

Do you provide a lot of input in rehearsal?

It varies enormously. When Les is working on stage, he's always watching you as well. If he gives notes to an actor—this is during the first stages, getting the play on its feet—he's always talking to the actor and to you, checking that you agree, including you in the process. I remember in the beginning thinking, "Don't look at me, I just want to watch you work," because I think he's such a marvelous director. When he looked at me, he called on me to respond and I didn't want to. But it depends how fully the director is in charge. If I choose the director well I'm freed to step back and have a more objective attitude. And I always have an apprentice playwright on the production with whom I work out a lot.

Do you do much rewriting in rehearsal?

It varies a lot. It's not the amount of rewriting, it's the kind of rewriting that matters. On *Ghost on Fire* I did very little. But it was the best kind because it was alert to what was going on in the show and not an attempt to cram through a truth.

There's a subtle element of show biz in a lot of American directors. How to make this work really means how to make it show biz—commerce. That's not a bad instinct. I think it's great, in fact, if it's harnessed to real imagination and talent. The British have a slightly different idea—maybe all the Europeans do—which is "The author means this. He's saying that." The purpose is not to do generalized show biz, it's to do the specific philosophy and thought and feeling of the playwright.

How was working with Alan Schneider?

He was marvelous. When I was coming into the theatre, I suspected that the kind of plays I wrote might not be for the bulk of the theatregoing public. They might be for a younger crowd who got my references and attitudes. And I thought, "These young people aren't coming to the theatre. They're going to rock concerts and movies. So how the hell am I going to get to them?" The wonderful thing about Alan was that he was a translator of the plays. He had his take on them. Like everything with Alan, it was a very intense one. He was great at translating the plays into the kind of event that other people could understand. He made them accessible. The audience would be broader when Alan directed them. But people have gotten used to the conventions and now anyone can watch a play of mine with some degree of comprehension and interest.

How does this compare with Les Waters' work?

Les Waters' direction is more observationally accurate. It's less about the emotional *sturm und drang* of the characters, and much more about the way people behave with each other. He's very precise and clear, in that way. I like to see that kind of interpretation because I get a lot of my pleasure in writing out of making those things clear. He's very aware of what people are doing with each other all the time, not just what they're feeling.

Have you done much rewriting after first productions?

It varies a lot.

Say, with Ghost on Fire?

I did a rewrite of it. To the unsubtle eye, it wouldn't seem that much was changed, but a lot was—the way a line was phrased, the emphasis.

And you're open to different interpretations of your work?

I like to be surprised. I'd written in the introduction to my book that I like it naturalistic, almost like eavesdropping. But that's only half true. I'm getting much more interested now in a more imaginative kind of stage space.

The direct addresses in **Ghost on Fire.**

It breaks all sorts of conventions, but hopefully without being self-conscious. I wondered how to make a play soar into a nonnaturalistic convention yet never abandon the comfort of recognizable people. I was proud when I figured out that I could get this guy going to heaven in a car. That allowed something that would have been really weird without that scene: to have a guy dying and yet addressing the audience with a normal, healthy voice again. If you took the scene of flying out of the play, it would never work. I can't explain why that scene gave you a new freedom, but it did. I'm more and more interested to see how you can make things seem comfortable and familiar and inevitable while being more and more full of conventions and unreality, like Elizabethan plays. They could do whole plays about spirits and fairies but there's such an ease with the convention that you feel the magic world is just there.

Do you read the critics?

No I don't, not anymore.

Why did you stop?

I never believed the good reviews and I was always hurt by the bad ones. I was putting myself through such agony and doubt. So other people tell me if they were good or bad. And I get angry and depressed anyway.

Do you think they provide any useful function?

Presumably they help people decide whether to go to the theatre or not. I've never needed to read the critics but that's because I'm in the theatre and my friends tell me what's good. The workaday public needs some guidance. But I think too much emphasis is put on the critics. They can stop you from making a living and in that sense, they're dangerous to your well-being. And they can help you make a living and in that way, they can be dangerous to you as well, because the choice is in their hands. But in terms of how you write or how you finally get across to the public, it doesn't matter very much. Your work makes its way somehow.

A great deal of power has passed into the hands of critics—in New York, at any rate. And since New York is a model for the rest of the country, I've noticed it creeping a bit into other cities. You used to have stars, and if you had them in a play, the play ran. It didn't matter what the critics said. Because it was going to run, the critics knew that a lot of people were going to see the play and make up their own minds about it, so if they were wildly irresponsible it would have been noticed. They had an obligation to be good.

And to be in touch with the audience.

That's the same thing. I ran into a wonderful old playwright who said to me, "You guys have it tough. Every time you write a play, it has to be good. We could write garbage and get the Lunts in it and it would run for six months anyway. You've got to be good every time you go out. It's impossible." You had protection when you had people who really drew audiences. In the days when I read theatre reviews, I noticed that when a critic reviewed something that was going to bring an audience in, his tone changed distinctly. They were frightened into a sort of respect.

How do you see the American theatre today?

I think it's going into regional houses. In New York it's simply dying. I work mainly in the regions, so I consider myself a regional playwright. It seems to me that things are very well set-up for theatre to develop and thrive in places like Seattle and Chicago and possibly Washington, D.C.—although Washington's a little close to New York. Possibly L.A.

The days when theatre could be commercially viable seem to be over. There are few playwrights still working in a tradition that's been usurped by television. I suppose Neil Simon is the last great television writer who's writing his television plays for the stage. A young writer with Simon's talents wouldn't waste his time on the theatre. I think the newer batch of playwrights are thinking of a career in the theatre as a regional career. It's a nonprofit arena, which means that the calculations have to be different. For instance, there's absolutely no economic need to do new plays. They can do old ones. The only thing that will keep them doing new writing is realizing that if they don't, their theatres will simply be the last death gasp of the American theatre. Because, finally, no one's interested in old drama. In America, those people end up being opera buffs. If you're interested in a familiar and moribund art, you're interested in opera. If you're radical in your tastes, you're interested in old opera done by radical directors. But you don't go to the opera to find out about the world we live in and how to respond to it. If the regional theatres become resistant to new plays, they'll slowly cut their throats.

Americans are a bustling and social people and when we write plays with four or five characters, we subtly give audiences a clue that it would be better to go to the movies—because it means you're not going to see spectacle and imaginative landscapes. You're going to get to see the inner worlds of four or five people and that's okay once in a while. But I don't think you can keep audiences coming back to hear string quartets. Every now and then you have to give them a festival overture or a symphony. Otherwise, you reduce the audience to aficionados. And then it becomes an effete and irrelevant art.

285

The regional theatres have to make a clear commitment to do new plays with large casts.

Regional theatres are not run by people who want to be playwrights. They're run by people who want to direct. So they're attentive to and aware of directors, actors and set designers but not so attentive to the evolution of playwriting. On the other hand, the playwright has to be eager to show his world to the audience. If the audience feels abandoned by the way the art's being practiced, they'll turn their backs. And playwrights will get protective and their references will become self-congratulatory and a little obscure and they'll slowly withdraw. If the playwright's desire is not to show them the best goddam time they ever had—and I don't mean in a show-biz way—he'll lose his audience.

The problem with the more defensive sort of writing is that in a funny way it's saying, "I'm not going to put my idea clearly enough for you to judge it. When I present my world, I'm going to leave a lot of loopholes so that if you go 'Ugh,' I can always say, 'You didn't understand it.' " I would say these writers haven't done their work. If you're not clear and entertaining—and entertainment applies to *Hamlet* or *Marat/Sade* or *True West*—then why should an audience go see your play? They've paid you their money and you're going to be clever and obscure on them? I think there has to be a robust and healthy desire to reach an audience.

We're probably going to pass through a time where the people with a popular urge go into other arts, movies and TV. It's a pitfall because we then think, to be distinct, that we can't be clear, we can't just entertain—the other media do that. But that's abandoning half of your arsenal.

Which is why you spoke of the ingratiating surface of your work which draws people in so that they can then deal with the more serious issues raised.

I hesitate to say yes only because if that were a technique it would seem manipulative, whereas in fact I think I have basically an ingratiating temperament so that's how my work comes out. If I had a truculent temperament, I would probably write truculent plays.

What are your plans, goals for the future?

[Laughs] To make a living. To keep writing. I have a lot of plans and I feel that now I've finally figured out how to write a play. I'm ready to really write. I think to a certain degree I've just been testing the waters. Now I have a lot of stuff I want to put in plays. So the strategy is going to be to balance making a living with writing the plays I want to write.

I enjoy getting out of New York because the intellectual life here is very constricted. The orthodoxies in the air are so overwhelmingly present and so unimportant in terms of what the rest of the country is thinking and feeling. When you go out and work in the regions, you find such sophisticated people, in terms of where theatre fits in their lives. In New York people know people in their own profession and that's all. Subscribers to regional theatres tend to have a variety of contacts, so the discussions you have with them about your play are much more interesting. Theatre fits in their lives as a way to start discussions with themselves. It's an entertainment that serves as the beginning of a discussion with wife, husband, children, neighbors. In New York it's "Loved him, hated her," or "Oh, God, not more of so and so."

Milos Forman said about the American film industry: "You know it's healthy because of the variety of types of films that are made." Everything from horror pictures to the most artistic, low-budget thing is possible in this country. The mark of health is that variety is acceptable. And New York is still healthy in that you do have all sorts of different theatre. But there's a center missing now which is your solid Broadway fare. Economics have killed that possibility. It was inevitable once movies and television happened. People like Woody Allen are writing what amount to serious Broadway plays but they're being seen in movie houses. But, you know, God has tricks up his sleeve. You never know which way these things will go. Look what they said about dance twenty years ago.

AUGUST WILSON

Born and raised on The Hill, a black slum in Pittsburgh, August Wilson dropped out of school in the ninth grade, dividing his time between the street and the public library. There he first encountered the works of black American writers, which he read vociferously, supporting himself as a cook and stock clerk. With the twenty dollars he earned writing a term paper for his sister, he bought a used Royal typewriter and began to compose poems and stories. Deeply aware of both the changing texture of race relations in America and the violence circulating within the black community, he turned to writing as a way of effecting social change. In the late sixties he cofounded a black theatre in Pittsburgh but did not secure a production of a play of his own until the late seventies, after he moved to St. Paul, Minnesota. In 1981 *Ma Rainey's Black Bottom* was accepted at the O'Neill Theatre Center. It opened on Broadway three years later to critical acclaim, followed by *Fences*, which won the 1987 Pulitzer Prize, *Joe Turner's Come and Gone* (1986) and *The Piano Lesson* (1987).

All four plays are part of a series in progress, each work set in a different decade of the twentieth century. With this project Wilson is writing a new history of black America, probing what he perceives to be the crucial opposition in black culture: between those who acknowledge and celebrate the black American's African roots and those who attempt to deny that historical reality. *Ma Rainey*, for example, set in 1927, centers on the conflict between two of the legendary blues singer's sidemen, Levee and Toledo, the former brash, self-destructive and charismatic, always willing to accomodate the white man, the latter thoughtful and politically aware. "We done sold ourselves to the white man in order to be like him," Toledo says. "We's imitation white men." Levee never understands, however, and he remains incapable of expressing his discontent to those who are oppressing him. Instead of dealing with his anger and pain directly, he turns on one who could help him, knifing Toledo for stepping on his shoe.

Joe Turner's Come and Gone, which takes place in 1911, performs a ritual of purification, setting African religious tradition against American Christianity. It documents the liberation of the spiritually bound Herald Loomis, who years before had been pressed into illegal servitude by the bounty hunter named in the play's title. In the course of the play the details of everyday life in a Pittsburgh boarding house give way to the patterns of African religion and ritual. With the help of Bynum, an African healer, a "Binder of What Clings," Loomis effects his own liberation. He recognizes that his enslavement has been self-imposed; this man "who done forgot his song" finds it again. Bynum explains to him: "You bound on to your song. All you got to do is stand up and sing it, Herald Loomis. It's right there kicking at your throat. All you got to do is sing it. Then you be free."

Wilson's 1950s play, *Fences*, an examination of the nature and dynamic of inheritance, is his most structurally conservative work, centered upon the steadily escalating conflict between Troy Maxson and his teenage son, Cory. Following the well-made play model, the first act climaxes in Troy's revelation of the events that have been crucial in shaping his life: his break with his father and the murder that put him in the penitentiary for fifteen years, wiping out the possibility of a career as a baseball player. The second act ends with Cory's reconciliation with the shadow of his father, now dead. As Cory's mother explains, "That shadow wasn't nothing but you growing into yourself. You either got to grow into it or cut it down to fit you. But that's all you got to make life with." Rose has come to understand the dogged persistence of the past, in all its irony: "Your daddy wanted you to be everything he wasn't...and at the same time he tried to make you into everything he was."

Each of Wilson's plays is modeled on the well-made play, developing conflict step by step to a crisis that hinges on the disclosure of a crucial and traumatic incident from the protagonist's past. However, Wilson is subtly and powerfully transforming the problematic protagonist inherited from Ibsen and Miller. In *Ma Rainey* and *Fences* the central character is revealed to be both victim and victimizer, intellectually astute yet spiritually or emotionally crippled. His ambiguous moral status allows Wilson to use him to undermine and question, in a concrete and visceral way, the workings of oppressive systems—institutionalized racism in *Ma Rainey*, the mechanics of patriarchy in *Fences*.

In all of Wilson's dramas, the conflict between African and European plays itself out not simply on the level of character and theme, but formally as well, in a tension between the strictures of the well-made play and an impulse toward jazz-inspired improvisation and poetic form. Consistently Wilson fractures the narrative line with ingenious theatrical devices: in *Ma Rainey*, the songs; in *Fences*, Gabriel's extraordinary ritual dance; in *Joe Turner*, the Juba dancing and exorcism. Each play mixes European and African elements, keeping them intact, to create not a homogeneous synthesis but a complex and plural whole. It is as if each play, both formally and thematically, reflects Wilson's vision of a more equitable and respectful society, one that will not simply integrate African-Americans by forcing them to renounce their cultural heritage and their history, but will encourage them to build upon and celebrate their past.

■ ■ ■

MARCH 13, 1987—WEST BANK CAFE, NEW YORK CITY

What were your early experiences in theatre?

I was a participant in the Black Power movement in the early sixties and I wrote poetry and short fiction. I was interested in art and literature and I felt that I could alter the relationship between blacks and society through the arts. There was an explosion of black theatre in the late sixties—theatre was a way of politicizing the community and raising the consciousness of the people. So with my friend, Rob Penny, I started the Black Horizons Theatre in Pittsburgh in 1968.

I knew nothing about theatre. I had never seen a play before. I started directing but I didn't have any idea how to do this stuff, although I did find great information in the library. We started doing Baraka's plays and virtually anything else out there. I remember *The Drama Review* printed a black issue, somewhere around '69, and we did every play in the book. I tried to write a play but it was disastrous. I couldn't write dialogue. Doing community theatre was very difficult—rehearsing two hours a night after people got off work, not knowing if the actors were going to show up. In '71, because of having to rely so much on other people, I said "I don't need this," and I concentrated on writing poetry and short stories.

Then in 1976 a friend of mine from Pittsburgh, Claude Purdy, was living in L.A. He came back to Pittsburgh and came to a reading of a series of poems I'd written about a character, Black Bart, a kind of Western satire. He said, "You should turn this into a play." He kept after me and eventually I sat down and wrote a play and gave it to him. He went to St. Paul to direct a show and said, "Why don't you come out and rewrite the play?" He sent me a ticket and I thought, "A free trip to St. Paul, what the hell?" So I went out and did a quick rewrite of the play. That was in November '77. In January of '78, the Inner City Theatre in Los Angeles did a staged reading of it.

What's it called?

Black Bart and the Sacred Hills—a musical satire. In 1981 we did a production in St. Paul at Penumbra Theatre, for which Claude Purdy worked. When I moved to St. Paul I got a job in the Science Museum of Minnesota as a script writer—they had a theatre troupe attached to the museum. That was the first job where someone was actually paying me to write. We dramatized tales of the Northwest Indians—how Peyote got his name, how Spiderwoman taught the Navahoes to read—which were very popular. Then I started doing Profiles of Science—I went around to all the curators asking who can I write a play about. The biology guy suggested William Harvey, who discovered the circulation of the blood, so I wrote a one-man show on Harvey, one on Charles Darwin, one on Margaret Mead. I was writing scripts without knowing that I was becoming a playwright. Then I found out about the Eugene O'Neill Theatre Center's National Playwrights Conference and wrote a play called *Jitney* that I sent in along with *Black Bart*. They sent them back. Then I submitted *Jitney* to the Playwrights' Center in Minneapolis. They accepted it and gave me twenty-five hundred dollars.

I remember walking into a room there containing sixteen playwrights and thinking, "Wow, I must be a playwright." The Playwrights' Center was a very helpful experience. We did a reading of *Jitney* and I felt encouraged. So I wrote *Fullerton Street*, which was set in the forties. We did a staged reading of it and I sent it off to the O'Neill and they sent it back. I sent *Jitney* to them again because I thought, "You guys didn't read this play," and they sent it back a second time. I was forced to look at it again and I thought, "Maybe it's not as good as I think it is. I have to write a better play but how the hell do you do that?" I felt I was writing the best I could. A workshop of *Fullerton Street* had been very helpful, so I felt confident. *Jitney*—okay, it wasn't quite big enough. *Fullerton Street* was epic and too unwieldy. I decided to try for something right in the middle. I sat down and wrote *Ma Rainey's Black Bottom* and sent that off to the O'Neill and they accepted it.

When you first started writing plays, what playwrights influenced you most strongly?

None, really. Baraka wrote a book called *Four Revolutionary Plays* which I liked—I liked the language, I liked everything about them. In my early one-acts I tried to imitate that and then I discovered I wasn't him and that wasn't going to work. Other than Baraka, the first black playwright I found who wrote anything that even approached what was, to my ear, realistic dialogue for black folks was Philip Hayes Dean. I directed his play *The Owl-Killer* for the theatre in Pittsburgh. I don't want to judge it as a play, but I thought the dialogue was good. Likewise, *The Sty of the Blind Pig*. I haven't read Ibsen, Shaw, Shakespeare—except *The Merchant of Venice* in ninth grade. The only Shakespeare I've ever seen was *Othello* last year at Yale Rep. I'm not familiar with *Death of a Salesman*. I haven't read Tennessee Williams. I very purposefully didn't read them.

The first professional production I saw was *The Taking of Miss Janie* by Ed Bullins in New York. I think it's his best work but I didn't really care for the play. But something happened when I saw *Sizwe Bansi Is Dead* at the Pittsburgh Public Theater in 1976. I thought, "This is great. I wonder if I could write something like this?" Most of the plays that I have seen are Fugard plays, so he's probably had an influence on me without my knowing it. Among the fourteen or so plays I've seen have been *Blood Knot, Sizwe Bansi, "Master Harold"...and the boys* and *Boesman and Lena*.

I'm surprised to hear that you know so few plays. I'm struck by how linear your plays are, how traditional the protagonist-antagonist opposition is and how smoothly they build to a final confrontation. Especially in Joe Turner. *It's like Ibsen.*

The foundation of my playwriting is poetry. Not so much in terms of the language but in the concept. After writing poetry for twenty-one years, I approach a play the same way. I think Robert Duncan said form equals content. So each play is specific, each is different, each has its own form. But the mental process is poetic: you use metaphor and condense. I try to find a metaphor to carry the work.

I approach playwriting as literature, as opposed to a craft—though craft is important. It occurred to me one day that when I sit down to write, I am sitting in the same chair as Ibsen, Shaw, Miller, Beckett—every playwright. You're confronted with the same problems: what to do with this space and how to articulate your ideas in two hours of public time, moving characters about in an environment designed specifically for them. It gives you a sense of power, sitting in this hallowed and well-worn chair. I get comfortable and write from the feeling that I'm free to do anything I choose to do, to create this thing called literature.

What was the most important experience in your training as a playwright?

The O'Neill. I first went with *Ma Rainey* when it was a fifty-nine page, ill-organized script—some people say it's still ill-organized—and was fortunate enough to work with Michael Feingold as my dramaturg. The important thing I learned was to rewrite. Not just patchworking here and fixing there, but exactly what the word means—re-writing. When you write, you know where you want to go—you know what a scene, a particular speech is supposed to accomplish. Then I discovered that it's possible to go back and rewrite this speech, to find another way to say it. In a poem you rewrite six or seven times before you end up with what you want. But I didn't think of theatre as being like that. And I learned to respect the stage and trust that it will carry your ideas. The intensity of the O'Neill process—working in four days, working fast—was also good experience. It comes down to problem solving. But there's no one correct solution.

The O'Neill made me more conscious of what theatre is about. There's nothing like encountering the problems of costume, lighting, set design—What do you mean by this? Where is this? Where is the window?—which make you more aware of the totality of what you're doing. I discovered with *Fences*, for example, that I had a character exiting upstage and coming back immediately with a different costume. That's really sloppy but I was totally unaware. I never thought, "The guy's got to change his costume." I've become conscious of things like that and it's made me a better playwright. But I don't want to lose the impulse, the sense, as with *Ma Rainey*, that anything goes, that you may do whatever you desire to do. Maybe I wouldn't have written *Ma Rainey* as I did, had I been aware of the problems with casting and with the music.

In Ma Rainey *the instruments the characters play become metaphors. Toledo the pianist sounds a broad compass of experience and Levee the trumpet player expresses individual subjectivity more aggressively.*

With the trumpet you have to blow and force yourself out through the horn. Half-consciously, I tried to make Levee's voice be a trumpet. I was conscious when I was writing the dialogue that this is the bass player talking, this is the trombonist talking. Levee is a brassy voice.

How do you start a play?

I generally start with an idea, something that I want to say. In *The Piano Lesson* the question was, "Can one acquire a sense of self-worth by denying one's past?" (I think I place myself on one side of the question.) So then, how do you put this question on stage, how do you narrate it? Next I got the title from a Romare Bearden painting called *The Piano Lesson*. His painting is actually a piano teacher with a kid. I wanted a woman character as large as Troy is in *Fences*. I wanted to write it for Mary Alice to challenge her talent. I think she's a wonderful actress and there are not many roles for black actresses of that magnitude. From the painting I had a piano, and I just started writing a line of dialogue and had no idea who was talking. First I had four guys moving the piano into an empty house. I discarded that because people would be offstage too much, getting other pieces of furniture.

Someone says something to someone else, and they talk, and at some point I say, "Well, who is this?" and I give him a name. But I have no idea what the story line of the play is. It's a process of discovery. While writing *The Piano Lesson* I came up with the idea of tracing the history of the piano for a hundred and thirty-five years, with the idea that it had been used to purchase members of this family from slavery. But I didn't know how that was going to tie in. I knew there was a story, but I didn't know what the story was. I discovered it as the characters began to talk: one guy wants to sell the piano, the sister doesn't want to. I thought, why doesn't she want to sell it? Finding all those things helped me to find the story. I put off writing the history of the piano—one character tells the whole story—until I found it out in the process of writing dialogue. As it turned out, the female character is not as large as I intended. I'm not sure the play's about the idea I started with. I think the central question ended up being "How do you use your legacy?"

I write in bars and restaurants. At the start of the day, I take my tablet and I go out and search for a play. I get some coffee and sit down. If I feel like writing something, I do. If I don't, I go about my day. I've started writing a play called *Two Trains Running*, set in the sixties. I have no idea what it's about. I started with a line of dialogue. I was in rehearsals in New Haven and this line came to me. I said, "Not now, please, I'm busy," but I had to go with it. It may or may not end up in the play. But having discovered it, I know something central to the character who is speaking. The story and the character will grow out of that one line of dialogue.

Then I will place the character within the sociology of the sixties, keeping in mind that I am trying to write plays that contain the sum total of black culture in America, and its difference from white culture. Once you put in the daily rituals of black life, the play starts to get richer and bigger. You're creating a whole world in the process of telling your story, of writing this character. Once you place him down in his environment, you have to write about his whole philosophical approach to life. And then you can uncover, from a black perspective, the universalities of life. Some questions will emerge that man has been asking himself ever since he's been on the planet. One of my favorite lines in *Joe Turner* is, "Why God got to be so big? Why he got to be bigger than me?" I think this is one of the first questions man asked himself when he found out that he wasn't God. Why am I not the biggest thing in the universe? Romare Bearden said, "I try to explore, in terms of the life I know best, those things common to all culture." You discover that the black experience is as valuable, rich and varied as anybody else's and that there's been so little written about it.

Blacks do not have a history of writing—things in Africa were passed on orally. In that tradition you orally pass on your entire philosophy, your ideas and attitudes about life. Most of them were passed along in blues. You have to make the philosophy interesting musically and lyrically, so that someone will want to repeat it, to teach it to someone else as soon as they've heard it. If you don't make it interesting, the information dies. I began to view blues as the African-American's response to the world before he started writing down his stuff. James Baldwin has a beautiful phrase—"field of manners and rituals of intercourse." An African man has a whole different field of manners. All cultures have their mythology, their creative motifs and social and political organizations. To my mind, people just gloss over these things in the black community without really examining it and seeing what's there.

I'm interested to hear you talk about history. One line from Ma Rainey *could, I think, stand as an epigraph to your work: "The white man...done the eating and he know what he done ate. But we don't know that we been took and made history of."*

We're leftovers from history—history that happened when there was a tremendous need for manual labor, when cotton was king. But history and life progress, you move into the industrial age, and now we're moving into the computer age. We're left over. We're no longer needed. At one time we were very valuable to America—free labor.

So what you're doing with your series of plays is rediscovering history, rewriting history.

Yes, because the history of blacks in America has not been written by blacks. And whites, of course, have a different attitude, a different relationship to the history. Writing our own history has been a very valuable tool, because if we're going to be pointed toward a future, we must know our past. This is so basic and simple yet it's a thing that Africans in America disregard. For instance, the fact of slavery is something that blacks do not teach their kids —they do not tell their kids that at one time we were slaves. That is the most crucial and central thing to our presence here in America. It's nothing to be ashamed of. Why is it, after spending hundreds of years in bondage, that blacks in America do not once a year get together and celebrate the Emancipation and remind ourselves of our history? If we did that, we would recognize our uniqueness in being African. One of the things I'm trying to say in my writing is that we can never really begin to make a contribution to the society except as Africans.

If you took Africans and said, "Here's all the money and resources you need, solve the problems of society," things would be totally different. The social organization would be different. We'd probably all live in round houses, as opposed to square ones. I don't think society would be as consumer-oriented. Now, if you can't buy anything, you're worthless. You don't count if you can't consume. I don't think it would be that kind of society because of the differences in our values and our attitudes toward ownership.

To make inroads into society, you have to give up your African-ness. You can be doctors, lawyers, be middle-class, but if you want to go to Harvard, you have to give up the natural way that you do things as blacks. Let me give you an example. I was in a bus station in St. Paul. I saw six Japanese-American guys having breakfast at the counter. They chatted among themselves and then the check came and they—I'll make a joke here—they all reached for their American Express cards. It was nice and they embraced and there was a slight bow and off they went.

What would be the difference if six black guys came in and ordered breakfast? The first thing they'd notice is the jukebox. This is very important: it never entered the mind of those Japanese guys to play the jukebox. Six black guys walk in, somebody's going to the jukebox. He's gonna drop a quarter. Another guy's gonna say, "Hey Rodney, play this." And he's gonna say, "Man, get out of here, play your own record. I ain't playin' with you." Another thing I notice, none of the Japanese guys said anything to the waitress. But a black guy would say: "Hey, mama, don't talk to him. Look, baby, where ya from? Why don't you give me your phone number?" A guy gets up to play another record, somebody steals a piece of bacon off his plate: "Don't mess with my food. Who took my food?" It comes time to pay the bill, it's only two dollars: "Hey, man, lend me two dollars. I ain't got no money. Come on, man, give me a dollar."

If you're a white observer you say, "They don't know how to act. They're loud. They're boisterous. They don't like one another. The guy won't let him play a song. They're thieves. He stole a piece of bacon." The Japanese have their way of eating breakfast. Blacks have their way. If you bring in six white characters, an entirely different dynamic would go on. White society tells Africans, "You can't act like that. If you act like that, you won't get anywhere in society. If you want to make progress, you have to learn to act like us. Then you can go to school, we'll hire you for a job, we'll do this, that and the other." I don't see that said to other ethnic groups. Asians are allowed to maintain their Asian-ness and still participate in society. That suppression of blacks does not allow you the impulse, does not allow you to respond to the world without encumbrance. I try to reveal this and to allow my characters to be as African as they are and to respond to the world as they would.

How closely do you work with Lloyd Richards?

Generally I will meet with him an hour before rehearsal and talk about what happened yesterday and what we're going to do today. I don't talk to actors in rehearsal. I talk to Lloyd and he understands and communicates my concerns to the actors. Other than that, I just look at the way things are going and I listen. Some things might strike my ear wrong. I might find a certain scene doesn't build the way I thought it did. So I make changes when necessary and come back the next day with new pages.

How extensive are these changes?

Usually the changes are minor. For example, in *Ma Rainey* Levee had to put his shoes on and there weren't lines to cover that action. That's the only thing I can remember actually adding to the script in the rehearsal process.

Fences was a bit different because we were cutting a four-hour play down to two hours and ten minutes. Sometimes in watching it I'd say, "We cut this, but I need it back." One part I cut out for the Yale and Goodman productions I put back because I needed a moment between father and son that was not a conflict. Cory asks Troy, "Hey, Pop, why don't you buy a TV?" And Troy tells him that the roof needs tarring. He's teaching him a lesson about priorities. "If you don't fix the roof, the water's going to run all over your brand-new TV. So if you had twenty dollars, what would you do?" You need that moment to balance the conflict. Rehearsals were more cutting and adding to shape it, as opposed to major rewriting.

I do a major rewrite before the O'Neill Conference and then, after the two-day staged readings, I've got a bunch of notes and ideas and I do another major rewrite and that is generally the play that we go into rehearsal with. I don't mind cutting. I'll say, "If that's not working, what do you need? Let's put something else in here," because this is theatre. Nobody writes a perfect play by just sitting down and writing. You find out what's there when the actors begin to move around in the space.

With *Joe Turner* people had been saying before rehearsals that we should see Loomis find his song. After a read-through I knew that moment was missing. We went into rehearsal and it remained an unsolved problem.

Then I came up with the idea of ending the first act with him on the floor unable to stand up. When he stands at the end, you can read that as him finding his song. That's one thing I discovered in rehearsal that was crucial to the play. I never would have found it sitting at home.

Is there a favorite among your plays?

Not really, it's like comparing your kids. They're all mine. Although I always consider the last thing I've done the best. So I think *Piano Lesson* is my best play. After that, it would be *Joe Turner* and then *Fences*. I think I was able to get more things through in *Joe Turner*. Among my plays, *Fences* is the odd one, more conventional in structure with its large character. I kept hearing *Ma Rainey* described as oddly structured and I thought, "I can write one of those plays where you have a big character and everything revolves around him." I like *Joe Turner* for the ideas and for Loomis's accepting responsibility for his own salvation and his own presence in the world. Those kinds of statements are not present in *Fences*. So of those three, I like *Joe Turner* best. I hope that it shows a growth, a maturing.

I find that sexual politics comes into more prominence in **Joe** **Turner,** *when Bynum says, "When you grab hold to a woman, you got something there. You got a whole world there."*

A way of life kicking up under your hand.

There and in your other plays I get a sense of the interconnection between racial politics and sexual politics. Can you describe your goal in portraying black men?

I'm trying to write an honest picture of the black male in America. I try to present positive images, strong black male characters who take a political stand, if only in the sense of Loomis in *Joe Turner*: one, Joe Turner's come and gone, it ain't gonna happen no more; two, I don't need anyone to bleed for me, I can bleed for myself. I can accept responsibility for my presence in the world. The idea of responsibility is crucial because, I believe, white Americans basically see black males as irresponsible, which I think is incorrect. They say, you should be responsible in the same way we are, without understanding that we have different ideas of responsibility.

I try to position my characters so they're pointed toward the future. I try to demonstrate the spirit of the character. For instance, in *Ma Rainey*, Levee's a very spirited character who does a terrible thing. He murders someone. He's going to spend the next twenty years in the penitentiary. But he's willing to confront life with a certain zest and energy. It's the same with

Troy. He wrestles with death. I try to make them heroic. I've experienced it and I'm just trying to uncover it, pulling layer after layer from the stereotype.

In reading Fences, *I came to view Troy more and more critically as the play progressed, sharing Rose's point of view. We see that Troy has been crippled by his father. That's being replayed in Troy's relationship with Cory. Do you think there's a way out of that cycle?*

Surely. First of all, we're all like our parents. The things we are taught early in life, how to respond to the world, our sense of morality—everything, we get from them. Now you can take that legacy and do with it anything you want to do. It's in your hands. Cory is Troy's son. How can he be Troy's son without sharing Troy's values? I was trying to get at why Troy made the choices he made, how they have influenced his values and how he attempts to pass those along to his son. Each generation gives the succeeding generation what they think they need. One question in the play is, "Are the tools we are given sufficient to compete in a world that is different from the one our parents knew?" I think they are—it's just that we have to do different things with the tools. That's all Troy has to give. Troy's flaw is that he does not recognize that the world was changing. That's because he spent fifteen years in a penitentiary.

As African-Americans, we should demand to participate in society as Africans. That's the way out of the vicious cycle of poverty and neglect that exists in 1987 in America, where you have a huge percentage of blacks living in the equivalent of South African townships, in housing projects. No one is inviting these people to participate in society. Look at the poverty levels— $8,500 for a family of four, if you have $8,501 you're not counted. Those statistics would go up enormously if we had an honest assessment of the cost of living in America. I don't know how anybody can support a family of four on $8,500. What I'm saying is that 85 or 90 percent of blacks in America are living in abject poverty and, for the most part, are crowded into what amount to concentration camps. The situation for blacks in America is worse than it was forty years ago. Some sociologists will tell you about the tremendous progress we've made. They didn't put me out when I walked in the door. And you can always point to someone who works on Wall Street, or is a doctor. But they don't count in the larger scheme of things.

Do you have any idea how these political changes could take place?

I'm not sure. I know that blacks must be allowed their cultural differences. I think the process of assimilation to white American society was a big mistake. We don't want to be like you. Blacks living in housing projects are isolated from the society, for the most part—living as they choose, as Africans. Only they don't realize the value in what they're doing because they have accepted their victimization. They've marked themselves as victims. Once they recognize that, they can begin to move through society in a different manner, from a stronger position, and claim what is theirs.

A project of yours is to point up what happens when oppression is internalized.

Yes, transfer of aggression to the wrong target. I think it's interesting that the two roads open to blacks for "full participation" are entertainment and sports. *Ma Rainey* and *Fences*, and I didn't plan it that way. I don't think that they're the correct roads. I think Troy's right. Now with the benefit of historical perspective, I can say that the athletic scholarship was actually a way of exploiting. Now you've got two million kids who think they're going to play in the NBA. In the sixties the universities made a lot of money off of athletics. You had kids playing for free who, by and large, were not getting educated, were taking courses in basketweaving. Some of them could barely read.

Troy may be right about that issue, but it seems that he has passed on certain destructive traits in spite of himself. Take the hostility between father and son.

I think every generation says to the previous generation: you're in my way, I've got to get by. The father-son conflict is actually a normal generational conflict that happens all the time.

So it's a healthy and a good thing?

Oh, sure. Troy is seeing this boy walk around, smelling his piss. Two men cannot live in the same household. Troy would have been tremendously disappointed if Cory had not challenged him. Troy knows that this boy has to go out and do battle with that world: "So I had best prepare him because I know that's a harsh, cruel place out there. But that's going to be easy compared to what he's getting here. Ain't nobody gonna whip your ass like I'm gonna whip it." He has a tremendous love for the kid. But he's not going to say, "I love you," he's going to demonstrate it. He's carrying garbage for seventeen years just for the kid. The only world Troy knows is the one that he made. Cory's going to go on to find another one, he's going to arrive at the same place as Troy. I think one of the most important lines in the play is when Troy is talking about his father: "I got to the place where I could feel him kicking in my blood and knew that the only thing that separated us was the matter of a few years."

Hopefully, Cory will do things a bit differently with his son. For Troy, sports was not the way to go, the white man wouldn't let him get away with that. "Get you a job, with your hands, something that nobody can take away from you." The idea of school—he doesn't know what that is. That's for white folks. Very few blacks had paperwork jobs. But if you knew how to fix cars, you could always make some money. That's what Troy wants for Cory. There aren't many people who ever jumped up in Troy's face. So he's proud of the kid at the same time that he expresses a hurt that all men feel. You got to cut your kid loose at some point. There's that sense of loss and separation. You find out how Troy left his father's house and you see how Cory leaves his house. I suspect with Cory it will repeat with some differences and maybe, after five or six generations, they'll find a different way to do it.

Where Cory ends up is very ambiguous, as a marine in 1965.

Yes. For the average black kid on the street, that was an alternative. You went into the army because you could learn how to do something. I can remember my parents talking about the son of some friends: "He's in the navy. He *did* something"—as opposed to standing on the street corner, shooting drugs, drinking wine and robbing stores. Lyons says to Cory, "I always knew you were going to make something out of yourself." It really wounds me. He's a corporal in the marines. For blacks, that is a sense of accomplishment. Therein lies one of the tragedies of blacks in America. Cory says, "I don't know. I put in six years. That's enough." Anyone who goes into the army and makes a career out of it is a loser. They sit there and are nurtured by the army and they don't have to confront life. Then they get out of the army and find there's nothing to do. They didn't learn any skills. And if they did, they can't find a job. Four months later, they're shooting dope. In the sixties a whole bunch of blacks went over, fought and died in the Vietnam War. The survivors came back to the same street corners and found out nothing had changed. They still couldn't get a job.

At the end of *Fences* every person, with the exception of Raynell, is institutionalized. Rose is in a church. Lyons is in a penitentiary. Gabriel's in a mental hospital and Cory's in the marines. The only free person is the girl, Troy's daughter, the hope for the future. That was conscious on my part because in '57 that's what I saw. Blacks have relied on institutions which are really foreign—except for the black church, which has been our saving grace. I have some problems with it but I recognize it as a central social organization and sometimes an economic organization for the black community. I would like to see blacks develop their own institutions that respond to their needs.

That religious element is so important in Joe Turner. *At the end of that play, when Loomis "shines," the moment of fulfillment and salvation has such strong*

*religious overtones—both African and Christian—as well as social and po-
litical ones. How do you see the relationship between the religious and the
political?*

I think blacks are essentially a religious people. Whites see man against a
world that needs to be subdued. Africans see man as a part of the world, as
a natural part of their environment. Blacks have taken Christianity and bent
it to serve their African-ness. In Africa there's ancestor worship, among kinds
of religious practices. That's given blacks, particularly southern blacks, the
idea of ghosts, magic and superstition—for example, the horseshoe as a good-
luck symbol. It's not the shape, it's the iron, the god of iron which protects
your house. Relating to the spirit worlds is very much a part of African and
Afro-American culture.

I try to approach people with an anthropologist's eye. That's why I make
constant references to food. If you study culture, you want to know what
people eat, what their social organization is. In my plays you can see what
the economics are—that's an important part of any culture. In *Fences*, for
example, Gabriel goes to work every day. He goes and collects his fruits and
vegetables to sell and he's trying so hard to be self-sufficient, even though
he's gravely wounded. He's my favorite character because he still wants to
contribute and work. I'm trying to illuminate the culture, so that you're able
to see the "field of manners and rituals of intercourse that can sustain a man
once he's left his father's house."

What I want is that you walk away from my play, whether you're black
or white, with the idea that these are Africans, as opposed to black folks in
America. Yet I have found a tremendous resistance to that. I talked with an
audience at Yale Rep after *Joe Turner* and I actually lost my temper. I said,
"How many recognize these people as Africans?" There were two hundred
people sitting there and about eight raised their hands. I'm very curious as
to why they refuse—I have to say it's a refusal because it's so obvious. So
many people blocked that, wanting to recognize them as black Americans. I
was really surprised to find that.

Do you read the critics?

Sure. Do I value them? I have mixed opinions about critics. I've been fortunate
to have gotten mostly good reviews. If you have six hundred people at a play,
you have six hundred different opinions. But critics should have an informed
opinion and therein lies their value—they can bring a lot, not to a particular
play, but to the development of theatre. The bad reviews that I've gotten are
the ones I study. I think the guy's misread the play and I want to know, how
did he see it this way? I'm trying to communicate to everyone. If I missed

communicating with someone with an informed opinion, then I try to look at it through his eyes and see how he arrived at his opinion. I don't place a whole hell of a lot of value on the critical response. I'm glad when anyone who sees my work says, "I really enjoyed that." A critic's saying that is no different from an ordinary person walking up and saying that to me.

How do you see the American theatre today?

I'm relatively new to theatre. I can speak most about playwriting because I've been a participant at the O'Neill for four years. I'm a member of New Dramatists. For the most part, I've been disappointed in the work, even from some very talented playwrights. First, it's the influence of television. A whole generation of playwrights has been raised on television. I think it's a bad influence on theatre, which in many ways is almost an archaic art form. I'm fearful it may go the way of opera, which is an elitist art, one that doesn't engage the larger society.

Theatre engages very few people. I don't think it has to be that way. I think it should be a part of everyone's life, the way television is. But it's not. It's moving the other way. As it costs more and more to produce plays, you see fewer and fewer. Fewer playwrights are given the opportunity to fail. You can learn immeasurably from a failure. You should at least be given the opportunity to bat—if you strike out, you strike out. The cost of production, the price of tickets, all of these things further remove theatre from the people and make it an elitist art form, which I think is wrong. But I don't know how you correct it.

The second main problem is society's attitude toward playwriting. It's not considered a part of literature. What has been missing from the new plays I've seen is metaphor. The story often reads like a TV sitcom—it's slight, there's no character development. Writing for the stage is very different. If playwriting was reconnected to the idea of literature, I think you would begin to see better plays. If you're giving the audience the same thing they're getting on TV, there's no reason to come to the theatre.

If every regional theatre would select a playwright and commit themselves to doing a play of his or hers every year, by the third year you're going to have a better playwright. There's nothing like writing a play knowing that it's going to be produced and working to reward the faith that's been placed in you. New plays are looked at in a disparaging way. A theatre will do its fifth Shaw in five years on the mainstage without even considering whether a new play deserves more attention than a staged reading or a second-stage production. You say "new play" and people run the other way. Theatres should be encouraging and nurturing, providing a home for playwrights and providing audiences with an alternative. Of course they say there isn't the material there. I'm saying if you work with what you have, five years from now you're going to have different and better material.

The playwright has a responsibility to the audience. I'm asking people to hire a babysitter, get dressed, find the car keys, find a place to park, pay money—more than it costs to go see a movie. When they get there, I should have something to say to them that's worth all their trouble. I discovered my responsibility sitting in the theatre at Yale, watching the audience. You can't do that with workshops or staged readings. Playwrights are not like fiction writers. They need living bodies. One thing I'll never forget is my confrontation with a set designer at the O'Neill who asked me a thousand difficult questions about the play. Unless you go through that process, you're working in a vacuum.

I'm not sure what to do about production costs. I do think the American people would subsidize the theatre if it was made a part of their life. They subsidize television, simply by watching it. Maybe we have to have commercials in the theatre. There has to be some financial basis to allow all the people involved in the production to make a living.

What are your goals for the future?

What's important for me is to write plays, as opposed to movies or television. After *Ma Rainey* I was offered work on this and that movie. But I want to establish myself as a playwright first. I hope to write one play a year and finish my series. I'm working on the sixties play now. I have my forties play. I'll either rewrite it or throw it out and come up with a better idea. Then I'll do contemporary plays. But I've enjoyed the benefit of the historical perspective. I have an idea for a novel that I've been tossing around. A novel, for me, was always a vast, uncharted sea. It was like being lost on the ocean. So was a play, for that matter, at one point. So I feel confident coming from plays and I'd like to try my novel. I still write poetry.

You said that when you first got interested in theatre, you thought it could be an effective political tool. Do you still think it can be?

Absolutely. All art is political. It serves a purpose. All of my plays are political but I try not to make them didactic or polemical. Theatre doesn't have to be agitprop. I hope that my art serves the masses of blacks in America who are in desperate need of a solid and sure identity. I hope my plays make people understand that these are African people, that this is why they do what they do. If blacks recognize the value in that, then we will be on our way to claiming our identity and participating in society as Africans.

And one other thing: the blues is the core. All American popular music, especially in 1987, is influenced by the blues. This is the one contribution everyone admits that Africans have made. But the music has been pulled so far out of context that it's no longer recognizable. Any attempt to claim it is met with tremendous resistance. The music is ours, since it contains our soul, so to speak—it contains all our ideas and responses to the world. We need it to help us claim this African-ness and we would be a stronger people for it. It's presently in the hands of someone else who sits over it as custodian, without even allowing us its source.

When Loomis finds his song, he can stand up again.

Yes.

LANFORD WILSON

Born in Lebanon, Missouri, in 1937, Lanford Wilson was five when his parents divorced. His father moved to California (he wasn't to see him again for thirteen years) and he lived with his mother in a succession of rented houses before going to Chicago in 1956. There he took several jobs and finally moved to New York to become a playwright. Working at the Caffe Cino, Wilson quickly became one of the most active figures in the Off-Off Broadway movement of the mid-sixties. There, in 1964, he enjoyed his first major success with *The Madness of Lady Bright*. This was followed by a succession of full-length plays, most directed by his longtime associate Marshall Mason, including *Balm in Gilead* (1965), *The Gingham Dog* (1966) and *The Rimers of Eldritch* (1967). In 1968 he cofounded Circle Repertory Company, which since has premiered most of his work. His later plays include *Lemon Sky* (1970), *The Hot l Baltimore* (1973), *The Mound Builders* (1975), *Serenading Louie* (1976), *Angels Fall* (1982), *Burn This* (1986) and the "Talley Trilogy," consisting of *Fifth of July* (1978), the Pulitzer Prize-winning *Talley's Folly* (1980) and *A Tale Told* (1981), later revised as *Talley and Son* (1985).

Wilson is a skilled craftsman with a keen ear for dialogue and eye for strong characterization. From the beginning, he has employed a lyrical realism particularly apt for the expression of rich and fluent interpersonal dynamics. Although using a familiar realistic framework, he has appropriated devices, particularly in his early work, to break the naturalistic texture. He has run scenes in counterpoint against each other or interrupted the action with various stylized devices: direct address, narrative, genre painting and music. Throughout his career, he has developed plot primarily by allowing it to evolve almost invisibly out of conversation and then leading it to an emotionally or physically violent climax (confrontation, death, separation). Despite his plays' punctuation by these moments of violence (sometimes aestheticized, as at the end of *Balm in Gilead*), his drama characteristically moves toward reconciliation or the acceptance of loss. Tirelessly, it encourages approbation both of the anomalous individual—in the belief that all individuals are wayward—and of middle-class culture—in the belief that it promises a future in which the individual can fully realize himself.

Despite the diversity of characters in Wilson's plays and his facility in portraying group dynamics, his drama characteristically opposes two approaches to the past, linking each to a character or group of characters. *Balm in Gilead*, for example, is drawn with a particularly large and colorful dramatis personae and is filled with a vigorous dramatic counterpoint among various social misfits: junkies, drug dealers, pimps, whores, hustlers and drag queens. Far more than simply a cross section of New York lowlife, however, the play juxtaposes those who know themselves and survive by celebrating their identity and their past against those who have never confronted their past—or present—and lose badly. Even the dramatic center of the play—Darlene's long monologue describing the failure of a relationship which she still does not understand—is focused on the past. In the autobiographical *Lemon Sky*, the conflict is centered on a young protagonist and his estranged father, who is never able to reach his son or deal with his own problems. The play's double time scheme, balancing action and recollection, 1957 and 1970, offers perspective and distance on the past, but by the end it seems that even the passage of time has not provided Alan with the power to work out and accept the events of that California summer thirteen years before.

Wilson's serious study of the well-made play in the late seventies and his subsequent use of the form hasn't significantly changed his approach to the past (the revelation of information about the past is, of course, as crucial to the well-made play as it is to his own early works). His study did, however, encourage him to use a more diagrammatic dramatic form and more concentrated interpersonal conflict. *Talley's Folly*, his most well-made play, is an unabashedly romantic presentation of Matt Friedman's wooing of Sally Talley, completed only after they overcome the differences between them and reveal pivotal facts about their pasts: Matt's victimage by anti-Semitism and Sally's infertility. *Angels Fall* is even more schematic, a play in the tradition of *Bus Stop*. An allegory of modern crisis both ecological and psychological, the play features a cross section of middle-class America taking refuge in a New Mexico mission during a minor nuclear accident. The characters' confrontations with themselves and each other build, through a series of revelations, to climaxes just as the emergency ends and, more mindfully than before, they go back into the world.

Among the many playwrights to have emerged from the Off-Off Broadway movement, Wilson has unquestionably been the most successful commercially. His work has been seen extensively on Broadway and has become a staple of regional theatre. Certainly his warmly realistic style and the tenderness of his characters are major factors in his success. His is a theatre without villains, one in which emotionality is highlighted against witty repartee. His work does not probe psychological horror and, as a result, is accessible to many who find much contemporary drama too emotionally wrenching. Wilson remains a skilled writer of romantic fictions, providing audiences with a modicum of self-examination and thereby facilitating their return to a world less poised and graceful than his own.

■ ■ ■

DECEMBER 1, 1986—CIRCLE REP OFFICES, NEW YORK CITY

What were your early experiences in the theatre? And what prompted you to become a playwright?

I thought I was going to be a painter. I had been writing stories from the time I was ten or twelve, but I drew and painted so much that I thought I would do that.

When I was nineteen, after one year at San Diego State, I hit Chicago and said, "I'm not going back to California." I fell in love with big towns. So, planning to be an artist, I got a job with an advertising agency doing illustration. On lunch hours I wrote story after story and sent them out to magazines. I had rejection slips from the best magazines in the country. One day I came up with an idea and I thought, "That's not a story, that's a play." So I started writing it as a play and within two pages I said, "Oh, I'm a playwright." It was just as easy as that. I've told that story a hundred thousand times and I've written it as Zappy's story in *Angels Fall* about becoming a tennis player. Since that day I discovered I was a playwright, I have hardly drawn or painted at all. I've written very little else besides plays.

My interest in theatre began long before that. In high school I acted in all the plays. I had fallen in love with the theatre. Also in high school I saw some major plays—the local college did *Death of a Salesman,* a touring company did *Brigadoon.* But it never really occurred to me that plays were written. They were just handed down in those Samuel French books. So when I wrote a play in Chicago, I wrote it as three-fourths farce. I didn't have any idea what a farce was—I had never seen one—but I wrote one. It was quite stupid. And then I wrote a full-length play that was really very bad.

I decided I better find out what a play was so I went to one term of the downtown center of the University of Chicago, where I took a very basic adult education course. A play has conflict, write a scene of conflict. This is exposition, write a scene of exposition. We had great fun having actors from the Goodman Theatre come over and read the scenes. They would discuss them, we would discuss them, and our teacher Dr. Rhuby would discuss them. We ended by writing a one-act play. I decided if I was a playwright, I'd better go to New York.

When was that?

I got here on July 5th, 1962. I didn't remember that until years after I wrote *Fifth of July.* I was twenty-five.

That was just the beginning of Off-Off Broadway.

The Caffe Cino was down there. And Julie Bovasso had already done *The Maids.* I had written a revue while I was in Chicago and didn't have enough nerve to give it to Second City. So when I came here, I did it for the guy who ran Upstairs at the Downstairs. He offered me a job acting. But I turned it down because I knew the two actors I had come to New York with would kill me if I got an acting job. I was taking part-time jobs and writing. And I saw every play in New York. I hated everything. I had so looked forward to seeing plays. But it wasn't what I thought it was going to be. They weren't doing *Death of a Salesman* and *Long Day's Journey into Night.* They were doing *Bye Bye, Birdie.* The only play that was any good was *Night of the Iguana* and I had already seen that in Chicago on tour before it opened.

My first production here was down at the Caffe Cino—*Home Free,* a one-act play by a completely different person from the person who wrote those things in school in Chicago. I've never quite known what it was...maybe the atmosphere in New York. There was a huge leap. I was reading more. Maybe I had read something that said you're better off writing about your own experiences, or people you observe.

During those years, what playwrights were particularly important to you?
You mentioned Miller, Williams.

I read them all, but only the Americans. I was in New York before I discovered
any of the European writers. My source in Ozark and Springfield, Missouri
was mainly *Theater Arts* magazine and those twenty-play anthologies. So I
read the best twenty plays of Europe and liked them all. They were all by
the same person as far as I was concerned. The first thing I saw at the Caffe
Cino was Ionesco's *The Lesson* and it blew me completely away because I
had never seen anything like that. I loved Ionesco and immediately looked
up everything he had done.

I started working in the office at the Phoenix Theatre, where they did
Next Time I'll Sing to You by James Saunders, which was important to me at
the time. I hadn't realized that you could talk to the audience, and admit that
you were on stage. With my art history background, it seemed as important
to me as admitting that what you were working with was paint on canvas. So
some of the early things I wrote had a lot of actors talking to the audience.
It's very strange though, because years later I took the talking to the audience
out. It never seemed to work. They always talked in character. Only in
Serenading Louie did I drop the character and have them talk to the audience
as actors. But I changed that in rehearsal because you were so convinced they
were the characters that it didn't make any sense, you didn't know what in
hell they were talking about.

What about Tennessee Williams?

I always loved Tennessee's work. One of the first plays I acted in was *The
Glass Menagerie* and I thought it was just the greatest thing I had ever
encountered. I was reading his short stories when I came to New York. That's
about the time he wrote *Sweet Bird of Youth*, which has an absolutely sensational first act and an absolutely sensational third act...and the second act
in between. I never responded to Inge at all. From the first play of his I read,
I laughed out loud because I thought it was so incredibly stupid that a woman
was telling her husband they had a daughter who was sixteen years old. And
Miller I liked.

Strangely enough, I did not read *Hedda Gabler* for fifteen years and I
missed Chekhov completely. I didn't read Chekhov until '68 or so—very,
very late. I got the complete plays of Chekhov and was blown completely out
of the water by him. I had never read anything like that in my life. That
finally was what I thought a play should be.

I read somewhere in these formative years that Miller took the ordinary speech of the common man and transformed that subtly into a poetry for the stage. So I expected Swinburne, and I read Miller and said, "No he doesn't." But I think that statement influenced me more than anything else, reading that and thinking, "That's a wonderful thing and should be done." That's exactly what I had a talent for, which was probably why I responded to it. That idea and the fiction and the poetry I was reading—Swinburne and Gerard Manley Hopkins and André Gide and Dickens—were much stronger influences on me than any playwrights except James Saunders and Brendan Behan.

I was more influenced by Behan than anybody. *Balm in Gilead* is my attempt to do something as good as *The Hostage*, which I saw in Chicago. It had been the most exciting thing I had ever seen in theatre. I came to New York saying that theatre should be a three-ring circus. God knows I've changed a lot since then, but those early plays were an attempt to create that kind of life, from *Rimers of Eldritch* through *Lemon Sky*.

Tennessee said I was doing something quite different from what he was doing and I always agreed. I rarely have the violence that he has. Yes, in some of them, in *Gilead* and *Rimers*. But it's a very different kind of violence. He uses a very different subject. He used himself and I was using me, what I saw and what I had experienced several years before. But only *Lemon Sky* is autobiographical in the same way that his plays are autobiographical. "Where I am now as an artist" is what he always wrote about. I wouldn't have the chutzpa to do that. It's just not the way I think or what I ever thought theatre should be.

Your plays, especially the early ones, tend to have group protagonists rather than a single, overshadowing hero. That's also the difference between Chekhov and Miller.

Exactly. I think it has something to do with being essentially an only child, so I'm drawn more to the group. It's either the lonely child or cockroach syndrome.

I think probably the first of my plays influenced by Chekhov was *Hot l Baltimore*—I was writing it as quickly as I could for Circle Rep, not thinking about it, and when I got to the third act I thought "What in hell happens here?" because I hadn't mapped it out. I went to *The Cherry Orchard* and said, "Of course, we'll have some champagne and leave." That's where Suzie leaving and throwing the party came from.

But you don't really have to read Chekhov to be influenced by him because you are influenced by people who have been influenced by him. It's in the air. I knew Chekhov because of takeoffs of Chekhov I had seen. I had just never bothered to read him myself. But I had no idea that you could do

311

what he was doing on stage and that you could hide a plot as cleverly as he does. All of his plays are plotted, of course, but the plots are hidden so incredibly beautifully, in symbols and metaphors.

When you think back on your training, what is the most striking element to you?

I think a lot of us were trained like gardeners—by doing. At the Caffe Cino we had to do everything ourselves—sets, lights. We had to get the actors, we had to get replacements when the actors got jobs, we had to act ourselves when the replacements got jobs. It spoiled us incredibly because we thought we were always going to get to do everything. It was great fun and an enormous amount of work. Four and five one-act plays a year. But we had no idea that we were serving an apprenticeship.

After doing about six or eight one-act plays with two or three characters, because that was all you could fit on stage at Caffe Cino or La Mama, I finally wrote *Balm in Gilead* as something you could not possibly do at the Caffe Cino. I thought of it being published but never produced. I just sat in the coffee shop and took down every word I heard, then tried to make it into a design using a circle. A strong influence on that play was the Judson Poets' Theater, the dances and some of the musicals, Gertrude Stein's *In Circles* and *What Happened*—that's where I got the idea of lifting the stage and turning it halfway around, then turning it back at the end. We did that at La Mama. It's wonderfully effective. Much of the structure of *Balm in Gilead* was based on the fact that you saw the outside of the counter at the beginning. Then when they turned it around and repeated some of the scenes, you saw that the guy had a baseball bat in his hand when he was arguing, that's why he wasn't frightened. And the other guy probably knows he has a bat in his hand. It was very poignant when they started turning it back around again. So that play is constructed in circles. We used circular physical actions. And a lot of those shaggy-dog stories come back on themselves, so I think of them as circles. Darlene's long story is like that.

One night I got out of a subway in the pouring rain. I didn't have a quarter on me and this guy who later became Fick was trying to get some money or trying to get me to be his buddy—I couldn't really figure it out at the time. He ran alongside me like Ratso Rizzo during this incredible rainstorm at four in the morning, and I went into my shabby little hotel room and took a hot bath because I was freezing cold and got out and spent the rest of the night writing down everything he had said.

Several years later, when I took a step back and looked at what I had done, I began not quite to trust all this technique. I reread *Rimers of Eldritch* about three years after I wrote it and said, "God, I haven't touched the surface of Josh." He has ten lines and most of them are to his sister, but from his actions we know he's a terribly complicated character. With this flashy technique and all these characters, I hadn't had time to develop him. I decided to concentrate on depth of character.

In which plays?

The Gingham Dog and *Serenading Louie*. *Louie* gets a little flashy but I had only four characters and I was using them to examine and question each other and go as far as I could. I was working on *Serenading Louie* in '67 and *Lemon Sky* came from nowhere and I said, "No, I don't want to work like that anymore," but I had to finish it anyway because it was just all there. Then I went back to *Serenading Louie*. And then Circle Rep came into being and that changed everything again.

When?

1969. I was in the middle of a massive writer's block at the time, which is no fun. I had had all these plays done on Broadway and it was clear that I was supposed to write The Great American Play. As soon as that was clear, I couldn't write a damn thing. It took about a year and a half, coming back to my friends and working in the office to take my mind off of result and put it back on process. Caffe Cino was gone and until I got comfortable at Circle Rep I really didn't have any reason to write.

I finally came up with *Hot l Baltimore*. I was trying to do something else but didn't trust my motive. The time got shorter and shorter because Circle Rep wanted a play for the following year. Marshall and I were painting flats and "The City of New Orleans" came on—I'm a train freak—and I said, "I'm going to write a play about this girl train freak who is a prostitute...I have to write that sometime." Marshall said, "Why don't you write it now." I started it the next day and it went nowhere for about three weeks, then suddenly caught fire and went very, very quickly.

What about the Talley plays?

Up to *The Mound Builders*, I felt that I never had a complete formal education. People like me read too much, see too much, over-compensate all over the place. I had never really studied writing and I didn't know what a well-made play was. I had come up with the idea of writing about my family in 1945, when my uncle came back from the war. I said, "It should be a 1945 play, one of those old-fashioned, well-made plays." Then I said, "What in hell is an old-fashioned, well-made play?" All I knew is that it's based on Ibsen instead of Chekhov. So I reread Ibsen—and finally read *Hedda Gabler*—and realized, "He writes more like Chekhov than Chekhov."

I made the mistake of getting that book by George Pierce Baker. I read it and said, "If that's what people are expecting in the theatre, no wonder no one likes my work." So I tried to work on this 1945 play, but I couldn't do what he said and ended up writing *Fifth of July*, which straddled the fence between a well-made play and the way I had always written. I started out to write about these quite poor people but my brain wouldn't have any of it. In working on *Fifth of July*, I realized that there are about twenty plays in that house. But in working out the reason why Matt and Sally did not have children and so had brought up Shirley, and what that had meant to them, I had, of course, worked out the history of Matt and Sally and said, "That would be a very nice play too." I was still aiming to write that 1945 play about my uncle, but by now it wasn't my uncle because the Talleys were very wealthy and ran the town. So they are based on the people my mother worked for.

Talley's Folly is more of a well-made play. It locks into place, you can actually hear it click. And you have that wonderful satisfaction of hearing the click and the incredible disappointment at the same time that it is that kind of play. It's very strange.

What do you mean by disappointment?

It's like "Oh, it's all been just a design. It's not really people at all, just this incredibly well-made piece of machinery." You have that in Ibsen from time to time, but a completely different grand design in Chekhov. His is not all worked out on paper, but comes from natural impulses, which was always the way I had worked.

Determined to write that well-made play, I worked out *A Tale Told*, as it was then called. Now it's *Talley and Son*. Moments in the story drove me crazy. I like some of it a lot, but it was the most difficult thing I ever did. That and *Angels Fall*. I said, "Now I have had my well-made play experience and I'm curious what that's going to do to the way I used to write." I found out that once you know how a play is supposed to be built, it's not easy to shake. And I had to write a play in about four months because I had said yes to a commission two years earlier from a festival down in Miami. They had called me up and said, "We have a yes from Tennessee Williams and a yes from Edward Albee, would you like to be the third one?" I said, "I'm supposed to say no?" It was great fun because they said they were giving Edward and Tennessee $15,000 and me $10,000. I said, "In a pig's eye." And they said, "Oh, we'll give you the same." So I had to do this and I didn't have a damn idea in my head.

I came back to New York from California in a panic and got an idea—bam!—in a bar. I saw a picture of New Mexico and I saw the entire play, all of the characters and the situation. The plays have often been a metaphor for where I think we're at, but usually I don't know that until I'm three-quarters of the way through them. This one I knew from the beginning, which is not as easy. If we're not people in a church that very few people go to, huddling there in a minor nuclear emergency, I don't know where in the fuck we are. It didn't cross the mind of a single critic. They can only find metaphors, those giant designs, in English plays like *Plenty*. We're making them continually and they never see it. I don't think they saw it in *American Buffalo*. What assholes.

Anyway, simultaneously with the idea I thought, "That is a locked-door play. And I hate a locked-door play." That's *Bus Stop* and *Outward Bound* and I didn't want to write another genre play. But I ended up trying to write that locked-door play just as well as I possibly could. And it took everything out of me. It usually takes me a year to write a play and I wrote *Angels Fall* in four months. And then I rewrote it between Miami and New York. The last month I was working ten hours a day, seven days a week. With a secretary yet. It burned me out completely. I said I didn't want to have another original thought in my head for a year...and I didn't, for two.

Finally after that—I was helped by doing a translation of *Three Sisters*—I threw over the well-made play. The new one, *Burn This*, is back to *Serenading Louie* or *Balm in Gilead*, although it's only a four-character play. I wouldn't want to be without those six years of study, but it's important now to lose that. I'm happy to be back working in contemporary times and in the city with strong people to whom I don't quite know what's going to happen.

How do you write a play now?

For *Burn This* I had an idea about four years ago of a very interesting kind of coincidence and I had the two central characters. I was working on too many other things and didn't have a chance to write it. Four years later I was a little panicked because I wasn't working on anything. In three years I had written one one-act play and the translation of *Three Sisters*. It took me five times longer to translate it than it took Chekhov to write it, because he had the benefit of knowing Russian. I had to learn the goddam thing. So I was feeling real physical anxiety, getting as stiff as poured concrete. Usually I say, "Stop that," and I stop. But I couldn't not feel this anxiety. So I said, "Describe that." I started describing my physical symptoms and within half a page it turned into a character and I no longer felt any of that anxiety. So what I look for first is a character. And eventually someone says, "I can help you" or "Oh shut up," and then you have two points of view.

I think *Burn This* is the best thing I've done. It's a love story. But it's not at all like any love story that I've ever written or seen. It's a love story in which people say "I don't want this" instead of "I love you." It's very contemporary. After all the damn dance I've seen since Judson, and talking to dancers and having all these dancer friends—and of course Joe Cino was a dancer, too—I can finally write a dancer. And even at that I had to interview. This is modern dance and of course it isn't at all like classical ballet, where you start when you're nine and never see your mother again.

After I finally came up for air in this character I said, "What in the hell is that? Oh yeah, that's the idea from four years ago with that clever little gimmick." So I worked it out with the gimmick. We had a first reading and I said, "Cut it." So the thing I started with for the plot is gone and there is no plot, only character development—except there is a plot. It's just that I managed to hide it as well as I ever have. And it's convoluted in exactly the same way those early plays are. But this isn't circles, it's mirrors and land-scapes. It's strange that the one thing I thought I had for sure, this nice little gimmick, was the first thing to go. The second thing to go was the very first page I had written, that had started me back to work and got me to find those four characters.

Do you rewrite a lot before the first rehearsal?

I did a lot more on *Angels Fall* and on *Talley and Son* than I did on this, which is a good sign. I also did very little on *Hot l Baltimore*. *Burn This* has taken forever because I wanted John Malkovich, and he couldn't do it for the longest time. I finished it in December and we got him for a reading in August. So I rewrote it some for the first reading we had here, and some for the reading in August, and some for California for December. But not a whole lot. We'll probably be paring it down during rehearsals—it's a little wordy —and clarifying and changing some things. I've rewritten the first scene about five times. It's only the first half of the first act that keeps changing and will keep changing. The rest stays exactly the same.

How long now have you worked with Marshall Mason?

'65, I think, was the first time we worked together.

What is your working relationship?

It's great. He'll say, "I'll take care of this and you take care of that." It's like two heads instead of one. It's especially terrific on the large-cast plays. He'll say, "I'll never get that girl to do that." So I say, "I'll talk to her, if you can get him to do what he's supposed to do." He has seen a play at least fifteen times over the year I've been working on it. We've seen readings of it. He has read scenes. I've read scenes to him. He knows more or less what the play is, so we both know exactly what we want. And then in casting we find ourselves very, very close every time. And since we both know what we want, we trust either to get it. And so if I'm talking to someone over in the corner, he knows I'm not telling them something that is going to undermine his purpose. He says, "Good, that's taken care of." I don't do that too much, but it gives him maybe a quarter more time than he would normally have.

Do you normally go to all of the rehearsals?

All except for the first two or three when they're improvising. They need to do that for scenes like "the first time she met Burt." And that's very nice because if they improvise it, they'll always have that experience in their minds when they're playing, to fall back on. I would rather die than see them improvise. I always think it's better than the scene I wrote. But when they start saying my words, I'm there. Because they may need me. Or I may need them.

Do you do much rewriting in rehearsal?

Clarification. If someone says something for the fourth time and isn't making sense out of it, I'll say, "Do you know what that means?" He'll say no. I'll ask, "Who knows what that means?" And the other three people will say what they think it means and if they're right, the first person will say, "Oh, of course, what an asshole I am." If no one quite knows I say, "That means this, in other words." And they all go, "Why didn't you say that?" Then I usually go back to the typewriter to clarify because I don't think there's a point in being misunderstood. I hate not understanding something...unless it's the sort of play you're not supposed to understand, which is a whole different thing. But I'm not writing *Last Year at Marienbad* and neither is anyone else I know.

And do you rewrite often after a first production?

I wish I didn't, but I do. I keep writing. The trade edition of *Fifth of July* is quite different from the last rewrite of the play, published by Dramatists Play Service. I have a horror of anyone doing the hardback version instead of the actors' version.

What production are you particularly happy with?

There are about six or seven. We've done some very good work. We did *Hot l Baltimore* here and then we did it in California, and I came back from California thinking I had seen the ultimate production. But the production here was forty times better and I didn't know it until we came back to it. I was hyperventilating. I completely forgot that I had written it. I just had not seen anything like that on the American stage before. *Angels Fall*...I told you of

317

the reservations I have with that kind of play, but the production was stunning. You wanted to fuck the lights. I am still incredibly pleased with the costumes, with Nancy Snyder walking across the stage leading with her pelvis in that dress that kept flipping back and forth around her waist. Peeling that green apple, the only green on the set.

I thought Malkovich's production of *Balm in Gilead* was absolutely stunning. Our first production of *Balm in Gilead* was stunning, too, and very much like Malkovich's. We used music that was contemporary then. We didn't use Bruce Springsteen because Bruce Springsteen didn't exist then...he probably wasn't even born. Both *Lemon Skys* have been terrific. *Serenading Louie* at Second Stage was the most difficult rehearsal period I ever went through because I didn't want to go back to that place again. I rewrote a couple of scenes and I think I improved them but I couldn't really tell. It's a pain in the ass to be questioned as closely as those incredibly serious actors questioned me.

Who directed?

John Tillinger. It looked like shit all during rehearsals but the first preview was pretty damn good and the second preview was pretty damn amazing and after that it was just astonishing. But that play has always been difficult for me. I hyperventilate for all the wrong reasons. I like the play, but I don't like my experience of the play.

Do you read the critics?

Oh yeah. It's a business so you want to know if you're going to run. Also, Marshall and I are better at finding quotes in a review than any of the people who are paid to do it. We're shameless at it because we really don't take it that seriously. We don't let the actors read them because it can fuck up their performance. The critics never say anything enlightening about the writing —unless of course they like it in which case it's wonderful. I read reviews of productions I haven't even seen. Pittsburgh Public Theater sent me the reviews of *Serenading Louie* and I had great fun reading those. But I haven't taken any advice from any of them.

What direction do you see the American theatre going in now? It seems that both Broadway and Off Broadway are changing.

Have they? How?

Broadway is no longer a forum for serious drama, with a few exceptions.

Name one.

Glengarry Glen Ross.

And *Hurlyburly.* That's about it. Even *Benefactors* didn't do it for me. *Glengarry, 'night, Mother* and *Hurlyburly.* Especially *Hurlyburly.* What do you know? A good play on Broadway. Good Lord, it's enough to put you in a time warp. As I said, when I got here, I hated everything on Broadway. I don't think there have been more than two good plays on Broadway since '62. Good God, that's twenty-four years! So many things are bombed before anyone has a chance to see them. And something else isn't very good but gets praised. And something else squeaks through for a short while. I don't suppose anyone makes any money. Of the plays I've had done on Broadway, only *Talley's Folly* returned its investment. *Fifth of July* ran fourteen months and ended up costing money. *Angels Fall* is starting to return some money from around the country, but it was a total wash. So as far as the business goes, that's lousy. Off Broadway? I have difficulty finding Off Broadway right now.

Well, the Public for instance.

I can get only so interested in Czechoslovakian theatre. There are some...they did an Innaurato last year that was astonishing. And the Kramer play. *Tracers* was wonderful and good to see.

In your letter to me you mentioned Irene Fornes's work.

She's unlike anyone else, which is amazing to see. And she's like me in that one play is not much like the next, as opposed to say Chekhov or Sam Shepard, who seem to be writing the same play over and over again. So I'm crazy about her work.

I have a lot of energy but I am not by nature positive. But I am positive about the theatre. I can't think of a time that has had so many theatre artists of the quality that we have working right now. There just isn't another period that has Irene Fornes and David Rabe and David Mamet and Sam Shepard and Lanford Wilson and about ten others. Now three-fourths of them aren't getting the recognition they deserve. And that none of their plays are running is really beside the point. We will go down as a Golden Age—I sound like a fucking Chekhov—in American theatre. Not one of those writers is writing like any other. We're all working our own turf, our own brain, our own dream, our own vision. And I think that is very, very exciting.

We're building a strong theatre literature that is being done across the country—it's not being done in New York except for about two weeks or sometimes all of three or four months—but it's being done in every regional theatre, all the work that goes from being a failure with the New York critics to being extremely important to everyone throughout the country. *Serenading Louie* ran twice as long in a 700-seat theatre in Pittsburgh as it did in a 70-seat theatre in New York. So I don't feel particularly good about New York theatre—the finances are totally fucked. But I feel very good about theatre across the country. After all, that's what we're talking about. We can't be bothered about New York theatre.

What are your plans for the future?

I would hope to write a decent play. I've been getting involved with these damn actors who can't move with a play for an extended life. It happens time and again. I'd like to stop doing that, write for unknowns. The next play will be for unknown actors or else I'm going to sign them to a two-year contract. When you work on something very hard and do it correctly with no compromises, you want it to be seen that way by as many people as possible. Only in one case, with Richard Thomas coming into *Fifth of July* and Joe Bottom who followed him, have I had a production with replacements as good or better than the original. Both guys were not only dynamite, they fit into the ensemble. But that almost never happens when you're doing an ensemble piece.

Do you have a favorite among your plays?

I don't really. It depends on my mood. Until I see it on its feet in front of an audience, I'll like *Burn This* the best. I might even like *Hot l Baltimore* if I read it. I've not read it since it closed Off Broadway, twelve years ago or whatever, so I don't know what that play is anymore. But really, whichever one I'm going to do next is my favorite.